Voices of the American Past

Voices of the American Past

Documents in U.S. History

Volume I

FIFTH EDITION

RAYMOND M. HYSER
J. CHRIS ARNDT
James Madison University

WADSWORTH
CENGAGE Learning™

Australia • Brazil • Japan • Korea • Mexico • Singapore • Spain • United Kingdom • United States

WADSWORTH
CENGAGE Learning™

Voices of the American Past: Documents in U.S. History, Volume I, Fifth Edition

Raymond M. Hyser and
J. Chris Arndt

Senior Publisher: Suzanne Jeans

Senior Sponsoring Editor: Ann West

Development Editor: Larry Goldberg

Assistant Editor: Megan Chrisman

Editorial Assistant: Patrick Roach

Senior Media Editor: Lisa Ciccolo

Senior Marketing Manager: Katherine Bates

Marketing Coordinator: Lorreen Pelletier

Marketing Communications Manager: Caitlin Green

Content Project Management: PreMediaGlobal

Senior Art Director: Cate Rickard Barr

Manufacturing Buyer: Sandee Milewski

Rights Acquisition Specialist, Images: Jennifer Meyer Dare

Senior Rights Acquisition Specialist, Text: Katie Huha

Production Service: PreMediaGlobal

Cover Designer: Lori Leahy, Mighty Quinn Graphics

Cover Image: North Wind Picture Archives/Alamy

Compositor: PreMediaGlobal

For product information and technology assistance, contact us at **Cengage Learning Customer & Sales Support, 1-800-354-9706**

For permission to use material from this text or product, submit all requests online at **www.cengage.com/permissions**. Further permissions questions can be emailed to **permissionrequest@cengage.com.**

Library of Congress Control Number: 2010943277

ISBN-13: 978-1-111-34124-4

ISBN-10: 1-111-34124-9

Wadsworth
20 Channel Center Street
Boston, MA 02210
USA

Cengage Learning is a leading provider of customized learning solutions with office locations around the globe, including Singapore, the United Kingdom, Australia, Mexico, Brazil and Japan. Locate your local office at **international.cengage.com/region**

Cengage Learning products are represented in Canada by Nelson Education, Ltd.

For your course and learning solutions, visit **www.cengage.com.**

Purchase any of our products at your local college store or at our preferred online store **www.cengagebrain.com.**

Instructors: Please visit **login.cengage.com** and log in to access instructor-specific resources.

Printed in the United States of America
1 2 3 4 5 6 7 15 14 13 12 11

To our children,
Kelsey, Marshall, and Christopher Hyser
and Olivia and Ruby Arndt
Thanks for all of your love
and inspiration

Contents

Preface to the Fifth Edition

We are delighted with the opportunity to produce a revised fifth edition of *Voices of the American Past*. This allows us to better represent the ever-evolving approaches that historians employ to interpret the past, as well as provide more documents covering a greater variety of issues.

CHANGES TO THE FIFTH EDITION

Those who use this edition will find significant changes. Our selection of new documents was guided by a desire to provide greater diversity of voices while also offering readable selections that spoke to larger issues. The revised reader offers well-known primary sources such as *Federalist 10*, Walker's Appeal, the Seneca Falls Declaration of Sentiments, the Populist Platform, President Eisenhower's farewell address, and Martin Luther King Jr.'s "Letter from Birmingham Jail." But this edition includes substantial changes with over fifty new documents and images. These include an indentured servant's letter describing conditions in seventeenth-century Virginia; a contemporary newspaper report on the 1741 New York slave conspiracy; George Washington's instructions on conducting war against the Iroquois during the American Revolution; an 1840s African American petition to integrate schools in Massachusetts; the American Party Platform of 1856; a woman's description of farm life in Illinois at the turn of the twentieth century; Eleanor Roosevelt's commentary on New Deal policies; an editorial on the 1955 Emmitt Till murder trial; a description of illegal immigrants crossing into Arizona in 2000; and an economist's commentary on the looming financial crisis in 2007.

We have also added images to the fifth edition. As historians have increasingly expanded the types of sources they use both as scholars and in the classroom, we have added pictures and drawings, but especially political cartoons, to the written documents. The result is a number of images that provide a unique approach to interpreting and understanding the key issues of U.S. history. These include drawings of Native American life in the late sixteenth century; European views of the American Revolution; political cartoons about the election of 1860; perspectives on American overseas expansion; advertisements in the 1920s; political cartoons on the New Deal; and viewpoints on the war in Vietnam.

ACKNOWLEDGMENTS

We are again indebted to our colleagues in the James Madison University Department of History for their contributions and inspiration. Their high standards of teaching excellence coupled with their strong sense of collegiality provide the perfect atmosphere for quality instruction. Our students have contributed greatly by showing us where a document was contradictory or less readable, and perhaps more important, for helping to make us aware of the issues that are central to the current generation of young people. Many of our colleagues in the profession, particularly those who participate in the annual Advanced Placement U.S. History Reading, have made more important contributions than they could ever realize. The criticisms and suggestions of reviewers did much to improve this edition, enabling us to refocus our attention in some areas and leading us to some excellent documents in others. We wish to thank the following reviewers:

Brandon Buck, Mountain Pointe High School

Stacy Cordery, Monmouth College

Aley Ginette, University of Southern Indiana

Edward Gutierrez, University of Hartford

Timothy Kelly, Saint Vincent College

Marianne McKnight, Salt Lake Community College

Keshia Medellin, Los Medanos College

James Paradis, Arcadia University

George Sochan, Bowie State University

Special thanks go to our friends at Wadsworth/Cengage Publishing. Ann West has been remarkable as an editor. The fifth edition could not have been completed without her professionalism and support. Larry Goldberg is a terrific editor who patiently guided us through the final stages of the writing and editing process. His keen insights and steadfast support made this a much better book than it would have been otherwise. Finally, we thank our wives, Pamela and Andi, for their love and support.

We are eager to hear from readers of *Voices of the American Past*. Please feel free to offer your comments by contacting us at the Department of History, James Madison University, 58 Bluestone Drive MSC 2001, Harrisonburg, VA 22807, or through our e-mail addresses: J. Chris Arndt, arndtjc@jmu.edu; Raymond M. Hyser, hyserrm@jmu.edu.

A Guide to Reading and Interpreting Documents and Images

This volume contains edited documents about American history. Historians refer to such documents as written *primary sources*. These are the raw materials, the basic building blocks to reconstructing past events. In the same way that a detective searches a crime scene for clues, a historian draws on primary sources and uses the weight of the evidence to determine what happened and to help support an interpretation of the event. Although primary sources might be described as any evidence that is contemporary to the event described, historians rely heavily on firsthand, eyewitness accounts or recollections of events of the time, as well as speeches or official reports produced at that time. All primary sources, however, are not created equal. The closer the evidence is in time and space to the event described, the less bias that it contains, the more reliable it tends to be. The interpretations that historians produce from these primary sources are called *secondary sources*. Secondary sources are books and articles written about past events, such as a textbook, the introductions to the documents in this volume, or a history of the American Civil War.

Reading and analyzing documents require particular skills. You should examine documents with a critical eye; that is, ask questions about the document. We recommend that you develop the ability to perform a twofold reading of a document. First, try to understand the document as the people in the time and place in which it was produced would have comprehended it. What did the document mean to them? Always remember that people live within a historical context—they inhabit a time and place different from what exists today. They do not know what the future holds. Careful analysis of a document will enable you to examine the thoughts and actions of the people of a particular time. Second, read the document and consider the similarities and differences between that time period and other time periods, including your own. Students of history are often called upon to make judgments about the past. Documents should be analyzed to see how they fit into the broader sweep of history.

We have included the following suggestions that will be useful in introducing you to this spirit of historical inquiry and enable you to better understand documents. These guidelines will enable you to read primary sources in a critical manner. In so doing, you will gain more insight into past events, add some real-life views to historical facts, and better understand the complexities of the American past.

Interpreting Written Documents

1. **Context:** Each document has an introduction. You should read it as well as review notes from your instructor's lecture. These will provide some historical context about events, people, and ideas of the time period in which the document was created.

    - What major political, social, economic, and/or cultural trends may have affected the author of the document?

    - How does this document fit into the historical context?

    - How does this document better our understanding of the event?

    - Does the document help to explain the cause-and-effect relationship of this event?

2. **Thesis:** Most documents have a central point that is being conveyed. This is known as the thesis. It is critical for any reader to understanding the core argument—the thesis—of a document. Identifying the thesis is the important first step in making sense of a document's overall impact.

    - Can you summarize the document in three or four sentences?

    - What is the thesis? Can you express it in a sentence or two?

    - What does the author emphasize?

    - What are the key words that define the argument?

    Keep in mind that the meaning of words changes over time, so try to understand the use of language in the historical time period of the document. For example, students in the twenty-first century might refer to "icon" as a clickable symbol on their computer's desktop, but prior to the widespread use of computers, "icon" would refer to a sacred, religious image.

3. **Perspective:** The author's point of view, including his or her prejudices and beliefs, can affect dramatically the content of a document. It is essential to consider the author of a document when reading. Biographical information can be helpful in deciding the author's point of view. For example, a slave owner would have a different view of slavery than a slave. Factory workers would certainly have a different perception of life in America than the owner of the factory where they worked.

    - Who is the author of the document?

    - What is his or her background?

- When was the document created? How does historical context affect the author at the time the document was created?

- Was it prepared during the event, immediately afterwards, within a short time period, or years later? Such timing is important, as memories often fade or become distorted over time.

An individual's life experience often shapes perspective or views about events in his or her time. Seek to determine the authors' gender, class, ethnicity (where appropriate), their regional background, and their political, economic, or social position.

- Do you detect any prejudices or preferences?

- What evidence indicates the bias of the author?

- Can you determine the author's motive in producing the document?

- What did he or she hope to accomplish?

4. **Audience:** Knowing the intended audience of an account can be useful in better understanding why the document was created.

- Was the document prepared for a specific audience—women, members of Congress, African Americans, wealthy businessmen, immigrants, a friend, for example?

- Was the document prepared for public distribution?

- Was it a speech, a newspaper or a magazine article or editorial, an official government report, a published memoir or autobiography, to name a few possibilities?

- Was it produced for personal and private reflection, such as a diary, journal entry, or an exchange of letters between friends?

Public consumption documents tend to be carefully worded, often guarded in presentation, while private ones tend to be less cautious and more honest. Classifying or identifying the document can be helpful in understanding its contents.

5. **Significance:** Finally, one should determine why a document is important.

- Why is the document important or significant?

- How has it shaped our understanding of the event?

- How has it shaped our understanding of historical change or continuity over time?

- What does it tell us about the historical time period?

Interpreting Visual Images

Many of the techniques used to interpret visual images are similar to those used to make sense of written documents. It is as important to ask questions about context, thesis, perspective, audience, and significance when analyzing an image as it is when reviewing a written text. The major difference with visual images is that there is more room for interpretation since the author/artist/photographer does not specifically describe what he or she is thinking. In addition to considering context, thesis, perspective, audience, and significance, one should also consider the following when analyzing visual images:

- Carefully study the image. What is your overall impression? What thoughts or emotions does it conjure?

- How are individuals or groups depicted? Does their dress indicate anything significant about them?

- What activities are depicted in the image? How and why are these activities significant?

- Does the artist make use of symbols? If so, what are they? What is the significance of these symbols?

- Who or what is portrayed positively? Negatively? What can you infer from this?

About the Authors

J. Chris Arndt is a professor of history at James Madison University in Harrisonburg, Virginia, where he teaches courses in U.S. history, the American Revolution, the early Republic, and historical methods. He focuses his research interests on the study of states' rights and economic change in antebellum America.

Raymond M. Hyser is a professor of history at James Madison University in Harrisonburg, Virginia, where he teaches courses in U.S. history, U.S. business history, Gilded Age America, and historical methods. He focuses his research interests on the study of race and ethnicity in the Gilded Age.

1

Diverse Beginnings

American history began not in 1607, but tens of thousands of years earlier with the first arrivals, the Native Americans. Native Americans spent millennia living beyond the contact of the outside world until the late fifteenth-century arrival of European explorers. The contact of cultures initiated a process that radically transformed societies throughout the world. The rush to conquer and colonize the area of the present-day United States began with the Spanish, but soon came to include other Europeans. Native Americans were not passive bystanders in the process, and they responded to the contact in a variety of ways. The following documents collectively reveal European motives in North America and provide a glimpse of the impact this presence had upon the native population.

1

The Spanish Letter of Columbus to Luis Sant' Angel (1493)

Christopher Columbus was born Cristoforo Colombo in Genoa, Italy, in either 1451 or 1452. He went to sea early in life and by the early 1490s had sailed as far north as Iceland, and as far south as the modern-day country of Ghana, West Africa. By the mid-1480s, he began to seek support for a voyage of exploration westward into the Atlantic, primarily to open a trade route with East Asia. In 1492 the Spanish kingdom of

Castile, under the leadership of Queen Isabella, was ready to support his endeavor. He left Palos, Spain, on August 3; and on October 12, 1492, his three ships—the Niña, Pinta, *and* Santa María—*touched land in the West Indies. After three months of sailing and exploring the Caribbean, he returned to Spain. Three later voyages would establish the primary transatlantic sailing routes and allowed Columbus to conduct a thorough reconnaissance of the Caribbean. Although he went to his grave believing he was skirting the coast of Asia, his legacy was the discovery of a continent formerly unknown to Europeans. This letter describes what Columbus saw on his first visit.*

Questions to Consider

1. What is the perspective of the author of this document?
2. According to this account, what does Christopher Columbus seem interested in achieving?
3. What can you deduce about Spanish attitudes toward Native Americans from this document?
4. Compare Columbus's letter to the description of Pennsylvania found in "Pennsylvania, the Poor Man's Paradise," (Document 14).

… There are wonderful pine-groves, and very large plains of verdure, and there is honey, and many kinds of birds, and many various fruits. In the earth there are many mines of metals; and there is a population of incalculable number. Spanola is a marvel; the mountains and hills, and plains, and fields, and land, so beautiful and rich for planting and sowing, for breeding cattle of all sorts, for building of towns and villages. There could be no believing, without seeing, such harbours as are here, as well as the many and great rivers, and excellent waters, most of which contain gold. In the trees and fruits and plants, there are great differences from those of Juana. In this, there are many spiceries, and great mines of gold and other metals. The people of this island, and of all the others that I have found and seen, or not seen, all go naked, men and women, just as their mothers bring them forth; although some women cover a single place with the leaf of a plant, or a cotton something which they make for that purpose. They have no iron or steel, nor any weapons than the stems of reeds in their seeding state, on the end of which they fix little sharpened stakes.… I gave gratuitously a thousand useful things that I carried, in order that they may conceive affection, and furthermore may be made Christians; for they are inclined to the love and service of their Highnesses and of all the Castilian nation, and they strive to combine in giving us things which they have in abundance, and of which we are in need. And they knew no sect, nor idolatry; save that they all believe that power and goodness are in the sky; and in such opinion, they received me at every place where I landed, after they had lost their terror. And this comes not because they are ignorant; on the contrary, they are men of very subtle wit, who navigate

SOURCE: "The Spanish Letter of Columbus to Luis Sant' Angel" (February 15, 1493), *Personal Narrative of the First Voyage of Columbus to America* (Boston, 1827), 303.

all those seas, and who give a marvellously good account of everything—but because they never saw men wearing clothes nor the like of our ships. And as soon as I arrived in the Indies, in the first island that I found, I took some of them by force to the intent that they should learn [our speech] and give me information of what there was in those parts. And so it was, that very soon they understood [us] and we them, what by speech or what by signs; and those [Indians] have been of much service. To this day I carry them [with me] who are still of the opinion that I come from heaven, [as appears] from much conversation which they have had with me. And they were the first to proclaim it wherever I arrived; and the others went running from house to house and to the neighbouring villages, and loud cries of "Come! come to see the people from heaven!" Then, as soon as their minds were reassured about us, every one came, men as well as women, so that there remained none behind big or little; and they all brought something to eat and drink, which they gave with wondrous lovingness. They have in all the islands very many canoes, after the manner of rowing-galleys, some larger, some smaller; and a good many are larger than a galley of eighteen benches. They are not so wide, because they are made of a single log of timber, but a galley could not keep up with them in rowing, for their motion is a thing beyond belief. And with these, they navigate through all those islands which are numberless, and ply their traffic. I have seen some of those canoes with seventy, and eighty, men in them, each one with his oar. In all those islands, I saw not much diversity in the looks of the people, nor in their manners and language; but they all understand each other, which is a thing of singular towardness for what I hope their Highnesses will determine, as to making them conversant with our holy faith, unto which they are well disposed....

2

Images of Sixteenth-Century Native American Life

Artists have left important clues about the Native American societies that existed before they had extensive contact with Europeans. The first image depicts members of the Timucua tribe planting crops in what is now Florida. The second image is an engraving by Theodore DeBry, based on a painting by John White. It shows a Native American village in what is now North Carolina. Taken together, these images dispel later claims by whites that Indians were an "uncivilized" people who had not yet mastered agriculture and who lacked the sophisticated social structures necessary for urban life.

Questions to Consider

1. What can you deduce about Timucua gender roles from the first image?
2. How well organized does the town of Secoton appear? What types of institutions would likely be necessary to support what you see in the picture?
3. What conclusions can you draw from these images about sixteenth-century Native American life?
4. Compare and contrast Mary Rowlandson's description of Native Americans with what you see here ("'Captivity Account' of Mary Rowlandson," Document 9). What seems different? How do you account for this?

"Timucua planting crops"

SOURCE: [LC-USZ62-31869]/Library of Congress Prints and Photographs Division

The town of Secoton, Sixteenth-century North Carolina
SOURCE: [LC-USZ62-52444]/Library of Congress Prints and Photographs Division

3

Powhatan and John Smith (1608)

Initial English attempts at colonization met with failure until the successful settlement at Jamestown in 1607. John Smith was among the first group of settlers. He was an adventurer and soldier of fortune whose experiences had taken him from the Low Countries to wars against the Turks, and, in 1607, to Virginia. The activities of the new arrivals quickly drew the attention of Powhatan, a paramount chief who had built a powerful Chesapeake Bay area confederacy of 30 tribes and 10,000–15,000 people that bore his name. In the following excerpt, Powhatan and Smith exchange views on the impact of English settlement.

Questions to Consider

1. How does the depiction of European–Indian relations in this document differ from that found in "Images of Sixteenth-Century Native American Life" (Document 2)?

2.   What are the major points of disagreement between Powhatan and John Smith?

3.   What impact has English settlement had upon the Powhatan?

Captaine Smith, you may understand that I having seene the death of all my people thrice, and not any one living of these three generations but my selfe; I know the difference of Peace and Warre better than any in my Country. But now I am old and ere long must die, my brethren, namely Opitchapam, Opechancanough, and Kekataugh, my two sisters, and their two daughters, are distinctly each others successors. I wish their experience no lesse then mine, and your love to them no lesse then mine to you. But this bruit from Nandsamund, that you are come to destroy my Country, so much affrighteth all my people as they dare not visit you. What will it availe you to take that by force you may quickly have by love, or to destroy them that provide you food. What can you get by warre, when we can hide our provisions and fly to the woods? whereby you must famish by wronging us your friends. And why are you thus jealous of our loves seeing us unarmed, and both doe, and are willing still to feede you, with that you cannot get but by our labours? Thinke you I am so simple, not to know it is better to eate good meate, lye well, and sleepe quietly with my women and children, laugh and be merry with you, have copper, hatchets, or what I want being your friend: then be forced to flie from all, to lie cold in the woods, feede upon Acornes, rootes, and such trash, and be so hunted by you, that I can neither rest, eate, nor sleepe; but my tyred men must watch, and if a twig but breake, every one cryeth there commeth Captaine Smith: then must I fly I know not whether: and thus with miserable feare, end my miserable life, leaving my pleasures to such youths as you, which through your rash unadvisednesse may quickly as miserably end, for want of that, you never know where to finde. Let this therefore assure you of our loves, and every yeare our friendly trade shall furnish you with Corne; and now also, if you would come in friendly manner to see us, and not thus with your guns and swords as to invade your foes. To this subtill discourse, the President thus replyed.

Capt. Smiths Reply.

Seeing you will not rightly conceive of our words, we strive to make you know our thoughts by our deeds; the vow I made you of my love, both my selfe and my men have kept. As for your promise I find it every day violated by some of your subjects: yet we finding your love and kindnesse, our custome is so far from being ungratefull, that for your sake onely, we have curbed our thirsting desire of revenge; els had they knowne as well the crueltie we use to our enemies, as our true love and courtesie to our friends. And I thinke your judgement sufficient to conceive, as well by the adventures we have undertaken, as by the advantage we have (by our Armes) of yours: that had we intended you any hurt, long ere this we could have effected it. Your people comming to James Towne are entertained with their Bowes and Arrowes without any exceptions;

SOURCE: John Smith, *The Generall Historie of Virginia, New England & The Summer Isles* (Glasgow, Scotland, 1907), 1: 158–59.

we esteeming it with you as it is with us, to weare our armes as our apparell. As for the danger of our enemies, in such warres consist our chiefest pleasure: for your riches we have no use: as for the hiding your provision, or by your flying to the woods, we shall not so unadvisedly starve as you conclude, your friendly care in that behalfe is needlesse, for we have a rule to finde beyond your knowledge.

4

An Indentured Servant Writes Home (1623)

The overwhelming majority of English settlers who came to seventeenth-century Virginia were indentured servants. Drawn from the ranks of criminals, the poor, and in some cases tricked or coerced into servitude, the indentures received transportation to the colony in exchange for their labor over a period of between three and seven years. The new settlers faced brutal conditions due to the threat of Indian attack, lawlessness among the settlers, and their often dehumanizing treatment at the hands of masters who sought to squeeze as much from the labor as possible. Most indentured servants died before their contracts were completed. Here Richard Frethorne writes his parents about his experiences as a new colonist. Other than this and a few other letters, little is known of what became of Frethorne.

Questions to Consider

1. To what extent might Richard Frethorne describe Virginia as a "land of opportunity"?
2. What seem to be the major problems facing the Virginia colony in 1623?
3. Why is Frethorne asking his father to send food?
4. Compare and contrast the reasons for the conditions of the settlement in 1623 Virginia with those described in "Early New York" (Document 5), "Jesuit Comparison of French and Native Life" (Document 6), and "General Considerations for the Plantation in New England" (Document 7). How do you account for these similarities? Differences?

March 20 1623

Loving and kind father and mother:

My most humble duty remembered to you, hoping in God of your good health, as I myself am at the making hereof. This is to let you understand that I your child am in a most heavy case by reason of the nature of the country, [which] is such that it causeth much sickness, [such] as the scurvy and the bloody flux and diverse other diseases, which maketh the body very poor and weak. And when we are sick there is nothing to comfort us; for since I came out of the ship I never ate anything but peas, and loblollie (that is, water gruel). As for deer or venison I never saw any since I came into this land. There is indeed some fowl, but we are not allowed to go and get it, but must work hard both early and late for a mess of water gruel and a mouthful of bread and beef. A mouthful of bread for a penny loaf must serve for four men which is most pitiful.... For we live in fear of the enemy every hour, yet we have had a combat with them on the Sunday before Shrovetide, and we took two alive and made slaves of them. But it was by policy, for we are in great danger; for our plantation is very weak by reason of the death and sickness of our company. For we came but twenty for the merchants, and they are half dead just; and we look every hour when two more should go. Yet there came some four other men yet to live with us, of which there is but one alive; and our Lieutenant is dead, and [also] his father and his brother. And there was some five or six of the last year's twenty, of which there is but three left, so that we are fain to get other men to plant with us; and yet we are but 32 to fight against 3000 if they should come....

And I have nothing to comfort me, nor is there nothing to be gotten here but sickness and death, except [in the event] that one had money to lay out in some things for profit. But I have nothing at all—no, not a shirt to my back but two rags (2), nor no clothes but one poor suit, nor but one pair of shoes, but one pair of stockings, but one cap, [and] but two bands. My cloak is stolen by one of my own fellows, and to his dying hour [he] would not tell me what he did with it; but some of my fellows saw him have butter and beef out of a ship, which my cloak, I doubt [not], paid for. So that I have not a penny, nor a penny worth, to help me to either spice or sugar or strong waters, without the which one cannot live here. For as strong beer in England doth fatten and strengthen them, so water here doth wash and weaken these here [and] only keeps [their] life and soul together. But I am not half [of] a quarter so strong as I was in England, and all is for want of victuals; for I do protest unto you that I have eaten more in [one] day at home than I have allowed me here for a week....

And indeed so I find it now, to my great grief and misery; and [I] saith that if you love me you will redeem me suddenly, for which I do entreat and beg. And if you cannot get the merchants to redeem me for some little money, then for God's sake get a gathering or entreat some good folks to lay out some little sum of money in meal and cheese and butter and beef. Any eating meat will yield great profit. Oil and vinegar is very good; but, father, there is great loss in leaking. But for God's sake send beef and cheese and butter, or the more of one sort and none of another.... I will send it over and beg the profit to redeem me; and if I die before it come, I have entreated Goodman Jackson to send you the worth of it, who hath promised he will. If you send, you must direct your letters to Goodman Jackson, at Jamestown, a gunsmith. (You must set down his freight,

SOURCE: Richard Frethorne, letter to his father and mother, March 20, 1623, in Susan Kingsbury, ed., *The Records of the Virginia Company of London* (Washington, DC: Government Printing Office, 1935), 4: 58–62.

because there be more of his name there.) Good father, do not forget me, but have mercy and pity my miserable case. I know if you did but see me, you would weep to see me; for I have but one suit.... Wherefore, for God's sake, pity me. I pray you to remember my love to all my friends and kindred. I hope all my brothers and sisters are in good health, and as for my part I have set down my resolution that certainly will be; that is, that the answer of this letter will be life or death to me. Therefore, good father, send as soon as you can; and if you send me any thing let this be the mark.

ROT
Richard Frethorne
Martin's Hundred

The names of them that be dead of the company [that] came over with us to serve under our Lieutenants:

John Flower	George Goulding
John Thomas	Jos. Johnson
Thos. Howes	our lieutenant, his father and brother
John Butcher	
John Sanderford	Thos. Giblin
Rich. Smith	George Banum
John Olive	a little Dutchman
Thos. Peirsman	one woman
William Cerrell	one maid
	one child

All these died out of my master's house, since I came; and we came in but at Christmas, and this is the 20th day of March. And the sailors say that there is two-thirds of the 150 dead already. And thus I end, praying to God to send me good success that I may be redeemed out of Egypt. So *vale in Christo*.

5

Early New York (1626)

By the late sixteenth and early seventeenth centuries, several European countries had begun a reconnaissance of the North American coast in search of sites for trade and agriculture. In 1609, a Dutch East India Company ship captained by English-born Henry Hudson sailed into the river that later bore his name, claiming the region for the Netherlands. Five years later the Dutch would establish a trading post (Fort Orange) near present-day Albany, New York. In 1624, they established New Amsterdam at the mouth of the Hudson, where it would quickly blossom into an important commercial center for the fur trade. In the following document, Nicolaes van Wassenaer provides an eyewitness account of life, commerce, and the meeting ground of cultures in early New Amsterdam. Van Wassenaer, an early resident of New Amsterdam, wrote the Historisch Verhael *[Historical Narrative], which provides historians with an excellent collection of firsthand observations of the Dutch in early New York.*

Questions to Consider

1. What seems to be the central economic activity in early New Amsterdam? How might such activity shape the development of this town?

2. How are American Indians depicted in this document?

3. How do these depictions of American Indians compare with those found in the "Jesuit Comparison of French and Native Life" (Document 6), and the "'Captivity Account' of Mary Rowlandson" (Document 9)? What conclusions might you draw about the similarities? Differences?

4. What does the author say about local government? What does he say about local religious practices? What conclusions can you draw from these depictions?

November 1626

... The colony is now established on the Manhates, where a fort has been staked out by Master Kryn Frederycks, an engineer. It is planned to be of large dimensions. The ship which has returned home this month [November] brings samples of all sorts of produce growing there, the cargo being 7246 beaver skins, 675 otter skins, 48 mink, 36 wild cat, and various other sorts; many pieces of oak timber and hickory.

The counting-house there is kept in a stone building, thatched with reed; the other houses are of the bark of trees. Each has his own house. The Director and *Koopman* [merchant] live together; there are thirty ordinary houses on the east side of the river, which runs nearly north and south. The Honorable Pieter Minuit is Director there at present; Jan Lempou *schout*; Sebastiaen Jansz. Crol and Jan Huych, comforters of the sick, who, whilst awaiting a clergyman, read to the commonalty there, on Sundays, texts of Scripture and the commentaries. François Molemaecker is busy building a horse-mill, over which shall be constructed a spacious room sufficient to accommodate a large congregation, and then a tower is to be erected where the bells brought from Porto Rico will be hung.

The council there administers justice in criminal matters as far as imposing fines, but not as far as corporal punishment. Should it happen that any one deserves that, he must be sent to Holland with his sentence. Cornelis May of

SOURCE: Nicolaes van Wassenaer, from "The *Historisch Verhael* [Historical Narrative]," *Narratives of New Netherland, 1609–1664,* ed. J. Frank Jameson (New York, 1909), 82–87.

Hoorn was the first Director there, in the year 1624; Willem van Hulst was the second, in the year 1625. He returns now. Everyone there who fills no public office is busy about his own affairs. Men work there as in Holland; one trades, upwards, southwards and northwards; another builds houses, the third farms. Each farmer has his farmstead on the land purchased by the Company, which also owns the cows; but the milk remains to the profit of the farmer; he sells it to those of the people who receive their wages for work every week. The houses of the Hollanders now stand outside the fort, but when that is completed, they will all repair within, so as to garrison it and be secure from sudden attack.

Those of the South River will abandon their fort, and come hither. At Fort Orange, the most northerly point at which the Hollanders traded, no more than fifteen or sixteen men will remain; the remainder will come down [to the Manhates]. Right opposite is the fort of the Maykans which they built against their enemies, the Maquaes, a powerful people.

It happened this year, that the Maykans, going to war with the Maquaes, requested to be assisted by the commander of Fort Orange and six others. Commander Krieckebeeck went up with them; a league from the fort they met the Maquaes who fell so boldly upon them with a discharge of arrows, that they were forced to fly, and many were killed, among whom were the commander and three of his men. Among the latter was Tymen Bouwensz, whom they devoured, after having well roasted him. The rest they burnt. The commander was buried with the other two by his side. Three escaped; two Portuguese and a Hollander from Hoorn. One of the Portuguese was wounded by an arrow in the back whilst swimming. The Indians carried a leg and an arm home to be divided among their families, as a sign that they had conquered their enemies.

Some days after the worthy Pieter Barentsz, who usually was sent upwards and along the coast with the sloops, visited them; they wished to excuse their act, on the plea that they had never set themselves against the whites, and asked the reason why the latter had meddled with them; otherwise, they would not have shot them.

There being no commander, Pieter Barentsen assumed the command of Fort Orange by order of Director Minuit. There were eight families there, and ten or twelve seamen in the Company's service. The families were to leave there this year—the fort to remain garrisoned by sixteen men, without women—in order to strengthen with people the colony near the Manhates, who are becoming more and more accustomed to the strangers. The natives are always seeking some advantage by thieving. The crime is seldom punished among them. If any one commit that offence too often he is stript bare of his goods, and must seek fresh means. The husband who abandons his wife without cause must leave all her goods; in like manner the wife the husband's. But as they love the children ardently, these are frequently the cause of their coming again together. The girls allow their hair to be shaved all around, like the priests, when they are unwell for the first time. They are set apart from all in a separate house, where food is furnished them on a stick. They remain therein until they are sick a second time. Then they make their appearance among their relatives again, and are caused to marry. They then again dress their hair, which before they may not touch. The married women let their hair grow to the waist and smear it with oil. When they are unwell they do not eat with their husbands, and they sup their drink out of the hand. The men let the hair grow on one side of the head into a braid; the rest is cut off. If one kill the other, it is not punished; whoever it concerns sets vengeance on foot; if not, nothing is done. In the month of August a universal torment seizes them, so that they run like men possessed, regarding neither hedges nor ditches, and like mad dogs resting not till exhausted. They have in such men a singular sight. The birds most common are wild pigeons; these are so numerous that they shut out the sunshine.

When the fort, staked out at the Manhates, will be completed, it is to be named Amsterdam. The fort at the South River is already vacated, in order to strengthen the colony. Trading there is carried on only in yachts, in order to avoid expense.

6

Jesuit Comparison of French and Native Life (1657–1658)

France established its most important North American outposts in Nova Scotia and along the St. Lawrence River valley. Faith and fortune were the primary reasons for French involvement along the St. Lawrence. Control of the region enabled French traders to tap the lucrative fur trade of the interior, while the conversions of many local tribes to Roman Catholicism enhanced French influence in the region. The bulk of the French missionaries were Jesuits. Created in response to the Protestant Reformation, the Society of Jesus sought to convert individuals to Roman Catholicism and fight heresy; by the seventeenth century, the Jesuits had become a formidable missionary force. Often sent alone to live among those who they sought to convert, the Jesuits endured years of hardship to achieve their mission. The accounts left by the missionaries in the Jesuit Relations *provide excellent insights into the structure and folkways of American Indian life. In the following account, a Jesuit compares French and native habits.*

Questions to Consider

1. How do European and American Indian dress, eating habits, and social customs differ?

2. Why do you think this account was written?

3. What can you deduce about European and American Indian contact from this selection?

4. In what ways does this description of Native culture differ from that contained in "Early New York" (Document 5), "'Captivity Account' of Mary Rowlandson" (Document 9), and "The Pueblo Revolt" (Document 10)? How do you account for these differences?

… In Europe, the seam of stockings is behind the leg.… Among the Savages it is otherwise; the seam of stockings worn by men is between the legs, and here they fasten little ornaments—made of porcupine quills, stained scarlet, and in the form of fringe or of spangles—which meet when they walk, and make … a pretty effect, not easily described. The women wear this ornamentation on the outer side of the leg.

In France, patterns and raised shoes are considered the most beautiful.… The Savages' shoes are as flat as tennis-shoes, but much wider, especially in winter, when they stuff and line them amply to keep away the cold.

Shirts are in Europe worn next to the skin, under the other garments. The Savages wear them usually over their dress, to shield it from snow and rain.…

The end of a shirt protruding from under the coat is an indecorous thing; but not so in Canadas. You will see Savages dressed in French attire, with worsted stockings and a cloak, but without any breeches; while before and … behind are seen two large shirt-flaps hanging down below the cloak.… That fashion seems all the more tasteful in their eyes because they regard our breeches as an encumbrance.…

Politeness and propriety have taught us to carry handkerchiefs. In this matter the Savages charge us with filthiness—because, they say, we place what is unclean in a fine white piece of linen, and put it away in our pockets as something very precious, while they throw it upon the ground.…

Most Europeans sit on raised seats, using round or square tables. The Savages eat from the ground.…

In France, food and drink are taken together. The Algonquins follow quite the contrary custom in their feasts, first eating what is served them, and then drinking, without touching food again.…

We wash meat to cleanse it of blood and impurities; the Savages do not wash it, for fear of losing its blood and a part of its fat.… We usually begin the dinner with soup, which is the last dish among the Savages, the broth of the pot serving them for drink. Bread is eaten here with the meat and other courses; if you give some to a Savage, he will make a separate course of it and very often eat it last. Yet they are gradually adapting themselves to our way.

In most parts of Europe, when any one makes a call he is invited to drink; among the Savages he is invited to eat.…

When the Savages are not hunting or on a journey, their usual posture is to recline or sit on the ground. They cannot remain standing, maintaining that their legs become swollen immediately. Seats higher than the ground they dislike; the

SOURCE: *The Jesuit Relations and Allied Documents*, ed. Reuben G. Thwaites, *Iroquois, Lower Canada, 1656–58*, vol. 44 (Cleveland, 1899), 293–309.

French, on the contrary, use chairs, benches, or stools, leaving the ground and litter to the animals.

A good dancer in France does not move ... his arms much, and holds his body erect, moving his feet so nimbly that, you would say, he spurns the ground and wishes to stay in the air. The savages, on the contrary, bend over in their dances, thrusting out their arms and moving them violently as if they were kneading bread, while they strike the ground with their feet so vigorously that one would say they are determined to make it tremble, or to bury themselves in it up to the neck....

In France, children are carried on the arm, or clasped to the breast; in Canadas, the mothers bear them behind their backs. In France, they are kept as well covered as possible.... The cradle, in France, is left at home; there the women carry it with their children; it is composed merely of a cedar board, on which the poor little one is bound like a bundle.

... In France, a Workman does not expect his pay until he completes his task; the Savages ask it in advance....

Europeans have no hesitation about telling their names and conditions, but you embarrass a Savage by asking him his name; if you do ask him, he will say that he does not know, and will make a sign to some one else to tell it....

In France, when a father gives his daughter in marriage, he allows her a dowry. There, it is given to the girl's father.

In Europe, the children inherit from their parents; among the Hurons the nephews, sons of the father's sister, are their uncle's heirs; and the Savage's small belongings will be given to the friends of the deceased, rather than to his children....

In France, the man usually takes to his house the woman whom he marries; there, the man goes to the woman's house to dwell.

In France, if any one fall into a fit of anger, or harbor some evil purpose, or meditate some harm, he is reviled, threatened, and punished; there, they give him presents, to soothe his ill-humor, cure his mental ailment, and put good thoughts into his head again. This custom, in the sincerity of their actions, is not a bad one; for if he who is angry, or is devising some ill ... to resent an offense, touch this present, his anger and his evil purpose are immediately effaced from his mind.

In a large part of Europe, ceremonies and compliments are indulged in to such an excess as to drive out sincerity. There quite on the contrary sincerity is entirely naked....

In Europe, we unclothe the dead as much as we can, leaving them only what is necessary to veil them and hide them from our eyes. The Savages, however, give them all that they can, anointing and attiring them as if for their wedding, and burying them with all their favorite belongings.

The French are stretched lengthwise in their graves, while the Savages, ... in burying their dead make them take in the grave the position which they held in their mothers' wombs. In some parts of France, the dead are placed with their heads turned toward the East; the Savages make them face the West.

7

General Considerations for the Plantation in New England (1629)

The Puritans established the first extensive English settlement in North America at Massachusetts Bay in 1630. Dissatisfied with the Church of England and determined to create a church free of corruption, the Puritans became interested in the region with the establishment of a fishing concern on Cape Ann, Massachusetts, in 1623. By the end of the decade many Puritans, whose attempts to create a purified church had alienated the Crown, sought to establish a model community where they could practice their religion without interference. In 1629, they obtained a charter for the Massachusetts Bay Company. In the selection excerpted below, the leaders of the company give their reasons for establishing a colony in New England. The Massachusetts Bay Colony attracted 20,000 Englishmen in the ensuing Great Migration of 1630–1643.

Questions to Consider

1. What is the thesis of this document?
2. Why was the Massachusetts Bay colony established?
3. What role do economic factors play in this colony? What might that say about the Puritans?
4. Why would this colony be so attractive to English settlers?

First, it will be a service to the Church of great consequence, to carry Gospel into those parts of the world, and to raise a bulwark against the kingdom of Antichrist, which the Jesuits labor to rear up in all places of the world.

Secondly, all other churches of Europe are brought to desolation, and it may be justly feared that the like judgment is coming upon us; and who knows but that God hath provided this place to be a refuge for many whom he means to save out of the general destruction?

Thirdly, the land grows weary of her inhabitants, so that man, which is the most precious of all creatures, is here more vile and base than the earth they tread upon; so as children, neighbors and friends, especially of the poor, are counted the greatest burdens, which, if things were right, would be the chiefest earthly blessings.

SOURCE: "General Considerations for the Plantation in New England; with an Answer to Several Objections," *Chronicles of the First Planters of the Colony of Massachusetts Bay, from 1623–1636*, ed. Alexander Young (Boston, 1846), 271–73.

Fourthly, we are grown to that excess and intemperance in all excess of riot, as no mean estate almost will suffice [a man] to keep sail with his equals; and he that fails in it, must live in scorn and contempt. Hence it comes to pass, that all arts and trades are carried in that deceitful manner and unrighteous course, as it is almost impossible for a good, upright man to maintain his charge, and live comfortably in any of them.

Fifthly, the schools of learning and religion are so corrupted as, (besides the unsupportable charge of their education), most children, even the best, wittiest, and of fairest hopes, are perverted, corrupted, and utterly overthrown by the multitude of evil examples and licentious governors of those seminaries.

Sixthly, the whole earth is the Lord's garden, and he has given it to the sons of Adam to be tilled and improved by them. Why then should we stand starving here for places of habitation, (many men spending as much labor and cost to recover or keep sometimes an acre or two of lands as would procure him many hundreds of acres, as good or better, in another place) and in the mean time suffer whole countries, as profitable for the use of man, to lie waste without improvement?

Seventhly, what can be a better work, and more noble, and worthy a Christian, than to help to raise and support a particular church while it is in its infancy, and to join forces with such a company of faithful people as by a timely assistance may grow stronger and prosper, and for want of it may be put to great hazard, if not wholly ruined?

Eighthly, if any such as are known to be godly, and live in wealth and prosperity here, shall forsake all this to join themselves with this church, and run in hazard with them of a hard and mean condition, it will be an example of great use both for the removing of scandal and sinister and worldly respects, to give more life to the faith of God's people in their prayers for the Plantation, and also to encourage others to join the more willingly in it.

8

William Bradford on Sickness Among the Natives (1633)

The arrival of Europeans had a devastating impact on Native Americans. European demand for land, the introduction of new flora and fauna, and the disruption of traditional intertribal relations all created severe dislocation for America's original inhabitants, but European diseases had the greatest repercussions. Long isolated from the disease pool shared by Europeans, Asians, and Africans, American Indians had no resistance to the microbial invaders that accompanied the newcomers after 1492. The following account, written by William Bradford, describes the catastrophic effect of disease upon the New England tribes. A native of England,

Bradford had become a Pilgrim as a youth and lived in the Netherlands before arriving in North America aboard the Mayflower. *As leader of Plymouth during most of the period from 1622 until 1656, he greatly influenced the development of the Pilgrim colony.*

Questions to Consider

1. What was the impact of smallpox on the American Indians?
2. How does William Bradford explain why Indians die and Europeans survive the disease? What does this say about the seventeenth-century Pilgrim worldview?
3. How did the American Indians react?
4. In what ways would disease assist European conquest of the New World?

I am now to relate some strange and remarkable passages. There was a company of people [who] lived in the country, up above in the river of Conigtecut [Connecticut], a great way from their trading house there, and were enemies to those Indians which lived about them, and of whom they stood in some fear (being a stout people). About a thousand of them had enclosed them selves in a fort, which they had strongly palisaded about. 3. or 4. Dutch men went up in the beginning of winter to live with them, to get their trade, and prevent them for bringing it to the English, or to fall into amity with them; but at spring to bring all down to their place. But their enterprise failed, for it pleased God to visit these Indians with a great sickness, and such a mortalitie that of a 1000. above 900. and a half of them died, and many of them did rot above ground for want of burial, and the Dutch men almost starved before they could get away, for ice and snow. But about Feb: they got with much difficulty to their trading house; whom they kindly relieved, being almost spent with hunger and cold. Being thus refreshed by them diverse days, they got to their own place, and the Dutch were very thankful for this kindness.

This spring, also, those Indians that lived about their trading house there fell sick of the small pox, and died most miserably; for a sorer disease cannot befall them; they fear it more than the plague; for usually they that have this disease have them in abundance, and for want of bedding and lining and other helps, they fall into a lamentable condition, as they lie on their hard mats, the pox breaking and mattering, and running one into another, their skin cleaving (by reason thereof) to the mats they lie on; when they turn them, a whole side will flee of at once, (as it were,) and they will be all of a gore blood, most fearful to behold; and then being very sore, what with cold and other distempers, they die like rotten sheep. The condition of this people was so lamentable, and they fell down so generally of this disease, as they were (in the end) not able to help one another; no, not to make a fire, nor to fetch a little water to drink, nor any to bury the dead; but would strive as long as they could, and when they could procure no other means to make fire, they would burn the wooden trays and dishes they ate their meat in, and their very bows and arrows; and some would crawl out on all four to get a little water, and some times die by the way, and

SOURCE: William Bradford, *History of Plimouth Plantation* (Boston, 1898), 388–89.

not be able to get in again. But those of the English house, (though at first they were afraid of the infection,) yet seeing their woeful and sad condition, and hearing their pitiful cries and lamentations, they had compassion of them, and daily fetched them wood and water, and made them fires, got them victuals whilst they lived, and buried them when they died. For very few of them escaped, notwithstanding they did what they could for them, to the hazard of them selves. The chief Sachem him self now died, and almost all his friends and kindred. But by the marvelous goodness and providence of God not one of the English was so much as sick, or in the least measure tainted with this disease, though they daily did these offices for them for many weeks together. And this mercy which they showed them was kindly taken, and thankfully acknowledged of all the Indians that knew or heard of the same; and their mrs. here did much commend and reward them for the same.

9

"Captivity Account" of Mary Rowlandson (1675)

The spread of white settlement in southern New England had placed many of the native tribes in a precarious position. Pressed by white land hunger and decimated by European diseases, a coalition of the Wampanoag, Narragansett, Nipmuck, Mohegan, and Podunk allied under the leadership of the Wampanoag sachem (leader) Metacom, or King Philip, to attack the white settlements. During the 1675–1676 campaign, the natives enjoyed great success, including the burning of Lancaster, Massachusetts, in 1676. As they fled the town, they left with several captives, including Mary White Rowlandson. The daughter of one of Lancaster's wealthiest proprietors and wife of the village's first minister, Mary spent her captivity making shirts and stockings. After she had spent eleven weeks with the natives, a ransom freed her. The following excerpt describes some of her experiences and reveals how her captors managed to feed themselves while on the run.

Questions to Consider

1. To what audience is this document addressed?
2. What is Mary Rowlandson's opinion of the American Indians?
3. Why does Rowlandson place the American Indians and their actions within a religious context?

4. How does this description of Native culture differ from that contained in "Early New York" (Document 5), the "Jesuit Comparison of French and Native Life" (Document 6), and "The Pueblo Revolt" (Document 10)? How do you account for these differences?

It was thought, if their corn were cut down, they would starve and die with hunger; and all that could be found was destroyed and they driven from that little they had in store, into the woods, in the midst of winter; and yet how to admiration did the Lord preserve them for his holy ends, and the destruction of many still among the English! Strangely did the Lord provide for them, that I did not see (all the time I was among them) one man, woman or child die with hunger. Though many times they would eat that, that a hog or a dog would hardly touch; yet by the God strengthened them to be a scourge to his people.

Their chief and commonest food was ground-nuts, they eat also nuts and acorns, artichokes, lily roots, ground beans, and several other weeds and roots that I know not.

They would pick up old bones, and cut them in pieces at the joints, and if they were full of worms and maggots, they would scald them over the fire, to make the vermin come out, and then boil them, and drink up the liquor, and then beat the great ends of them in a mortar, and so eat them. They would eat horses' guts, and ears, and all sorts of wild birds which they could catch. Also bear, venison, beavers, tortoise, frogs, squirrels, dogs, skunks, rattle-snakes. Yea, the very bark of trees; besides all sorts of creatures and provision which they plundered from the English. I can but stand in admiration to see the wonderful power of God, in providing for such a vast number of our enemies in the wilderness, where there was nothing to be seen, but from hand to mouth.

10

The Pueblo Revolt (1680)

By 1598, Spanish expansion north from the Valley of Mexico had established settlements in the Rio Grande Valley of modern-day New Mexico. For nearly a century, the Pueblo Indian villages in the region tolerated Spanish demands for labor and Spanish insistence on conversion to Roman Catholicism. By the 1670s, a group of Pueblo Indian leaders began to emphasize a reassertion of traditional customs as a means of resisting outside domination. In 1675, Spanish authorities rounded up forty-seven leaders, executing three and publicly

SOURCE: Mary Rowlandson, *A Narrative … of Mrs. Mary Rowlandson* (Boston, 1856), 104–105. Reprinted by permission.

whipping the rest. Resistance continued in secret; and by the summer of 1680, insurgent leader Popé was prepared to drive out the Spanish and resurrect traditional Pueblo Indian practices. The Pueblos revolted on August 11, 1680; within just a few days, the Spanish fled south to El Paso and would not reassert their control over the region until the mid-1690s. In the meantime, the Pueblo Indians set about destroying all elements of Spanish culture. The following excerpt discusses a Spanish official's account of the revolt.

Questions to Consider

1. From this document, what can you deduce about Spanish attitudes toward American Indians?

2. Why are the Spanish under attack? Why do some of the American Indians cooperate with the Spanish?

3. Why are priests being killed? What might this say about the role of religion in Spanish and Native cultures?

On the eve of the day of the glorious San Lorenzo, having received notice of the said rebellion from the governors of Pecos and Tanos, who said that two Indians had left the Teguas, and particularly the pueblos of Tesuque, to which they belonged, to notify them to come and join the revolt, and that they [the governors] came to tell me of it and of how they were unwilling to participate in such wickedness and treason, saying that they now regarded the Spaniards as their brothers, I thanked them for their kindness in giving the notice and told them to go to their pueblos and remain quiet. I busied myself immediately in giving the said orders, which I mentioned to your reverence, and on the following morning as I was about to go to mass there arrived Pedro Hidalgo, who had gone to the pueblo of Tesuque, accompanying Father Fray Juan Pio, who went there to say mass. He told me that the Indians of the said pueblo had killed the said Father Fray Pio and that he himself had escaped miraculously. He told me also that the said Indians had retreated to the sierra with all the cattle and horses belonging to the convent, and with their own.

The receipt of this news left us all in the state that may be imagined. I immediately and instantly sent the maese de campo, Francisco Gomez, with a squadron of soldiers sufficient to investigate this case and also to attempt to extinguish the flame of the ruin already begun. He returned here on the same day, telling me that the report of the death of the said Fray Juan Pio was true. He said also that there had been killed that same morning Father Fray Tomas de Torres, guardian of Nambe, and his brother, with the latter's wife and a child, and another resident of Taos, and also Father Fray Luis de Morales, guardian of San Ildefonso, and the family of Francisco de Ximenez, his wife and family, and Dona Petronila de Salas with ten sons and daughters; and that they had been robbed and profaned the convents and had robbed all

SOURCE: "Letter of the Governor and Captain-General, Don Antonio de Otermin, 8 September 1680," C. W. Hackett, ed., *Historical Documents Relating to New Mexico, Nueva Vizcaya, and Approaches Thereto, to 1773* (Washington, DC, 1937), 3: 327–35. Reprinted by permission.

the haciendas of those murdered and also all the horses and cattle of that juris-diction and La Canada.

Upon receiving this news I immediately notified the alcalde mayor of that district to assemble all the people in his house in a body, and told him to advise at once the alcalde mayor of Los Taos to do the same. On this same day I received notice that two members of a convoy had been killed in the pueblo of Santa Clara, six others having escaped by flight. Also at the same time the sargento mayor, Bernabe Marquez, sent to ask me for assistance, saying that he was surrounded and hard pressed by the Indians of the Queres and Tanos nations. Having sent the aid for which he asked me, and an order for those fam-ilies of Los Cerrillos to come to the villa, I instantly arranged for all the people in it and its environs to retire to the casas reales. Believing that the uprising of the Tanos and Pecos might endanger the person of the reverend father custodian, I wrote to him to set out at once for the villa, not feeling reassured even with the escort which the lieutenant took, at my orders, but when they arrived with the letter they found that the Indians had already killed the said father custodian; Father Fray Domingo de Fernando de Velasco, guardian of Los Pecos, near the pueblo of Galisteo, he having escaped that far from the fury of the Pecos. The latter killed in that pueblo Fray Juan de la Pedrosa, two Spanish women, and three children. There died also at the hands of the said enemies in Galisteo Joseph Nieto, two sons of Maestre de Campo Leiva, Francisco de Anaya, the younger, who was with the escort, and the wives of Maestre de Campo Leiva and Joseph Nieto, with all their daughters and families. I also learned definitely on this day that there had died, in the pueblo of Santo Domingo, Fathers Fray Juan de Talaban, Fray Francisco Antonio Lorenzana, and Fray Joseph de Mon-tesdoca, and the alcalde mayor, Andres de Peralta, together with the rest of the men who went as escort.

Seeing myself with notices of so many and such untimely deaths, and that not having received any word from the lieutenant general was probably due to the fact that he was in the same exigency and confusion, or that the Indians had killed most of those on the lower river, and considering also that in the pueblo of Los Taos the father guardians of that place and of the pueblo of Pecuries might be in danger, as well as the alcalde mayor and the residents of that valley, and that at all events it was the only place from which I could obtain any horses and cattle—for all these reasons I endeavored to send a relief of soldiers. Marching out for that purpose, they learned that in La Canada, as in Los Taos and Pecuries, the Indians had risen in rebellion, joining the Apaches of the Achos nation. In Pecuries they had killed Francisco Blanco de la Vega; a *mulata* belonging to the maese de campo, Francisco Xavier; and a son of the said *mulata*. Shortly thereafter I learned that they also killed in the pueblo of Taos the father guardian, Fray Francisco de Mora; and the Father Fray Mathias Rendon, the guardian of Pecuries; and Fray Antonio de Pro; and the alcalde mayor, as well as another fourteen or fifteen soldiers, along with all the families of the inhabitants of that valley, all of whom were together in the convent....

11

The Indians and Missions
of Florida (1675)

By the late seventeenth century, the establishment of English settlements along the North American coast posed a threat to the tenuous Spanish hold over Florida. Spain had established a small garrison town in Florida named San Augustín (St. Augustine) in 1565, to secure the shipping lanes from pirates and to protect the region from colonization by other European powers. The Spanish had cultivated the support of local Native American tribes, primarily through the use of missions, to secure their hold on the region. The following document provides a detailed description of the Florida Indians. The author, Gabriel Diaz Vara Calderón, Bishop of Santiago, Cuba, visited Apalachee, a tribal confederation of about twenty towns located near present-day Tallahassee, Florida, in 1664. During his visit, he established five new missions. Neither Calderón nor the Apalachee would long survive this account: Calderón died in 1676, while forces under the leadership of South Carolina Governor James Moore conducted the Apalachee Massacre in 1704.

Questions to Consider

1. How do these depictions compare with those found in "Images of Native American Life" (Document 2), the "Jesuit Comparison of French and Native Life" (Document 6), and the "'Captivity Account' of Mary Rowlandson" (Document 9)? What conclusions might you draw about the similarities? Differences?

2. What are living conditions like in late seventeenth-century Florida? How do they compare with other colonies?

3. Are the Apalachee good Catholics? Why do you think they might embrace a foreign religion?

In the four provinces of Guale, Timuqua, Apalache and Apalachocoli there are 13,152 Christianized Indians to whom I administered the holy sacrament of confirmation. They are fleshy, and rarely is there a small one, but they are weak and phlegmatic as regards work, though clever and quick to learn any art they see done, and great carpenters as is evidenced in the construction of their wooden

SOURCE: Lucy L. Wenhold, "A 17th Century Letter of Gabriel Diaz Vara Calderón, Bishop of Cuba, Describing the Indians and Indian Missions of Florida," *Smithsonian Miscellaneous Collections* (Washington, DC, 1936), 95, no. 16: 12–14.

churches which are large and painstakingly wrought. The arms they employ are bow and arrows and a hatchet they call *macâna*. They go naked, with only the skin [of some animal] from the waist down, and, if anything more, a coat of serge without a lining, or a blanket. The women wear only a sort of tunic that wraps them from the neck to the feet, and which they make of the pearl-colored foliage of trees, which they call *guano* and which costs them nothing except to gather it. Four thousand and eighty-one women, whom I found in the villages naked from the waist up and from the knees down, I caused to be clothed in the grass like the others.

Their ordinary diet consists of porridge which they make of corn with ashes, pumpkins, beans which they call *frijoles*, with game and fish from the rivers and lakes which the well-to-do ones can afford. Their only drink is water, and they do not touch wine or rum. Their greatest luxury is [a drink] which they make from a weed that grows on the seacoast, which they cook and drink hot and which they call *cazina*. It becomes very bitter and is worse than beer, although it does not intoxicate them and is beneficial. They sleep on the ground, and in their houses only on a frame made of reed bars, which they call *barbacoa*, with a bear skin laid upon it and without any cover, the fire they build in the center of the house serving in place of a blanket. They call the house *bujío*. It is a hut made in round form, of straw, without a window and with a door a *vara* high and half a *vara* wide. On one side is a granary supported by 12 beams, which they call a *garita*, where they store the wheat, corn and other things they harvest.

During January they burn the grass and weeds from the fields preparatory to cultivation, surrounding them all at one time with fire so that deer, wild ducks and rabbits, fleeing from it fall into their hands. This sort of hunting they call *hurimelas*. Then they enter the forests in pursuit of bears, bison and lions which they kill with bows and arrows, and this they call *ojêo*. Whatever they secure in either way they bring to the principal cacique, in order that he shall divide it, he keeping the skins which fall to his share. Offering is made to the church of the best parts, and this serves for the support of the missionary priest, to whom they are in such subjection that they obey his orders without question.

In April they commence to sow, and as the man goes along opening the trench, the woman follows sowing. All in common cultivate and sow the lands of the caciques. As alms for the missionaries and the needy widows, they sow wheat in October and harvest it in June. This is a crop of excellent quality in the provinces of Apalache, and so abundant that it produces seventy *fanegas* from one *fanega* sown.

Each village has a council house called the great *bujío*, constructed of wood and covered with straw, round, and with a very large opening in the top. Most of them can accommodate from 2,000 to 3,000 persons. They are furnished all around the interior with niches called *barbacôas*, which serve as beds and as seats for the caciques and chiefs, and as lodgings for soldiers and transients. Dances and festivals are held in them around a great fire in the center. The missionary priest attends these festivities in order to prevent indecent and lewd conduct, and they last until the bell strikes the hour of *las ánimas*.

These Indians do not covet riches, nor do they esteem silver or gold, coins of which do not circulate among them, and their only barter is the exchange of one commodity for another, which exchange they call *rescate*. The most common articles of trade are knives, scissors, axes, hoes, hatches, large bronze rattles, glass beads, blankets which they call *congas*, pieces of rough cloth, garments and other trifles.

As to their religion, they are not idolaters, and they embrace with devotion the mysteries of our holy faith. They attend mass with regularity at 11 o'clock on the holy days they observe, namely, Sunday, and the festivals of Christmas, the Circumcision, Epiphany, the Purification of Our Lady, and the days of Saint Peter, Saint Paul and All Saints Day, and before entering the church each one brings to the house of the priest as a contribution a log of wood. They do not talk in the church, and the women are separated from the men; the former on the side of the Epistle, the latter on the side of the Evangel. They are very devoted to the Virgin, and on Saturdays they attend when her mass is sung. On Sundays they attend the *Rosario* and the *Salve* in the afternoon. They celebrate with rejoicing and devotion the Birth of Our Lord, all attending the midnight mass with offerings of loaves, eggs and other food. They subject themselves to extraordinary penances during Holy Week, and during the 24 hours of Holy Thursday and Friday, while our Lord is in the Urn of the Monument, they attend standing, praying the rosary in complete silence, 24 men and 24 women and the same number of children, both male and female, go to the church on work days, to a religious school where they are taught by a teacher whom they call the *Athequi* of the church; [a person] whom the priests have for this service; as they have also a person deputized to report to them concerning all parishioners who live in evil.

Your Majesty's most humble servant and chaplain,
GAB'L Bishop of Cuba.

2

Emerging Colonial Societies

Colonists came to North America in the seventeenth and early eighteenth centuries for a variety of reasons. Some sought the right to worship as they wished; others came for economic opportunity; still others arrived as forced labor or slaves. By 1740, much of the Atlantic coastline of what is now the United States came under English control, but the local population was not necessarily like that of Britain. The American colonies exhibited far more ethnic diversity than found in England, while providing many of its white inhabitants with greater personal freedom and more social mobility. As such, an increasingly American society had begun to emerge. The following documents offer insights into the diverse nature of colonial society and culture.

12

A Treaty Between the Five Nations and the New England Colonies (1689)

In 1689, Britain engaged in the first of a series of wars against the French. Known as King William's War, the conflict had European roots but quickly spilled across the Atlantic. American Indians often held the balance of power in this and later conflicts. The Five Nations of the Iroquois (Mohawk, Oneida, Onondaga, Cayuga, and Seneca) dominated the fur trade along the northern frontier and controlled the region of upstate New York between New England and New France. Their support was vital in a conflict between Britain and France. In the following excerpted account, the New England colonies negotiate a treaty with the Five Nations. The author of this tract was a leading figure in colonial America. Scottish-born Cadwallader Colden was one of America's leading scientists and a major figure in New York politics. His works on the Iroquois are among the best surviving accounts of the Five Nations.

Questions to Consider

1. Why are the Five Nations willing to fight the French? Why are they unwilling to fight Indian tribes from New England?
2. What can you deduce from this document about the religious views of the Iroquois?
3. What items seem valuable to the Five Nations? Why?
4. Compare and contrast this document with "The Treaty of Lancaster" (Document 20) and "The Pontiac Manuscript" (Document 24). What similarities do you notice? Differences?

About the beginning of September 1689, Colonel John Pynchon, Major John Savage, and Captain Jonathan Bull, Agents for the Colonies of Massachuset's Bay, New Plymouth, and Connecticut, arrived at Albany, to renew the Friendship with the Five Nations, and to engage them against the Eastern Indians, who made War on the English of those Colonies, and were supported by the French....

"*Brethren,*

"You are welcome to this House, which is appointed for our Treaties and publick Business with the Christians; we thank you for renewing the Covenant-chain. It is now no longer of Iron and subject to Rust, as formerly, but of pure Silver, and includes in it all the King's Subjects, from the Senekas Country eastward to Virginia. Here he gave a Bever.

"We are glad to hear of the good Success our great King has had over the French by Sea, in taking and sinking so many of their Men of War. You tell us in your Proposals that we are one People, let us then go hand in hand together, to ruin and destroy the French in our common Enemy. Gives a Bever.

"The Covenant-chain between us is ancient (as you tell us) and of long standing, and it has been kept inviolably by us. When you had Wars some time ago with the Indians, you desired us to help you; we did it readily, and to the Purpose; for we pursued them closely, by which we prevented the Effusion of much of your Blood. This was a certain Sign that we loved truly and sincerely, and from our Hearts. Gives a Belt.

"You advise us to pursue our Enemies, the French, vigorously; this we assure you we are resolved to do to the utmost of our Power: But since the French are your Enemies likewise, we desire our Brethren of the three Colonies to send us an hundred Men for the Security of this Place, which is ill provided, in Case of an Attack from the French; the Christians have Victuals enough for their Entertainment. Gives one Belt.

SOURCE: Cadwallader Colden, "A Treaty between the Agents of Massachuset's Bay, New-Plymuth, and Connecticut, and the Sachems of the Five Nations, at Albany, in the Year 1689," *The History of the Five Indian Nations of Canada* (New York, 1922), 1: 119–26.

"We patiently bore many Injuries from the French, from one Year to another, before we took up the Axe against them. Our Patience made the Governor of Canada think, that we were afraid of him, and durst not resent the Injuries we had so long suffered; but now he is undeceived. We assure you, that we are resolved never to drop the Axe, the French never shall see our Faces in Peace, we shall never be reconciled as long as one Frenchman is alive. We shall never make Peace, though our Nation should be ruined by it, and every one of us cut in Pieces. Our Brethren of the three Colonies may depend on this. Gives Bever.

"As to what you told us of the Owenagungas and Uragees, we answer: That we were never so proud and haughty, as to begin a War without just Provocation. You tell us that they are treacherous Rogues, we believe it, and that they will undoubtedly assist the French. If they shall do this, or shall join with any of our Enemies, either French or Indians, then we kill and destroy them. Gives a Bever."

... the Speaker continued his Speech, and said: "We have spoke what we had to say of the War, we now come to the Affairs of Peace: We promise to preserve the Chain inviolably, and wish that the Sun may always shine in Peace over all our Heads that are comprehended in this Chain. We give two Belts, one for the Sun, the other for its Beams.

"We make fast the Roots of the Tree of Peace and Tranquility, which is planted in this Place. Its Roots extend as far as the utmost of your Colonies; if the French should come to shake this Tree, we would feel it by the Motion of its Roots, which extend into our Country: But we trust it will not be in the Governor of Canada's Power to shake this Tree, which has been so firmly and so long planted with us. Gives two Bevers."

Lastly, He desired the Magistrates of Albany to remember what he had said, and gave them a bever.

But the Agents perceiving, that they had not answered any Thing about the Owenagunga messengers, and had answered indistinctly about the War with the Eastern Indians, desired them to explain themselves fully on these two points, about which the Agents were chiefly concerned.

The Five Nations answered:

"We cannot declare War against the Eastern Indians, for they have done us no Harm; Nevertheless our Brethren of New-England may be assured, that we will live and die in friendship with them. When we took up the Axe against the French and their Confederates, we did it to revenge the Injuries they had done us; we did not make War with them at the Persuasions of our Brethren here; for we did not so much as acquaint them with our Intention, till fourteen Days after our Army had begun their March."

... Now we assure our Brethren, that we are resolved to look on your Enemies as ours, and that we will first fall on the Owaragees; and then on the Owenagungas, and lastly on the French; and that you may be convinced of our Intention, we design to send five of our young Men along with our Brethren to New-England, to guard them, who have Orders to view the Country of the Owaragees, to discover in what Manner it can be attacked with the most Advantage. This we always do before we make an Attempt on our Enemies. In a Word, Brethren, your War is our War, for we will live and dye with you....

"WE have a hundred and forty Men out skulking about Canada; it is impossible for the French to attempt any Thing, without being discovered and harassed by these Parties: If the French shall attempt any Thing this Way, all the Five Nations will come to your Assistance, for our Brethren and we are but one, and we will live and dye together.... The Great God hath sent us Signs in the Sky to confirm this. We have heard uncommon Noise in the Heavens, and have seen heads fall down upon Earth, which we look upon as a certain Presage of the Destruction of the French: Take Control! On this they all immediately joined in singing and crying out, Courage! Courage!"

13

Petition of an Accused Witch (1692)

The Salem witchcraft trials are one of the most compelling events in American history. The cause for the hysteria remains an area of lively debate, as theories of causation have looked at the event from political, social, economic, geographic, gender, and chemical perspectives. The historical record does show that the craze began early in 1692 when a group of adolescent girls experienced "fits" and claimed that they had been bewitched. Widespread belief in witches (over three hundred individuals had been accused of witchcraft in seventeenth-century New England) combined with community stresses to fuel the frenzy. Over the next ten months, authorities in Salem Village, Massachusetts, condemned twenty individuals to death and jailed over one hundred more on charges of witchcraft. In the following account, Mary Esty responds to the charges of witchcraft leveled against her.

Questions to Consider

1. What is the historical context of this document?
2. In what ways does Mary Esty defend herself from the charges of witchcraft?
3. Why would Esty (or someone else) be accused of witchcraft?
4. What can you deduce from this document about the status of women in late seventeenth-century Massachusetts?

To the Honorable Judge and Bench now sitting in Judicature in Salem and the Reverend Ministers, humbly sheweth, That whereas your humble poor Petitioned being Condemned to die, doth humbly beg of you, to take it into your Judicious and Pious Consideration, that your poor and humble Petitioned knowing my Innocency (blessed be the Lord for it) and seeing plainly the Wiles and Subtilty

SOURCE: *Narratives of the Witchcraft Cases, 1648–1706*, ed. George L. Burr (New York, 1914), 368–69.

of my Accusers, by my self, cannot but judge charitably of others, that are going in the same way with my self, if the Lord step not mightily in. I was confined a whole Month on the same account that I am now condemned for, and then cleared by the Afflicted persons, as some of your Honours know, and in two days time I was cried out upon by them, and have been confined, and now am condemned to die. The Lord above knows my innocency then, and likewise doth now, as at the great day will be known to Men and Angels. I Petition to your Honours not for my own Life, for I know I must die, and my appointed time is set; but the Lord he knows it is, if it be possible, that no more Innocent blood be shed, which undoubtedly cannot be avoided in the way and course you go in. I question not, but your Honours do to the utmost of your powers, in the discovery and detecting of witchcraft and Witches, and would not be guilty of Innocent Blood for the World; but by my own Innocency I know you are in the wrong way. The Lord in his infinite Mercy direct you in this great work, if it be his blessed will, that Innocent Blood be not shed; I would humbly beg of you, that your Honours would be pleased to Examine some of those confessing Witches, I being confident there are several of them have belyed themselves and others, as will appear, if not in this World, I am sure in the World to come, whither I am going; and I question not, but your selves will see an alteration in these things: They say, my self and others have made a league with the Devil, we cannot confess. I know and the Lord he knows (as will shortly appear) they belye me, and so I question not but they do others; the Lord alone, who is the searcher of all hearts, knows that as I shall answer it at the Tribunal Seat, that I know not the least thing of Witchcraft, therefore I cannot, I durst not belye my own Soul. I beg your Honours not to deny this my humble Petition, from a poor dying Innocent person, and I question not but the Lord will give a blessing to your Endeavours.

— Mary Esty

14

"Pennsylvania, the Poor Man's Paradise" (1698)

William Penn established the colony of Pennsylvania on land he received from the Crown in lieu of a debt owed to his father. The colony was initially founded as a religious haven and land of opportunity for English Quakers; its 1692 proclamation supporting liberty of conscience and Penn's extensive promotion of the area attracted immigrants from throughout western Europe. One of these early settlers was Gabriel Thomas. A Quaker, he lived in Pennsylvania and western New Jersey from 1682 until 1697. His An Historical and Geographical Account of the Province and Country of Pensilvania and West New Jersey, *published in 1698, was among the more widely read works by an American author. In the following excerpt, Thomas discusses conditions facing those who chose to colonize Pennsylvania.*

Questions to Consider

1. What was the intended audience for this document?
2. According to Thomas, what made Pennsylvania attractive to settlers?
3. Was Pennsylvania a "poor man's paradise"?
4. In what ways was late seventeenth-century Pennsylvania different from early seventeenth-century Virginia ("An Indentured Servant Writes Home," Document 4)? Why was it different?
5. In what ways was late seventeenth-century Pennsylvania different from early eighteenth-century New France ("The Dilemma of New France" Document 16)? Why was it different?

And now for their Lots and Lands in City and Country, in their great Advancement since they were first laid out, which was within the compass of about Twelve Years, that which might have been bought for Fifteen or Eighteen Shillings, is now sold for Fourscore Pounds in ready Silver; and some other Lots, that might have been then Purchased for Three Pounds, within the space of Two Years, were sold for a Hundred Pounds a piece....

Now the true Reason why this Fruitful Country and Flourishing City advance so considerably in the Purchase of Lands both in the one and the other, is their great and extended Traffic and Commerce both by Sea and Land, viz. to New-York, New-England, Virginia, Maryland, Carolina, Jamaica, Barbadoes, Nevis, Monsserat, Antigua, St. Christophers, Bermuda, New-Foundland, Madeiras, Saletudeous, and Old-England; besides several other places. Their Merchandize chiefly consists in Horses, Pipe-Staves, Pork and Beef Salted and Barreled ... Bread, and Flower, all sorts of Grain, Peas, Beans, Skins, Furs, Tobacco, or Pot-Ashes, Wax &c. which are Barter'd for Rum, Sugar, Molasses, Silver, Negroes, Wine, Linen, Household-Goods, &c....

... the Countrey at the first, laying out, was void of Inhabitants (except the Heathens, or very few Christians not worth naming) and not many People caring to abandon a quiet and easy (at least tolerable) Life in their Native Country (usually the most agreeable to all Mankind) to seek out a new hazardous, and careful one in a Foreign Wilderness or Desert Country, wholly destitute of Christian Inhabitants, and even to arrive at which, they must pass over a vast Ocean, expos'd to some Dangers, and not a few Inconveniences: But now all those Cares, Fears and Hazards are vanished, for the Country is pretty well Peopled, and very much Improv'd, and will be more every Day, now the Dove is return'd with the Olive-branch of Peace in her Mouth.

SOURCE: Gabriel Thomas, *An Historical and Geographical Account of the Province and Country of Pensilvania* ... (London, 1698), 23–45.

I must needs say, even the Present Encouragements are very great and inviting, for Poor People (both Men and Women) of all kinds, can here get three times the Wages for their Labor they can in England or Wales....

Corn and Flesh, and what else serves Man for Drink, Food and Rayment, is much cheaper here than in England, or elsewhere; but the chief reason why Wages of Servants of all sorts is much higher here than there, arises from the great Fertility and Produce of the Place; besides, if these large Stipends were refused them, they would quickly set up for themselves, for they can have Provision very cheap, and Land for a very small matter, or next to nothing in comparison of the Purchase of Lands in England; and the Farmers there, can better afford to give that great Wages than the Farmers in England can, for several Reasons very obvious.

As first, their Land costs them (as I said but just now) little or nothing in comparison, of which the Farmers commonly will get twice the increase of Corn for every Bushel they sow, that the Farmers in England can from the richest Land they have.

In the Second place, they have constantly good price for their Corn, by reason of the great and quick vent into Barbadoes and other Islands; through which means Silver is become more plentiful than here in England, considering the Number of People, and that causes a quick Trade for both Corn and Cattle; and that is the reason that Corn differs now from the Price formerly, else it would be at half the Price it was at then; for a Brother of mine (to my own particular knowledge) sold within the compass of one Week, about One Hundred and Twenty fat Beasts, most of them good handsome large Oxen.

Thirdly, They pay no Tithes, and their Taxes are inconsiderable; the Place is free for all Persuasions, in a Sober and Civil way; for the Church of England and the Quakers bear equal Share in the Government. They live Friendly and Well together; there is no Persecution for Religion, nor ever like to be; 'tis this that knocks all Commerce on the Head, together with high Imposts, strict Laws, and cramping Orders. Before I end this Paragraph, I shall add another Reason why Womens Wages are so exorbitant; they are not yet very numerous, which makes them stand upon high Terms for their several Services, in Sempstering, Washing, Spinning, Knitting, Sewing, and in all the other parts of their Employments; for they have for Spinning either Worsted or Linen, Two Shillings a Pound, and commonly for Knitting a very Coarse pair of Yarn Stockings, they have half a Crown a pair; moreover they are usually Marry'd before they are Twenty Years of Age, and when once in that Noose, are for the most part a little uneasy, and make their Husbands so too, till they procure them a Maid Servant to bear the burden of the Work, as also in some measure to wait on them too....

... what I have here written, is not a Fiction, Flam, Whim, or any sinister Design, either to impose upon the Ignorant, or Credulous, or to curry Favor with the Rich and Mighty, but in mere Pity and pure Compassion to the Numbers of Poor Laboring Men, Women, and Children in England, half starv'd, visible in their meager looks, that are continually wandering up and down looking for Employment without finding any, who here need not lie idle a moment. ... Here are no Beggars to be seen (it is a shame and Disgrace to the State that there are so many in England) nor indeed have any here the least Occasion or Temptation to take up that Scandalous Lazy Life....

15

Of the Servants and Slaves in Virginia (1705)

During the seventeenth century, the English colonies hoped to meet their labor with inden-tured servants. Individuals entered into a contractual relationship promising to serve a mas-ter for a fixed number of years, after which the servants became free. Many individuals entered into such arrangements to gain passage to North America, but some convicts could escape imprisonment or execution by agreeing to become indentured labor in America. Despite the numerous indentured servants who crossed the Atlantic, they were too few and their labor too temporary to serve the needs of the South's emerging plantation econ-omy. Virginia and other southern colonies responded by turning to African slaves for their workforce. The first Africans arrived at Jamestown in 1619, but it was not until later in the century that distinctions emerged between the institutions of slavery and indentured servitude. In the following excerpt, Robert Beverly differentiates between the two. Virginia-born and English-educated, Beverly served as clerks of the General Court and the Assembly and Council, and he represented Jamestown in the House of Burgesses.

Questions to Consider

1. What is the thesis of this document?
2. What are the similarities and differences between the statuses of slaves and indentured servants ("An Indentured Servant Writes Home," Document 4)?
3. In what ways were women slaves and servants treated differently?
4. What does this document tell you about emerging racial consciousness in Virginia? What conclusions can you draw about attitudes toward women?

Their servants they distinguish by the names of slaves for life, and servants for a time.

Slaves are the negroes and their posterity, following the condition of the mother.... They are called slaves, in respect of the time of their servitude, because it is for life.

Servants, are those which serve only for a few years, according to the time of their indenture, or the custom of the country. The custom of the country takes place upon such as have no indentures. The law in this case is, that if

SOURCE: Robert Beverly, *The History of Virginia, in Four Parts*, 2nd rev. ed. (Richmond, VA, 1855), 219–22.

such servants be under nineteen years of age ... they must serve until they reach four and twenty; but if they be adjudged upwards of nineteen, they are then only to be servants for the term of five years.

... The male servants, and slaves of both sexes, are employed together in tilling and manuring the ground, in sowing and planting tobacco, corn, &c. Some distinction indeed is made between them in their clothes, and food; but the work of both is no other than what the overseers, the freemen, and the planters themselves do.

Sufficient distinction is also made between the female servants, and slaves; for a white woman is rarely or never put to work in the ground, if she be good for anything else; and to discourage all planters from using any women so, their law makes female servants working in the ground tithables, while it suffers all other white women to be absolutely exempted; whereas, on the other hand, it is a common thing to work a woman slave out of doors, nor does the law make any distinction in her taxes, whether her work be abroad or at home.

... Because I have heard how strangely cruel and severe the service of this country is represented in some parts of England, I can't forebear affirming, that the work of their servants and slaves is no other than what every common freeman does; neither is any servant required to do more in a day than his overseer; and I can assure you, with great truth, that generally their slaves are not worked near so hard, nor so many hours in a day, as the husbandmen, and day laborers in England. An overseer is a man, that having served his time, has acquired the skill and character of an experienced planter, and is therefore entrusted with the direction of the servants and slaves.

But to complete this account of servants, I shall give you a short relation of the care their laws take, that they be used as tenderly as possible:

BY THE LAWS OF THEIR COUNTRY,

1. All servants whatsoever have their complaints heard without fee or reward; but if the master be found faulty, the charge of the complaint is cast upon him, otherwise the business is done *ex officio*.

2. Any justice of the peace may receive the complaint of a servant, and order everything relating thereto, till the next country court, where it will be finally determined.

3. All masters are under the correction and censure of the county courts, to provide for their servants food and wholesome diet, clothing and lodging.

4. They are always to appear upon the first notice given of the complaint of their servants, otherwise to forfeit the service of them until they do appear.

5. All servants' complaints are to be received at any time in court, without process, and shall not be delayed for want of form; but the merits of the complaint must be immediately enquired into by the justices; and if the master may cause any delay therein, the court may remove such servants, if they see cause, until the master will come to trial.

6. If a master shall at any time disobey an order of court, made upon any complaint of a servant, the court is empowered to remove such servant forthwith to another master who will be kinder, giving to the former

master the produce only, (after fees deducted,) of what such servants shall be sold for by public outcry.

7. If a master should be so cruel, as to use his servant ill, … and thereby rendered unfit for labor, he must be removed by the church wardens out of the way of such cruelty, and boarded in some good planter's house, till the time of his freedom, the charge of which must be laid before the next county court, which has power to levy the same, from time to time, upon the goods and chattels of the master, after which, the charge of such boarding is to come upon the parish in general.

8. All hired servants are entitled to these privileges.

9. No master of a servant can make a new bargain for service, or other matter with his servant, without the privity and consent of the county court, to prevent the masters overreaching, or scaring such servant into an unreasonable compliance.

10. The property of all money and goods sent over thither to servants, or carried in with them, is reserved to themselves, and remains entirely at their disposal.

11. Each servant at his freedom receives of his master ten bushels of corn, (which is sufficient for almost a year,) two new suits of clothes, both linen and woolen, and a gun, twenty shillings value, and then becomes as free in all respects, and as much entitled to the liberties and privileges of the country, as any of the inhabitants or natives are, if such servants were not aliens.

12. Each servant has then also a right to take up fifty acres of land, where he can find any unpatented.…

16

The Dilemma of New France (1724)

By the early eighteenth century, French and English settlement patterns in North America were markedly different. While the opportunity for land and religious freedom had boosted the English North American population to 234,000 by 1700, the combination of a short growing season that prevented the cultivation of the desired cash crops coupled with France's prohibition on the emigration of dissenters to New France limited its population to approximately 15,000. The author of the following account is Pierre François Xavier de Charlevoix, a Jesuit who taught at the Collège Louis le Grand in Paris and the Jesuit College in Quebec. His account of his early 1720s trip to New Orleans by way of the Great Lakes and Mississippi River, and his descriptions of early New France, have given him the title "first historian of New France." In the following document, Charlevoix reports to French authorities on the dilemma of New France.

Questions to Consider

1. Compare the description of the fur trade's impact as described in this document with that found in "Early New York" (Document 5). Is the fur trade a blessing or a curse?

2. Why do you think the author compares New France with English settlements in North America?

3. How would you compare life in 1720s New France with that described in Pennsylvania ("Pennsylvania, the Poor Man's Paradise" Document 14) or Virginia ("Of the Servants and Slaves in Virginia" Document 15) during this period? Which area seems to offer the most opportunity? For whom?

4. Why do you think a Jesuit priest is reporting to French officials about problems in New France and offering suggestions on how these might be improved?

The two Intendants first assume that the chief, and almost sole object in fact, aimed at in the colony of Canada, has been the Fur Trade, especially that in beaver-skins; which is true, however, only of individuals; but they remark justly, that it should have been foreseen that in course of time the beaver-skins would be exhausted, or become too common, and that consequently, they would not suffice to sustain a colony of that importance; that it has, in fact, fallen into the latter of these two difficulties, the abundance of beaver having ruined it. Private individuals, who had no object except to enrich themselves speedily, disregarded this. It mattered little to them what became of New France, after they had drawn from it wherewith to live at ease in Old France.

They then observe that the Beaver trade has never been able to maintain more than a very limited number of settlers; that the use of this commodity can never be sufficiently general to maintain and enrich a whole colony; and if the consumption were sure, they could avoid the difficulty just stated, only to fall into the first; that for want of making these reflections, the colonists of New France had devoted themselves almost exclusively to this trade, as if they had been certain that the beavers would reproduce as rapidly as codfish in the sea, and that the sale of their skins would equal the sale of that fish. They have accordingly made it their chief business to roam through woods and lakes in pursuit of furs. These long and frequent voyages have accustomed them to a life of indolence, which they renounce reluctantly, although their journeys now produce very little, in consequence of the low price of beaver. The English, they continue, have pursued a very different course. Without wasting time on such long excursions, they have tilled their soil, established manufactures, set up

SOURCE: Pierre François Xavier de Charlevoix, "Narrative of Pierre François Xavier de Charlevoix," *History and General Description of New France*, ed. John Gilmary Shea (New York, 1900), 5: 287–88.

glass-works, opened iron mines, built ships, and have never regarded furs but as an accessory on which little dependence was placed.

Necessity has, it is true, at last opened the eyes of the Canadians; they have been forced to cultivate flax and hemp, to make linen cloth and inferior druggets of the wool of their old clothes mixed with thread; but the long contracted habit of doing nothing, prevented their rising completely from want. All, indeed, have grain and live stock enough to live, but many lack covering for their bodies, and are forced to pass the long severe winter clad in deer-skins.

Yet the King expends in that colony a hundred thousand crowns a year: the furs are worth about two hundred and eighty thousand livres; the oils and other minor products bring in twenty thousand livres; the pensions on the royal treasury paid by the King to individuals, and the revenues held by the bishop and seminaries in France, amount to fifty thousand francs. This makes six hundred and fifty thousand livres, on which all New France rolls. On this sum alone can it conduct its trade; and it is evident that this cannot be sufficiently great to maintain a colony of twenty or twenty-five thousand souls, and furnish what they are obliged to draw from France.

Its affairs were formerly on a better footing, the King spending a great deal more there; it shipped beaver to France to the amount of about a million, and was not so thickly settled; but it always drew more than it was able to pay, which ruined its credit with mercantile men, who are in our days not disposed to send goods to Canadian merchants without letters of exchange or a good security. From this, and the low price to which beaver has fallen, it followed that all the money in Canada had to go to France to obtain goods; so that there was a time when there was not, perhaps, a thousand crowns in silver coin in the country. Paper money made up the deficiency. I will not repeat here what I have said in my Journal as to this money; its advantages, its drawbacks, and the reasons for suppressing it.

The Messieurs Raudot, after thus exposing the state in which New France stood till the year 1708, in regard to its trade and its faculties, give the means which they devised to render it more flourishing. This colony, they say, might carry on a trade in its own products, which would enrich it. These products are salt meats, masts, planks, sheathing, timber for building and staves, tar, pitch, whale, seal and porpoise-oil, codfish, hemp and flax; to which might be added iron and copper. It only requires to find an opening for all this, and to reduce the price of labor.

The difficulty on the last score, arises from the indolence of the inhabitants and the high price of French goods. At times, when work is scarcest, the workman expects twenty-five sous a day, for the reason that he uses up more clothes in working than he can replace by his labor. On the other hand, goods in Canada are at double French prices. This seems exorbitant, but after reckoning twenty-five per cent for assurance, (though this is only in war time, at least at that rate,) expenses of commission, freight, which some-times exceeds forty crowns a ton, interest on money advanced, charges to be paid to agents, and which are heavy when drafts are not met at maturity, as is often the case, and exchange on Paris, it will be found that the merchant does not gain much. In fact, none in the country are rich.

To raise up the colony of Canada, all the people must be employed, each according to his ability, and every individual enabled to subsist by diminishing the price of goods. Now this might apparently be attained by finding a place to which they could cheaply and conveniently carry their produce and obtain French goods to take home. They will thus gain a part of the freight of both, and that part of the people who rust out in inaction or roam the woods, would be employed in navigation.

17

New York Slave Conspiracy (1741)

Following an unusually cold winter in 1740–41 which created great hardships among New York's poor, a number of fires broke out the following March and April. Amid fears exacerbated by the War of Jenkins's Ear with Spain, by late spring rumors of a slave conspiracy abetted by poor whites swept the city. Under the leadership of Provincial Supreme Court Daniel Horsmanden, the hysteria culminated in a series of trials that would incriminate half of the city's adult black men as saboteurs and resulted in the execution of thirty African Americans and seven whites. Historians remain divided as to whether the events of the spring of 1741 constituted a real or imagined conspiracy. Excerpted below is New York Lieutenant Governor George Clark's proclamation and the New York Weekly Journal's *description of the conspiracy.*

Questions to Consider

1. What can you deduce from this document about race relations in New York?
2. Can you explain why free whites and enslaved Africans might be working together in such a conspiracy?
3. Where do officials place the blame for this conspiracy?
4. What actions did the newspaper believe should be taken to prevent future conspiracies?
5. Compare and contrast these events with those described in "Petition of an Accused Witch" (Document 13)?

By the HONOURABLE. George Clarke, Elq; His Majesty's Lieutenant Governour and Commander in Chief of the Province of New York, and the Territories thereon depending in America.

A PROCLAMATION

Whereas a most Wicked and Dangerous Conspiracy has been lately formed and set on foot in this City and Province, abetted, encouraged and carried on by several *White People*, in Conjunction with divers *Spanish Negroe's* lately brought over from the *West Indies*, and a greater Number of the other *Negroes* within this City and Country, for burning and destroying of this whole Town and City, and for the Murdering the Inhabitants thereof, to the utter Ruin and Destruction of the whole Province. For which Diabolical Scheme and Conspiracy a great Number of *Slaves* and others, have already been Convicted and Executed, and many others are now indicted and Imprisoned, in order for their Tryal for the said Offences.

But to the End that Mercy may be shewn to such as may merit and deserve the same, I have thought it necesary, and I do hereby, by and with Advice of His Majesty's Council, in His Majesty's Name, issue this Proclamation, hereby Offering and Promising His Majesty's most Gracious Pardon to any and every Person or Persons, whether White People, Free Negroes, Slaves or others, who have been or are concerned in the said Conspiracy, who shall, on or before the first Day of July next, voluntarily, freely and fully discover and Confession make of his, her or their Confederates, Accomplices, or others concerned in the said Conspiracy, and his, her or their part of share, actings and doings therein, so that the Persons making such discovery and Confession be not before Convicted, Arreigned or Indicted for the same.

Given under my Hand and Seal at New York, the Nineteenth Day of June, in the Fifteenth year of His Majesty's Reign, Annoq; Domini, 1741.

GEORGE CLARK.

On the 12th Instant a Petition was presented to the Assembly setting forth.

That a horrid Conspiracy has been lately formed by some Wicked White People, in Confederacy with a great number of Negro Slaves, to lay this City to Ashes, and to Murder and destroy the Inhabitants thereof, which has been, in part, executed, by burning His Majesty's House, and Publick buildings in the Fort, and by setting fire to sundry other Houses in this City, by which Conspiracy great Terror and Distress, and very considerable Loss and Damage has been brought upon the Inhabitants of this City. And that upon strict Enquiry, the great Number of Publick Houses in which Negroes have been entertained and encouraged to buy Rum and other strong Liquors, has been a principal Instrument to their Diabolical Vilanies. And that the horrid Conspiracy to burn this City and to Murder the People, was formed and agreed to by great Numbers of Negroes meeting together on diverse Sundays, and was intended to be put in Execution on some Sunday Morning during the Time of Publick Service; as also fetching Tea-Water on Sundays, has been found to tend to the forming of the said Conspiracy, by giving Occasion to great Numbers of them to meet in the

SOURCE: *New York Weekly Journal*, 29 June 1741.

same Place, that some further Provision by Law to prevent the like Evils for the future, will be of absolute necessity for the Peace and Saftey of this City, and worthy of the immediate Care of the Legislature, and therefore humbly pray, that a Law may be obtained to limit the Number of Publick Houses within the City of New York; also to oblige all Keepers of Publick Houses, under severe Penalties, to keep good Order in such Houses; and to prohibit them to sell any sort of strong Liquors to Negroes, unless by express Leave from their Masters in writing first had and obtained. Also, a more effectual Law to prohibit the receiving any goods from Negroes, upon any pretence whatsoever, unless by express leave or Licence from their Masters in Writing, as aforesaid. Also a Law to restrain Negroes from fetching Tea-Water on Sundays, and more effectually to punish such Persons and shall harbour and entertain them—and the prevent their being absent from their Masters Houses on Sundays, unless at the Publick Worship of God, or by the express Leave of their Masters, for some necessary Service signified in Writing, and to be delivered to such Negro. And also, that such further Provision be made in the Premisses, as to the Honourable House shall seem meet.

Upon reading of which it was ordered That during the Recess of the General Assembly, the Members for the City and County of New York, and the Members of the County of Westchester, do prepare proper Bills for the Purposes recommended by the grand Jury, in order to be brought in at the next meeting of the House.

The same day His Honour the Lieut. Governour gave his Assent to two Bills, entitled, *An Act for the better fortifying of this Colony*, and other *the Purposes therein mentioned*. And An Act for the more Equal keeping of Military Watches in the City of the New York, and other the Purposes therein mentioned.

18

Eliza Lucas, a Modern Woman (1741–1742)

First settled in 1669, the area around Charleston at the confluence of the Ashley and Cooper Rivers quickly became the hub of life in South Carolina. The young colony grew rapidly, attracting a cosmopolitan population of New Englanders, New Yorkers, Virginians, and West Indians. By the early eighteenth century, the establishment of plantation agriculture and slavery had begun to dominate the local economy. Many of the early planters came from the British West Indies to cultivate rice in the tidal flats along the coast. One of the more uncommon early planters was Eliza Lucas. The daughter of Antigua's Lieutenant Governor George Lucas, the English-educated Eliza came to South Carolina in 1738 when she was only sixteen. Over the next several years, she managed several family plantations. Among Lucas's most significant contributions to the local economy was her development of indigo cultivation, which soon became an important cash crop. In the following selection, Lucas discusses the business of running the plantations under her care, as well as other tasks she performs in the community.

Questions to Consider

1. What were some of the tasks that Eliza Lucas performed on her plantation and for the local community?

2. Were these responsibilities typical for women of the time?

3. How did Lucas acquire such authority?

4. How does the status of women in eighteenth-century South Carolina compare with that of mid-nineteenth-century America as described in "Sarah Grimké Argues for Gender Equality" (Document 82)?

June 4 [1741] … After a pleasant passage of about an hour we arrived safe at home as I hope you and Mrs. Pinckney did at Belmont. But this place appeared much less agreeable than when I left it, having lost the agreeable company & conversation of our friends—I am engaged now with the rudiments of the Law to w[hi]ch I am but a Stranger and what adds to my mortification is that Doctr Wood wants the Politeness of your Uncle who with a graceful ease & good nature peculiar to himself is always ready to instruct the ignorant—but this rustic seems by no means to court my acquaintance for he often treats me with such cramp phrases I am unable to understand him nor is he civil enough to explain them when I desire it. However I hope in a short time we shall be better friends nor shall I grudge a little pains and application that will make me useful to my poor neighbors. We have some in this Neighbourhood who have a little Land and a few slaves and Cattle to give their children, that never think of making a Will till they come upon a sick bed and find it too expensive to send to town for a Lawyer. If you will not laugh too immoderately at me I'll trust you with a secret. I have made two Wills ready. I know I have done no harm for I conn'd my lesson very perfect. and know how to convey by Will Estates real and personal and never forget in it's proper place him and his heirs for Ever. nor that tis to be sign'd by 3 Witnesses in presence of one another. but the most comfortable remembrance of all is that Doctr Wood says the Law makes great allowance for last Wills and Testaments presuming the Testator could not have Council learned in the Law. but after all what can I do if a poor creature lies a dying and the family takes it into their head that I can serve them, I cann[o]t refuse but when they are well and able to employ a Lawyer I always shall. A Widow

SOURCE: Eliza Lucas, *Journal and Letters*, ed. H. P. Holbrook (Wormsloe, GA, 1850), 13–16.

here abouts with a pretty little fortune teazed me intolerably to draw her a marriage settlement but it was out of my depth and I absolutely refused it—so she got an able hand to do it—indeed she could afford it—but I could not get off from being one of the Trustees to her settlement and an old Gent ... the other I shall begin to think myself an old woman before I am a young one having such weighty affairs upon my hands....

Septr 20. 1741. Wrote to my father on plantation business and Concerning a planter's importing negroes for his own use. Colo Pinckney thinks not—but thinks twas proposed in the assembly and rejected—promised to look over the act and let me know. also informed my father of the alteration tis Supposed there will be in the value of our money occasioned by a late Act of Parliament that Extends to all America w[hi]ch is to dissolve all private banks by the 30th of last Month or be liable to lose their Estates and put themselves out of the King's protection. informed him of the Tyranical Govrt at Georgia.

Octr 29. 1741 Wrote to my father acknowledging the receipt of a ps of rich yellow Lustring consisting of 19 yards for myself do of blue for my Mama. also for a ps of Holland and Cambrick received from London at the same time. Tell him we have had a moderate and healthy summer and preparing for the King's birth day next day. Tell him [we] shall send the rice by Bullard.

Novr. 11. 1741. Wrote to Mr. Murray to send down a boat load of white oak staves, bacon and salted beef for the West Indies. sent up at the same time a barl. salt 1/2 wt salt peter. some brown sugar for the bacon. Vinegar and a couple of bottles Wine for Mrs. Murray and desire he will send down all the butter and hogs lard.

Jany 1741/2 Wrote my father about the Exchange with Colo Heron. the purchasing [of] his house at Georgia.... Returned my father thanks for a present I received from him by Capt Sutherland of twenty pistols. and for the sweetmeats by Capt Gregory. Shall send the preserved fruit as they come in season ... shall try different soils for the Lucern grass this year. The ginger turns out but poorly. We want a supply of Indigo Seed. Sent by his Vessel a waiter of my own Japaning my first Essay. Sent also the Rice and beef. Sent Govr. Thomas of Philadelphia' Daughter a tea chest of my own doing also Congratulate my father on my brother's recovery from the small pox and having a Commission....

[Feb. 6] I received yesterday the favor of your advice as a physician and want no arguments to convince me I should be much better for both my good friends Company. a much pleasanter Prescription that Doctr Meads w[hi]ch I have just received. To follow my inclination at this time I must endeavor to forget that I have a Sister to instruct and a parcel of little Negroes whom I have undertaken to teach to read ... I am a very Dunce, for I have not acquird ye writing short hand yet with any degree of Swiftness but I am not always so for I give a very good proof of the brightness of my Genius when I can distinguish well enough to Subscribe my Self with great Esteem.

3

Toward an American Identity

By the eighteenth century, the American colonies had evolved from small, struggling outposts into prosperous, growing societies. During the first half of the century, American culture became increasingly distinct from that of Great Britain as large numbers of Germans, Scots-Irish, and West Africans joined the English in America. British authorities were eager to exercise some control over the American possessions; but with their authority constrained in part by a worldwide struggle for empire, Americans were relatively free to manage their own affairs. The prosperity and independence of the colonies caused some to ponder whether the colonies might ultimately sever their ties with Britain. The following excerpts detail the emergence of an increasingly American culture.

19

"Sinners in the Hands of an Angry God" (1741)

The Great Awakening was the single most important religious event in eighteenth-century America. Part of a larger movement that occurred in western Europe, the evangelical emotionalism of the Great Awakening enabled its adherents to experience a more intense religious fervor than that offered by most existing churches. While widespread throughout the colonies between 1730 and 1750, the movement was strongest in New England's

Connecticut River Valley, where Jonathan Edwards had begun to deliver sermons that ignited local religious fervor. Following his graduation from Yale, Edwards returned to his hometown of Northampton, Massachusetts, to serve in the Congregationalist (Puritan) church headed by his grandfather, Solomon Stoddard, whom he ultimately succeeded. Using Enlightenment rationalism to support traditional church beliefs, Edwards epitomized the New England Awakening. The movement divided established churches into the rationalist "Old Light" and the evangelical "New Light" factions, a split that anticipated some later divisions during the American Revolution. The following selection is an excerpt from Edwards's most famous work, "Sinners in the Hands of an Angry God."

Questions to Consider

1. What is Jonathan Edwards's view of humanity? Why might he be so concerned about people's behavior?

2. Why does Edwards frequently refer to God's control over people's lives, especially the sinners?

3. What impact did such sermons have on the people of New England?

4. How are Edwards's views similar to those found in "General Considerations for the Plantation in New England" (Document 7)? How are they different?

... This that you have heard is the case of every one of you that are out of Christ. That world of misery, that lake of burning brimstone, is extended abroad under you. There is the dreadful pit of the glowing flames of the wrath of God; there is hell's wide gaping mouth open; and you have nothing to stand upon, nor any thing to take hold of; there is nothing between you and hell but the air; 'tis only the power and mere pleasure of God that holds you up....

Your wickedness makes you as it were heavy as lead, and to tend downwards with great weight and pressure towards hell; and, if God should let you go, you would immediately sink, and swiftly descend and plunge into the bottomless gulf; and your healthy constitution, and your own care and prudence, and best contrivance, and all your righteousness, would have no more influence to uphold you and keep you out of hell, than a spider's web would have to stop a falling rock. Were it not that so is the sovereign pleasure of God, the earth would not bear you one moment; for you are a burden to it; the creation groans with you; the creature is made subject to the bondage of your corruption, not willingly; the sun don't willingly shine upon you, to give you light to serve sin and Satan; the earth don't willingly yield her to increase to satisfy your lusts, nor is it willingly a stage for your wickedness to be acted upon; the air don't willingly serve you for breath to maintain the flame of life in your vitals, while you spend your life in the service of God's enemies. God's creatures are good, and were made for men to serve God with, and don't willingly subserve to any other purpose, and groan when they are abused to purposes so directly contrary to their nature and end.

SOURCE: Jonathan Edwards, "Sinners in the Hands of an Angry God," *The Works of President Edwards*, ed. Samuel Austin (Worcester, MA, 1808), 2: 72–79.

And the world would spew you out, were it not for the sovereign hand of him who hath subjected it in hope. There are the black clouds of God's wrath now hanging directly over your heads, full of the dreadful storm, and big with thunder.... The sovereign pleasure of God for the present stays his rough wind; otherwise it would come with fury, and your destruction would come like a whirlwind, and you would be like the chaff of the summer threshing-floor....

Thus are all you that never passed under change of heart, by the mighty power of the spirit of God upon your souls; all that were never born again and made new creatures, and raised from being dead in sin, to a state of new, and before altogether unexperienced light and life. However you may have reformed your life in many things, and may have had religious affections, and may keep up a form of religion in your families and closets, and in the house of God, and may be strict in it, you are thus in the hands of an angry God; 'tis nothing but his mere pleasure that keeps you from being this moment swallowed up in everlasting destruction.

However unconvinced you may now be of the truth of what you hear, by and by you will be fully convinced of it. Those that are gone from being in the like circumstances with you, see that it was so with them; for destruction came suddenly upon most of them, when they expected nothing of it, and while they were saying, peace and safety. Now they see, that those things that they depended on for peace and safety, were nothing but thin air and empty shadows.

The God that holds you over the pit of hell, much as one holds a spider or some loathsome insect over the fire, abhors you, and is dreadfully provoked; his wrath towards you burns like fire; he looks upon you as worthy of nothing else but to cast into the fire; he is of purer eyes than to bear to have you in his sight; you are ten thousand times so abominable in his eyes as the most hateful venomous serpent is in ours. You have offended him infinitely more than ever a stubborn rebel did his prince; and yet 'tis nothing but his hand that holds you from falling into the fire every moment....

O' Sinner! Consider the fearful danger you are in .... you have no interest in any mediator, and nothing to lay hold of to save yourself, nothing to keep off the flames of wrath, nothing of your own, nothing that you ever have done, nothing that you can do, to induce God to spare you one moment....

How dreadful is the state of those that are daily and hourly in danger of this great wrath, and infinite misery! But this is the dismal case of every soul in this congregation that has not been born again, however moral and strict, sober and religious they may otherwise be. Oh that you would consider it, whether you be young or old! There is reason to think, that there are many in this congregation, now hearing this discourse, that will actually be the subjects of this very misery to all eternity. We know not who they are, or in what seats they sit, or what thoughts they now have. It may be they are now at ease, and hear all these things without much disturbance, and are now flattering themselves that they shall escape.... And it would be a wonder if some that are now present should not be in hell in a very short time, before this year is out; and it would be no wonder if some person that sits here in some seat of this meeting-house, in health, and quiet and secure, should be there before tomorrow morning....

20

Chief Canassatego Speaks at the Treaty of Lancaster (1744)

Despite an earlier agreement to restrict white settlement east of the Blue Ridge Mountains, by 1740 settlers had begun to spill into the Shenandoah Valley of Virginia. These incursions led to skirmishes between American Indians and whites that threatened all out war. With another war with mutual enemy France on the horizon, both sides needed peace. Officials from Virginia, Maryland, and the Iroquois Confederacy met in Lancaster, Pennsylvania, to hammer out a new agreement. The Treaty of Lancaster appeared to settle these differences but simply opened another controversy—whether Iroquois had simply given up claim to the She-nandoah Valley or all land south and east of the Ohio River. Here, Canassatego, a leading Onondaga chief, offers an Indian interpretation of Native–white relations.

Questions to Consider

1. According to Canassatego, to what extent have Indians become reliant on white trade goods?
2. How would you describe the symbolism employed by Canassatego describing the ways in which Natives and whites are tied together?
3. Why do you think Canassatego is willing to give up Indian lands at Lancaster?
4. Compare and contrast white–Indian relations described here with the description found in "A Treaty Between the Five Nations and the New England Colonies" (Document 12). How do you account for the similarities? Differences?

Brother, the Governor of Maryland,

WHEN you mentioned the Affair of the Land Yesterday, you went back to old Times, and told us, you had been in Possession of the Province of *Maryland* above One Hundred Years; but what is One Hundred Years in Comparison of the Length of Time since our Claim began? Since we came out of this Ground? For we must tell you, that long before One Hundred Years our Ancestors came out of this very Ground, and their Children have remained here ever since. You came out of the Ground in a Country that lies beyond the Seas, there you may have a just Claim, but there you must allow us to be your elder Brethren, and the Lands to belong to us long before you knew any thing of them. It is true, that above One Hundred Years ago the *Dutch* came here in a Ship, and brought

SOURCE: Treaty, Held at the Town of Lancaster, in Pennsylvania, Philadelphia: Ben Franklin, 1744.

with them several Goods; such as Awls, Knives, Hatchets, Guns, and many other Particulars, which they gave us; and when they had taught us how to use their Things, and we saw what sort of People they were, we were so well pleased with them, that we tied their Ship to the Bushes on the Shore; and afterwards, liking them still better the longer they staid with us, and thinking the Bushes too slender, we removed the Rope, and tied it to the Trees; and as the Trees were liable to be blown down by high Winds, or to decay of themselves, we, from the Affection we bore them, again removed the Rope, and tied it to a strong and big Rock and not content with this, for its further Security we removed the Rope to the big Mountain and there we tied it very fast, and rowll'd Wampum about it; and, to make it still more secure, we stood upon the Wampum, and sat down upon it, to defend it, and to prevent any Hurt coming to it, and did our best Endeavours that it might remain uninjured for ever. During all this Time the New-comers, the *Dutch*, acknowledged our Right to the Lands, and solicited us, from Time to Time, to grant them Parts of our Country, and to enter into League and Covenant with us, and to become one People with us.

After this the *English* came into the Country, and, as we were told, became one People with the *Dutch*. About two years after the Arrival of the *English*, an *English* Governor came to *Albany*, and finding what great Friendship subsisted between us and the *Dutch*, he approved it mightily, and desired to make as strong a League, and to be upon as good Terms with us as the *Dutch* were, with whom he was united, and to become one People with us: And by his further Care in looking into what had passed between us, he found that the Rope which tied the Ship to the great Mountain was only fastened with Wampum, which was liable to break and rot, and to perish in a Course of Years; he therefore told us, he would give us a Silver Chain, which would be much stronger, and would last forever. This we accepted, and fastened the Ship with it, and it has lasted ever since. Indeed we have had some small Differences with the *English*, and, during these Misunderstanding, some of their young Men would, by way of Reproach, be every now and then telling us, that we should have perished if they had not come into the Country and furnished us with Strowds and Hatchets, and Guns, and other Things necessary for the Support of Life; but we always gave them to understand that they were mistaken, that we lived before they came amongst us, and as well, or better, if we may believe what our Forefather have told us. We had then Room enough, and Plenty of Deer, which was easily caught; and tho' we had not Knives, Hatchets, or Guns, such as we have now, yet we had Knives of Stone, and Hatchets of Stone, and Bows and Arrows, and those served our Uses as well then as the *English* ones do now. We are now straitened, and sometimes in want of Deer, and liable to many other Inconveniencies since the *English* came among us, and particularly from that Pen-and-Ink work that is going on at the Table (*pointing to the Secretary*) and we will give you an Instance of this. Our Brother *Onas*, a great while ago, came to *Albany* to buy the *Sasquahannah* Lands of us, but our Brother, the Governor of *New-York*, who, as we suppose, had not a good Understanding with our Brother *Onas*, advised us not to sell him any Land, for he would make an ill Use of it; and, pretending to be our good Friend, he advised us, in order to prevent *Onas's*, or any other

Person's imposing upon us, and that we might always have our Land when we should want it, to put it into his Hands; and told us, he would keep it for our Use, and never open his Hands, but keep them close shut, and not part with any of it, but at our Request. Accordingly we trusted him, and put our Land into his Hands, and charged him to keep it safe for our Use; but, some Time after, he went to *England*, and carried our Land with him, and there sold it to our Brother *Onas* for a large Sum of Money; and when, at the Instance of our Brother *Onas*, we were minded to sell him some Lands, he told us, we had sold the *Sasquahannah* Lands already to the Governor of *New-York*, and that he had bought them from him in *England*; tho', when he came to understand how the Governor of *New-York* had deceived us, he very generously paid us for our Lands over again.

THO' we mention this Instance of an Imposition put upon us by the governor of *New-York*, yet we must do the *English* the Justice to say, we have had their hearty Assistances in our Wars with the *French*, who were no sooner arrived amongst us than they began to render us uneasy, and to provoke us to War, and we have had several Wars with them; during all which we constantly received Assistance from the *English*, and, by their Means, we have always been able to keep up our Heads against their Attacks.

WE now come nearer home. We have had your Deeds interpreted to us, and we acknowledge them to be good and valid, and that the *Conestogoe* or *Sasquahannah Indians* had a Right to sell those Lands to you, for they were then theirs; but since that Time we have conquered them, and their Country now belongs to us, and the Lands we demanded Satisfaction for are no Part of the Lands comprised in those Deeds; they are the *Cohongorontas* Lands; those, we are sure, you have not possessed One Hundred Years, no, nor above Ten Years, and we made our Demands so soon as we knew your People were settled in those Parts. These have never been sold, but remain still to be disposed of; and we are well pleased to hear you are provided with Goods, and do assure you of our Willingness to treat with you for those unpurchased Lands; in Confirmation whereof, we present you with this Belt of Wampum.

21

Pennsylvania Assembly Comments on German Immigration (1755)

In 1700, roughly 250,000 people inhabited the American colonies; by 1775, the population had increased to 2.5 million. While natural increase accounted for much of the tenfold rise in population, immigration also contributed to the American colonies' explosive growth. Where seventeenth-century immigrants had been overwhelmingly English, the new immigration was more diverse, including large numbers of Scots-Irish, West Africans, and Germans. Chronic warfare, religious persecution, and crop failures forced many Germans to flee to America. The first group of German settlers came to Pennsylvania in the late seventeenth century, lured by the colony's cheap, fertile soil and religious tolerance. Pennsylvania continued to attract large numbers of Germans in the eighteenth century, and many of them came to be known as Pennsylvania Dutch—a corruption of Deutsch. The following selection contains an excerpt of a resolution issued by the Pennsylvania Assembly in 1755.

Questions to Consider

1. What changes were taking place in the German immigration?

2. Why was the Pennsylvania Assembly issuing this resolution?

3. Compare this response to immigration with the earlier description found in "Pennsylvania, the Poor Man's Paradise" (Document 14) and the later description found in "What Is an American?" (Document 25).

4. What characteristics does the Pennsylvania Assembly seem to value in immigrants? Why?

… The German Importations were at first and for a considerable Time of such as were Families of Substance and industrious sober People, who constantly brought with them their Chests of Apparel and other Necessaries for so long a voyage. But these we apprehend have for some time past been shipped on board other Vessels in order to leave more Room for crowding their unhappy Passengers in greater Numbers, and to secure the Freights of such as might perish during the voyage, which experience has convinced us must be the Case of very many where such Numbers (as have been lately imported in each Vessel) are crowded together without Change of Raiment or any other Means of keeping themselves sweet and clean. But this Provision the Governor has been pleased to throw out of our Bill; and yet we think it so essentially necessary that the Want of it must necessarily poison the Air those unhappy Passengers breathe on Shipboard, and spread it wherever they land to infect the Country which receives them, especially as the Governor has likewise altered the Provision We had made by the Advice of the Physicians for accommodating them with more Room and Air upon their Arrival here.

We have reason to believe the Importations of Germans have been for some Time composed of a great Mixture of the Refuse of their People, and that the very Jails have contributed to the Supplies We are burthened with. But as there are many of more Substance and better Character, We thought it reasonable to hinder the Importer from obliging such as had no connections with one another to become jointly bound for their respective Freights or Passages; but the Governor has thought fit to alter this also in such a manner as to elude the good Purposes intended by the Act, by which means those who are of more Substance are involved in the Contracts and Debts of Others, and the Merchants secured at the Expence of the Country where they are necessitated and do become very

SOURCE: "Message to the Governor from the Assembly," 15 May 1755, *Minutes of the Provincial Council of Pennsylvania,* 6: 384–86.

frequently common Beggars from Door to Door, to the great Injury of the Inhabitants and the Increase and Propagation of the Distempers they have brought among us. Many who have indented themselves for the Payment of their Passages have frequently been afflicted with such secret and loathsome Diseases at the Time as have rendered them altogether unfit for the Services they had contracted to perform.…

22

The Albany Plan of Union (1754)

As the threat of yet another war with France loomed on the horizon, colonial officials sought to improve their relations with the powerful Iroquois Confederacy that dominated the region of upstate New York lying between British and French settlements. The ensuing meeting in Albany would, however, become better known for the Albany Plan of Union. Proposed by Benjamin Franklin, the plan called for closer intercolonial cooperation in managing affairs in North America. Opposition to the plan in both Great Britain and the colonies prevented it from being implemented. In the following letter, William Shirley offers his views on the plan. Shirley had served as the royal governor of Massachusetts since 1741, and he assumed the role of Military Commander in America in 1755. Charges of military incompetence led to his recall to Britain in 1756, but he was exonerated and went on to serve as governor of the Bahamas.

Questions to Consider

1. What authority does William Shirley have to comment on colonial issues?
2. Based on the sentiments expressed here, how do you think Shirley would have responded to the "Stamp Act Riots" (Document 28) in 1765?
3. What views does Shirley have on the extent of imperial power in North America? Compare his views with those found in "The Articles of Confederation" (Document 37) and "*Federalist Number 10*" (Document 46). What similarities do you notice? Differences?

William Shirley To Sir Thomas Robinson
    Boston, New England, December 24th, 1754
Sir,
    I suppose Gov. Delancey may have sent you a copy of the proceedings of the Commissioners of several of His Majesty's Governments upon this Continent

SOURCE: "William Shirley to Sir Thomas Robinson," 24 December 1754, *Correspondence of William Shirley*, ed. Charles H. Lincoln (New York, 1912), 2: 111–18.

lately assembled at Albany in the Province of New York; least that, by any accident should have miscarry'd, I inclose you one here....

As to the plan of the Union form'd at Albany, I would beg leave, Sir, to submit the following remarks upon it to your consideration, vizt

1.   That the reason of committing to the several Houses of Representatives *solely* the choice of the members which each Colony is allowed to send to the Grand Council seems to be because it is propos'd that the Council should have power to levy taxes upon the People, which it is thought could not be exercis'd by any Council whatsoever in the Colonies which should not be wholly chosen by the People, or at least by their Representatives, without raising a general dissatisfaction.

2.   That on the other hand it is clear that as such Council can be consider'd no otherwise than as the General Representative body of all the people of the Colonies compriz'd in the Union, the giving to them a share in making peace and war with the Indians and concluding treaties with them, in the disposal of military commissions, in the power of raising troops and erecting Forts, would be a great strain upon the prerogative of the Crown and contrary to the English Constitution.

3.   That the command over the Militia, power of raising them by warrant of impress, marching them upon any service at least within the limits of the several Colonies, appointing all military Officers, erecting and demolishing of Forts, declaring war against the Indians and making treaties of peace with them; are vested soley in the respective Governours of all of them, proprietary and charter, as well as those whose government is founded on His Majesty's commission, except in the two Colonies of Connecticut and Rhode Island, whose governments stand upon their old charters, by which the Crown hath divested itself almost of the whole prerogative, and transferr'd it to the populace in whom the several above mention'd powers are lodg'd, the Governours not having so much as a negative in any election of officers or Act of Legislature.

4.   That the institution of these old Charter Governments in the Colonies during the state of their infancy, tho' well accommodated to draw together numbers of the settlers in the beginning of the English Plantations and for the regulation of each settlement whilst it consisted of but an handful of people, yet seems by no means well calculated for the government of them when the inhabitants considerably increas'd in numbers and wealth, The present state of the government of Rhode Island is an instance of this....

5.   That the unfitness of these old Charter Governments for the Colonies when they are grown up and come out of their infancy, was I suppose the reason why in the beginning of King William and Queen Mary's reign the government at home refus'd to the old Massachusetts Colony to renew their Charter which had been vacated by a judgment in the

Court of Chancery in Westminster Hall in a late reign, tho' their principles and loyalty to the Crown at that time greatly recommended them to its favour; but instead of that it was thought good policy to put an end likewise to the Charter Colony of New Plymouth and to erect and incorporate the old colonies of the Massachusetts Bay and New Plymouth, together with the Provinces of Main and Nova Scotia into one Province, but which is now the present Province of the Massachusetts Bay, saving that the Crown hath disannex'd Nova Scotia from it, and to grant them a new Charter, ...

The result from these observations, Sir, which I would submit to your consideration is, that if the old charter form of government, such as that is which is proposed in the Albany plan of Union, is unfit for ruling a particular Colony, it seems much more improper for establishing a General Government and *Imperium* over all the Colonies to be comprised in the Union.

The only material difference between an old charter government and the Albany Plan appears to be, that by the latter it is propos'd that the Governour General shall be appointed and supported by His Majesty and have a negative Every Act of the Grand Council (as it is there called) whereas in the former the Governour is annually elected by the People, dependent upon them for his support and hath no negative in the Acts of Assembly.

This is relied upon as a most favourable circumstance on the part of the Crown in the following remarks, drawn up by a gentleman who had a principle hand in forming the Albany Plan, vizt. "That the Government or Constitution propos'd to be form'd by the plan consists of two branches, a President General appointed by the Crown and a Council chosen by the People or by the People's Representative" which is the same thing.

That by a subsequent article the Council chosen by the "People can effect nothing without the consent of the President General appointed by the Crown; the Crown possesses therefore full one half of the power of this Constitution." ...

But it seems an obvious answer to say *that the* power of the President General which in the remarks is called *one half of the Power of the Constitution*, is only a *Negative* one, stripped of every branch of the prerogative, and is at best only a preventative power in a small degree. It may control the other half of the constitution from doing mischief by any act of theirs, but it can't prevent mischiefs arising from their inactivity, neglect or obstinacy....

I have I am afraid, Sir, been too diffuse in my remarks upon the Albany Plan, and it may perhaps be expected that I should offer some other plan in lieu of it.... But as I understood the Lords Commissioners for Trade and Plantations were forming a plan themselves, I did not think it proper for me to transmit my crude sentiments to you upon so difficult and delicate a work.

23

Edmund Burke on British Motives in the Seven Years' War (1762)

Great Britain's and France's struggle for empire culminated in the Seven Years' (or French and Indian) War. Britain's victory in the worldwide conflict established it as the leading European power. The following selection comes from the Annual Register of World Events, *a periodical established in 1759. Edmund Burke served as its principal author and editor. After studying law at Great Britain's prestigious Middle Temple, the Dublin native abandoned the legal profession for a career as a writer. Burke later established himself as the leading conservative political theorist of his time. In the ensuing excerpt, Burke reviews the proposed treaty to end the Seven Years' War and discusses the importance of North America in England's future considerations.*

Questions to Consider

1. What is the historical context of this document?
2. According to Edmund Burke, what are the advantages in keeping the British colonies after this war? Who would be the chief beneficiary?
3. For what reasons does Burke support removing France from North America?
4. How are relations strained between mother country and colony in the years after this war?

… That the original object of the war was the security of our colonies upon the continent; that the danger to which these colonies were exposed, and in consequence of that danger, the immense waste of blood and treasure which ensued to Great Britain, together with the calamities, which were from the same source, derived upon the four quarters of the world, left no sort of doubt that it was not only our best, but our only policy, to guard against all possibility of the return of such evils. Experience has shown us that while France possesses any single place in America, from whence she may molest our settlements, they can never enjoy any repose, and of course that we are never secure from being plunged again into those calamities, from which we have at length, and with so

SOURCE: *A Complete History of the Late War: From the Annual Register of World Events* [Edmund Burke] (Dublin, 1774): 621–22.

much difficulty, happily emerged. To remove France from our neighborhood in America, or to contract her power within the narrowest limits possible, is therefore the most capital advantage we can obtain; and is worth purchasing by almost any concessions.

They insisted that the absolute security derived from this plan, included itself an indemnification. First; by saving us, more effectually than any other method could, from the necessity of another war, and consequently by giving us an opportunity of increasing our trade, and lowering our debt. Secondly; by permitting our colonies on the continent to extend themselves without danger or molestation. They showed the great increase of population in those colonies within a few years. They showed, that their trade with the mother country had uniformly increased with this population. That being now freed from the molestation of enemies, and the emulations of rivals, unlimited in their possessions, and safe in their persons, our American planters would, by the very course of their natural propagation in a very short time, furnish out a demand of our manufactures, as large as all the working hands of Great Britain could possibly supply. That there was therefore no reason to dread that want of trade, which their adversaries insinuated, since North America alone would supply the deficiencies of our trade in every other part of the world.

… That the value of our conquests thereby ought not to be estimated by the present produce, but by their probable increase. Neither ought the value of any country to be solely tried on its commercial advantages; that extent of territory and a number of subjects, are of as much consideration to a state attentive to the sources of real grandeur, as the mere advantages of traffic.…

24

"The Pontiac Manuscript" (1763)

At the end of the Seven Years' (or French and Indian) War, Native Americans in the Great Lakes region faced a difficult choice. As long-time trading partners with the French, they were allies during the war. British efforts to reduce the tribes to dependence and the tribes' feared loss of land had led to some sporadic frontier attacks as early as 1761. Native Americans began planning for a coordinated rising in 1763. The Ottawa leader Pontiac was nearly fifty when he hammered out an alliance between his tribe, the Potawatomies and some Wyandots. He struck at Detroit in May 1763, laying a siege that would not be lifted until October. Attacks against other frontier posts were more successful, and other tribes joined in. By midsummer, nine of Britain's eleven western posts had been taken and the other two (Detroit and Pitt) were under siege. After the failure of the rebellion,

Pontiac concluded a peace in July 1766. The following excerpt describes Pontiac's reasons for war and his plans for its prosecution.

Questions to Consider

1. What role do the French appear to play in the formation of this Native American alliance?
2. What is the nature of the relationship between Native Americans and the English? What are the major sources of complaint in this relationship?
3. Why might other tribes be willing to cooperate with Pontiac?
4. What does Pontiac hope to accomplish?

The day fixed having arrived, all the Ottawas, with Pondiak at their head, and the band of the Hurons, with Také [Yaka] at their head, all proceeded to the village of the Foxes [Potawatomies], where the council was intended to be held, taking care to send the women out of the village so as not to be interrupted in their deliberations. After all these precautions had been made, each Indian took his place in a circle, in accordance with his rank, and Pondiak at the head, as the great chief of all. He took the floor, and, as chief of the league, said:

"It is important for us, my brothers, that we exterminate from our land this nation which only seeks to kill us. You see, as well as I do, that we cannot longer get our supplies as we had them from our brothers, the French. The English sell us the merchandise twice dearer than the French sold them to us, and their wares [are worth] nothing. Hardly have we bought a blanket, or something else to cover us, than we must think of having another of the kind. When we want to start for our winter quarters they will give us no credit, as our brothers, the French, did. When I go to the English chief to tell him that some of our comrades are dead, instead of weeping for the dead, as our brothers, the French, used to do, he makes fun of me and of you. When I ask him for something for our sick, he refuses, and tells me that he has no need of us. You can well see by that that he seeks our ruin. Well, my brothers, we must all swear to destroy them! Nor will we wait any longer, nothing impedes us. There are very few of them, and we can easily overcome them. All the nations who are our brothers are ready to strike a blow at them; why should we not? Are we not men like them? Have I not shown you the war-belts which I have received from our great father, the Frenchman? He tells us to strike; why should we not listen to his words? Whom fear we? It is time. Are we afraid that our brothers, the French, who are here amongst us, would hinder us? They know not our designs, and could not if they wanted to. You know as well as I do, that when the English came to our country to drive out our father, Bellestre, they took away all the guns of the Frenchmen, and that they have no weapons to defend

SOURCE: "The Pontiac Manuscript," in *Historical Collections*, coll. by Michigan Pioneer and Historical Society (Lansing, MI, 1900–1913), 8: 273–74.

themselves. Thus it is. Let us strike all together! If there are any French who take up for them, we shall strike them as we do the English. Remember what the Master of Life has said to our brother, the Wolf. That concerns us all as well as them. I have sent war-belts and word to our brothers, the Sauteux, of the Saginaw, and to our brothers, the Ottawas, of Michelimakinak, and to those of the river's mouth to join them with us, and they will not tarry to come. While waiting for them, let us commence the attack. There is no more time to lose, and when the English shall be defeated, we shall see what to do, and we shall cut off the passage so that they cannot come back to our country."

This address, which Pondiak delivered with a voice full of energy, made upon the whole assembly the full effect which he had desired, and all swore, as in one voice, the complete extermination of the English nation.

It was decided at the end of the council that Pondiak, at the head of sixty picked men, should go into the fort to ask the English commander for a great council, that those should have weapons concealed under their blankets and that the rest of the village should follow them, armed with tomahawks, dirks and knives hid under their clothes and enter the fort as if taking a walk, so as not to create any suspicion, while the first should hold council with the commander. The women of the Ottawas should also enter, carrying guns, cut short, and other arms of attack hid under their blankets and take position in the back of the street of the fort, waiting for the signal, which should be a [war] cry uttered by the great chief, when all together should throw themselves upon the English and take good care not to hurt the Frenchmen who lived in the fort. The Hurons and Foxes [Potawatomies] should divide into bands, one to go down the river to stop those who might come, and the other band to be around the fort at a distance to kill those who were at work outside the fort, and that each one should shout the war song in his own village. All these measures being taken, each nation returned to their village with the resolution to execute the orders of their great chief; but although they had taken all these precautions not to be discovered, God permitted that they were discovered, as I am going to tell....

25

"What Is an American?" (1770)

By the middle of the eighteenth century, America's bounty of opportunity had attracted large numbers of immigrants. While many of these new arrivals came in search of religious freedom, the bulk sought economic opportunity, specifically land. The possibility for upward mobility profoundly affected the outlook of those who ventured across the Atlantic. In the ensuing selection, J. Hector St. John Crèvecoeur [Michel-Guillaume-Jean de Crèvecoeur] describes how the American environment transformed Europeans into Americans. A native of France, he fought with Montcalm's army in the Seven Years' War before moving to the British colonies in 1759. Crèvecoeur received his naturalization papers in 1765 and four years later settled on a New York frontier farm, where he probably wrote much of his famous Letters of an American Farmer. *He remained loyal to the Crown during the Revolution and left America from 1780 until 1783.*

Questions to Consider

1. According to Crèvecoeur, what are the differences between Europe and America?

2. In what ways are Europeans transformed into Americans?

3. What are the characteristics of an American? How does this help shape a distinct American identity?

4. How do you think Alexander Falconbridge ("Account of the African Slave Trade," Document 26) would respond to this document?

... The rich stay in Europe, it is only the middling and the poor that emigrate. Would you wish to travel in independent idleness, from north to south, you will find easy access, and the most cheerful reception at every house; society without ostentation, good cheer without pride, and every decent diversion which the country affords, with little expense. It is no wonder that the European who has lived here a few years, is desirous to remain; Europe with all its pomp, is not to be compared to this continent, for men of middle stations, or laborers.

An European, when he first arrives, seems limited in his intentions, as well as in his views; but he very suddenly alters his scale; two hundred miles formerly appeared a very great distance, it is now but a trifle; he no sooner breathes our air than he forms schemes, and embarks in designs he never would have thought of in his own country. There the plenitude of society confines many useful ideas, and often extinguishes the most laudable schemes which here ripen into maturity. Thus Europeans become Americans.

But how is this accomplished in that crowd of low, indigent people, who flock here every year from all parts of Europe? I will tell you; they no sooner arrive than they immediately feel the good effects of that plenty of provisions we possess: they fare on our best food, and they are kindly entertained; their talents, character, and peculiar industry are immediately inquired into; they find countrymen everywhere disseminated, let them come from whatever part of Europe. Let me select one as an epitome of the rest; he is hired, he goes to work, and works moderately; instead of being employed by a haughty person, he finds himself with his equal, placed at the substantial table of the farmer, or else at an inferior one as good; his wages are high, his bed is not like that bed of sorrow on which he used to lie: if he behaves with propriety, and is faithful, he is

SOURCE: Hector St. John de Crèvecoeur, *Letters from an American Farmer* (London, 1782), 58–65.

caressed, and becomes as it were a member of the family. He begins to feel the effects of a sort of resurrection; hitherto he had not lived, but simply vegetated; he now feels himself a man, because he is treated as such; the laws of his own country had overlooked him in insignificancy; the laws of this cover him with their mantle. Judge what an alteration there must arise in the mind and thoughts of this man; he begins to forget his former servitude and dependence, his heart involuntarily swells and glows; this first swell inspires him with those new thoughts which constitute an American.... He looks around, and sees many a prosperous person, who but a few years before was as poor as himself. This encourages him much, he begins to form some little scheme, the first, alas, he ever formed in his life. If he is wise he thus spends two or three years, in which time he acquires knowledge, the use of tools, the modes of working the lands, felling trees, etc. This prepares the foundation of a good name, the most useful acquisition he can make. He is encouraged, he has gained friends; he is advised and directed, he feels bold, he purchases some land; he gives all the money he has brought over, as well as what he has earned, and trusts to the God of harvests for the discharge of the rest. His good name procures him credit. He is now possessed of the deed, conveying to him and his posterity the fee simple and absolute property of two hundred acres of land, situated on such a river. What an epocha in this man's life! He is become a freeholder, from per-haps a German boor—he is now an American, a Pennsylvanian, an English sub-ject. He is naturalized, his name is enrolled with those of the other citizens of the province.... From nothing to start into being; from a servant to the rank of a master; from being the slave of some despotic prince, to become a free man, invested with lands, to which every municipal blessing is annexed! ... It is in consequence of that change that he becomes an American.... Ye poor Europeans, ye, who sweat, and work for the great—ye, who are obliged to give so many sheaves to the church, so many to your lords, so many to your government, and have hardly any left for yourselves—ye, who are held in less estimation than favorite hunters or useless lap-dogs—ye, who only breathe the air of nature, because it cannot be withheld from you; it is here that ye can con-ceive the possibility of those feelings I have been describing; it is here the laws of naturalization invite every one to partake of our great labors and felicity, to till unrented, untaxed lands! Many, corrupted beyond the power of amendment, have brought with them all their vices, and disregarding the advantages held to them, have gone on in their former career of iniquity, until they have been overtaken and punished by our laws. It is not every emigrant who succeeds; no, it is only the sober, the honest, and industrious: ... Others again, have been led astray by this enchanting scene; their new pride, instead of leading them to the fields, has kept them in idleness; the idea of possessing lands is all that satisfies them—though surrounded with fertility, they have mouldered away their time in inactivity, misinformed husbandry, and ineffectual endeavors. How much wiser, in general, the honest Germans than almost all other Europeans; they hire themselves to some of their wealthy landsmen, and in that apprenticeship learn everything that is necessary. They attentively consider the prosperous industry of others, which imprints in their minds a strong desire of possessing the same advantages. This forcible idea never quits them, they launch forth, and by dint of sobriety, rigid parsimony, and the most persevering industry, they commonly succeed.

26

Account of the African Slave Trade (1788)

The first Africans arrived in the English colonies in 1619 when a Dutch vessel brought a group to Jamestown. The status of the Africans was initially murky, but by the end of the seventeenth century, Africans were legally classified as slaves who filled European demands for cheap labor. The African slave trade, which predated the arrival of the Europeans in Africa, became an enormous business in which traders became rich through the sale of human beings. The slave trade created a cycle of violence in West Africa that devastated many groups and virtually depopulated certain regions. The following account by British surgeon Alexander Falconbridge vividly describes the horrors of the trade. Falconbridge made four trips to the coast of Africa before becoming an abolitionist in the late 1780s.

Questions to Consider

1. According to Alexander Falconbridge, how do most Africans come to be enslaved?
2. To what extent do West Africans participate in the slave trade? In what ways?
3. What impact has the slave trade had in West Africa?
4. What can you deduce from this essay about European views on race and gender?
5. What are the conditions like on the ship?

After permission has been obtained for *breaking trade*, as it is termed, the captains go ashore, from time to time, to examine the negroes who are exposed to sale, and to make their purchases. The unhappy wretches thus disposed of are bought by the black traders at fairs, which are held for that purpose, at the distance of

SOURCE: Alexander Falconbridge, *An Account of the Slave Trade on the Coast of Africa* (London, 1788), 12–21.

upwards of two hundred miles from the sea coast; and these fairs are said to be supplied from an interior part of the country. Many Negroes, upon being questioned relative to the places of their nativity, have asserted that they have travelled during the revolution of several moons (their usual method of calculating time) before they have reached the places where they were purchased by the black traders. At these fairs, which are held at uncertain periods, but generally every six weeks, several thousands are frequently exposed to sale who had been collected from all parts of the country for a very considerable distance around. When I was upon the coast, during one of the voyages I made, the black traders brought down, in different canoes, from twelve to fifteen hundred Negroes who had been purchased at one fair. They consisted chiefly of men and boys, the women seldom exceeding a third of the whole number. From forty to two hundred Negroes are generally purchased at a time by the black traders, according to the opulence of the buyer, and consist of all ages, from a month to sixty years and upwards. Scarcely any age or situation is deemed an exception, the price being proportionable. Women sometimes form a part of them, who happen to be so far advanced in their pregnancy as to be delivered during their journey from the fairs to the coast; and I have frequently seen instances of deliveries on board ship....

There is great reason to believe, that most of the negroes shipped off the coast of Africa are *kidnapped*.... Continual enmity is thus fostered among the negroes of Africa, and all social intercourse between them destroyed....

When the Negroes, whom the black traders have to dispose of, are shown to the European purchasers, they first examine them relative to their age. They then minutely inspect their persons and inquire into the state of their health; if they are inflicted with any disease or are deformed or have bad eyes or teeth; if they are lame or weak in the joints or distorted in the back or of a slender make or narrow in the chest; in short, if they have been ill or are afflicted in any manner so as to render them incapable of much labour; if any of the foregoing defects are discovered in them they are rejected. But if approved of, they are generally taken on board the ship the same evening. The purchaser has liberty to return on the following morning, but not afterwards, such as upon re-examination are found exceptionable....

The men Negroes, on being brought aboard the ship, are immediately fastened together, two and two, by handcuffs on their wrists and by irons riveted on their legs. They are then sent down between the decks and placed in an apartment partitioned off for that purpose. The women also are placed in a separate apartment between the decks, but without being ironed. An adjoining room on the same deck is appointed for the boys. Thus they are all placed in different apartments.

But at the same time, however, they are frequently stowed so close, as to admit of no other position than lying on their sides. Nor with the height between decks, unless directly under the grating, permit the indulgence of an erect posture; especially where there are platforms, which is generally the case. These platforms are a kind of shelf, about eight or nine feet in breadth, extending from the side of the ship toward the centre. They are placed nearly midway between the decks, at the distance of two or three feet from each deck. Upon these the Negroes are stowed in the same manner as they are on the deck underneath.

In each of the apartments are placed three or four large buckets, of a conical form, nearly two feet in diameter at the bottom and only one foot at the top and in depth of about twenty-eight inches, to which, when necessary, the Negroes have recourse. It often happens that those who are placed at a distance from the buckets, in endeavoring to get to them, tumble over their companions, in consequence of their being shackled. These accidents, although unavoidable, are productive of continual quarrels in which some of them are always bruised. In this distressed situation, unable to proceed and prevented from getting to the tubs, they desist from the attempt; and as the necessities of nature are not to be resisted, ease themselves as they lie. This becomes a fresh source of boils and disturbances and tends to render the condition of the poor captive wretches still more uncomfortable. The nuisance arising from these circumstances is not infrequently increased by the tubs being too small for the purpose intended and their being emptied but once every day. The rule for doing so, however, varies in different ships according to the attention paid to the health and convenience of the slaves by the captain....

The diet of the Negroes while on board, consists chiefly of horse beans boiled to the consistency of a pulp; of boiled yams and rice and sometimes a small quantity of beef or pork. The latter are frequently taken from the provisions laid in for the sailors. They sometimes make use of a sauce composed of palm-oil mixed with flour, water and pepper, which the sailors call *slabber-sauce*. Yams are the favorite food of the Eboe or Bight Negroes, and rice or corn of those from the Gold or Windward Coast; each preferring the produce of their native soil....

4

Coming of the Revolution

While the roots of the American Revolution can be traced back to the first half of the eighteenth century, it was not until the 1760s that differences between Britain and the colonies became obvious. After the Seven Years' War, British policymakers were determined to consolidate their empire and raise funds to pay their enormous war debts. They turned to the American colonies as a source of revenue. Americans saw British attempts to exercise authority—for example, levying taxes on such varied items as public documents, tea, newspapers, and playing cards—as a tyrannical encroachment on their liberty. British officials, on the other hand, interpreted opposition to their policies as a potential source of anarchy. The following documents illustrate the various positions taken by those on both sides of the Atlantic and provide insights into the growing intensity of the confrontation.

27

John Locke on Political Society and Government (1689)

John Locke was one of the leading philosophers of the Enlightenment. Educated at Oxford, Locke eschewed a career as a physician to become one of the most influential thinkers of his day. As an advisor to Anthony Ashley Cooper (later Lord Shaftesbury), Locke helped to create the "Fundamental Constitutions" for early South Carolina. The Constitutions were aristocratic, but did guarantee religious toleration and the right to representative assemblies. As Shaftesbury emerged as a leading opponent of the Crown in the early 1680s, Locke was pulled into the constitutional crisis and even fled to Holland in 1683. By this time, he had begun to write Two Treatises of Government, *which called for a limited government. Following the Glorious Revolution in 1688–1689, Locke published his work. His ideas would influence Anglo-American concepts of liberty over the next century. The selection here is excerpted from* Two Treatises of Government.

Questions to Consider

1. What is the historical context for this document?
2. According to John Locke, what is the chief purpose of government?
3. What limits does the author wish to place on government?
4. What does Locke consider to be the greatest threats to liberty?

OF THE ENDS OF POLITICAL SOCIETY
AND GOVERNMENT

123. If Man in the state of Nature be so free, as has been said; if he be absolute Lord of his own Person and Possessions, equal to the greatest and subject to no Body, why will he part with his Freedom? Why will he give up this Empire, and subject himself to the Dominion and Controul of any other Power? To which 'tis obvious to answer, that though in the state of Nature he hath such a Right, yet the Enjoyment of it is very uncertain, and constantly exposed to the Invasion of others. For all being Kings as much as he, every man his Equal and the greater Part no strict Observers of Equity and Justice, the enjoyment of the Property he has in this State, is very unsafe, very unsecure. This makes him willing to quit this Condition, which however free, is full of Fears and continual Dangers: And 'tis not without Reason, that he seeks out, and is willing to joyn in Society with others, who are already united, or have a Mind to unite, for the mutual *Preservation* of their Lives, Liberties and Estates, which I call by the general Name, *Property*.

124. The great and *chief End* therefore, of Mens uniting into Commonwealths, and putting themselves under Government, *is the Preservation of their Property*. To Which in the state of Nature there are many things wanting.

First, There wants an *establish'd*, settled, known *Law*, received and allowed by common consent to be the Standard of right and wrong, and the common Measure to decide all Controversies between them. For though the Law of

SOURCE: John Locke, "Two Treatises of Government," *Works of John Locke* (London, 1714), 2: 193–94, 226–27.

Nature be plain and intelligible to all rational Creatures; yet Men being biassed by their Interest, as well as ignorant for want of Study of it, are not apt to allow of it as a Law binding to them in the application of it to their particular Cases.

125. *Secondly*, In the State of Nature there wants *a known and indifferent Judge*, with Authority to determine all Differences according to the established Law. For every one in that State being both Judge and Executioner of the Law of Nature, Men being partial to themselves, Passion and Revenge is very apt to carry them too far, and with too much Heat, in their own Cases; as well as Negligence, and unconcernedness, to make them too remiss in others Mens.

126. *Thirdly*, In the State of Nature there often wants *Power* to back and support the Sentence when right, and to *give* it due *Execution*. They who by any Injustice offended, will seldom fail, where they are able, by Force to make good their Injustice; such Resistance many times makes the Punishment dangerous, and frequently destructive, to those who attempt it.

127. Thus Mankind, notwithstanding all the Privileges of the State of Nature, being but in an ill Condition, while they remain in it, are quickly driven into Society. Hence it comes to pass, that we seldom find any number of Men live any time together in this State. The Inconveniences that they are therein exposed to, by the irregular, and uncertain exercise of the Power every Man has of punishing the transgressions of others, make them take Sanctuary under the establish'd Laws of Government, and therein seek the *preservation of their Property*. 'Tis this makes them so willingly give up every one his single Power of punishing, to be exercised by such alone, as shall be appointed to it, amongst them; and by such Rules as the Community, or those authorized by them to that purpose, shall agree on. And in this we have the original *right and rise of both the Legislative and Executive power,* as well as of the Governments, and Societies themselves....

128. But though Men when they enter into Society, give up the Equality, Liberty, and Executive Power they had in the State of Nature, into the hands of the Society, to be so far disposed of by the Legislative, as the good of the Society shall require; yet it being only with an intention in every one the better to preserve himself his Liberty and Property; (For no rational Creature can be supposed to change his condition with an intention to be worse) the Power of the Society, or *Legislative* constituted by them, can *never be suppos'd to extend farther than the common good*; but is obliged to secure every ones Property, by providing against those three defects above-mentioned, that made the State of Nature so unsafe and uneasie. And so whoever has the Legislative or supream Power of any Commonwealth, is bound to govern by establish'd *standing Laws*, promulgated and known to the People, and not by Extemporary Decrees; by *indifferent* and upright *Judges*, who are to decide Controversies by those Laws, And to imploy the force of the Community at home, *only in the Execution of such Laws,* or abroad to prevent or redress Foreign Injuries, and secure the Community from Inroads and Invasion. And all this to be directed to no other *End,* but the *Peace, Safety,* and *publick good* of the People....

28

Stamp Act Riots (1765)

British officials had been considering imperial reorganization since 1750, but the experience of the Seven Years' War (or French and Indian War) served as the catalyst for reform. In addition to governing newly conquered French territories, the government also had to find a way to reduce the staggering debt amassed during the war. English leaders, reluctant to tax an already burdened population at home, turned to the American colonies. Following the war, Parliament passed several pieces of legislation to raise money in North America and to enforce existing taxes. The passage of the Stamp Tax was one of these revenue-producing laws. Similar to an existing British tax, the new law required that a duty be placed on legal documents and nearly all forms of printed materials. Many of Boston's citizens found the new tax threatening. Mired in an economic slump that the tax might exacerbate, fearful of encroachments against their rights, the well-organized and highly politicized Boston mob offered their response, described in this document.

Questions to Consider

1. What is the mob trying to accomplish? Are they successful?

2. Does the mob seem organized?

3. How do you think Joseph Galloway, author of "A Loyalist Perspective on the Coming of the Revolution" (Document 33), responded to news of the mob in Boston?

4. Explain the symbolism in the mob's use of effigies discussed in the first paragraph.

Extracted from a letter from Boston, in New England, August 26.

"Very early on Wednesday morning, the 14th instant, were discovered hanging, on a limb of the great tress, so called, at the South part of this town, two effigies, one of which, by the labels, appeared to be designed to represent a stamp officer; the other a jack boot with a head and horns peeping out of the top. The report of the images soon spread through the town, brought a vast number of spectators, and had such an effect on them, that they were immediately inspired with a spirit of enthusiasm, which diffused itself through the whole concourse; so much were they affected with a sense of liberty, that scarce any could attend to the task of day-labor. About dusk, the images were taken down, placed on a bier (not covered with a sheet, except a sheet of paper which bore the inscription) supported in procession by ... men, followed by a great concourse of

SOURCE: John Almon, comp., *A Collection of Interesting, Authentic Papers Relative to the Dispute Between Great Britain and America* (London, 1777), 10–11.

people, and in the greatest order, echoing forth, Liberty and Prosperity! No Stamp, &c.—Having passed through the town-house, they proceeded with their pageantry down King-street, and thro' Kilby-street, where an edifice had been lately erected, which was supposed to be designed for a stamp-office. Here they halted, and went to work to demolish that building, which they soon effected, without receiving any hurt, excepting one of the spectators, who happened to be rather too nigh the brick wall when it fell. This being finished, many of them loaded themselves with the wooden trophies, and proceeded (bearing the two effigies) to the top of Fort-hill, where a fire was soon kindled, in which one them was burnt. The populace after this went to work on the barn, fence, garden, &c. and here it would have ended had not some indiscretions, to say the least, been committed by his friends within, which so enraged the people they were to be restrained, though hitherto no violence had been offered to any one. But it is very remarkable, though they entered the lower part of the house in multitudes, yet the damage done to it was not so great as might have been expected.

The next day the honourable gentleman, who had been appointed to the duty of distributor of the stamps when they should arrive, supposing himself to be the object of their derision, informed the principal gentlemen of the town, that as it appeared to disagreeable to the people, he should request the liberty of being excused from that office, and in the evening the populace re-assembled, erected a pyramid, intending a second bonfire; but upon hearing of the resignation, they desisted, and repaired to the gentleman's gate, gave three cheers, and took their departure without damage; but having heard it propagated that an honourable gentleman, at the north part of town, had been accessory in laying on the stamp duties, &c. they repaired to his house, where, upon being informed by some gentlemen of integrity and reputation, that he had not only spoke, but wrote to the contrary, they retired, and having patrolled the streets, returned to their respective habitations, as quietly as they had done the night before."

29

Images of Colonial Resistance (1760s–1770s)

As divisions over British policy in the colonies intensified, both sides began to employ propaganda to advance their cause. Some of the most useful came in the form of images, which

SOURCE: Paul Revere, The bloody massacre perpetrated in King Street Boston on March 5th 1770 by a party of the 29th Regt., 1770. Library of Congress, http://hdl.loc.gov/loc.pnp/ppmsc.00174

went beyond depicting opponents as mere brutes, by advancing both direct and subtle hints regarding events in the colonies. The ensuing images epitomize the best of this genre. The first is Paul Revere's famous engraving of the 1770 Boston Massacre that soon found its way to publishers throughout the colonies. A devoted supporter of the revolutionary cause, Revere would become famous as one of the riders who warned of the British approach before the Battle of Lexington in 1775. The second image is The Bostonian's paying the excise-man, *or tarring & feathering. A 1774 British cartoonist's depiction of the tarring and feathering of a British customs official by Bostonians, it offers a very different interpretation of colonial resistance to British authority.*

The bloody massacre perpetrated in King Street Boston on March 5th 1770 by a party of the 29th Regt.

SOURCE: [LC-DIG-ppmsca-01657]/Library of Congress Prints and Photographs Division

The Bostonian's paying the excise-man, or tarring & feathering
SOURCE: [LC-USZ62-9487]/Library of Congress Prints and Photographs Division

Questions to Consider

1. How would the author of the "Stamp Act Riots" (Document 28) and Catharine Macauley ("Englishwoman's Appeal to the People of Great Britain on the Crisis in America," Document 31) respond to these images?

2. What allusions to revolutionary and loyalist ideology can you find in these images?

3. How accurate do you think these images are in portraying events and ideas in 1770s Boston?

4. What sorts of symbols does each image use to vilify its opponents? Why do you think these symbols were chosen?

30

Ann Hulton, Loyalist View of Colonial Unrest (1774)

Colonial opposition to British authority grew more heated following the passage of the Tea Act in 1773. Designed as a means to bail out the financially troubled East India Company and provide Americans with inexpensive tea, the act instead elicited heated opposition. Colonists, believing that the act was yet another attempt by British officials to force their will on America, responded by refusing to allow the tea to be imported. Colonial intimidation made it impossible to land the tea anywhere other than Charleston, South Carolina. In Philadelphia, opponents of the tax organized tar-and-feathering committees; at the Boston Tea Party, British tea was dumped in the harbor. In New York, Governor William Tryon was determined to land the tea; its late arrival prevented a showdown with the local Sons of Liberty. By 1774, physical intimidation of those loyal to British authority became increasingly common in many colonial towns. In the ensuing document, Ann Hulton describes treatment meted out to a New York loyalist.

Questions to Consider

1.   What is the historical context of this document?
2.   What were the reasons for tarring and feathering this man?
3.   Why was Ann Hulton fearful of mob actions?
4.   How does Hulton's view of the mob differ with that described in the "Stamp Act Riots" (Document 28)?

The most shocking cruelty was exercised a few nights ago, upon a poor old man, a tidesman, one Malcolm.... A quarrel was picked with him. He was afterward taken, and tarred and feathered. There's no law that knows a punishment for the greatest crimes beyond what this is, of cruel torture. And this instance exceeds any other before it. He was stripped stark naked, one of the severest cold nights this winter, his body covered all over with tar, then with feathers, his arm dislocated in tearing off his clothes. He was dragged in a cart, with thousands attending, some beating him with clubs and knocking him out of the cart, then in again. They gave him several severe whippings, at different parts of the town. This spectacle of horror and sportive cruelty was exhibited for about five hours.

SOURCE: Ann Hulton, *Letters of a Loyalist Lady* (Cambridge, MA, 1927), 70–71. Reprinted by permission of Harvard University Press. Copyright © 1927 by the President and the Fellows of Harvard College.

The unhappy wretch they say behaved with the greatest intrepidity and fortitude. All the while before he was taken, he defended himself a long time
against numbers; and afterwards, when under torture they demanded of him to
curse his masters, the king, governors, etc. which they could not make him do,
but still he cried, Curse all Traitors. They brought him to the gallows and put a
rope about his neck saying that they would hang him; he said he wished they
would, but that they could not for God was above the Devil. The doctors say his
flesh comes off his back in stakes.

It is the second time he has been tarred and feathered and this is looked
upon more to intimidate the judges and others than a spite to the unhappy victim, though they owe him a grudge for some things, particularly, he was with
Governor Tryon in the Battle with the Regulators.... The Governor has
declared that he was of great service to him in that affair, by his undaunted spirit
encountering the greatest dangers.

Governor Tryon had sent him a gift of ten guineas just before this inhuman
treatment. He has a wife and family and an aged father and mother who, they
say, saw the spectacle which no indifferent person can mention without horror.

These few instances among many serve to show the abject state of government and the licentiousness and barbarism of the times. There's no magistrate
that dare or will act to suppress the outrages. No person is secure. There are
many objects pointed at, at this time, and when once marked out for vengeance,
their ruin is certain.

31

Englishwoman's Appeal
to the People of Great Britain
on the Crisis in America (1775)

*The Seven Years' War (or French and Indian War) gave Great Britain control of the
North American continent, but simultaneously drained its treasury. In the decade following
the war's end in 1763, Parliament had sought a variety of means to raise funds through
taxes on her North American colonies. Such efforts were met with increasing belligerence in
North America, culminating in the destruction of tea in Boston Harbor by colonists who
resented the recently passed Tea Act. Britain responded to the so-called Boston Tea Party
with several acts that shut down local government and provincial courts and closed the port*

of Boston until the city paid for the destruction of the tea. Colonists would soon refer to this legislation as the Coercive or Intolerable Acts. Parliament's subsequent passage of the Quebec Act, which sought to reorganize the former French colony, led to more unrest as many of its provisions were seemingly another attempt to undermine colonial liberties. Some in Britain agreed with the colonists, including Catharine Sawbridge Macauley. Born to an affluent gentry family in 1731, she would emerge as an early advocate of republicanism and an important supporter of English radicals in the 1760s and 1770s. She would eventually become a renowned historian. In the ensuing document, she responds to the Coercive or Intolerable Acts.

Questions to Consider

1. Based on this document, how much freedom of expression is available in Great Britain in the mid-1770s? What does this tell you about Britain at this time?
2. How do you think Catharine Macauley would interpret the events described by Abigail Smith Adams in "Abigail Smith Adams on the British Occupation of Boston" (Document 32)?
3. In what ways do Macauley and Adams seem similar? Different?
4. What conclusions can you draw about Macauley and Adams's similarities and differences? Based on these two documents, in which society do women appear to experience greater equality?

It can be no secret to you, my friends and fellow citizens, that the Ministry, after having exhausted all those ample sources of corruption which your own tameness under oppressive taxes have afforded, either fearing the unbiased judgment of the people, or impatient at the slow but steady progress of despotism, have attempted to wrest from our American Colonists every privilege necessary to freemen;—privileges which they hold from the authority of their charters and the principles of the constitution.

With an entire supineness, England, Scotland, and Ireland have seen the Americans, year by year, stripped of the most valuable of their rights; and, to the eternal shame of this country, the Stamp Act, by which they were to be taxed in an arbitrary manner, met with no opposition, except from those who are particularly concerned that the commercial intercourse between Great Britain and her Colonies should meet with no interruption.

With the same guilty acquiescence, my countrymen, you have seen the last Parliament finish their venal course, with passing two acts for shutting up the Port of Boston, for indemnifying the murders of the inhabitants of Massachusetts-Bay, and changing their chartered constitutions of government: And to show that none of the fundamental principles of our boasted constitution are held sacred by the government or the people, the same Parliament, without any interruption either by petition or remonstrance, passed another act for

SOURCE: Catharine Macauley, *An Address to the People of England, Scotland, and Ireland, on the Present Important Crisis of AFFAIRS* (Bath, England, 1775).

changing the government of Quebec; in which the Popish religion, instead of being tolerated as stipulated by the treaty of peace, is established; in which the Canadians are deprived of the right to an assembly, and of trial by jury; in which the English laws in civil cases are abolished, the French laws established, and the Crown empowered to erect arbitrary courts of judicature: and in which for the purpose of enlarging the bounds where despotism is to have its full sway, the limits of that province are extended so as to comprehend those vast regions that lie adjoining to the northerly and westerly bounds of our colonies....

These men have asserted that unlimited obedience is stipulated in the acceptance of protection; and though such an assertion involves you and the subjects of every state in unlimited slavery, and unlimited slavery excludes every idea of right and power, yet they have also told you that it is in vindication of your authority that your Governors have exerted an arbitrary power over your brethren in America.

In order to confound your ideas on the merits of the dispute, and to stifle your feelings of humanity, they have told you that the Americans, though neither adequately or inadequately represented in the case of taxation, stand on the same predicament with yourselves, and that there is no more injustice in inflicting a severe punishment on the whole town of Boston, for the supposed offence of a few of its inhabitants, than in the bombarding a town in the possession of an enemy, when by such an act of hostility, a few of our won people dwelling in the down might accidentally be destroyed....

In the act for the government of the province of Quebec, my friends and fellow citizens, we read despotism in every line. The poor Canadians, instead of being put in possession of all the privileges and immunities of English subjects, according to his majesty's proclamation in 1763, are indeed favored with the full possession of their religion as long as his Majesty, who is at the head of their church, is graciously inclined to continue to them such indulgence; yet in respect both to their civil and religious rights, they are in a more abject state of slavery than when they were under the French government.

The conquests of foreign nations are dangerous triumphs, even to the liberty of republican states; but in limited monopolies; when on the conquered are imposed laws opposite and hostile to the limitations of power in these governments, it never fails of subjecting the conquerors to the same measure of slavery which they have imposed on the conquered....

It was the Canada bill, and other transactions of the government, which equally threatened your security and welfare; that engaged the city of London to exact from those they elected into the representative office an engagement by which their members were bound to endeavor, to the utmost of their abilities, [to secure] the repeal of the unconstitutional laws which passed in the last session of the last parliament respecting America. And as septennial parliaments are found to be the root from whence all our political grievances spring, they were also bound to endeavor the restoration of our ancient privileges in respect to the duration of parliaments.

Surely, my friends and fellow citizens, this is a conduct which, at such a crisis of our affairs, was laudable and necessary; and a conduct which, it all the electors of Great Britain had followed, we should not now have been at the eve of a civil war with America; nor such an interruption give to our commerce as threatens the immediate ruin of thousands of families....

Suffer me again to remind you of the imminent danger of your situation:— Your Ministers, by attacking the rights of all America, have effected that which the malicious policy of more judicious minds would have avoided. Your colonists, convinced that their safety depends on their harmony, are now united in one strong bond of union; nor will it be in the power of a Machiavel to take any advantage of those feuds and jealousies which formerly subsided among them, and which exposed their liberties to more real danger than all the fleets and armies we are able to sent against them....

Rouse, my countrymen! rouse from that state of guilty dissipation in which you have too long remained, and in which, if you longer continue, you are lost for ever. Rouse! and unite in one general effort; 'till, by your unanimous and repeated Addresses to the Throne, and to both Houses of Parliament, you draw the attention of every part of the government to their own interests, and to the dangerous state of the British empire.

32

Abigail Smith Adams on the British Occupation of Boston (1775)

By the fall of 1774, British authorities in Boston found so much resistance to their rule that they had begun to fortify the city. But efforts to quell the brewing insurrection in Massachusetts met with little success. In April 1775, British efforts to seize colonial arms and leaders at Concord failed, resulting in a humiliating retreat to Boston. In early June, the British declared martial law in the city. When local insurgents fortified Breed's Hill overlooking Boston, the British determined to assault the colonial positions. On June 17, 1775, the Battle of Bunker Hill (so named because the colonists had originally planned to fortify it rather than the nearby, but less defensible, Breed's Hill) cost the British over one thousand casualties before they finally drove off the colonial defenders. Abigail Smith Adams watched the battle and bombardment of neighboring Charlestown with her young son, John Quincy. The wife of a leading figure in the independence movement, the self-educated Abigail conducted a lively and insightful correspondence with her husband and would later emerge as an early voice for women's rights. In the following letter to her husband, Abigail recounts the battle and describes the effects of the British occupation of the city.

Questions to Consider

1. To what extent might these letters corroborate colonial Whig charges of British "tyranny"?

2. How might a person loyal to British authority interpret these letters?

3. Based on these letters, what might you conclude about the level of equality between Abigail and her husband? Do you think their relationship was typical of the time?

Letter from Abigail Smith Adams to John Adams, 25 June 1775

DEAREST FRIEND.

My father has been more afflicted by the destruction of Charlestown than by any thing which has heretofore taken place. Why should not his countenance be sad, when the city, the place of his father's sepulchre, lieth waste, and the gates thereof are consumed with fire? Scarcely one stone remaineth upon another; but in the midst of sorrow we have abundant cause of thankfulness, that so few of our brethren are numbered with the slain, whilst our enemies were cut down like the grass before the scythe. But one officer of all the Welsh fusileers remains to tell his story. Many poor wretches die for want of proper assistance and care of their wounds.

Every account agrees in fourteen or fifteen hundred slain and wounded upon their side, nor can I learn that they dissemble the number themselves. We had some heroes that day, who fought with amazing intrepidity and courage.

> "Extremity is the trier of spirits;
> —common chances common men can bear;"
> And "when the sea is calm, all boats alike
> Show mastership in floating. But fortune's blows,
> When most struck home, being *bravely* warded, crave
> A noble cunning."

I hear that General Howe has said, that the battle upon the plains of Abram was but a bauble to this. When we consider all the circumstances, attending this action, we stand astonished that our people were not all cut off. They had but one hundred feet intrenched, the number who were engaged did not exceed eight hundred, and they with not half ammunition enough; the reinforcement not able to get to them seasonably. The tide was up, and high, so that their floating batteries came upon each side of the causeway, and their row-galleys kept a continual fire. Added to this, the fire from Cops Hill, and from the ships; the town in flames, all around them, and the heat from the flames so intense as scarcely to be borne; the day one of the hottest we have had this season, and the wind blowing the smoke in their faces, —only figure to yourself all

SOURCE: Letters from Abigail Smith Adams to John Adams, 25 June 1775, 5 July 1775, 16 July 1775; *Letters of Mrs. Adams, The Wife of John Adams*, 4th ed., ed. Charles Francis Adams (Boston, 1848), 34–54.

these circumstances, and then consider that we do not count sixty men lost. My heart overflows at the recollection.

Letter from Abigail Smith Adams to John Adams, July 05, 1775

I should have been more particular, but I thought you knew every thing that passed here. The present state of the inhabitants of Boston is that of the most abject slaves, under the most cruel and despotic of tyrants. Among many instances I could mention, let me relate one. Upon the 17th of June, printed handbills were posted up at the corners of the streets and upon houses, forbidding any inhabitants to go upon their houses, or upon any eminence, on pain of death; the inhabitants dared not to look out of their houses, nor to be heard or seen to ask a question. Our prisoners were brought over to the Long Wharf, and there lay all night, without any care of their wounds or any resting-place but the pavements, until the next day, when they exchanged it for the jail, since which we hear they are civilly treated. Their living cannot be good, as they can have no fresh provisions; their beef, we hear, is all gone, and their own wounded men die very fast, so that they have a report that the bullets were poisoned. Fish they cannot have, they have rendered it so difficult to procure; and the admiral is such a villain as to oblige every fishing schooner to pay a dollar every time it goes out. The money that has been paid for passes is incredible. Some have given ten, twenty, thirty, and forty dollars, to get out with a small proportion of their things. It is reported and believed, that they have taken up a number of persons and committed them to jail, we know not for what in particular. Master Lovell is confined in the dungeon; a son of Mr. Edes is in jail, and one Wiburt, a ship carpenter, is now upon trial for his life. God alone knows to what length these wretches will go, and will I hope restrain their malice.

Letter from Abigail Smith Adams to John Adams, 16 July 1775

... I am much surprised that you have not been more accurately informed of what passes in the camps. As to intelligence from Boston, it is but very seldom we are able to collect any thing that may be relied on; and to report the vague, flying rumors, would be endless. I heard yesterday, by one Mr. Roulstone, a goldsmith, who got out in a fishing schooner, that their distress increased upon them fast. Their beef is all spent; their malt and cider all gone. All the fresh provisions they can procure, they are obliged to give to the sick and wounded. Thirteen of our men who were in jail, and were wounded at the battle of Charlestown, were dead. No man dared now to be seen talking to his friend in the street. They were obliged to be within, every evening, at ten o'clock, according to martial law; nor could any inhabitant walk any street in town after that time, without a pass from Gage. He has ordered all the molasses to be distilled up into rum for the soldiers; taken away all licenses, and given out others, obliging to a forfeiture of ten pounds, if any rum is sold without written orders from the general. He gives much the same account of the killed and wounded we have from others. The spirit, he says, which prevails among the soldiers, is a spirit of malice and revenge; there is no true courage and bravery to be observed among them. Their duty is hard, always mounting guard with their packs at their backs, ready for an alarm, which they live in continual hazard of. Dr. Eliot is not on board a man-of-war, as has been reported, but perhaps was left in town, as the comfort and support of those who cannot escape. He was constantly with our prisoners. Messrs. Lovell and Leach, with others, are certainly in jail. A poor milch [milk] cow was last week killed in town, and sold for a shilling sterling per pound.

33

A Loyalist Perspective on the Coming of the Revolution (1780)

Many Americans refused to support the Whig cause during the American Revolution and remained loyal to the Crown. Disparate in background and without real organization, Loyalists had numerous reasons for their stance. Many ultimately fled America, leaving all behind. Joseph Galloway was one of the most prominent Loyalists. A prominent figure in the Quaker party (along with his close friend, Benjamin Franklin) that represented the Philadelphia establishment, he served as the Speaker of the Pennsylvania Assembly from 1766 until 1775. A firm believer that colonial liberties could be preserved only within an imperial union, Galloway offered his Plan for Union that the First Continental Congress rejected in the fall of 1774. Determined to remain loyal to Britain, he refused election to the Second Continental Congress and left the Pennsylvania Assembly. In 1778, he and his family abandoned their home and moved to London. In the following selection, Galloway presents his views on the cause of the American Revolution.

Questions to Consider

1. What is the author's purpose in writing this document?
2. Does the author see widespread support for the Revolution?
3. What does Joseph Galloway see as the leading cause of the American Revolution?
4. To what extent are Galloway's views influenced by "John Locke on Political Society and Government" (Document 27)?

When the Tea-act passed, the same men, determined to lose no opportunity of promoting their favourite scheme of independence, stirred up the rabble in several of the sea-ports, headed by the smuggling merchants, whose interest alone was affected by the act, to seize the Tea, and in one of the Colonies to destroy it. But in this the people at large took no part.

In consequence of the illegal and unjustifiable destruction of the Tea in Boston, the Act for stopping up that port was passed; this afforded another opportunity for the exercise of violent spirits. Every art was used to draw the people of that town into violent measures. The country was called upon to join them, but in vain; far from any views of independence, the people honestly declared, that a violent act of injustice had been committed, and that reparation ought to be made.

These daring spirits having, however, by various arts and incessant exertions, procured in most of the Colonies, a party of men immediately interested in the repeal of the Tea-act, of the most restless dispositions,—of bankrupt fortunes, and dishonest principles, proposed a general Congress, under pretence of uniting in *decent and proper measures*, for obtaining a repeal of these statutes. But they carefully concealed their principle design of separating the two countries, and establishing independent Governments, because they knew the minds and affections of the people, and even of some of those who were zealous opposers of the acts, were too firmly attached to the British government to endure the thought; and they had not as yet obtained a power sufficient to enforce the measure.

This proposal of a Congress was by no means generally approved by the people. They thought, that their respective Assemblies were most proper to petition, and to obtain a redress of their grievances; they knew, that the Assemblies were their legal Representatives, that the appointment of a Congress would be by themselves a violation of those rights which they complained of in others; and they were apprehensive, that persons illegally appointed, might not pursue reasonable and legal measures; or if they did, that they would not be so successful in the event, as if proposed and pursued under a constitutional authority. For these reasons they relied on their Assemblies. But, while the great bulk of the people acted on such rational and loyal principles, the violent few proceeded to chuse their Committees and Conventions, and these to chuse their Delegates in Congress. Under this circumstance, it was an easy task for the independent faction, to prevail on a few restless and weak men to appoint many of their own number. However zealous the electors might be in opposing the Statutes of which they wished for a repeal, yet there were many among them whose opposition was meant to extend no further; and therefore we find, that the instructions given to the Delegates in Congress were too far from authorising them to promote the independence of the Colonies, or to take up arms, that all of them, either expressly, or by the fullest implication, prohibited it. I have inclosed, for your Lordship's perusal, extracts of those instructions, from which it will clearly appear, that the Congress were not authorised to pursue any measures, except those that were *legal*, that perfectly corresponded with their *allegiance to their Sovereign*, and that tended to *unite, and not to separate* the two countries. Your Lordship will perceive, on comparing these instructions with the proceedings of Congress, particularly in their approbation of the Suffolk resolves, inciting the

SOURCE: Joseph Galloway, *Letters to a Nobleman on the Conduct of the War in the Middle Colonies*, 3rd ed. (London, 1780), 12–15.

people to arms, their resolve to make reprisals, and their seditious letters to the people of England, Ireland, and Canada, that the Delegates violated their trust, acted in every measure which tended to violence and sedition, without authority, and contrary to the directions of those who appointed them; and that the people in general were so far from intending the least deviation from their loyalty, that all they fought for was a redress of what they thought grievances, by "prudent and legal measures, and a more perfect union of the two countries upon constitutional principles."

34

Introduction to *Common Sense* (1776)

The publication of the forty-seven-page pamphlet Common Sense *in early 1776 marked an important turning point in the American colonists' decision to leave the British Empire. Despite the outbreak of hostilities in 1775, many Americans were hesitant to support independence. It was* Common Sense *that questioned the colonies' relationship with England and influenced many previously wavering Americans to support the Revolution. The author of* Common Sense, *Thomas Paine, grew up in a humble English household and received only a rudimentary education. After failing in a variety of jobs, including that of a lobbyist for British excise collectors, Paine left for Philadelphia in 1774 with letters of introduction from Benjamin Franklin. After arriving in America, Paine landed a job writing for the* Pennsylvania Magazine. *(Among his first articles was a call for the abolition of slavery.) The following selection contains excerpts from the introduction to* Common Sense.

Questions to Consider

1. To what audience is this document addressed?
2. On what basis does Thomas Paine argue for American independence?
3. In what ways would this presentation help convince wavering colonists to support the Revolution?
4. To what extent was Paine influenced by John Locke ("On Political Society and Government," Document 27))? How are his views different than those of Joseph Galloway ("A Loyalist Perspective on the Coming of the Revolution," Document 33)?

...The cause of America is in a great measure the cause of all mankind. Many circumstances have, and will arise, which are not local, but universal, and through which the principles of all lovers of mankind are affected, and in the event of which their affections are interested. The laying a country desolate with fire and sword, declaring war against the natural rights of all mankind, and extirpating the defenders thereof from the face of the earth, is the concern of every man to whom nature hath given the power of feeling....

... government; namely, [is] a mode rendered necessary by the inability of moral virtue to govern the world; here too is the design and end of government, viz. freedom and security. And however our eyes may be dazzled with show, or our ears deceived by sound; however prejudice may warp our wills, or interest darken our understanding, the simple voice of nature and reason will say, 'tis right....

The sun never shone on a cause of greater worth. 'Tis not the affair of a city, a county, a province, or a kingdom; but of a continent—of at least one eighth part of the habitable globe. 'Tis not the concern of a day, a year, or an age; posterity are virtually involved in the contest, and will be more or less affected even to the end of time, by the proceedings now. Now is the seed-time of continental union, faith and honor. The least fracture now will be like a name engraved with the point of a pin on the tender rind of a young oak; the wound would enlarge with the tree, and posterity read it in full grown characters.

By referring the matter from argument to arms, a new era for politics is struck—a new method of thinking has arisen. All plans, proposals, &c. prior to the nineteenth of April, i.e. to the commencement of hostilities, are like the almanacs of the last year; which tho' proper then, are superceded and useless now. Whatever was advanced by the advocates on either side of the question then, terminated in one and the same point, viz. a union with Great Britain; the only difference between the parties was the method of effecting it; the one proposing force, the other friendship; but it hath so far happened that the first has failed, and the second has withdrawn her influence....

I have heard it asserted by some, that as America has flourished under her former connection with Great Britain, the same connection is necessary towards her future happiness, and will always have the same effect. Nothing can be more fallacious than this kind of argument.... America would have flourished as much, and probably much more, had no European power taken any notice of her. The commerce by which she hath enriched herself are the necessaries of life, and will always have a market while eating is the custom of Europe....

We have boasted the protection of Great Britain, without considering, that her motive was interest not attachment; and that she did not protect us from our enemies on our account; but from her enemies on her own account, from those who had no quarrel with us on any other account, and those who will always be our enemies on the same account. Let Britain waive her pretensions to the continent, or the continent throw off the dependance, and we should be at peace with France and Spain, were they at war with Britain. The miseries of Hanover's last war ought to warn us against connections....

SOURCE: Thomas Paine, *The Writings of Thomas Paine*, ed. Moncure D. Conway (New York, 1902), 1: 68, 71, 84–87.

But Britain is the parent country, say some. Then the more shame upon her conduct. Even brutes do not devour their young, nor savages make war upon their families; wherefore, the assertion, if true, turns to her reproach; but it happens not to be true, or only partly so, and the phrase parent or mother country hath been jesuitically adopted by the king and the parasites, with a low papistical design of gaining an unfair bias on the credulous weakness of our minds. Europe, and not England, is the parent country of America. This new world hath been the asylum for the persecuted lovers of civil and religious liberty from every part of Europe. Hither have they fled, not from the tender embraces of the mother, but from the cruelty of the monster; and it is so far true of England, that the same tyranny which drove the first emigrants from home, pursues their descendants still.

In this extensive quarter of the globe, we forget the narrow limits of three hundred and sixty miles (the extent of England) and carry our friendship on a larger scale; we claim brotherhood with every European Christian, and triumph in the generosity of the sentiment.

35

A Speech against Independence (1776)

Before declaring independence in the summer of 1776, the Continental Congress was the scene of heated debate on whether the colonies should sever their relationship with Britain. John Dickinson was one of those who spoke on the issue. Born in Maryland, Dickinson began his professional training in a Philadelphia law office and continued his education at London's prestigious Middle Temple. Dickinson first gained notoriety in 1767–1768 with the publication of Letters from a Farmer in Pennsylvania. *Written in response to the Townshend Duties, the* Letters *distinguished between external and internal taxes and expressed colonial opposition to taxes levied on them by Parliament. In the ensuing excerpt, Dickinson offers his views just days before the signing of the Declaration of Independence. Dickinson ultimately supported American independence and later served in the 1787 Constitutional Convention.*

Questions to Consider

1. For what reasons does John Dickinson believe the colonies should resolve their differences with Great Britain?

2. What had Great Britain offered the American colonies that Dickinson did not want to lose?

3. What does Dickinson fear if the colonies declare independence?

4. Compare and contrast the views contained in this document with those found in Thomas Paine's "Introduction to *Common Sense*" (Document 34). How do you account for similarities? Differences?

... I know the name of liberty is dear to each one of us; but have we not enjoyed liberty even under the English monarchy? Shall we this day renounce that to go and seek it in I know not what form of republic, which will soon change into a licentious anarchy and popular tyranny? In the human body the head only sustains and governs all the members, directing them, with admirable harmony, to the same object, which is self-preservation and happiness; so the head of the body politic, that is the king, in concert with the Parliament, can alone maintain the union of the members of this Empire, lately so flourishing, and prevent civil war by obviating all the evils produced by variety of opinions and diversity of interests. And so firm is my persuasion of this that I fully believe the most cruel war which Great Britain could make upon us would be that of not making any; and that the surest means of bringing us back to her obedience would be that of employing none. For the dread of the English arms, once removed, provinces would rise up against provinces and cities against cities; and we shall be seen to turn against ourselves the arms we have taken up to combat the common enemy.

Insurmountable necessity would then compel us to resort to the tutelary authority which we should have rashly abjured, and, if it consented to receive us again under its aegis, it would be no longer as free citizens but as slaves. Still inexperienced and in our infancy, what proof have we given of our ability to walk without a guide?

... our union with England ... is no less necessary to procure us, with foreign powers, that condescension and respect which is so essential to the prosperity of our commerce, to the enjoyment of any consideration, and to the accomplishment of any enterprise.... From the moment when our separation shall take place, everything will assume a contrary direction. The nations will accustom themselves to look upon us with disdain; even the pirates of Africa and Europe will fall upon our vessels, will massacre our seamen, or lead them into a cruel and perpetual slavery....

Independence, I am aware, has attractions for all mankind; but I maintain that, in the present quarrel, the friends of independence are the promoters of slavery, and that those who desire to separate us would but render us more dependent, ... to change the condition of English subjects for that of slaves to the whole world is a step that could only be counseled by insanity....

But here I am interrupted and told that no one questions the advantages which America derived at first from her conjunction with England; but that the new pretensions of the ministers have changed all, have subverted all. If I should deny that, ... I should deny not only what is the manifest truth but

SOURCE: "Speech of John Dickinson of Pennsylvania, Favoring a Condition of Union with England, Delivered July 1, 1776," *Principles and Acts of the Revolution in America*, ed. Hezekiah Niles (Baltimore, 1822), 493–95.

even what I have so often advanced and supported. But is there any doubt that it already feels a secret repentance? These arms, these soldiers it prepares against us are not designed to establish tyranny upon our shores but to vanquish our obstinacy, and to compel us to subscribe to conditions of accommodation.

... to pretend to reduce us to an absolute impossibility of resistance, in cases of oppression, would be, on their part, a chimerical project.... [But only] an uninterrupted succession of victories and of triumphs could alone constrain England to acknowledge American independence; which, whether we can expect, whoever knows the instability of fortune can easily judge.

If we have combated successfully at Lexington and at Boston, Quebec and all Canada have witnessed our reverses. Everyone sees the necessity of opposing the extraordinary pretensions of the ministers; but does everybody see also that of fighting for independence?

... By substituting a total dismemberment to the revocation of the laws we complain of, we should fully justify the ministers; we should merit the infamous name of rebels, and all the British nation would arm, with an unanimous impulse, against those who, from oppressed and complaining subjects, should have become all at once irreconcilable enemies. The English cherish the liberty we defend; they respect the dignity of our cause; but they will blame, they will detest our recourse to independence, and will unite with one consent to combat us.

The propagators of the new doctrine are pleased to assure us that, out of jealousy toward England, foreign sovereigns will lavish their succors upon us, as if these sovereigns could sincerely applaud rebellion; as if they had not colonies, even here in America, in which it is important for them to maintain obedience and tranquility.... under the most benevolent pretexts they will despoil us of our territories, they will invade our fisheries and obstruct our navigation, they will attempt our liberty and our privileges. We shall learn too late what it costs to trust to those European flatteries, and to place that confidence in inveterate enemies which has been withdrawn from long tried friends.

There are many persons who, to gain their ends, extol the advantages of a republic over monarchy. I will not here undertake to examine which of these two forms of government merits the preference. I know, however, that the English nation, after having tried them both, has never found repose except in monarchy. I know, also, that in popular republics themselves, so necessary is monarchy to cement human society, it has been requisite to institute monarchical powers, ... Nor should I here omit an observation, the truth of which appears to me incontestible—the English constitution seems to be the fruit of the experience of all anterior time, in which monarchy is so tempered that the monarch finds himself checked in his efforts to seize absolute power; and the authority of the people is so regulated that anarchy is not to be feared. But for us it is to be apprehended that, when the counterpoise of monarchy shall no longer exist, the democratic power may carry all before it and involve the whole state in confusion and ruin. Then an ambitious citizen may arise, seize the reins of power, and annihilate liberty forever; ...

5

Creating the New Nation

The American Revolution pitted a large portion of the American population—people who believed their liberties were under attack—against the British and their American Loyalist supporters, who resolved to uphold the authority of Parliament. Militarily, the American strategy was to avoid losing while somehow luring France into the war, an act that would drain off British forces and likely assure American independence. To achieve this end, American forces first had to secure a major victory. Eighteenth-century battles could be particularly brutal, especially when American Whigs faced their Loyalist neighbors. In such engagements, victors sometimes left the field without prisoners. The principles over which the Americans fought the war—to preserve their liberty—became embedded in the political culture and would shape the political dialogue in the United States for decades to come. The following documents illustrate various aspects of the wartime experience and reveal the tensions over how to best preserve these liberties in the immediate aftermath of the Revolution.

36

German Doctor's Account of War and Surgery (1777)

Britain's controversial decision to use foreign auxiliaries against the Americans caused many colonists to forsake their loyalty to the Crown. England's determination to use mercenaries made sense in London; the German troops were well-trained professionals who could be rented from cash-hungry German sovereigns for a reasonable price. The largest number of these troops came from Hesse Kassel; hence, the term Hessian *became a synonym for all German mercenaries. The author of the ensuing account was Julius F. Wasmus, an army surgeon from the German state of Brunswick. Before coming to Canada in 1776, he had served in the Seven Years' War. A member of General John Burgoyne's force as it headed south along Lake Champlain in 1777, Wasmus was captured at the Battle of Bennington. The Bennington engagement contributed to Burgoyne's later defeat at Saratoga, and it resulted in four years of captivity for the doctor. Wasmus recalls the heat of the Bennington fight in the selection excerpted here.*

Questions to Consider

1. How does Julius Wasmus describe the battle?
2. How did Wasmus view his captors?
3. What seemingly surprised Wasmus about the American army?
4. Would Wasmus agree with the argument espoused in "Pennsylvania, the Poor Man's Paradise" (Document 14) and "What Is an American?" (Document 25)? How might the 1755 Pennsylvania Assembly ("Pennsylvania Assembly Comments on German Immigration," Document 21) have viewed someone like Wasmus?

16th … The enemy is marching in force against our right wing and it appears that they want to encircle us. There is also some shooting on our right wing. After 12 o'clock, a patrol was sent out from our lines and was driven off by the enemy, who fired at them. Half an hour later, a violent volley of fire erupted against the entrenchment that was occupied by 35 dragoons. Our dragoons fired up volleys on the enemy in cold blood and with much courage, and it

SOURCE: J. F. Wasmus, *An Eyewitness Account of the American Revolution and New England Life: The Journal of J. F. Wasmus, German Company Surgeon, 1776–1783*, trans. Helga Doblin, ed. Mary C. Lynn (Westport, CT, 1990), 71–73. ©1990 by Helga Doblin. Reproduced with permission of ABC-CLIO, LLC.

did not take them long to load their carbines behind the breastworks. But as soon as they rose up to take aim, bullets went through their heads. They fell backwards and no longer moved a finger. Thus, in a short time, our tallest and best dragoons were sent into eternity. The [German] cannon shot balls and grapeshot sometimes to the right, sometimes to the left and then again forward into the brush. The Savages made terrible faces and ran from one tree to the next. I had chosen a very big oak tree close behind our entrenchment, behind which I dressed the wounded. The Savages also came behind this tree and 4 or 5 of them lying down on top of me almost crushed me to death. From the enemy side, the fire became increasingly heavy and they [the enemy] pressed harder. When the Savages saw that, one of them, probably the oldest, emitted a strange cry, which cannot be described; whereupon they all ran down the mountain toward the barrage. The cannon in our entrenchment was quiet because the sergeant artificer, who commanded it, had been shot; the 8 men at the cannon were either shot or wounded. At the bridge, where our Lieut. Colonel Baum was standing, the cannon and volley fire had ceased. Capt. Dommes, who was covering our left flank and rear, was driven back with his few men and captured; we could see this quite well from our mountain. We were thus completely encircled. We too withdrew now with great speed while I was still busy dressing wounds. Then, following the regiment in a great hurry, I stumbled over a big, fallen tree about 300 paces from our entrenchment. When I got up, the enemy came rushing over our entrenchment and 3 quickly took aim and fired at me. I again fell to the ground behind the tree and the bullets were dreadful, whistling over and beyond me. I remained lying on the ground until the enemy urged me rather impolitely to get up. One grabbed me by the arm and another said he should kill me, whereupon he placed the bayonet of his gun with tightened trigger on my chest. He asked whether I was a Britisher or a Hessian. I told him I was a Braunschweig surgeon, shook hands with him, and called him my friend and brother; for what does one not do when in trouble. I was happy they understood me (Freund and Bruder) for that helped so much that he withdrew his gun. But he now took my watch, looked at it, held it to his ear and put it away [in his pocket]. After this, he made a friendly face and was so human that he urged me to take a drink from his wooden flask. He handed me over to his comrades, who started anew to search my pockets. One of them took nothing but my purse in which, however, were only 14 piasters (specie). He continued eagerly looking for money but then left, whereupon the third began searching my pockets. This one took all my small items as my knife, my paper, my lighter, but he did not find the best; they were so dumb that they did not see the pocket in my overcoat. Thus, I saved my Noble [sic] pipe. If I had put my watch and moneybag into this pocket, I would not have lost anything....

When one of the enemy heard that I was a CHIRURGUS [surgeon], he led me behind our entrenchment to dress the wound of his son, who had been shot through the thigh. Now I saw what effect our cannon and musket fire had had, since the enemy had suffered great losses here. General Stark, who in attire and posture was very similar to the tailor Muller in Wolfenbuttel, had commanded the corps of the Americans against us. As he now saw me dressing the wounds of the first, he ordered me to bandage several others of the enemy, but I hurried toward our entrenchment because there were dragoons and Hess-Hanau Artillerymen in need of my help. But the Americans did not allow me any time but pulled me along by force. We went past the trusty tree that had warded off so many bullets from me. Here I found some of my instruments and bandages etc. in a case. Putting all of it in a bag, I wanted to take it along, but my guide took it away from me and urged me to drink some strong rum with him. All the enemy were very well provided with it and I noticed that almost all of them were drunk. Each one had a wooden flask filled with rum hanging from his neck; they all were in shirt-sleeves, had nothing [to cover] their bodies but shirts, vests and long linen trousers, which reached down to their shoes; no stockings; [in addition] a powder horn, a bullet bag, a flask with rum and a gun—that was all they had on them. They all were well-shaped men of very healthy appearance and well-grown; better than the Canadians.... They [the Rebels] did not capture one single Savage; it is incomprehensible to me how they [the Savages] got through. The unfortunate Tories (Royalist Americans) who were not killed also fell into the hands of their countrymen. Like cattle, they were tied to each with cords and ropes and led away; it is presumed that they will be hanged.... These scenes cannot really be described—reading this, the best will perhaps be moved, but it is actually not possible to feel the horror of these scenes. A thought that makes your flesh creep! To see a friend or fellow creature lie bleeding on the ground who had been cruelly wounded by the murderous lead and approached his death shaking—crying for help, and then not be able, not be allowed to help him, is that not cruel?

37

Articles of Confederation (1777)

Even before the Continental Congress proclaimed independence, its members were contemplating how the thirteen former colonies would govern themselves. In July 1775, Benjamin Franklin proposed a plan of government, but it would be more than two years before the congressional delegates agreed on the Articles of Confederation. Since the articles required the unanimous consent of the states before going into effect, it was not until Maryland's acceptance in 1781 that the plan of union began to operate. The articles provide an example of the principles that Americans fought for during the American Revolution. Essentially a continuation of the Second Continental Congress, this new central government had limited powers. The perceived weakness of the Confederation led many prominent Americans to demand that the articles be amended and specifically that the central government be strengthened.

Questions to Consider

1. What powers were given to the Confederation government?
2. In what ways was the Confederation government weak?
3. Why might the individuals who drafted the Articles of Confederation have wanted a weak central government?
4. What specific features of the Confederation government will be retained in the Constitution?

ARTICLE I. "… this confederacy shall be 'The United States of America.'"

ARTICLE II. Each State retains its sovereignty, freedom and independence, and every power, jurisdiction and right, which is not by this confederation expressly delegated to the United States, in Congress assembled.

ARTICLE III. The said States hereby severally enter into a firm league of friendship with each other, for their common defense, the security of their liberties, and their mutual and general welfare …

ARTICLE IV…. the free inhabitants of each of these States, paupers, vagabonds, and fugitives from justice excepted, shall be entitled to all privileges and immunities of free citizens in the several States …

ARTICLE V…. No State shall be represented in Congress by less than two, nor by more than seven members; and no person shall be capable of being a delegate for more than three years in any term of six years….

In determining questions in the United States, in Congress assembled, each State shall have one vote.

Freedom of speech and debate in Congress shall not be impeached or questioned in any court, or place out of Congress, and the members of Congress shall be protected in their persons from arrests and imprisonments, during the time of their going to and from, and attendance on Congress, except for treason, felony, or breach of the peace.

ARTICLE VI. No State without the consent of the United States in Congress assembled, shall send any embassy to, or receive any embassy from, or enter into any conference, agreement, alliance or treaty with any king prince or state…. No State shall engage in any war without the consent of the United States in Congress assembled, unless such State be actually invaded by enemies, … and the danger is so imminent as not to admit of a delay, till the United States in Congress assembled can be consulted….

ARTICLE VIII. All charges of war, and all other expenses that shall be incurred for the common defense or general welfare, and allowed by the United States in Congress assembled, shall be defrayed out a common treasury, which shall be supplied by the several States, in proportion to the value of all land within each State….

ARTICLE IX. The United States in Congress assembled, shall have the sole and exclusive right and power of determining on peace and war, … [and] entering into treaties and alliances….

SOURCE: "The Articles of Confederation," *Old South Leaflets*, no. 2 (Boston, 1896), 1–9.

The United States in Congress assembled shall also be the last resort on appeal in all disputes and differences now subsisting or that hereafter may arise between two or more States concerning boundary, jurisdiction or any other cause whatever....

The United States in Congress assembled shall also have the sole and exclusive right and power of regulating the alloy and value of coin ... fixing the standard of weights and measures throughout the United States,—regulating the trade and managing all affairs with the Indians, not members of any of the States, provided that the legislative right of any State within its own limits be not infringed or violated—establishing and regulating post-offices from one State to another, throughout all the United States....

The United States in Congress assembled shall have authority to appoint a committee, to sit in the recess of Congress, to be denominated "a committee of the States," and to consist of one delegate from each State; and to appoint such other committees and civil officers as may be necessary for managing the general affairs of the United States under their direction—to appoint one of their number to preside, provided that no person be allowed to serve in the office of president more than one year in any term of three years; to ascertain the necessary sums of money to be raised for the service of the United States, and to appropriate and apply the same for defraying the public expenses—to borrow money, or emit bills on the credit of the United States, transmitting every half year to the respective States an account of the sums of money so borrowed or emitted,—to build and equip a navy—to agree upon the number of land forces, and to make requisitions from each State for its quota, in proportion to the number of white inhabitants in such State; which requisition shall be binding, and thereupon the Legislature of each State shall appoint the regimental officers, raise the men and clothe, arm and equip them in a soldier like manner, at the expense of the United States....

The United States in Congress assembled shall never engage in a war, ... nor enter into any treaties or alliances, nor coin money, nor regulate the value thereof, nor ascertain the sums and expenses necessary for the defense and welfare of the United States, or any of them, nor emit bills, nor borrow money on the credit of the United States, nor appropriate money, nor agree upon the number of vessels of war, to be built or purchased, or the number of land or sea forces to be raised, nor appoint a commander in chief of the army or navy, unless nine States assent to the same: nor shall a question on any other point, ... be determined, unless by the votes of a majority of the United States in Congress assembled....

ARTICLE X. The committee of the States, or any nine of them, shall be authorized to execute, in the recess of Congress, such of the powers of Congress as the United States in Congress assembled, by the consent of nine states....

ARTICLE XI. Canada acceding to this confederation, ... shall be admitted into, and entitled to all the advantages of this Union....

ARTICLE XII. All bills of credit emitted, monies borrowed and debts contracted by or under the authority of Congress, before the assembling of the United States, in pursuance of the present confederation, shall be deemed and considered as a charge against the United States....

ARTICLE XIII. Every State shall abide by the determinations of the United States in Congress assembled, on all questions which by this confederation are submitted to them. And the articles of this confederation shall be inviolably observed by every State, and the Union shall be perpetual: nor shall any alteration at any time hereafter be made in any of them; unless such alteration be agreed to in a Congress of the United States, and be afterwards confirmed by the Legislatures of every State....

38

The Revolution in Indian Country

The American Revolution was more than a war for independence from Great Britain; it dramatically reshaped relations in Indian Country. Nowhere was this more apparent than in upstate New York, where the Iroquois Confederacy had effectively held the balance of power between the British and French for a century. The conflict divided the Confederacy as the Mohawks, led by Theyandanagea (Joseph Brant), Cayugas, Onondagas, and Senecas supported the British, while Oneidas and Tuscaroras remained neutral. In 1778, the British-allied Iroquois joined Loyalists in raids against the Cherry Valley in New York and the Wyoming Valley of Pennsylvania, which resulted in considerable loss of life in the settlements. The following year, George Washington responded with the ensuing order. The resulting expedition destroyed at least 40 Iroquois towns and surrounding crop lands, effectively ending Iroquois resistance in the region. The Iroquois would thereafter refer to George Washington as "Town Destroyer."

Questions to Consider

1. Compare and contrast the views found in this document with those in "Chief Canassatego Speaks at the Treaty of Lancaster," (Document 20). What can you deduce about Indian–white relations from these two documents?

2. Why do you think most Iroquois supported the British during the Revolution? What does this say about the Revolution in Indian Country?

3. Why do you think all of the Iroquois were targeted for destruction instead of only those who sided with the British?

4. Does this document cause you to think about George Washington in a different way? How?

Head Quarters, Middle Brook, May 31, 1779.

Sir: The expedition you are appointed to command is to be directed against the hostile tribes of the six nations of Indians, with their associates and adherents. The immediate objects are the total distruction and devastation of their settlements and the capture of as many prisoners of every age and sex as possible. The troops to be employed under your command are: Clinton's, Maxwell's, Poor's and Hand's brigades and independent companies raised in the State of Pensylvania. In Hand's brigade, I comprehend all the detached corps of Continental troops now on the Susquehanna and Spencer's regiment. Cortlandt's I consider as belonging to Clinton's brigade; ... Clinton's brigade you are informed has been ordered to rendezvous at Conojoharie, subject to your orders either to form a junction with the main body on the Susquehanna by way of Otsego, or to proceed up the Mohock River and cooperate in the best manner circumstances will permit, as you judge most adviseable. So soon as your preparations are in sufficient forwardness, you will assemble your main body at Wyoming and proceed thence to Tioga, taking from that place the most direct and practicable route into the heart of the Indian settlements. You will establish such intermediate posts as you think necessary for the security of your communication and convoys, nor need I caution you, while you leave a sufficiency of men for their defence, to take care to diminish your operating force as little as possible. A post at Tioga will be particularly necessary, either a stockade fort or an intrenched camp; if the latter, a block-house should be erected in the interior.

I would recommd. that some post in the center of the Indian Country should be occupied with all expedition, with a sufficient quantity of provision; whence parties should be detached to lay waste all the settlements around, with instructions to do it in the most effectual manner; that the country may not be merely *overrun* but *destroyed*. I need not urge the necessity of using every method in your power to gain intelligence of the enemy's strength motions and designs; nor need I suggest the extraordinary degree of vigilance and caution which will be necessary to guard against surprises, from an adversary so secret desultory and rapid as the Indians.

If a detachment operates on the Mohock River, the Commanding officer should be instructed to be very watchful that no troops come from Oswegatchie and Niagara to Oswego without his knowledge; and for this purpose he should keep trusty spies at those three places, to advertise him instantly of the movement of any party and its force.... It should be previously impressed upon the minds of the men when ever they have an opportunity, to rush on with the

SOURCE: "Instructions to Major General Sullivan, May 31, 1779," *The Writings of George Washington from the Original Manuscript Sources*, ed. by John C. Fitzpatrick (Washington, 1931–44).

warhoop and fixed bayonet. Nothing will disconcert and terrify the indians more than this....

After you have very thoroughly completed the destruction of their settlements; if the Indians should shew a disposition for peace, I would have you to encourage it, on condition that they will give some decisive evidence of their sincerity by delivering up some of the principal instigators of their past hostility into our hands. Butler, Brandt, the most mischievous of the tories that have joined them, or any other they may have in their power that we are interested to get into ours.

... I have no power, at present, to authorise you to conclude a treaty of peace with them but you may agree upon the terms of one, letting them know that it must be finally ratified by Congress and giving them every proper assurance that it will.

I shall write to Congress on the subject and endeavour to obtain more ample and definitive authority. But you will not by any means, listen to any overture of peace before the total ruin of their settlements is effected. It is likely enough their fears if they are unable to oppose us, will compel them to offers of peace, or policy may lead them to endeavour to amuse us in this way to gain time and succour for more effectual opposition. Our future security will be in their inability to injure us; [the distance to wch. they are driven] and in the terror with which the severity of the chastizement they receive will inspire them. Peace without this would be fallacious and temporary. New presents and an addition of force from the enemy, would engage them to break it the first fair opportunity, and all the expence of our extensive preparations, would be lost.

When we have effectually chastized them we may then listen to peace and endeavour to draw further advantages from their fears. But even in this case great caution will be necessary to guard against the snares which their treachery may hold out. They must be explicit in their promises give substantial pledges for their performance and execute their engagements with decision and dispatch. Hostages are the only kind of security to be depended on. Should Niagara fall into your hands in the manner I have mentioned, you will do every thing in your power for preserving and maintaining it, by establishing a chain of posts in such a manner as shall appear to you most safe and effectual and tending as little to reduce our general force as possible. This however we shall be better able to decide as the future events of the campaign unfold themselves. I shall be more explicit on the subject hereafter....

Relying perfectly upon your judgment prudence and activity, I have the highest expectation of success equal to our wishes; and I beg leave to assure you, that I anticipate with great pleasure, the honor which will redound to yourself and the advantage to the common cause, form a happy Termination of this important enterprise.

39

The Battle of King's Mountain and Loyalism in the Carolinas (1780)

In the fall of 1778, the British opened up a southern theater when they landed at Savannah, Georgia. Convinced that the southern colonies were more valuable to Britain and sure that large numbers of Loyalists would support them, British forces quickly proved triumphant in the region. By 1780, the specter of British victory in the region had roused large numbers of local residents to resist through guerilla actions and organized battles. At King's Mountain, North Carolina, an army comprised of frontier settlers confronted a force of Loyalists. The following account, written by Banastre Tarleton, describes the battle and its impact. Tarleton, a British cavalry officer fighting under the leadership of Lord Cornwallis, had gained a reputation for brutality toward prisoners that led him to be called "No Quarter" Tarleton.

Questions to Consider

1. What impact did Ferguson's defeat have upon Loyalists in the Carolinas?

2. What impact did Ferguson's defeat have upon the British campaign in the Carolinas?

3. Why do you think Banastre Tarleton is so offended by American "insult and indignity"? What can you deduce about Tarleton from this document?

4. Why do you think the American forces at King's Mountain "exercised horrid cruelties on the prisoners"? How does this compare with the actions they took during the Sullivan Expedition ("The Revolution in Indian Country," Document 38)?

Near the end of September, Major Ferguson had intelligence of Clarke's having joined Sumpter, and that a swarm of backwoodsmen, by an unexpected and rapid approach to Gilbert town, now threatened his destruction. He dispatched information to Earl Cornwallis of the superior numbers to which he was opposed, and directly commenced his march to the Catawba. Notwithstanding the prudent plan of verging towards the royal army, and advertising the British general of this situation; owing to some communication, or the distance of his friends, a detachment did not march in time from Charlotte town to yield him assistance.

SOURCE: Banastre Tarleton, *A History of the Campaigns of 1780 and 1781 in the Southern Provinces of North America* (Dublin, Ireland, 1787), 167–69.

Colonels Campbell, Cleveland, Selby, Seveer, Williams, Brandon, and Lacy, being informed at Gilbert town, of the retreat of Ferguson by the Cherokee road, towards King's mountain, selected sixteen hundred chosen men on horseback, for a rigorous pursuit. The rapid march of this corps soon rendered an action inevitable. Major Ferguson heard of the enemy's approach at King's mountain: he occupied the most favourable position he could find, and waited the attack. The action commenced at four o'clock in the afternoon, on the 7th of October, and was disputed with great bravery near an hour, when the death of the gallant Ferguson threw his whole corps into total confusion. No effort was made after this event to resist the enemy's barbarity, or revenge the fall of their leader. By American accounts, one hundred and fifty officers and men of the provincials and loyal militias were killed, one hundred and fifty were wounded, and eight hundred were made prisoners. The mountaineers, it is reported, used every insult and indignity, after the action, towards the dead body of Major Ferguson, and exercised horrid cruelties on the prisoners that fell into their possession....

The destruction of Ferguson and his corps marked the period and the extent of the first expedition into North Carolina. Added to the depression and fear it communicated to the loyalists upon the borders, and to the southward, the effect of such an important event was sensibly felt by Earl Cornwallis at Charlotte town. The weakness of his army, the extent and poverty of North Carolina, the want of knowledge of his enemy's designs, and the total ruin of his militia, presented a gloomy prospect at the commencement of the campaign. A farther progress by the route which he had undertaken could not possibly remove, but would undoubtedly increase his difficulties; he therefore formed a sudden determination to quit Charlotte town, and pass the Catawba river. The army was ordered to move, and expresses were dispatched to recall Lieutenant-colonel Tarleton.

40

Women's Contributions to the War Effort (1780)

The contributions of American women were essential to the success of the American Revolution. Economic boycotts of British goods before the conflict were clearly made possible by American women's willingness to produce goods in the home to replace the loss of imported items. As many American men made the decision to fight for independence, American women took similar steps. Esther de Berdt Reed was an early supporter of the Whig cause. The wife of prominent Philadelphia politician Joseph Reed, in 1780 she organized a women's fund-raising committee in the Philadelphia area. Her effort to create similar organizations in other colonial towns was cut short by her untimely death from dysentery in September 1780. George Washington would laud the women's support of the war effort, but stopped short of arguing for the extension of greater legal rights or a political voice. The excerpt presented here discusses women's views toward the cause and their efforts to support the American Revolution.

Questions to Consider

1. To what audience is this document directed?
2. According to Esther de Berdt Reed, to what extent do American women share the principles of the American Revolution?
3. What can you deduce about the place of women in eighteenth-century America based on Esther de Berdt Reed's essay?
4. Do you think American women expected the promise of the American Revolution to affect their status? How?

On the commencement of actual war, the Women of America manifested a firm resolution to contribute as much as could depend on them, to the deliverance of their country. Animated by the purest patriotism, they are sensible of sorrow at this day, in not offering more than barren wishes for the success of so glorious a Revolution. They aspire to render themselves more really useful; and this sentiment is universal from the north to the south of the Thirteen United States....

Born for liberty, disdaining to bear the irons of a tyrannic Government, we associate ourselves to the grandeur of those Sovereign, cherished, and revered, who have held with so much splendour the scepter of the greatest States, The Batildas, the Elizabeths, the Maries, the Catharines, who have extended the empire of liberty, and contented to reign by sweetness and justice, have broken the chains of slavery, forged by tyrants in the times of ignorance and barbarity....

But I must limit myself to the recollection of this small number of achievements. Who knows if persons disposed to censure, and sometimes too severely with regard to us, may not disapprove our appearing acquainted even with the actions of which our sex boasts? We are at least certain, that he cannot be a good citizen who will not applaud our efforts for the relief of the armies which defend our lives, our possessions, our liberty? ...

Who, amongst us, will not renounce with the highest pleasure, those vain ornaments, when she shall consider that the valiant defenders of America will be able to draw some advantage from the money which she may have laid out in these; that they will be better defended from the rigours of the seasons, that after their painful toils, they will receive some extraordinary and unexpected relief; that these presents will perhaps be valued by them at a greater price, when

SOURCE: Esther de Berdt Reed, *The Sentiments of an American Woman* (Philadelphia, 1780), 1–2.

they will have it in their power to say: *This Is the offering of the Ladies.* The time is arrived to display the same sentiments which animated us at the beginning of the Revolution, when we renounced the use of teas, however agreeable to our taste, rather than receive them from our persecutors; when we made it appear to them that we placed former necessaries in the rank of superfluities, when our liberty was interested; when our republican and laborious hands spun the flax, prepared the linen intended for the use of our soldiers; when exiles and fugitives we supported with courage all the evils which are the concomitants of war. Let us not lose a moment; let us be engaged to offer the homage of our gratitude at the altar of military valour, and you, our brave deliverers, while mercenary slaves combat to cause you to share with them, the irons with which they are loaded, receive with a free hand our offering, the purest which can be presented to your virtue.

IDEAS, RELATIVE TO THE MANNER OF FORWARDING TO THE AMERICAN SOLDIERS, THE PRESENTS OF THE AMERICAN WOMEN

… 1st. All Women and Girls will be received without exception, to present their patriotic offering; and, as it is absolutely voluntary, every one will regulate it according to her ability, and her disposition. The shilling offered by the Widow or the young Girl, will be received as well as the most considerable sums presented by the Women who have the happiness to join to their patriotism, greater means to be useful.

2d. A Lady chosen by the others in each county, shall be the Treasuress; and to render her task more simple, and more easy, she will not receive but determinate sums, in a round number, from twenty hard dollars to any greater sum. The exchange forty dollars in paper for one dollar in specie.

It is hoped that there will not be one Woman who will not with pleasure charge herself with the embarrassment which will attend so honorable an operation.

3d. The Women who shall not be in a condition to send twenty dollars in specie, or above, will join in as great a number as will be necessary to make this or any greater sum, and one amongst them will carry it, or cause it to be sent to the Treasuress.

4th. The Treasuress of the county will receive the money, and will keep a register, writing the sums in her book, and causing it to be signed at the side of the whole by the person who has presented it.

5th. When several Women shall join together to make a total sum of twenty dollars or more, she amongst them who shall have the charge to carry it to the Treasuress, will make mention of all their names on the register, if her associates shall have so directed her, those whose choice it shall be, will have the liberty to remain unknown.

6th. As soon as the Treasuress of the county shall judge, that the sums which she shall have received, deserve to be sent to their destination, she will cause them to be presented with the lists, to the wife of the Governor or President of the State, who will be the Treasuress-General of the state; and she will cause it to be set down in her register, and have it sent to Mistress Washington. If the Governor or President are unmarried, all will address themselves to the wife of the Vice-President, if there is one, or of the Chief-Justice, &c.

7th. Women settled in the distant parts of the country, and not chusing for any particular reason as for the sake of greater expedition, to remit their Capital to the Treasuress, may send it directly to the wife of the Governor, or President, &c. or to Mistress Washington, who, if she shall judge necessary, will in a short answer to the sender, acquaint her with the reception of it.

8th. As Mrs. Washington may be absent from the camp when the greater part of the banks shall be sent there; the American Women considering, that General Washington is the Father and Friend of the Soldiery; that he is himself, the first Soldier of the Republic, and that their offering will be received at its destination as soon as it shall have come to his hands, they will pray him, to take the charge of receiving it, in the absence of Mrs. Washington.

9th. General Washington will dispose of this fund in the manner that he shall judge most advantageous to the Soldiery. The American Women desire only that it may not be considered as to be employed, to procure to the army, the objects of subsistence, arms or cloathing, which are due to them by the Continent. It is an extraordinary bounty intended to render the condition of the Soldier more pleasant, and not to hold place of the things which they ought to receive from the Congress, or from the States.

10th. If the General judges necessary, he will publish at the end of a certain time, an amount of that which shall have been received from each particular State.

11th. The Women who shall send their offerings, will have in their choice to conceal or to give their names; and if it shall be thought proper, on a fit occasion, to publish one day the lists, they only, who shall consent, shall be named; when with regard to the sums sent, there will be no mention made, if they so desire it.

41

European View of the American Revolution (1778/80, 1783)

The American Revolution had profound repercussions in Europe. The first image appeared between 1778 and 1780. It depicts an American sawing the horn off of a cow while the

Dutch, French, and Spanish sought to take advantage of the conflict by siphoning off trade that traditionally had belonged to the British. All the while, the British lion remains asleep.

The second cartoon appeared in London early in 1783. It depicts an Englishman, a Dutchman, an American Indian, a Spaniard, and a Frenchman urinating into a pot. The cartoon and accompanying text mock the peace process and the substantial British losses that resulted. These cartoons reveal the complex international dimension of the American Revolution.

Questions to Consider

1. What can you deduce from these cartoons about eighteenth-century stereotypes of national and ethnic groups?

2. Based on the first cartoon, what appear to be European attitudes toward American independence?

3. Based on the second image, what can you deduce from this cartoon about freedom of expression in 1783 Great Britain?

4. What can you deduce from the second cartoon about British attitudes toward the loss of America?

Wegens de staat der Engelsche natie, in't jaar 1778

SOURCE: [LC-USZ62-15755]/Library of Congress Prints and Photographs Division

The general p–s, or peace

42

Failure of the Continental Congress (1786)

Following the American Declaration of Independence, the Continental Congress created a permanent national government. The result was the Articles of Confederation, which passed the Congress in 1777 but were not ratified until 1781. The articles show the extent to which a fear of centralized authority dominated American political thinking in the early 1780s. David Ramsay, a native of Pennsylvania, gained public notice as a physician in Charleston, South Carolina. His connections to the local elite led him into politics, and he was an early and outspoken supporter of independence. Captured by the British during the conquest of Charleston, he was exiled to St. Augustine, Florida, for the duration of the war. Upon his return to South Carolina, he was elected to two terms in the Confederation Congress, serving as acting president in 1785–1786. In his capacity as acting president of the Confederation Congress, Ramsay sent the following letter to officials in Rhode Island, Delaware, Maryland, Virginia, North Carolina, and Georgia. It reveals some of the fundamental problems facing the government.

Questions to Consider

1. What are some of the problems facing the Continental Congress?
2. Why might many states neglect or ignore the Continental Congress?
3. Do you think that David Ramsay would have been interested in supporting a stronger central government?
4. What is the historical context of this document?

THE CHAIRMAN OF CONGRESS (DAVID RAMSAY)

TO CERTAIN STATES

New York January 31st, 1786.

Sir,

In conformity to the resolution enclosed it becomes my duty to write to the Executives of the several States which are at present unrepresented in Congress.

SOURCE: "The Chairman of Congress (David Ramsay) to Certain States," 31 January 1786, *Letters of the Members of the Continental Congress*, ed. Edmund C. Burnett (Washington, DC, 1936), 8: 290–91. Reprinted by permission.

Three months of the federal year are now completed and in that whole period no more than seven states have at any one time been represented. No question excepting that of adjourning from day to day can be carried without perfect unanimity. The extreme difficulty of framing resolutions against which no exception can be taken by any one State, can scarcely be conceived but by those whose unfortunate situation had led them to experience the perplexing embarrassment. Was the convenience of the present members only concerned your Excellency would not have been troubled with this letter. Sorry I am to add that the most essential interests of the United States suffer from the same cause. The languishing State of public credit is notorious both in Europe and America. What an additional wound must be given to it when it is known that no plans can be made for the payment of our debts, without the Unanimous consent of Nine States, and that only seven States have yet come forward with a representation. The disposition of our western Territory, An American Coinage, Commercial arrangements with European powers, particularly Great Britain, and a variety of other matters are of immense and pressing importance, but for want of an additional number of States nothing can be done.

I forbear to mention to your Excellency that even in private life where two persons agree to meet at a given time and place for the adjustment of their common concerns, the one who attends has a right to complain that he is not treated with common politeness by the other who breaks his appointment. I say nothing of the unequal burden imposed on the States who are present: They incur a heavy expence to maintain their delegates, and this expence is rendered inefficient, because that out of the other six no two have come forward to concur with them in dispatching the public business. Least of all would I insinuate that the present States might be justified in resolving that as they had attended three months to no purpose they would in their turn relinquish the public service, and leave the other states should they come on, to suffer a similar mortification to what they have long experienced of meeting and adjourning from day to day without having it in their power to enter on the most important and pressing national business.

The remissness of the States in keeping up a representation in Congress naturally tends to annihilate our Confederation. That once dissolved our State establishments would be of short duration. Anarchy, or intestine wars would follow till some future Caesar seized our Liberties, or we would be the sport of European politics, and perhaps parcelled out as appendages to their several Governments.

In behalf of Congress in the chair of which I at present have the honor to sit I beseech your Excellency by the regard you have for our federal Government to use your utmost endeavours to induce the delegates of your State to give their immediate attendance in Congress.

I have the honor to be Your Excellency's
Most obedient and most humble Servant,

— DAVID RAMSAY.

43

The Northwest Ordinance (1787)

Two of the most pressing issues facing the Confederation government were western lands and the need to raise revenue. Conflicting claims between the various states had delayed ratification of the Articles of Confederation for four years. But after several states abandoned their claims to territory north of the Ohio, the national government devised a method to dispose of the lands, thus raising much-needed funds. In 1785, Congress passed an ordinance that provided for the orderly disposal of lands in the Old Northwest (the present states of Ohio, Indiana, Illinois, Michigan, Wisconsin, and part of Minnesota). Two years later, a lobbyist representing land speculators spurred Congress into passing the Northwest Ordinance, which is excerpted here. The plan, which borrowed from an earlier proposal offered by Thomas Jefferson, described the process by which territories were to become states.

Questions to Consider

1. What are the steps in forming a government in new territory?
2. What must the territorial government provide its citizens?
3. What role does the federal government play in the formation of western states?
4. To what extent is the role of the federal government described different from the role envisioned in "The Articles of Confederation" (Document 37)? Why do you think this change occurred?

...Be it ordained by the authority aforesaid, That there shall be appointed, from time to time, by Congress, a governor, whose commission shall continue in force for the term of three years, unless sooner revoked by Congress; he shall reside in the district, and have a freehold estate therein in 1000 acres of land, while in the exercise of his office.

There shall be appointed, from time to time, by Congress a secretary, whose commission shall continue in force for four years unless sooner revoked; ... There shall also be appointed a court to consist of three judges, any two of whom to form a court, who shall have a common law jurisdiction, and reside in the district....

The governor and judges, or a majority of them, shall adopt and publish in the district such laws of the original States, criminal and civil, as may be necessary

SOURCE: "The Ordinance of 1787," *Old South Leaflets*, no. 13 (Boston, 1896), 1–7.

and best suited to the circumstances of the district, and report them to Congress from time to time....

Previous to the organization of the General Assembly, the governor shall appoint such magistrates and other civil officers....

So soon as there shall be 5000 free male inhabitants of full age in the district, upon giving proof thereof to the governor, they shall receive authority, with time and place, to elect representatives from their counties or townships to represent them in the General Assembly: Provided, That, for every 500 free male inhabitants, there shall be one representative, and so on progressively with the number of free male inhabitants, shall the right of representation increase, until the number of representatives shall amount to 25; after which, the number and proportion of representatives shall be regulated by the legislature: Provided, That no person be eligible or qualified to act as a representative unless he shall have been a citizen of one of the United States three years, and be a resident in the district, or unless he shall have resided in the district three years; and, in either case, shall likewise hold in his own right, in fee simple, 500 acres of land within the same: Provided, also, That a freehold in 50 acres of land in the district, having been a citizen of one of the States, and being resident in the district, or the like freehold and two years residence in the district, shall be necessary to qualify a man as an elector of a representative.

The representatives thus elected, shall serve for the term of two years....

Art. 1st. No person, demeaning himself in a peaceable and orderly manner, shall ever be molested on account of his mode worship or religious sentiments, in the said territory.

Art. 2d. The inhabitants of the said territory shall always be entitled to the benefits of the writ of habeas corpus, and of the trial by jury; of a proportionate representation of the people in the legislature; and of judicial proceedings according to the course of the common law....

Art. 3d. Religion, morality, and knowledge, being necessary to good government and the happiness of mankind, schools and the means of education shall forever be encouraged. The utmost good faith shall always be observed towards the Indians; their lands and property shall never be taken from them without their consent; and, in their property, rights, and liberty, they shall never be invaded or disturbed, unless in just and lawful wars authorized by Congress; but laws founded in justice and humanity, shall, from time to time, be made for preventing wrongs being done to them, and for preserving peace and friendship with them.

Art. 4th. The said territory, and the States which may be formed therein, shall forever remain a part of this confederacy of the United States of America, subject to the Articles of Confederation, and to such alterations therein as shall be constitutionally made; and to all the acts and ordinances of the United States in Congress assembled, conformable thereto....

Art. 5th. There shall be formed in the said territory, not less than three nor more than five States; and the boundaries of the States, as soon as Virginia shall alter her act of cession, and consent to the same, shall become fixed and established.... Provided, however, and it is further understood and declared, that the boundaries of these three States shall be subject so far to be altered, that, if Congress shall hereafter find it expedient, they shall have authority to form one or two States in that part of the said territory which lies North of an East and West line drawn through the Southerly bend or extreme of lake Michigan. And, whenever any of the said States shall have 60,000 free inhabitants therein, such State shall be admitted, by its delegates, into the Congress of the United States, on an equal footing with the original States in all respects whatever, and shall be at liberty to form a permanent constitution and State government: Provided, the constitution and government so to be formed, shall be republican, and in conformity to the principles contained in these articles; and, so far as it can be consistent with the general interest of the confederacy, such admission shall be allowed at an earlier period, and when there may be a less number of free inhabitants in the State than 60,000.

Art. 6th. There shall be neither slavery nor involuntary servitude in the said territory, otherwise than in the punishment of crimes, whereof the party shall have been duly convicted....

44

Grievances of the Shays Rebels (1786)

Whig concepts of liberty and their proclamations of "No taxation without representation" did not melt away following the American Revolution. Some inhabitants of the nation's backcountry believed that their respective state governments, dominated by eastern elites, ignored the problems of the interior. Feeling underrepresented and overtaxed, many balked at what they considered the overbearing control of a distant and unresponsive government. By the mid-1780s, the situation was particularly acute in western Massachusetts, where traditional resentment of eastern control was exacerbated by an economic depression. High taxes were more than just a nuisance; many local farmers thought the taxes threatened their ability to continue owning their land. Popular unrest broke out in August 1786 when citizens in Northampton disrupted a meeting of the court of common pleas. Daniel Shays, a revolutionary war hero and leader in the poor upland community of Pelham, soon emerged as the leader of the Regulators. The Shaysites succeeded in shutting down state courts in the interior, but the movement soon collapsed in the face of an aggressive military campaign mounted by state officials. The specter of Shays' Rebellion specifically, and agrarian unrest more generally, was a catalyst in the drafting of a stronger central government in 1787. The document presented here is part of a petition to the governor of Massachusetts that outlines rebel grievances.

Questions to Consider

1. What is the intended audience of this document?
2. Why do the rebels believe their liberty is under attack?
3. What similarities does the petition draw from the principles of the American Revolution?
4. Do you think that the individuals who drafted "The Northwest Ordinance" (Document 43) supported the Shaysites? Why or why not?

To his Excellency James BOWDOIN, Esq; Governour and Commander in Chief of said Commonwealth, and to the Honourable COUNCIL, convened at *Boston* in *December, 1786.*

The PETITION *of a Committee from several Towns in the County of* Worcester; *together with a Committee from a BODY of MEN, from the Counties of* Worcester, Hampshire *and* Berkshire, *all convened at* Worcester, *under the Command of Captain* SHAYS *and Captain* WHEELER, *who, on the 4th instant, did obstruct the sitting of the* COURT *of* COMMON PLEAS,

HUMBLY SHEWETH,

THAT the people first assembled, seeking a redress of public grievances, which they supposed in a great measure to be derived from the great expences and abuses of said Court, together with the General Sessions of the Peace, and from many other burthens, with which your Petitioners conceive the yeomanry unproportionably burthened: Notwithstanding, your Petitioners would have dutifully submitted, and waited for relief from the wisdom of the Hon. General Court, as they gratefully acknowledge the attention of that Body, in some instances, respecting their grievances, in the last session of the General Court:

Your Petitioners beg leave to mention their horrour of the suspension of the privilege of the writ of Habeas Corpus, that your Excellency and your Honours may be convinced your Petitioners are not of the wicked, dissolute and abandoned, as it is not confined to a factious few, but extended to towns and counties, and almost every individual who derives his living from the labour of his hands or an income of a farm. That the suspension of said privilege your Petitioners view as dangerous, if not absolutely destructive to a Republican Government. That under the cover of the suspension of said privilege, your Petitioners have been informed that the eyes and breasts of women and children have been wounded, if not destroyed; the house of the innocent broken open, their limbs mangled, their friends conveyed to gaol in another country, and now languishing (if alive) under their wounds.

In vindication of our liberties, your Petitioners beg leave to point to your Excellency and your Honours the arguments used by our virtuous asserters of liberty against the act of the British Parliament, in conveying our countrymen from county to county, and even beyond the sea for trial.

SOURCE: *"The* PETITION *of a Committee from several Towns in the County of Worcester,"* (Boston) *Independent Chronicle and the Universal Advertiser,* 15 December 1786.

Likewise the inhuman murder of Maverick and others, from mercenary principles under the ostensible right of government.

Your Petitioners, induced from a supreme love to peace, liberty and good order,

Humbly pray,

THAT your Excellency and your Honours would be graciously pleased to grant, That our friends that are under confinement out of the counties to which they belong, may have the favour of the Act of Indemnity, with your Petitioners, and that so long as they and your Petitioners shall behave orderly, both they and we may be safe in our persons and properties, and if consistent with your wisdom, that there may be an adjournment of the Courts of Common Pleas and General Sessions of the Peace, in the three Counties of *Berkshire, Hampshire,* and *Worcester,* until after the next May session of the Hon. General Court of this Commonwealth.

Your Petitioners, for themselves and party, engage to return to their respective homes, and conduct themselves as good and faithful subjects.

With the greatest uprightness, your petitioners assure your Excellency and Honours, that they were not induced to rise from a ... to the Commonwealth, or instigated by British Emissaries, but from those sufferings which disenabled them to provide for their wives and children, or to discharge their honest debts, tho' in possession of the lands of their country.

Your petitioners are not induced to petition in this way, from the mean fear of death, as they esteem one moment of liberty, to be worth an eternity of bondage; or from the uncertainty of war, the injuries of hunger, cold, nakedness, or the infamous name of rebel; as under all those disadvantages they once before engaged, and through the blessing of God have come off victorious. To that God they now appeal, conscious of the innocence of their intentions, expecting direction from that Being who is able to strengthen the counsels of the weak, and to turn the wisdom of the wise into foolishness; but from a love to the people, and a horror of the thoughts of the cruelties and devastations of a civil war. For the prevention of so great an evil, your petitioners *humbly pray* for the love, candour and interposition of your Excellency and Honours, in releasing our unfortunate and suffering friends from goal, your petitioners engaging for their good conduct as well as their own; waiting for a redress of grievances from your wisdom, both at the present time, and in all future elections.—And as in duty bound, shall ever pray.

45

Pennsylvania Dissent to the Ratification of the Constitution (1787)

The Constitutional Convention that met in Philadelphia during the summer of 1787 did its work in secrecy. When it presented the Constitution for ratification, supporters of the new government had the benefit of organization on their side. Pennsylvania quickly assented to the new pact, but not without opposition. Yeomen farmers in the state's interior bitterly opposed the new Constitution, believing that it instituted a form of tyranny similar to that previously exercised by Britain. The Constitution's opponents (known as Anti-Federalists) wanted stronger guarantees for individual liberties and state power; Federalists who supported the new government argued that the states enjoyed enough power and that state constitutions were sufficient to guarantee individual liberties. The following document, which appeared in Philadelphia's Pennsylvania Packet and Daily Advertiser, *records the dissent of Pennsylvania's Anti-Federalists and amendments proposed to improve the Constitution.*

Questions to Consider

1. For what reasons do the Anti-Federalists dissent about the Constitution?
2. How do you think the authors of this document reacted to Shays' Rebellion?
3. What additions to the Constitution are proposed by this document?
4. Which "propositions" eventually became parts of the Constitution?

The convention met, and the same disposition was soon manifested in considering the proposed constitution that had been exhibited in every other stage of the business. We were prohibited by an express vote of the convention from taking any question on the separate articles of the plan, and reduced to the necessity of adopting or rejecting *in toto*. It is true the majority permitted us to debate on each article, but restrained us from proposing amendments. They also determined not to permit us to enter on the minutes our reasons of dissent against any of the articles, nor even on the final question our reasons of dissent against the whole. Thus situated we entered on the examination of the proposed system

SOURCE: "Address and Reason of Dissent of the Minority of the Convention of Pennsylvania," (Philadelphia) *Pennsylvania Packet and Daily Advertiser*, 18 December 1787, 1–3.

of government, and found it to be such as we could not adopt without, as we conceived, surrendering up your dearest rights. We offered our objections to the convention, ... and closed our arguments by offering the following propositions to the convention.

1. The right of conscience shall be held inviolable, and neither the legislative, executive nor judicial powers of the United States shall have authority to alter, abrogate, or infringe any part of the constitution of the several states which provide for the preservation of liberty in matters of religion.

2. That in controversies respecting property, and in suits between man and man, trial by jury shall remain as heretofore, as well in the federal courts, as in those of the several states.

3. That in all capital and criminal prosecutions, a man has a right to demand the cause and nature of his accusation, as well in the federal courts, as in those of the several states; to be heard by himself and his counsel; to be con-fronted with the accusers and witnesses; to call for evidence in his favor, and a speedy trial by an impartial jury of his vicinage, without whose unanimous consent, he cannot be found guilty, nor can he be compelled to give evi-dence against himself; and that no man be deprived of his liberty, except by the law of the land or the judgment of his peers.

4. That excessive bail ought not to be required, nor excessive fines imposed, nor cruel nor unusual punishments inflicted.

5. That warrants unsupported by evidence, whereby any officer or messenger may be commanded or required to search suspected places, or to seize any person or persons, his or their property, not particularly described, are grievous and oppressive, and shall not I don't think this space belongs here be granted either by the magistrates of the federal government or others.

6. That the people have a right to the freedom of speech, of writing and pub-lishing their sentiments. Therefore, the freedom of the press shall not be restrained by any law of the United States.

7. That the people have a right to bear arms for the defense of themselves and their own state, or the United States, or for the purpose of killing game; and no law shall be passed for disarming the people or any of them, unless for crimes committed, or real danger of public injury from individuals; and as standing armies in the time of peace are dangerous to liberty, they ought not to be kept up; and that the military shall be kept under strict subordina-tion to and be governed by the civil powers.

8. The inhabitants of the several states shall have liberty to fowl and hunt in seasonable times, on the lands they hold, and on all other lands in the United States not enclosed, and in like manner to fish in all navigable waters, and others not private property, ...

9. That no law shall be passed to restrain the legislatures of the several states from enacting laws for imposing taxes, except imposts and duties on goods imported or exported, and that no taxes, except imposts and duties upon goods imported and duties upon goods imported and exported, and postage on letters shall be levied by the authority of Congress.

10. That the house of representatives be properly increased in number; that elections shall remain free; that the several states shall have power to regulate the elections for senators and representatives, without ... any interference on the part of the Congress; and that elections of representatives be annual.

11. That the power of organizing, arming, and disciplining the militia ... remain with the individual states, and that Congress shall not have authority to call or march any of the militia out of their own state, without the consent of such state, and for such length of time only as such state shall agree.

    That the sovereignty, freedom and independence of the several states shall be retained, and every power, jurisdiction and right which is not by this constitution expressly delegated to the United States in Congress assembled.

12. That the legislative, executive, and judicial powers be kept separate; and to this end that a constitutional council be appointed, to advise and assist the president, who shall be responsible for the advice they give, thereby the senators would be relieved from almost constant attendance; and also that the judges be made completely independent.

13. That no treaty which shall be directly opposed to the existing laws of the United States in Congress assembled, shall be valid until such laws shall be repealed, or made conformable to such treaty; neither shall any treaties be valid which are in contradiction to the constitution of the United States, or the constitutions of the several states.

14. That the judiciary power of the United States shall be confined to cases affecting ambassadors, other public ministers and consuls; to cases of admiralty and maritime jurisdiction; to controversies to which the United States shall be a party; to controversies between two or more states; between a state and citizens of different states; between citizens claiming lands under grants of different states; and between a state or the citizen thereof and foreign states, and in criminal cases, to such only as are expressly enumerated in the constitution, and that the United States in Congress assembled, shall not have power to enact laws, which shall alter the laws of descents and distribution of the effects of deceased persons, the titles of lands or goods, or the regulation of contracts in the individual states....

46

Federalist Number 10 (1788)

As the states deliberated on whether to agree to the Constitution, it became increasingly clear that ratification by New York and Virginia would be essential to the new government's success. During the hard-fought ratification debate in New York, Alexander Hamilton, James Madison, and John Jay wrote a series of essays under the pseudonym Publius in support of the Constitution. Known collectively as The Federalist, the essays have become classic expressions of Federalist thought and are among the most significant contributions to American political theory. The following excerpt is from as Federalist 10, the most important of the essays. The author of the selection, James Madison, had a keen interest in the subject. He had helped his home state of Virginia draft a new constitution in 1776, and he was an early advocate of reforming or replacing the Articles of Confederation with a stronger central government. Few individuals had a better understanding of the Constitution than did Madison, one of the document's principal creators.

Questions to Consider

1. What is significant about the historical context of this document?
2. According to James Madison, what are the problems with "factions"?
3. What are Madison's views on democracy?
4. Does the Constitution seem to be a radical document or a conservative one?

… By a faction, I understand a number of citizens, whether amounting to a majority or minority of the whole, who are united and actuated by some common impulse of passion, or of interest, adverse to the rights of other citizens, or to the permanent and aggregate interests of the community.

There are two methods of curing the mischiefs of faction: the one, by removing its causes; the other, by controlling its effects.

There are again two methods of removing the causes of faction: the one, by destroying the liberty which is essential to its existence; the other, by giving to every citizen the same opinions, the same passions, and the same interests.

It could never be more truly said than of the first remedy that it was worse than the disease. Liberty is to faction what air is to fire, an aliment without which it instantly expires. But it could not be less folly to abolish liberty, which is essential to political life, because it nourishes faction, than it would be to wish the annihilation of air, which is essential to animal life.…

SOURCE: "The Numerous Advantages of the Union," *The Federalist* (New York, 1901), 44–51.

The second expedient is as impracticable as the first would be unwise. As long as the reason of man continues fallible, and he is at liberty to exercise it, different opinions will be formed.... The diversity in the faculties of men, from which the rights of property originate, is not less an insuperable obstacle to a uniformity of interests. The protection of these faculties is the first object of government....

The latent causes of faction are thus sown in the nature of man; and we see them everywhere brought into different degrees of activity, according to the different circumstances of civil society.... But the most common and durable source of factions has been the various and unequal distribution of property.

Those who hold and those who are without property have ever formed distinct interests in society. Those who are creditors and those who are debtors fall under a like discrimination. A landed interest, a manufacturing interest, a mercantile interest, a moneyed interest, with many lesser interests, grow up of necessity in civilized nations and divide them into different classes, actuated by different sentiments and views. The regulation of these various and interfering interests forms the principal task of modern legislation and involves the spirit of party and faction in the necessary and ordinary operations of the government....

It is in vain to say that enlightened statesmen will be able to adjust these clashing interests and render them all subservient to the public good. Enlightened statesmen will not always be at the helm. Nor, in many cases, can such an adjustment be made at all without taking into view indirect and remote considerations, which will rarely prevail over the immediate interest which one party may find in disregarding the rights of another or the good of the whole.

The inference to which we are brought is that the causes of faction cannot be removed and that relief is only to be sought in the means of controlling its effects.

If a faction consists of less than a majority, relief is supplied by the republican principle, which enables the majority to defeat its sinister views by regular vote. ... When a majority is included in a faction, the form of popular government, on the other hand, enables it to sacrifice to its ruling passion or interest both the public good and the rights of other citizens. To secure the public good and private rights against the danger of such a faction, and at the same time to preserve the spirit and the form of popular government, is then the great object to which our inquiries are directed....

From this view of the subject it may be concluded that a pure democracy, by which I mean a society consisting of a small number of citizens who assemble and administer the government in person, can admit of no cure for the mischiefs of faction. A common passion or interest will, in almost every case, be felt by a majority of the whole; a communication and concert result from the form of government itself; and there is nothing to check the inducements to sacrifice the weaker party or an obnoxious individual. Hence it is that such democracies have ever been spectacles of turbulence and contention; have ever been found incompatible with personal security or the rights of property; and have in general been as short in their lives as they have been violent in their deaths. Theoretic politicians, who have patronized this species of government, have erroneously supposed that by reducing mankind to a perfect equality in their political rights, they would, at the same time, be perfectly equalized and assimilated in their possessions, their opinions, and their passions.

A republic, by which I mean a government in which the scheme of representation takes place, opens a different prospect and promises the cure for which we are seeking....

The two great points of difference between a democracy and a republic are: first, the delegation of the government, in the latter, to a small number of citizens elected by the rest; secondly, the greater number of citizens, and greater sphere of country, over which the latter may be extended.

The effect of the first difference is, on the one hand, to refine and enlarge the public views by passing them through the medium of a chosen body of citizens, whose wisdom may best discern the true interest of their country, and whose patriotism and love of justice will be least likely to sacrifice it to temporary or partial considerations.... Men of factious tempers, of local prejudices, or of sinister designs may, by intrigue, by corruption, or by other means, first obtain the suffrages, and then betray the interests of the people. The question resulting is, whether small or extensive republics are more favorable to the election of proper guardians of the public weal; and it is clearly decided in favor of the latter by two obvious considerations:

In the first place, it is to be remarked that, however small the republic may be, the representatives must be raised to a certain number, in order to guard against the cabals of a few; and that; however large it may be, they must be limited to a certain number, in order to guard against the confusion of a multitude....

In the next place, as each representative will be chosen by a greater number of citizens in the large than in the small republic, it will be more difficult for unworthy candidates to practice with success the vicious arts by which elections are too often carried; and the suffrages of the people being more free, will be more likely to center in men who possess the most attractive merit and the most diffusive and established character.

... By enlarging too much the number of electors, you render the representative too little acquainted with all their local circumstances and lesser interests; as by reducing it too much, you render him unduly attached to these and too little fit to comprehend and pursue great and national objects. The federal Constitution forms a happy combination in this respect: the great and aggregate interests being referred to the national, the local and particular to the state legislatures.

The other point of difference is the greater number of citizens and extent of territory which may be brought within the compass of republican than of democratic government; and it is this circumstance principally which renders factious combinations less to be dreaded in the former than in the latter. The smaller the society, the fewer probably will be the distinct parties and interests composing it; ... the more easily will they concert and execute their plans of oppression. Extend the sphere and you take in a greater variety of parties and interests; you make it less probable that a majority of the whole will have a common motive to invade the rights of other citizens; or if such a common motive exists, it will be more difficult for all who feel it to discover their own strength and to act in unison with each other....

Hence, it clearly appears that the same advantage which a republic has over a democracy, in controlling the effects of factions, is enjoyed by a large over a small republic—is enjoyed by the Union over the states composing it....

In the extent, and proper structure of the Union, therefore, we behold a republican remedy for the diseases most incident to republican government. And according to the degree of pleasure and pride we feel in being republicans, ought to be our zeal in cherishing the spirit and supporting the character of Federalists.

6

The Limits of Republicanism

The ratification of the Constitution inaugurated a new government for the United States, but ambiguities over the limits of state and national power left unanswered many questions concerning its power. Shortly after the government had been created, political factions emerged and soon crystallized into parties. These groups differed over a variety of issues, including the future of America's economy, the franchise, foreign policy, and the limits of federal authority. Despite these differences, all agreed that participation in the early republic should be limited to adult white males. The ensuing documents reveal some of the constitutional ambiguities facing the new government as well as the limits of republican values in post–Revolutionary America.

47

Cato Petitions for His Freedom (1781)

The American Revolution unleashed powerful forces of egalitarianism that would shake the foundations of traditional social institutions. Among these was the institution of slavery. In the Middle Atlantic states the Revolution gave rise to a gradual abolition movement. Pennsylvania was in many ways the birthplace of American antislavery as groups like the Quakers and German religious dissenters had opposed the institution for decades. In 1780, Pennsylvania passed a law that ended future enslavement and made free blacks equal under state law, but it did so without freeing any of the six thousand Pennsylvanians then in bondage. The following year the legislature considered reversing the law. The petition below appeared in the Freeman's Journal or North American Intelligencer.

Questions to Consider

1. To what extent does Cato seem to be motivated by the principles of the American Revolution?

2. To what extent do you think Cato and Judith Sargent Murray ("Judith Sargent Murray on the Equality of the Sexes," Document 48) would share views on the position of white males in eighteenth-century American society?

3. Why do you think the assembly wants to reverse the gradual emancipation law of the preceding year?

4. What does this document say about the limits of republicanism?

Mr. PRINTER.

I AM a poor negro, who with myself and children have had the good fortune to get my freedom, by means of an act of assembly passed on the first of March 1780, and should now with my family be as happy a set of people as any on the face of the earth, but I am told the assembly are going to pass a law to send us all back to our masters. Why dear Mr. Printer, this would be the cruellest act that ever a sett of worthy good gentlemen could be guilty of. To make a law to hang us all, would be *merciful*, when compared with this law; for many of our masters would treat us with unheard of barbarity, for daring to take the advantage (as we have done) of the law made in our favor.—Our lots in *slavery* were hard enough to bear: but having tasted the sweets of *freedom*, we should now be miserable indeed.—Surely no christian gentlemen can be so cruel! I cannot believe they will pass such a law.—I have read the act which made me free, and I always read it with joy—and I always dwell with particular pleasure on the following words, spoken by the assembly in the top of the said law. "We esteem it a particular blessing granted to us, that we are enabled this day to add one more step to universal civilization, by removing as much as possible the sorrows of those, who have lived in *undeserved* bondage, and from which, by the assumed authority of the kings of Great-Britain, no effectual legal relief could be obtained." See it was the king of Great-Britain that kept us in slavery before.—Now surely, after saying so, it cannot be possible for them to make slaves of us again—nobody, but the king of England can do it—and I sincerely pray, that he may never have it in his power.—It cannot be, that the assembly will take from us the liberty they have given, because a little further they go on and say, "we conceive ourselves, at this particular period, extraordinarily called upon, by the blessings which *we* have received, to make manifest the sincerity of our professions and to give a substantial proof of our gratitude." If after all this, *we*, who by virtue of this very law (which has those very words in it which

SOURCE: *Freeman's Journal or North American Intelligencer* (Philadelphia, Pennsylvania) September 21, 1781.

I have copied,) are now enjoying the sweets of that "substantial proof of gratitude" I say if we should be plunged back into slavery, what must we think of the meaning of all those words in the begining of the said law, which seem to be a kind of creed respecting slavery? but what is most serious than all, what will our great father think of such doings? But I pray that he may be pleased to tern the hearts of the honourable assembly from this cruel law; and that he will be pleased to make us poor blacks deserving of his mercies.

CATO

48

Judith Sargent Murray on the Equality of the Sexes (1790)

Despite American women's important contributions to the Revolution, after independence it appeared that they would reap few of the benefits for which the war had been fought. Most eighteenth-century American men believed women to be overly emotional and intellectually inferior to men, and argued that their place was within the home as republican mothers. Judith Sargent Murray's argument offered a powerful rejoinder to this type of thinking. The possessor of a classical education, Murray had suffered through a loveless first marriage, which ended with her husband's death. Her second husband, Universalist minister John Murray, encouraged Judith's intellectual pursuits following their marriage in 1788. After writing this pamphlet, Murray would become a prolific author of histories, biographies, short stories, and plays. But her most important work would remain her commentary On the Equality of the Sexes, *which is excerpted here.*

Questions to Consider

1. What are the main points of Judith Sargent Murray's argument? How do her views on women's roles compare to those of today? How are they different?

2. To what extent do you think Murray and Esther de Berdt Reed (Document 40, "Women's Contributions to the War Effort") would share views on the position of white males in eighteenth-century American society? How might they differ?

3. How do you think male contemporaries responded to Murray?

4. Why does this document seem important to us today?

... Is it upon mature consideration we adopt the idea, that nature is thus partial in her distributions? Is it indeed a fact, that she hath yielded to one half of the human species so unquestionable a mental superiority? I know that to both sexes elevated understandings, and the reverse, are common. But, suffer me to ask, in what the minds of females are so notoriously deficient, or unequal. May not the intellectual powers be ranged under these four heads—imagination, reason, memory and judgment. The province of imagination hath long since been surrendered to us, and we have been crowned and undoubted sovereigns of the regions of fancy. Invention is perhaps the most arduous effort of the mind; this branch of imagination hath been particularly ceded to us, and we have been time out of mind invested with that creative faculty. Observe the variety of fashions (here I bar the contemptuous smile) which distinguish and adorn the female world: how continually are they changing, insomuch that they almost render the wise man's assertion problematical, and we are ready to say, *there is something new under the sun*.... Are we deficient in reason? We can only reason from what we know, and if an opportunity of acquiring knowledge hath been denied us, the inferiority of our sex cannot fairly be deduced from thence. Memory, I believe, will be allowed us in common, since everyone's experience must testify, that a loquacious old woman is as frequently met with, as a communicative man; their subjects are alike drawn from the fund of other times, and the transactions of their youth, or of maturer life, entertain, or perhaps fatigue you, in the evening of their lives. "But our judgment is not so strong—we do not distinguish so well."—Yet it may be questioned, from what doth this superiority, in this determining faculty of the soul, proceed[?] May we not trace its source in the difference of education, and continued advantages? Will it be said that the judgment of a male of two years old, is more sage than that of a female's of the same age? I believe the reverse is generally observed to be true. But from that period what partiality! how is the one exalted, and the other depressed, by the contrary modes of education which are adopted! the one is taught to aspire, and the other is early confined and limited. As their years increase, the sister must be wholly domesticated, while the brother is led by the hand through all the flowery paths of science. Grant that their minds are by nature equal, yet who shall wonder at the *apparent* superiority, if indeed custom becomes *second nature*; nay if it taketh place of nature, and that it doth the experience of each day will evince. At length arrived at womanhood, the uncultivated fair one feels a void, which the employments allotted her are by no means capable of filling. What can she do? to books she may not apply; or if she doth, *to those only of the novel kind,* lest she merit the appellation of a *learned lady;* and what ideas have been affixed to this term, the observation of many can testify. Fashion, scandal, and sometimes what is still more reprehensible, are then called in to her relief; and who can say to what lengths the liberties she takes may proceed. Meantimes she herself is most unhappy; she feels the want of a cultivated mind.... Now, was she permitted the same instructors as her brother, (with an eye however to their particular departments) for the employment of a rational mind an ample field would be opened. In astronomy she might

SOURCE: Judith Sargent Murray, "On the Equality of the Sexes," *The Massachusetts Magazine, or, Monthly Museum Concerning the Literature, History, Politics, Arts, Manners, Amusements of the Age,* 2 (March 1790): 132–34.

catch a glimpse of the immensity of the Deity, and thence she would form amazing conceptions of the august and supreme Intelligence. In geography she would admire Jehovah in the midst of his benevolence; thus adapting this globe to the various wants and amusements of its inhabitants. In natural philosophy she would adore the infinite majesty of heaven, clothed in condescension; and as she traversed the reptile world, she would hail the goodness of a creating God. A mind, thus filled, would have little room for the trifles with which our sex are, with too much justice, accused of amusing themselves, and they would thus be rendered fit companions for those, who should one day wear them as their crown. Fashions, in their variety, would then give place to conjectures, which might perhaps conduce to the improvements of the literary world; and there would be no leisure for slander or detraction. Reputation would not then be blasted, but serious speculations would occupy the lively imaginations of the sex. Unnecessary visits would only be indulged by way of relaxation, or to answer the demands of consanguinity and friendship. Females would become discreet, their judgments would be invigorated, and their partners for life being circumspectly chosen, an unhappy Hymen would then be as rare, as is now the reverse....

Yes, ye lordly, ye haughty sex, our souls are by nature *equal* to yours; the same breath of God animates, enlivens, and invigorates us; and that we are not fallen lower than yourselves, let those witness who have greatly towered above the various discouragements by which they have been so heavily oppressed; and though I am unacquainted with the list of celebrated characters on either side, yet from the observations I have made in the contracted circle in which I have moved, I dare confidently believe, that from the commencement of time to the present day, there hath been as many females, as males, who, by the *mere force of natural powers,* have merited the crown of applause; who, *thus unassisted,* have seized the wreath of fame.

49

Alexander Hamilton Speaks in Favor of the National Bank (1791)

Fiscal instability and the weakness of the central government were two of the major criticisms leveled against the Articles of Confederation. While the Constitution clearly provided the new government with powers in these areas, the extent to which these powers would be exercised remained open to debate. Alexander Hamilton believed a strong central government was essential to the survival of the new government. A native of the British West

Indian island of Nevis, Hamilton rose to prominence as a protégé of George Washington during the Revolution and as a leading figure in New York City politics in its aftermath. Convinced of the need for a strong central government supported by the nation's leading creditors, Hamilton offered a financial plan that expanded national power at the expense of the states. In the following document, the United States' first secretary of the treasury argues that the Constitution could be interpreted to permit the establishment of the Bank of the United States.

Questions to Consider

1. To whom is this document addressed?
2. Why does Alexander Hamilton support a "loose construction" of the Constitution?
3. How do you suppose an eighteenth-century financier would have responded to this document?
4. How do you think Shays's rebels ("Grievances of the Shays Rebels," Document 44) would have responded to Hamilton's views of loose construction?

... In entering upon the argument, it ought to be premised that the objections of the secretary of state and attorney general are founded on a general denial of the authority of the United States to erect anything in the bill which is not warranted by the Constitution, it is the clause of incorporation.

Now it appears to the Secretary of the Treasury that this *general principle* is *inherent* in the very *definition* of government and *essential* to every step of the progress to be made by that of the United States, namely: that every power vested in a government is in its nature *sovereign* and includes, by *force* of the term, a right to employ all the *means* requisite and fairly applicable to the attainment of the *ends* of such power, and which are not precluded by restrictions and exceptions specified in the Constitution, or not immoral, or contrary to the *essential ends* of political society....

The circumstance that the powers of sovereignty are in this country divided between the National and State governments does not afford the distinction required. It does not follow from this, that each of the portion of *powers* delegated to the one or to the other, is not sovereign with *regard to its proper objects.* It will only *follow* from it, that each has sovereign power as to *certain things,* and not as to other things. To deny that the government of the United States has sovereign power, as to its declared purposes and trusts, because its power does not extend to all cases, would be equally to deny that the State governments have sovereign power in any case, because their power does not extend to every case. The tenth section of the first article of the Constitution exhibits a long list of very important things which they may not do. And thus the United States

SOURCE: "Hamilton to Washington: Opinion as to the Constitutionality of the Bank of the United States," 23 February 1791, *Works of Alexander Hamilton*, ed. Henry Cabot Lodge (New York, 1904), 4: 104–38.

would furnish the singular spectacle of a *political* society without *sovereignty,* or of a *people governed* without *government.*...

... the foundation of the Constitution is laid on this ground: "That all powers not delegated to the United States by the Constitution, nor prohibited to it by the states, are reserved for the States, or to the people." Whence it is meant to be inferred that Congress can in no case exercise any power not included in those not enumerated in the Constitution. And it is affirmed that the power of erecting a corporation is not included in any of the enumerated powers....

It is not denied that there are *implied* as well as *express powers* and that the *former* are as effectually delegated as the *latter.*...

Then it follows that as a power of erecting a corporation may as well be *implied* as any other thing, it may as well be employed as an *instrument* or mean of carrying into execution any of the specified powers as any other *instrument* or *mean* whatever. The only question must be, in this, as in every other case, whether the mean to be employed or, in this instance, the corporation to be erected, has a natural relation to any of the acknowledged objects or lawful ends of the government. Thus a corporation may not be erected by Congress for superintending the police of the city of Philadelphia, because they are not authorized to *regulate* the *police* of that city. But one may be erected in relation ... to a general *sovereign* or *legislative* power to regulate a thing, to employ all the means which relate to its regulation to the best and greatest advantage....

Through this mode of reasoning respecting the right of employing all the means requisite to the execution of the specified powers of the government, it is objected that none but necessary and proper means are to be employed; and the Secretary of the State maintains that no means are to be considered as *necessary* but those without which the grant of the power would be *nugatory.* Nay, so far does he go in his restrictive interpretation of the *word* as even to make the case of the *necessity* which shall warrant the constitutional exercise of the power to depend on *casual* and *temporary* circumstances; an idea which alone refutes the construction. The *expediency* of exercising a particular power at a particular time, must, indeed, depend on circumstances; but the constitutional right of exercising it must be uniform and invariable, the same today as tomorrow.

All the arguments, therefore, against the constitutionality of the bill derived from the accidental existence of certain State banks, institutions which happen to exist today and, for aught that concerns the government of the United States, may disappear tomorrow—must not only be rejected as fallacious but must be viewed as demonstrative that there is a *radical* source of error in the reasoning....

... *necessary* often means no more than *needful, requisite, incidental, usefull,* or *conductive to.* It is a common mode of expression to say that it is *necessary* for a government or a person to do this or that thing, when nothing more is intended or understood than that the interests of the government or person require, or will be promoted by, the doing this or that thing....

To understand the word as the secretary of state does would be to depart from its obvious and popular sense and to give it a restrictive operation, an idea never before entertained....

It may be truly said of every government, as well as that of the United States, that it has only a right to pass such laws as are necessary and a right to do *merely what it pleases....* Hence, by a process of reasoning similar to that of the Secretary of State, it might be proved that neither of the State governments has a right to incorporate a bank. It might be shown that all the public business of the state could be performed without a bank, and inferring thence it was unnecessary, it might be argued that it could not be done, because it is against the rule which has been just mentioned. A like mode of reasoning would prove that there was no power to incorporate the inhabitants of a town, with a view to a more perfect police....

This restrictive interpretation of the word *necessary* is also contrary to this maxim of construction; namely, that the powers contained in a constitution of government, especially those which concern the general administration of the affairs of a country, its finances, trade, defense, etc., ought to be construed liberally in advancement of the public good.... The means by which national exigencies are to be provided for, national inconveniences obviated, national prosperity promoted, are of such infinite variety, extent, and complexity that there must of necessity be great latitude of discretion in the selection and application of those means. Hence, consequently, the necessity and propriety of exercising the authorities intrusted to a government on principles of liberal construction....

The truth is that difficulties on this point are inherent in the nature of the Federal Constitution; they result inevitably from a division of the legislative power. The consequence of this division is that there will be cases clearly within the power of the national government; others, clearly without its powers; and a third class which will leave room for controversy....

But the doctrine which is contended for is not chargeable with the consequences imputed to it. It does not affirm that the national government is sovereign in all respects, but that it is sovereign to a certain extent; that is, to the extent of the objects of its specified powers.

It leaves, therefore, a criterion of what is constitutional and of what is not so. This criterion is the *end* to which the measure relates as a *mean.* If the *end* be clearly comprehended within any of the specified powers, and if the measure have an obvious relation to that *end,* and is not forbidden by a particular provision of the Constitution, it may safely be deemed to come within the compass of the national authority....

To establish such a right, it remains to show the relation of such an institution to one or more of the specified powers of the government. Accordingly, it is affirmed that it has a relation, more or less direct, to the power of collecting taxes, to that of borrowing money, to that of regulating trade between the states, and to those of raising and maintaining fleets and armies. To the two former the relation may be said to be immediate; and in the last place it will be argued that it is clearly within the provision which authorizes the making of all needful rules and regulations concerning the property of the United States, as the same has been practised upon by the government....

A hope is entertained that it has, by this time, been made to appear, to the satisfaction of the President, that a bank has a natural relation to the power of collecting taxes—to that of regulating trade—to that of providing for the common defense—and that, as the bill under consideration providing for the common defense—and that, as the bill under consideration contemplates the government in the light of a joint proprietor of the stock of the bank, it brings the case within the provision of the clause of the Constitution which immediately respects the property of the United States.

Under a conviction that such a relation subsists, the Secretary of the Treasury, with all defence, conceives that it will result as a necessary consequence from the position that all the specified powers of government are sovereign, as to the proper objects; that the incorporation of a bank is a constitutional measure; and that the objections taken to the bill, in this respect, are ill-founded....

50

Opposing Views of the Whiskey Rebellion (1794)

Secretary of the Treasury Alexander Hamilton wasted little time in attempting to raise money for the new government. Eager to placate seaboard merchants, Hamilton successfully pressed for an excise tax on whiskey despite opposition to similar taxes during the Confederation period. Western Pennsylvania farmers quickly protested the new duty, arguing that they were being taxed unfairly and that the excise would prove ruinous to farmers who depended on the sale of whiskey to make a living. The Whiskey Rebellion was an early test for the federal government. Could it quell backcountry unrest, and how would it do so? The ensuing document from the Pennsylvania Gazette *reveals differing perspectives of the excise. Governor Thomas Mifflin, the leading political figure in Pennsylvania during the 1790s, did not support action against the rebels until after President Washington officially declared the region in rebellion. The second part of this document reveals how western Pennsylvanians responded.*

Questions to Consider

1. Why is the governor of Pennsylvania determined to put down the rebellion? What threat do the rebels appear to pose?

2. In what ways are the inhabitants of Pittsburgh resisting the excise?

3. What similarities do the citizens of Pittsburgh share with the sentiments expressed in "Grievances of Shays Rebels" (Document 44)?

4. In what ways do you think the legacy of the American Revolution shapes the governor of Pennsylvania's response? The citizens of Pittsburgh's response?

In the name, and by the authority of the Commonwealth of Pennsylvania, by THOMAS MIFFLIN, Governor of the said Commonwealth,

A PROCLAMATION.

WHEREAS information has been received, that several lawless bodies of armed men have, at sundry times, assembled in the county of Allegheny, within the commonwealth of Pennsylvania, and being so assembled, have committed various cruel and aggravated acts of riot and arson; and more particularly, that on the 17th ultimo, one of the said lawless bodies of armed men attacked the dwelling house of John Nevill, Esq; Inspector of the Revenue for the fourth survey of the district of Pennsylvania; and after firing upon, and wounding sundry persons employed in protecting and defending the said dwelling-house, set fire to, and totally burned and destroyed the same, together with the furniture and effects therein, and the barns, stables, and other buildings thereto adjoining and appurtenant:

And whereas it appears from the Proclamation of the President of the United States, bearing date this day as well as from other evidence, that the outrages and criminal proceedings aforesaid, have been undertaken and prosecuted by certain unlawful combinations of persons, who thereby design to obstruct and have actually obstructed the execution of the laws of the United States; and that by reason thereof, in pursuance of the authority in him vested, he has resolved to call forth the militia, for the purpose of supressing the said unlawful combinations, and of enforcing the execution of the laws so obstructed as aforesaid.

And whereas every good and enlightened citizen must perceive how unworthy it is thus riotously to oppose the constitution and laws of our country, (the government and laws of the state being herein as much affected as the government and laws of the United States) which were formed by the deliberate will of the people, and which (by the same legitimate authority) can, in a regular course, be peaceably amended or altered. How incompatible it is with the principles of a republican government, and dangerous in point of precedent, that a minority should attempt to controul the majority, or a part of the community undertake to prescribe to the whole! how indispensible, though painful an obligation, is imposed upon the officers of government, to employ the public force for the purpose of subduing and punishing such unwarrantable proceedings, when the judiciary authority has proved incompetent to the task: And how necessary it is, that the deluded rioters aforesaid should forthwith be brought to a just sense of their duty, as a longer deviation from it must inevitably be destructive to their

SOURCE: (Philadelphia) *The Pennsylvania Gazette*, August 13, 1794.

own happiness, as well as injurious to the reputation and prosperity of their country.

AND WHEREAS, entertaining a just sense of my federal obligations, and feeling a perfect conviction of the necessity of pursuing immediate measures to suppress the spirit of insurrection, which has appeared as aforesaid, and to restore tranquillity and order—I have heretofore given instructions to the proper officers of the commonwealth, to investigate the circumstances of the said riots, to ascertain the names of the rioters, and to institute the regular process of the law, for bringing offenders to justice.

NOW THEREFORE, I have deemed it expedient also to issue this Proclamation, hereby publicly announcing my determination, by all lawful means, to cause to be prosecuted and punished, all persons whomever, that have engaged, or shall engage, in any of the unlawful combinations or proceedings aforesaid:

AND FURTHER DECLARING, that whatever requisition the President of the United States shall make, or whatever duty he shall impose in pursuance of his constitutional and legal powers, for the purpose of maintaining the authority, and executing the laws of the United States—will, on my part, be promptly undertaken and faithfully discharged: And all judges, justices, sheriffs, coroners, constables, and other officers of the commonwealth, according to the duties of their respective stations, are hereby required and enjoined to employ all lawful means for discovering, apprehending, securing, trying and bringing to justice, each and every person concerned in the said riots and unlawful proceedings.

Given under my hand, and the great seal of the state, at Philadelphia, this seventh day of August, in the year of our Lord, one thousand seven hundred and ninety-four, and of the commonwealth the nineteenth.

THOMAS MIFFLIN.

By the Governor,

A.J. DALLAS,

Secretary of the Commonwealth.

The following is the Copy of a hand bill, printed at Pittsburgh. The Post rider left that place without any letters or Newspapers—

AT A MEETING OF THE INHABITANTS OF PITTSBURGH. On Thursday Evening, July 31, 1794, to take into consideration the present situation of Affairs, and declare their sentiments on this delicate Crisis.

A GREAT majority, almost the whole of the inhabitants of the town, assembled. It being announced to the meeting, that certain gentlemen from the town of Washington, had arrived, and had signified that they were instructed with a message to the inhabitants of the town, relative to present affairs; a committee of three persons were appointed to confer with them, and report the message to the meeting; the persons appointed were George Wallace, H. H. Brackenridge, and John Wilkins, junr. these gentlemen made report to the meeting, to wit.

That in consequence of certain letters sent by the last mail, certain persons were discovered as advocates of the Excise Law, and enemies to the interests of the country; and that a certain Edward Day, James Brison, and Abraham Kirkpatrick, were particularly obnoxious, and that it was expected of the country should be dismissed from the town without delay; whereupon, it was resolved, that it should be so done, and a committee of twenty-one were appointed to see the resolution carried in effect, to wit. George Wallace, H. H. Brackenridge, Peter Audrain. John Scull, John McMasters, John Wilkins, Sen. Andrew McIntire, George Robinson, John Irwin, merchant, Andrew Watson, George Adams, David Evans, Josiah Tannehill, Matthew Ernest, William Farls, Alexander McNickle, Col. John Irwin, James Clow, William Gormly, Nathaniel Irish, A. Tannehill.

Also, That whereas it is a part of the message from the gentlemen of Washington that a great body of the people of the country will meet tomorrow at Braddock's fields, in order to carry into effect measures that may seem to them adviseable with respect to the Excise Law and the advocates of it, Resolved, That the above committee shall, at an early hour, wait upon the people on the ground, and assure the people that the above resolution, with respect to the proscribed persons, has been carried into effect.

Resolved, also, That the inhabitants of the town shall march out, and join the people on Braddock's Field, as brethren, to carry into effect with them any measure that may seem adviseable to the common cause.

Resolved, also, That we shall be watchful among ourselves of all characters, that by word or act may be unfriendly to the common cause, and when discovered, will not suffer them to live amongst us, but they shall instantly depart the town.

Resolved, also, That the above committee shall exist as a committee of information and correspondence, as an organ of our sentiments, until our next town meeting.

And that whereas a general meeting of delegates from the townships of the country on the west of the mountains, will be held at Parkinson's ferry, on the Monongahela, on the 14th of August next, Resolved, That delegates shall be appointed to that meeting, and that the 9th of August next be appointed for a town meeting, to elect such delegates.

Resolved also, That a number of handbills be struck off, at the expence of the committee, and distributed among the inhabitants of the town, that they may conduct themselves accordingly.

51

George Washington's "Farewell Address" (1796)

The ratification of the Constitution was, in part, made possible by the understanding that George Washington would be the nation's first president. During his eight-year tenure, Washington presided over a government riddled by factionalism. One of the most divisive issues was how to respond to events in Europe, where revolutionary France toppled the monarchy, created a republic, and engaged in a series of wars with many of its neighbors. The events in France horrified many conservative Americans; eventually they became supporters of the Federalist Party. The Democratic-Republicans supported France and urged the government to honor its treaty commitments to America's wartime ally. In his farewell, President Washington addressed the nation on what he saw as potential problems for the United States. In this selection, he advises the nation on its future approach to dealing with the European powers.

Questions to Consider

1. What is Washington's warning about foreign relations?
2. What did Washington see as the main purpose of American foreign policy? Why?
3. How was American politics affected by foreign affairs?
4. To what extent have Washington's views on foreign relations been a guide for American foreign policy in the nineteenth century? The twentieth century?

... Against the insidious wiles of foreign influence (I conjure you to believe me, fellow-citizens,) the jealousy of a free people ought to be constantly awake; since history and experience prove, that foreign influence is one of the baneful foes of Republican Government. But that jealousy, to be useful, must be impartial; else it becomes the instrument of the very influence to be avoided, instead of a defense against it. Excessive partiality for one nation, and excessive dislike of another, cause those whom they actuate to see danger only on one side, and serve to veil and even second the arts of influence on the other. Real patriots, who may resist the intrigues of the favorite, are liable to become suspected and

SOURCE: George Washington, "Farewell Address," *A Compilation of the Messages and Papers of the Presidents*, ed. James D. Richardson (Washington, DC, 1903), 1: 213–24.

odious; while its tools and dupes usurp the applause and confidence of the people, to surrender their interests.

The great rule of conduct for us, in regard to foreign nations is, extending our commercial relations, to have with them as little political connection as possible. So far as we have already formed engagements, let them be fulfilled with perfect good faith. Here let us stop.

Europe has her own set of primary interests, which to us have none, or a very remote relation. Hence she must be engaged in frequent controversies, the causes of which are essentially foreign to our concerns. Hence, therefore, it must be unwise in us to implicate ourselves, by artificial ties, in the ordinary vicissitudes of her politics, or the ordinary combinations and collusions of her friendships or enmities.

Our detached and distant situation invites and enables us to pursue a different course. If we remain one free people, under an efficient government, the period is not far off, when we may defy material injury from external annoyance; when we may take such an attitude as will cause the neutrality, we may at any time resolve upon, to be scrupulously respected; when belligerent nations, under the impossibility of making acquisitions upon us, will not lightly hazard the giving us provocation; when we may choose peace or war, as our interest, guided by justice, shall counsel.

Why forego the advantages of so peculiar a situation? Why quit our own to stand upon foreign ground? Why, by interweaving our destiny with that of any part of Europe, entangle our peace and prosperity in the toils of European ambition, rivalship, interest, humor, or caprice?

It is our true policy to steer clear of permanent alliances with any portion of the foreign world; so far, I mean, as we are now at liberty to do it; for let me not be understood as capable of patronizing infidelity to existing engagements. I hold the maxim no less applicable to public than to private affairs, that honesty is always the best policy. I repeat it, therefore, let those engagements be observed in their genuine sense. But, in my opinion, it is unnecessary and would be unwise to extend them.

Taking care always to keep ourselves, by suitable establishments, on a respectable defensive posture, we may safely trust to temporary alliances in extraordinary emergencies.

Harmony, liberal intercourse with all nations, are recommended by policy, humanity, and interest. But even our commercial policy should hold an equal and impartial hand; neither seeking nor granting exclusive favors or preferences; consulting the natural course of things; diffusing and diversifying by gentle means the streams of commerce, but forcing nothing; establishing, with powers so disposed, in order to give trade a stable course, to define the rights of our merchants, and to enable the government to support them, conventional rules of intercourse, the best the present circumstances and mutual opinion will permit, but temporary, and liable to be from time to time abandoned or varied, as experience and circumstances shall dictate; constantly keeping in view, that it is folly in one nation to look for disinterested favors from another; that it must pay with a portion of its independence for whatever it may accept under that character;

that, by such acceptance, it may place itself in the condition of having given equivalents for nominal favors, and yet of being reproached with ingratitude for not giving more. There can be no greater error than to expect or calculate upon real favors from nation to nation. It is an illusion, which experience must cure, which a just pride ought to discard....

52

Description of a Conversion Experience at Cane Ridge, Kentucky (1801)

By the dawn of the nineteenth century, growing numbers of Americans felt alienated from their well-educated, rationalist-minded clergy. This factor, coupled with a rapidly expanding frontier population and a shortage of ordained ministers, led some churches (especially the Baptists and Methodists) to ordain ministers with less-formal education. These individuals used revivals to appeal emotionally to their converts. Revivals, which became a hallmark of the Second Great Awakening, began on the frontier but ultimately spread through much of the country. Not only did converts develop closer community bonds, but with the new religion's emphasis on emotion and a personal approach to God, they helped to democratize American Christianity. The following selection contains an excerpt from the writings of James B. Finley, who describes his experiences immediately after attending the great Cane Ridge, Kentucky, revival in 1801.

Questions to Consider

1. Why was James B. Finley curious about the revival at Cane Ridge?
2. What impact would revivals such as Cane Ridge have on religion in America?
3. What would those present at the revivals have thought of the Whiskey Rebellion ("Opposing Views of the Whiskey Rebellion," Document 50)?
4. Compare and contrast the description of this event with the Rochester Revival ("Charles G. Finney Describes the Rochester Revival," Document 73). How are they similar? Different? How do you account for these similarities and differences?

... About this time a great revival of religion broke out in the state of Kentucky. It was attended with such peculiar circumstances as to produce great alarm all over the country. It was reported that hundreds who attended the meetings were suddenly struck down, and would lie for hours and, sometimes, for days, in a state of insensibility; and that when they recovered and came out of that state, they would commence praising God for his pardoning mercy and redeeming love. This exercise was accompanied with that strange and unaccountable phenomenon denominated the jerks, in which hundreds of men and women would commence jerking backward and forward with great rapidity and violence, so much so that their bodies would bend so as to bring their heads near to the floor, and the hair of the women would crack like the lash of a driver's whip. This was not confined to any particular class of individuals, but saint, seeker, and sinner were alike subject to these wonderful phenomena.

The excitement created by these reports, was of the most intense and astonishing character. Some thought that the world was coming to an end; others that some dreadful calamity was coming upon the country as a judgment of God on the nation; others still, that it was the work of the devil, who had been unchained for a season, and assuming the garments of an angel of light, was permitted to deceive the ministers of religion and the very elect themselves. Many of the preachers spent whole Sabbaths in laboring to show that it was the work of the devil, and nothing but the wildest fanaticism, produced through the means of an overheated and distempered imagination....

In the month of August, 1801, I learned that there was to be a great meeting at Cane Ridge, in my father's old congregation. Feeling a great desire to see the wonderful things which had come to my ears, and having been solicited by some of my old schoolmates to go over into Kentucky for the purpose of revisiting the scenes of my boyhood, I resolved to go.... We arrived upon the ground, and here a scene presented itself to my mind not only novel and unaccountable, but awful beyond description. A vast crowd, supposed by some to have amounted to twenty-five thousand, was collected together. The noise was like the roar of Niagara. The vast sea of human beings seemed to be agitated as if by a storm. I counted seven ministers, all preaching at one time, some on stumps, others in wagons, and one—the Rev. William Burke, now of Cincinnati—was standing on a tree which had, in falling, lodged against another. Some of the people were singing, others praying, some crying for mercy in the most piteous accents, while others were shouting most vociferously. While witnessing these scenes, a peculiarly-strange sensation, such as I had never felt before, came over me. My heart beat tumultuously, my knees trembled, my lip quivered, and I felt as though I must fall to the ground. A strange supernatural power seemed to pervade the entire mass of mind there collected. I became so weak and powerless that I found it necessary to sit down. Soon after I left and went into the woods, and there I strove to rally and man up my courage. I tried to philosophize in regard to these wonderful exhibitions, resolving them into mere sympathetic excitement—a kind of religious enthusiasm, inspired by songs and eloquent harangues. My pride was wounded, for I had supposed that my mental and physical strength and vigor could most successfully resist these influences.

SOURCE: *Autobiography of the Reverend James B. Finley*, ed. W. P. Strickland (Cincinnati, 1854), 165–70.

After some time I returned to the scene of excitement, the waves of which, if possible, had risen still higher. The same awfulness of feeling came over me. I stepped up on to a log where I could have a better view of the surging sea of humanity. The scene that then presented itself to my mind was indescribable. At one time I saw at least five hundred swept down in a moment, as if a battery of a thousand guns had been opened upon them, and then, immediately followed shrieks and shouts that rent the very heavens. My hair rose up on my head, my whole frame trembled, the blood ran cold in my veins, and I fled for the woods a second time, and wished I had stayed at home. While I remained here my feelings became intense and insupportable. A sense of suffocation and blindness seemed to come over me, and I thought I was going to die.... In this state I wandered about from place to place, in and around the encampment. At times it seemed as if all the sins I had ever committed in my life were vividly brought up in array before my terrified imagination, and under their pressure I felt that I must die if I did not get relief. Then it was that I saw clearly through the thin veil of Universalism, and this refuge of lies was swept away by the Spirit of God. Then fell the scales from my sin-blinded eyes, and I realized, in all its force and power, the awful truth, that if I died in my sins I was a lost man forever....

As soon as day broke I went to the woods to pray, and no sooner had my knees touched the ground than I cried aloud for mercy and salvation and fell prostrate. My cries were so loud that they attracted the attention of the neighbors, many of whom gathered around me. Among the number was a German from Switzerland, who had experienced religion. He, understanding fully, my condition, had me carried to his house and laid on a bed. The old Dutch saint directed me to look right away to the Savior. He then kneeled at the bedside and prayed for my salvation most fervently, in Dutch and broken English. He then rose and sung in the same manner, and continued singing and praying alternately till nine o'clock, when suddenly my load was gone, my guilt removed, and presently the direct witness from heaven shone full upon my soul....

53

Marbury v. Madison (1803)

By 1800, even the federal judiciary had become politicized. During the late 1790s, Federalist-controlled federal courts used their power for political ends against their Democratic-Republican enemies. When Jefferson became president in 1801, he sought to settle old scores while simultaneously reducing Federalist influence in the courts. One of his first actions was to instruct Secretary of State James Madison to withhold several of the "midnight appointments" that outgoing President Adams had made shortly before leaving office. William Marbury, Adams's selection to serve as the District of Columbia's justice of peace, filed a writ of mandamus demanding delivery of his commission. Chief Justice John Marshall, a Virginia Federalist, issued the response excerpted here that helped establish the precedent of judicial review.

Questions to Consider

1. What is John Marshall's decision about William Marbury's appointment?

2. What powers does Marshall determine are the Supreme Court's? What is the basis of this decision?

3. How might partisan politics have influenced the Court's decision?

4. Why is this Court case so significant?

... In the order in which the court has viewed this subject, the following questions have been considered and decided.

1st. Has the applicant a right to the commission he demands?

2d. If he has a right, and that right has been violated, do the laws of his country afford him a remedy?

3d. If they do afford him a remedy, is it a mandamus issuing from this court? The first object of inquiry is,

1st. Has the applicant a right to the commission he demands? ...

It appears, from the affidavits, that in compliance with this law, a commission for William Marbury, as a justice of the peace for the county of Washington, was signed by John Adams, then President of the United States; after which the seal of the United States was affixed to it; but the commission has never reached the person for whom it was made out....

SOURCE: *"Marbury v. Madison," The Constitutional Decisions of John Marshall*, ed. Joseph P. Cotton Jr. (New York, 1905), 1: 7–43.

It is, therefore, decidedly the opinion of the court, that when a commission had been signed by the President, the appointment is made; and that the commission is complete when the seal of the United States has been affixed to it by the Secretary of State....

Mr. Marbury, then, since his commission was signed by the President, and sealed by the Secretary of State, was appointed; and as the law creating the office, gave the officer a right to hold for five years, independent of the executive, the appointment was not revocable, but vested in the officer legal rights, which are protected by the laws of his country.

To withhold his commission, therefore, is an act deemed by the court not warranted by law, but violative of a vested legal right.

This brings us to the second inquiry; which is,

2d. If he has a right, and that right has been violated, do the laws of his country afford him a remedy? ...

It is, then, the opinion of the Court, ...

That, having this legal title to the office, he has a consequent right to the commission; a refusal to deliver which is a plain violation of that right, for which the laws of his country afford him a remedy.

It remains to be inquired whether,

3d. he is entitled to the remedy for which he applies. This depends on,

1st. The nature of the writ applied for; and,

2d. The power of this court.

1st. The nature of the writ....

It is true that the mandamus, now moved for, is not for the performance of an act expressly enjoined by statute.

It is to deliver a commission; on which subject the acts of congress are silent. This difference is not considered as affecting the case. It has already been stated that the applicant has, to that commission, a vested legal right, of which the executive cannot deprive him. He has been appointed to an office, from which he is not removable at the will of the executive; and being so appointed, he has a right to the commission which the secretary has received from the President for his use. The act of congress does not indeed order the Secretary of State to send it to him, but it is placed in his hands for the person entitled to it; and cannot be more lawfully withheld by him than by any other person....

In the distribution of this power it is declared that "the Supreme Court shall have original jurisdiction in all cases affecting ambassadors, other public ministers and consuls, and those in which a state shall be a party. In all other cases, the Supreme Court shall have appellate jurisdiction."...

To enable this court, then, to issue mandamus, it must be shown to be an exercise of appellate jurisdiction, or to be necessary to enable them to exercise appellate jurisdiction.

It has been stated at the bar that the appellate jurisdiction may be exercised in a variety of forms, and that if it be the will of the legislature that a mandamus should be used for that purpose, that will must be obeyed. This is true, yet the jurisdiction must be appellate, not original.

It is the essential criterion of appellate jurisdiction, that it revises and corrects the proceedings in a cause already instituted, and does not create that cause. Although, therefore, a mandamus may be directed to courts, yet to issue such a writ to an officer for the delivery of a paper, is in effect the same as to sustain an original action for that paper, and, therefore, seems not to belong to appellate, but to original jurisdiction. Neither is it necessary in such a case as this, to enable the court to exercise its appellate jurisdiction.

The authority, therefore, given to the Supreme Court, by the act establishing the judicial courts of the United States, to issue writs of mandamus to public officers, appears not to be warranted by the constitution; and it becomes necessary to inquire whether a jurisdiction so conferred can be exercised.

The question, whether an act, repugnant to the constitution, can become the law of the land, is a question deeply interesting to the United States....

The constitution is either a superior paramount law, unchangeable by ordinary means, or it is on a level with ordinary legislative acts, and, like other acts, is alterable when the legislature shall please to alter it.

If the former part of the alternative be true, then a legislative act contrary to the constitution is not law: if the latter part be true, then written constitutions are absurd attempts, on the part of the people, to limit a power in its own nature illimitable.

Certainly all those who have framed written constitutions contemplate them as forming the fundamental and paramount law of the nation, and, consequently, the theory of every such government must be, that an act of the legislature, repugnant to the constitution, is void.

This theory is essentially attached to a written constitution, and, is consequently, to be considered, by this court, as one of the fundamental principles of our society. It is not therefore to be lost sight of in the further consideration of this subject....

Thus, the particular phraseology of the constitution of the United States confirms and strengthens the principle, supposed to be essential to all written constitutions, that a law repugnant to the constitution is void; and that courts, as well as other departments, are bound by that instrument.

The rule must be discharged.

54

Resolutions of the Hartford Convention (1815)

Federalist-dominated New England had opposed "Mr. Madison's War" from the start. The center of the American mercantile trade was New England, whose shippers had struggled economically since Jefferson's embargo of 1807. In addition, the region contained a rump of arch-Federalists who contemplated disunion. The British sought to take advantage of the region's hostility to the war by conducting a "hands-off" policy in 1812–1813. By 1814, however, British operations increasingly focused on the New England coast. Shipping interests faced with mounting losses combined with local disunionists to demand changes in the federal compact that would protect minority interests. New England Federalists issued the document excerpted here from their meeting at Hartford, Connecticut.

Questions to Consider

1. What is the historical context of this document?
2. How does the Hartford Convention justify its proposed changes to the Constitution?
3. Why do they want two-thirds majorities of both houses of Congress to determine actions?
4. What do you think President Madison thought when he saw this document?

… Resolved, That it be and hereby is recommended to the said Legislatures, to authorize an immediate and earnest application to be made to the government of the United States, requesting their consent to some arrangement, whereby the said states may, separately or in concert, be empowered to assume upon themselves the defense of their territory against the enemy; and a reasonable portion of the taxes, collected within said States, may be paid into the respective treasuries thereof, and appropriated to the payment of the balance due said states, and to the future defense of the same. The amount so paid into the said treasuries to be credited, and the disbursements made as aforesaid to be charged to the United States.

Resolved, That it be and hereby is recommended to the legislatures of the aforesaid states, to pass laws (where it has not already been done) authorizing the

SOURCE: Theodore Dwight, *History of the Hartford Convention* (New York, 1833), 376–79.

governors or commanders-in-chief of their militia to make detachments from the same, or to form voluntary corps, as shall be most convenient and conformable to their constitutions, and to cause the same to be well armed, equipped, and disciplined, and held in readiness for service; and upon the request of the governor of either of the other states to employ the whole of such detachment or corps, as well as the regular forces of the state, or such part thereof as may be required and can be spared consistently with the safety of the state, in assisting the state, making such request to repel any invasion thereof which shall be made or attempted by the public enemy.

Resolved, That the following amendments of the constitution of the United States be recommended to the states represented as aforesaid, to be proposed by them for adoption by the state legislatures, and in such cases as may be deemed expedient by a convention chosen by the people of each state....

First. Representatives and direct taxes shall be apportioned among the several states which may be included within this Union, according to their respective numbers of free persons, including those bound to serve for a term of years, and excluding Indians not taxed, and all other persons.

Second. No new state shall be admitted into the Union by Congress, in virtue of the power granted by the constitution, without the concurrence of two thirds of both houses.

Third. Congress shall not have power to lay any embargo on the ships or vessels of the citizens of the United States, in the ports or harbors thereof, for more than sixty days.

Fourth. Congress shall not have power, without the concurrence of two thirds of both houses, to interdict the commercial intercourse between the United States and any foreign nation, or the dependencies thereof.

Fifth. Congress shall not make or declare war, or authorize acts of hostility against any foreign nation, without the concurrence of two thirds of both houses, except such acts of hostility be in defense of the territories of the United States when actually invaded.

Sixth. No person who shall hereafter be naturalized, shall be eligible as a member of the senate or house of representatives of the United States, nor capable of holding any civil office under the authority of the United States.

Seventh. The same person shall not be elected president of the United States a second time nor shall the president be elected from the same state two terms in succession.

Resolved, That if the application of these states to the government of the United States, recommended in a foregoing resolution, should be unsuccessful, and peace should not be concluded, and the defense of these states should be neglected, as it has been since the commencement of the war, it will, in the opinion of this convention, be expedient for the legislatures of the several states to appoint delegates to another convention, to meet at Boston in the state of Massachusetts, on the third Thursday of June next, with such powers and instructions as the exigency of a crisis so momentous may require....

7

The New Nation and Its Place in the World

In addition to having to work out the details of how the new government would operate, the United States also had to establish a pattern of relations with foreign states. During much of this period, the United States attempted to remain neutral, while simultaneously keeping the Europeans from meddling in America's affairs. With the European flank covered, the young nation remained free to acquire land in the West and more than doubled its territorial size during the first quarter of the century. Westward expansion often involved foreign relations of another sort—negotiating with Native Americans. The following documents demonstrate the American policy of neutrality and territorial acquisition as well as the opposition to these policies.

55

Military Disaster on the Ohio Frontier (1791)

As a result of the Treaty of Paris in 1783, Great Britain had ceded all claim to territory east of the Mississippi River. Although the new nation might claim these western lands and sought to open them to speculators and settlers, American Indians who lived there had other ideas. In the region north of the Ohio River, Miami leader Little Turtle (or Michikinikwa) and the Shawnee war chief Blue Jacket (or Weyapiersenwah) led a confederacy of western tribes that sought to stop white encroachment on their lands. In 1790, this Native American force had defeated an American army on the Maumee River in present-day Ohio. The following year, President Washington sent a force under Arthur St. Clair to destroy the resistance. St. Clair seemed an excellent choice. A native of Scotland, he had stayed in North America following the Seven Years' War and would serve with distinction in the Continental Army during the Revolution. After the war, St. Clair served as President of the Confederation Congress before being appointed Governor of the Northwest Territory. As the nation's highest-ranking military officer, he led American forces to the Wabash River in present-day Indiana, where they engaged the Indian confederacy. The following excerpt from the diary of Major Ebenezer Denny, Aide-de-Camp to General St. Clair, describes the battle, which was the largest defeat of U.S. forces by Indians in the nation's history. A subsequent expedition led by Anthony Wayne would result in the defeat of the confederacy at Fallen Timbers in 1794. The next year, the U.S. government forced the cession of much of present-day Ohio in the Treaty of Greenville.

Questions to Consider

1. Based on this document, what can you deduce about white attitudes toward American Indians during this time?

2. How do you think the Whiskey rebels ("Opposing Views of the Whiskey Rebellion," Document 50) and the participants in the Cane Ridge revival ("Description of a Conversion Experience at Cane Ridge, Kentucky," Document 52) responded to news of the battle?

3. What impact do you think this defeat had upon the prestige of the new government?

The troops paraded this morning at the usual time, and had been dismissed from the lines but a few minutes, and the sun not up, when the woods in front rung with the yells and fire of the savages. The poor militia, who were but three hundred yards in front had scarcely time to return a shot—they fled into our camp. The troops were under arms in an instant, and a smart fire from the front line met the enemy. It was but a few minutes, however, until the men engaged in every quarter. The enemy from the front filed off to the right and left, and completely surrounded the camp, killed and cut off nearly all the guards, and approached close to the lines. They advanced from one tree, log, or stump to another, under cover of the smoke of our fire. The artillery and musketry made a tremendous noise, but did little execution.... Our left-flank, probably from the nature of the ground, gave way first; the enemy got possession of that part of the encampment, but, it being pretty clear ground, they were too exposed, and were soon repulsed. Was at this time with the General engaged toward the right; he was on foot, and led the party himself that drove the enemy and regained our ground on the left. The battalions in the rear charged several times and forced the savages from their shelter, but they always turned with the battalions and fired upon them back; indeed, they seemed to fear any thing we could do. They could skip out of reach of the bayonet, and return as they pleased. They were visible only when raised by a charge. The ground was literally covered with the dead. The wounded were taken to the center where it was thought most safe, and where a great many who had quit their post unhurt had crowded together. The General, with other officers, endeavored to rally these men, and twice they were taken out of the lines. It appeared as if the officers had been singled out; a very great proportion fell, or were wounded.... The men, being thus left with few officers, became fearful, despaired of success, gave up the fight and, to save themselves for the moment, abandoned entirely their duty and ground, and crowded in toward the center of the field, and no exertions could put them in any order even for defense; perfectly ungovernable. The enemy at length got possession of the artillery, though not until the officers were all killed but one, and he badly wounded, and the men almost all cut off, and not until the pieces were spiked. As our lines were deserted the Indians contracted theirs until their shot centered from all points, and now, meeting with little opposition, took more deliberate aim and did great execution. Exposed to a cross fire, men and officers were seen falling in every direction; the distress, too, of the wounded made the scene such as can scarcely be conceived; a few minutes longer, and a retreat would have been impracticable. The only hope left was, that perhaps the savages would be so taken up by the camp as not to follow. Delay was death; no preparation could be made; numbers of brave men must be left a sacrifice—there was no alternative. It was past nine o'clock, when repeated orders were given to charge toward the road. The action had continued between two and three hours. Both officers and men seemed confounded, incapable of doing anything; they could not move until it was told that a retreat was intended. A few officers put themselves in front, the men followed, the enemy gave way, and perhaps not being aware of the design, we were for a few minutes

SOURCE: "The Campaign in the Indian Country," from the Diary of Major Ebenezer Denny, Aide-de-Camp to General St. Clair, *The St. Clair Papers*, ed. William Henry Smith (Cincinnati, OH, 1882), 2: 259–61.

undisturbed. The stoutest and most active now took the lead, and those who were foremost in breaking the enemy's line were soon left behind. At the moment of the retreat, one of the few horses saved had been procured for the General; he was on foot until then; I kept by him, and he delayed to see the rear. The enemy soon discovered the movement and pursued, though not more than four or five miles and but a few so far; they turned to share the spoil. Soon after the firing ceased, I was directed to endeavor to gain the front, and, if possible, to cause a short halt that the rear might get up.... By this time the remains of the army had got somewhat compact, but in the most miserable and defenseless state. The wounded who came off left their arms in the field, and one-half of the others threw theirs away on the retreat. The road for miles was covered with firelocks, cartridge-boxes and regimentals. How fortunate that the pursuit was discontinued; a single Indian might have followed with safety upon either flank. Such a panic had seized the men, that I believe it would not have been possible to have brought any of them to engage again.... Stragglers continued to come in for hours after we reached the fort.

56

Jefferson's Instructions to Robert Livingston, Minister to France (1802)

Large numbers of settlers migrated to the area beyond the Appalachians after the American Revolution. By 1800, Kentucky and Tennessee had achieved statehood. Westerners considered the right to navigate the Mississippi River and to deposit goods at New Orleans as necessities. Thomas Jefferson, who counted on the West for political support, was eager to preserve these privileges. American access to the "Father of Waters" seemed threatened in October 1802 when Spain transferred the Louisiana Territory to the more militarily powerful French and suspended the right of American traders to deposit goods in New Orleans. Americans, many of whom believed that Napoleon had ordered the revocation of the right of deposit, feared the establishment of a French empire in the Mississippi Valley. In the following dispatch, President Thomas Jefferson provides Robert E. Livingston, the American minister to France, with instructions for negotiating the issue.

Questions to Consider

1. Why does Thomas Jefferson believe that French control of Louisiana "works most sorely on the United States"?

2.   How can you reconcile this document with the views expressed by George Washington in his "Farewell Address" (Document 51)?

3.   Why are events in St. Domingo important to American interests? Does Livingston complete Jefferson's instructions?

… The cession of Louisiana and the Floridas by Spain to France, works most sorely on the United States. On this subject the Secretary of State has written to you fully, yet I cannot forbear recurring to it personally, so deep is the impression it makes on my mind. It completely reverses all the political relations of the United States, and will form a new epoch in our political course. Of all nations of any consideration, France is the one which, hitherto, has offered the fewest points on which we could have any conflict of right, and the most points of a communion of interests. From these causes, we have ever looked to her as our natural friend, as one with which we never could have an occasion of difference. Her growth, therefore, we viewed as our own, her misfortunes ours. There is on the globe one single spot, the possessor of which is our natural and habitual enemy. It is New Orleans, through which the produce of three-eighths of our territory must pass to market, and from its fertility it will ere long yield more than half of our whole produce, and contain more than half of our inhabitants. France, placing herself in that door, assumes to us the attitude of defiance. Spain might have retained it quietly for years. Her pacific dispositions, her feeble state, would induce her to increase our facilities there, so that her possession of the place would be hardly felt by us, and it would not, perhaps, be very long before some circumstance might arise, which might make the cession of it to us the price of something of more worth to her. Not soon can it ever be in the hands of France: the impetuosity of her temper, the energy and restlessness of her character, placed in a point of eternal friction with us, and our character, which though quiet and loving peace and the pursuit of wealth, is high-minded, despising wealth in competition with insult or injury, enterprising and energetic as any nation on earth; these circumstances render it impossible that France and the United States can continue long friends, when they meet in so irritable a position. They, as well as we, must be blind if they do not see this; and we must be very improvident if we do not begin to make arrangements on that hypothesis. The day that France takes possession of New Orleans, fixes the sentence which is to restrain her forever within her low-water mark. It seals the union of two nations, who, in conjunction, can maintain exclusive possession of the ocean. From that moment, we must marry ourselves to the British fleet and nation. We must turn all our attention to a maritime force, for which our resources place us on very high ground; and having formed and connected together a power which may render reinforcement of her settlements here impossible to France, make the first cannon which shall be fired in Europe the signal for the tearing up any settlement she may have made, and for holding the two

SOURCE: "To the United States (Robert E. Livingston) Minister to France," *The Works of Thomas Jefferson*, ed. Paul Leicester Ford (New York, 1905), 9: 363–68.

continents of America in sequestration for the common purposes of the United British and American nations. This is not a state of things we seek or desire....

If France considers Louisiana, however, as indispensable for her views, she might perhaps be willing to look about for arrangements which might reconcile it to our interests. If anything could do this, it would be the ceding to us the island of New Orleans and the Floridas. This would certainly, in a great degree, remove the causes of jarring and irritation between us, and perhaps for such a length of time, as might produce other means of making the measure permanently conciliatory to our interests and friendships. It would, at any rate, relieve us from the necessity of taking immediate measures for counter-vailing such an operation by arrangements in another quarter. But still we should consider New Orleans and the Floridas as no equivalent for the risk of a quarrel with France, produced by her vicinage....

The idea here is, that the troops sent to St. Domingo, were to proceed to Louisiana after finishing their work in that island. If this were the arrangement, it will give you time to return again and again to the charge. For the conquest of St. Domingo will not be a short work. It will take considerable time, and wear down a great number of soldiers. Every eye in the United States is now fixed on the affairs of Louisiana. Perhaps nothing since the revolutionary war, has produced more uneasy sensations through the body of the nation....

57

Heading West with Lewis and Clark (1804)

Thomas Jefferson's intense curiosity about the West predated his presidency. Once elected to the office, he wasted little time in planning an expedition to travel up the Missouri River to the Pacific Ocean. Meriwether Lewis and William Clark, both acquaintances of Jefferson, would lead the mission. Their task was enormous—to make their way into unmarked territory with little hope of outside support in an effort to report on prospects for trade, to collect scientific data on the region's flora and fauna, and to map their route. The purchase of Louisiana shortly before their debarkation from St. Louis did little to simplify the mission. The following account by Patrick Gass describes winter quarters among the Mandan Indians near modern-day Bismarck, North Dakota. A Pennsylvania native, Gass had served in the army before joining the expedition, where his construction skills were useful in building winter shelter. The Mandan had long had friendly relations with French

*traders, but in 1837 a smallpox epidemic virtually wiped out the tribe. Gass's account of
the expedition first appeared in 1807.*

Questions to Consider

1. What are the author's attitudes toward native life?

2. Compare and contrast Gass's view of Native Americans with those found in
    "Military Disaster on the Ohio Frontier" (Document 55) and Tecumseh
    ("Tecumseh on White Encroachment," Document 59). How do you
    account for these differences?

3. In what ways does weather appear to affect the expedition?

Saturday 27th.   The morning was clear and pleasant and we set out early. At
half past seven we arrived at the first village of the Mandans and halted about
two hours. This village contains 40 or 50 lodges built in the manner of those
of the Rickarees. These Indians have better complexions than most other
Indians, and some of the children have fair hair. We passed a bluff on the
south side with a stratum of black resembling coal. There is a bottom on the
north side, where the second Mandan village is situated. We went about a mile
above it, and encamped in the same bottom, for the purpose of holding a council
with the natives. This place is 1610 miles from the mouth of the river du Bois,
where we first embarked to proceed on the expedition. There are about the
same number of lodges, and people, in this village as in the first. These people
do not bury their dead, but place the body on a scaffold, wrapped in a buffaloe
robe, where it lies exposed....

Friday 2nd.   Captain Lewis, myself and some of the men, went up to the first
village of the Mandans, who gave us some corn. Captain Clarke and the rest of
our party, having dropt half a mile lower down the river, began to clear a place
for a camp and fort. We pitched our tents and laid the foundation of our line of
huts.

Saturday 3rd.   A clear day; we continued building, and six men went down
the river in a periogue to hunt. They will perhaps have to go 30 or 40 miles
before they come to good hunting ground.—The following is the manner in
which our huts and fort were built. The huts were in two rows, containing
four rooms each, and joined at one end forming an angle. When raised about
7 feet high a floor of puncheons or split plank were laid, and covered with
grass and clay; which made a warm loft. The upper part projected a foot over
and the roofs were made shed-fashion, rising from the inner side, and making
the outer wall about 18 feet high. The part not enclosed by the huts we intend
to picket. In the angle formed by the two rows of huts we built two rooms, for
holding our provisions and stores....

SOURCE: Patrick Gass, *Journal of the Lewis and Clark Expedition* (Chicago, 1904, reprint of 1811 ed.), 54–61.

Thursday 29th.   This day was clear, but cold. We went to unrig the boat, and by an accident one of the sergeants had his shoulder dislocated. The 30th the weather continued the same. Early in the morning of this day we saw an Indian on the opposite side of the river, and brought him over. He informed us, that a few days ago, eight of his nation were out hunting, and were attacked by a party of the Sioux tribe, who killed one and wounded two more; and also carried off their horses. Captain Clarke and twenty-three men immediately set out with an intention of pursuing the murderers. They went up to the first village of the Mandans, but their warriors did not seem disposed to turn out. They suggested the coldness of the weather; that the Sioux were too far gone to be overtaken: and put off the expedition to the spring of the year. Captain Clarke and his party returned the same evening to the fort. We have been daily visited by the Indians since we came here. Our fort is called Fort Mandan, and by observation is in N. latitude 47.21.33.8.

Saturday 1st December, 1804.   The day was pleasant, and we began to cut and carry pickets to complete our fort. One of the traders from the North West Company came to the fort, and related that the Indians had been trouble-some in his way through. An Indian came down from the first Mandan village, and told us that a great number of the Chien or Dog nation had arrived near the village....

Friday 7th.   A clear cold morning. At 9 o'clock, the Bigwhite head chief, of the first village of the Mandans, came to our garrison and told us that the buffa-loe were in the prairie coming into the bottom. Captain Lewis and eleven more of us went out immediately, and saw the prairie covered with buffaloe and the Indians on horseback killing them. They shoot them with bows and arrows, and have their horses so trained that they will advance very near and suddenly wheel and fly off in case the wounded buffaloe attempt an attack....

Monday 10th.   After breakfasting on marrow bones, Captain Lewis and four of us set out for the fort. Four hunters and another man to keep camp remained out. On our return we met one of our men, who said that a party had gone down with the horses for more meat. This day was very cold: an experiment was made with proof spirits, which in fifteen minutes froze into hard ice. In the evening two of our hunters came in with the horses, but had killed nothing. Five encamped out....

Sunday 16th.   A clear cold day; I went up with some of the men to the 1st and 2nd village of the Mandans, and we were treated with much kindness. Three of the traders from the N.W. Company came to our fort, and brought a letter to our commanding officers. They remained with us all night. The object of the visits we received from the N.W. Company, was to ascertain our motives for visiting that country, and to gain information with respect to the change of gov-ernment....

58

Jefferson And His Opponents (1800, 1807)

Thomas Jefferson was one of the most controversial politicians in American history. Much of this opposition was captured in political cartoons. The first image appeared during the heated election of 1800, when Jefferson's Federalist rivals accused him of adhering too closely to the tenets of the French Revolution and of even defaming Geroge Washington in a 1796 letter to Philip Mazzei. The second image appeared following the passage of the Embargo Act of 1807. Caught between the warring powers of France and Great Britain, which continually harassed American shipping, Jefferson determined to use economic rather than military means to force the European powers to back down. The embargo made it unlawful for American ships to leave port to engage in trade. Traders, many of them Federalists, bitterly opposed the law as made evident in the second image.

Questions to Consider

1. What beliefs are associated with Jefferson in "The Providential Detection"?

2. To what extent are the charges made in "The Providential Detection" accurate?

3. Why do you think the artist used a terrapin as the means to pinch the trader in the "Ograbme" cartoon?

4. What does "ograbme" spell backwards?

THE PROVIDENTIAL DETECTION

Etching by an unknown artist, c. 1800

SOURCE: Courtesy American Antiquarian Society

A Smuggler During the Embargo Act

SOURCE: (c) Bettmann/Corbis

59

Tecumseh on White Encroachment (1810)

The wave of settlement that swept over the Appalachians after the Revolution threatened Native Americans in the region. Earlier Indian leaders had attempted to create an alliance to resist white encroachment, but these efforts proved difficult given traditional animosities and conflicting political agendas among the various tribes. The Shawnee warrior Tecumseh, who had grown up in close proximity to white settlers and was familiar with American society, attempted to create such an alliance with the assistance of his brother Tenskwatawa. While Tenskwatawa preached a religious message, Tecumseh sought to create a military alliance with British support. In the excerpted speech that follows, Tecumseh summarizes many of the grievances that the natives had concerning their treatment at the hands of the white Americans.

Questions to Consider

1. According to Tecumseh, what are the reasons for Native American opposition to the whites?

2. To what extent might Washington's orders to General Sullivan ("The Revolution in Indian Country," Document 38) justify Tecumseh's fears?

3. How do you think white American contemporaries would react to this document?

4. Compare Tecumseh's views on white encroachment with those found in "The Pontiac Manuscript" (Document 24). What similarities do you note? Differences?

… You ought to know that after we agreed to bury the Tomahawk at Greenville we then found their new fathers in the Americans who told us they would treat us well, not like the British who gave us but a small piece of pork every day. I want now to remind you of the promises of the white people.…

Brother. Since the peace was made you have kill'd some of the Shawanese, Winebagoes, Delawares and Miamies and you have taken our lands from us and I do not see how we can remain at peace with you if you continue to do so. You have given goods to the Kickapoos for the sale of their lands to you which

SOURCE: "Speech of Tecumseh," *Governors Messages and Papers*, ed. Logan B. Esarey, Indiana Historical Society, *Collections* (Indianapolis, 1922), 7: 463–67.

has been the cause of many deaths amongst them. You have promised us assistance but I do not see that you have given us any.

You try to force the red people to do some injury. It is you that is pushing them on to do mischief. You endeavour to make destructions, you wish to prevent the Indians to do as we wish them to unite and let them consider their land as the common property of the whole you take tribes aside and advise them not to come into this measure and untill our design is accomplished we do not wish to accept of your invitation to go and visit the President.

The reason I tell you this is—You want by your distinctions of Indian tribes in allotting to each a particular track of land to make them to war with each other. You never see an Indian come and endeavour to make the white people do so. You are continually driving the red people when at last you will drive them into the great lake where they can't either stand or work.

Brother. You ought to know what you are doing with the Indians. Perhaps it is by direction of the President to make those distinctions. It is a very bad thing and we do not like it. Since my residence at Tippecanoe we have endeavoured to level all distinctions to destroy village chiefs by whom all mischief is done; it is they who sell our land to the Americans our object is to let all our affairs be transacted by Warriors.

Brother. This land that was sold and the goods that was given for it was only done by a few. The treaty was afterwards brought here and the Weas were induced to give their consent because of their small numbers. The treaty at Fort Wayne was made through the threats of Winamac but in future we are prepared to punish those chiefs who may come forward to propose to sell their land. If you continue to purchase of them it will produce war among the different tribes and at last I do not know what will be the consequences to the white people.

Brother. I was glad to hear your speech you said if we could show that the land was sold by persons that had no right to sell you would restore it, that that did sell did not own it was me. These tribes set up a claim but the tribes with me will not agree to their claim, if the land is not restored to us you will soon see when we return to our homes how it will be settled. We shall have a great council at which all the tribes shall be present when we will show to those who sold that they had no right to see the claim they set up and we will know what will be done with those Chiefs that did sell the land to you. I am not alone in this determination it is the determination of all the warriors and red people that listen to me.

I now wish you to listen to me. If you do not it will appear as if you wished me to kill all the chiefs that sold you this land. I tell you so because I am authorised by all the tribes to do so. I am at the head of them all. I am a Warrior and all the Warriors will meet together in two or three moons from this. Then I will call for those chiefs that sold you that land and shall know what to do with them. If you do not restore the land you will have a hand in killing them.

Brother. Do not believe that I came here to get presents from you if you offer us anything we will not take it. By taking goods from you you will hereafter say that with them you purchased another piece of land from us. If we want anything we are able to buy it, from your traders. Since the land was sold to you no traders come among us. I now wish you would clear all the roads and let the traders come among us. Then perhaps some of our young men will occasionally call upon you to get their guns repaired. This is all the assistance we ask of you....

Brother. It has been the object of both myself and brother from the beginning to prevent the lands being sold should you not return the land, it will occasion us to call a great council that will meet at the Huron Village where the council fire has already been lighted. At which those who sold the land shall be call'd and shall suffer for their conduct.

Brother. I wish you would take pity on all the red people and do what I have requested. If you will not give up the land and do cross the boundary of your present settlement it will be very hard and produce great troubles among us. How can we have confidence in the white people when Jesus Christ came upon the earth you kill'd and nail'd him on a cross, you thought he was dead but you were mistaken. You have shaken among you and you laugh and make light of their worship....

60

Margaret Bayard Smith on The Burning of Washington, DC (1814)

Freedom of the seas, western land hunger, and an assertion of national rights were among the factors that led the United States into the War of 1812. The nation managed to survive the conflict, but the British campaigns of 1814 placed such a result in doubt. The following letter describes the events following the American defeat at the Battle of Bladensburg, just east of the District of Columbia. Following the collapse of the American defense, British forces arrived and set fire to many of the public buildings in the city. The author of the letter was Margaret Bayard Smith. The wife of newspaper editor Samuel Harrison Smith, Margaret was a passionate Jeffersonian who became a leading fixture in Washington society, frequently dining with President Jefferson and eventually becoming a friend of Dolley Madison. Her letter to Maria Kirkpatrick, excerpted here, provides a glimpse into wartime Washington as well as Smith's fears for the city and nation's future.

Questions to Consider

1. How does Margaret Bayard Smith describe American defense forces before the battle?

2. How does Smith describe the city after the British occupation?

3. What are her fears for the future? Do they seem reasonable?

4. What can we deduce from this document about women's roles in the early nineteenth century?

Brookville. [Md.,] August, [1814.]

On Sunday we received information that the British had debark'd at Benedict. They seem'd in no haste to approach the city, but gave us time to collect our troops. The alarm was such that on Monday a general removal from the city and George Town took place. Very few women or children remain'd in the city on Tuesday evening, altho' the accounts then received were that the enemy were retreating. Our troops were eager for an attack and such was the cheerful alacrity they display'd that a universal confidence reign'd among the citizens and people. Few doubted our conquering. On Tuesday we sent off to a private farm house all our linen, clothing and other movable property, in the afternoon Dr. Bradley's family came from the city and took tea with us, ... we were roused on Tuesday night by a loud knocking, —on the opening of the door, Willie Bradley called to us, "The enemy are advancing, our own troops are giving way on all sides and are retreating to the city. Go, for Gods sake go." He spoke in a voice of agony, and then flew to his horse and was out of sight in a moment. We immediately rose, the carriage and horses were soon ready, we loaded a wagon with what goods remained and about 3 oclock left our house with all our servants, the women we sent to some private farm houses at a safe distance, while we pursued our course....

Thursday morning. This morning on awakening we were greeted with the sad news, that our city was taken, the bridges and public buildings burnt, our troops flying in every direction. Our little army totally dispersed. Good God, what will be the event! ... The President who was on the ground, escap'd and has gone into Virginia. *Winder* with all the men he can collect are at the court house. He has directed our poor broken militia to make the best of their way to Baltimore. Every hour the poor wearied and terrified creatures are passing by the door. Mrs. Bently kindly invites them in to rest and refresh. Major Ridgely's troop of horse all breakfasted in town, that not a man was left to breakfast in the tavern. Ann and I hasten'd to assist Mrs. B. in getting their breakfast,—and Julia and Susan wanted to do something, help'd to set the table, & c....

Thursday evening. Our anxiety has been kept alive the whole day.... They first march'd to the navy yard which is wholly consumed; then to Capitol Hill. They had great difficulty in firing the capitol, several houses on the hill were burnt by cinders from the Capitol, but none by design, the President's house, the Potomac bridge, and all the other public buildings. Mr. Lee went to their camp at Marlborough (as a citizen unmolested) conversed with the officers, several of whom he had known in London. They told him that resistance would be

SOURCE: Margaret Bayard Smith, "Margaret Bayard Smith to Maria Kirkpatrick, August, 1814," *The First Forty Years of Washington Society in the Family Letters of Margaret Bayard Smith*, ed. Gaillard Hunt (New York, 1906), 98–105.

vain; that instead of 7000, they wished we had 40,000 militia, as it would make the greater confusion. They bade Mr. Lee tell the citizens that private property would not be injured, if the houses were not deserted, or private persons molested, that they intended to destroy the public buildings and shipping, and then to march to Baltimore on one side while Lord Hill with his fleet would attack it by water. I left our house with reluctance, but when I urged Mr. Smith to let me remain to protect the house, he would not hear of it, his duty called him away, and my situation being so critical, he said no consideration would induce him to leave me, for altho' the troops when under their officers might behave well, yet small parties or drunken soldiers might alarm or injure me in my present situation. And Ann declared she would not leave me if she were to die by my side. I had therefore to yield. I am afraid the consequence of leaving the house empty will be its destruction. Our house in the city too is unprotected and contains our most valuable furniture. In a week more and we may be penniless! ... God only knows when the executive government will again be organized. But I can say with truth, the individual loss of property, has not given me a moment's uneasiness. But the state of our country, has wrung tears of anguish from me. I trust it will only be momentary. We are naturally a brave people and it was not so much fear, as prudence which caused our retreat. Too late they discovered the dispreparation of our troops. The enemy were 3 to 1. Their army composed of conquering veterans, ours of young mechanics and farmers, many of whom had never before carried a musket. But we shall learn the dreadful, horrid trade of war. And they will make us a martial people, for never, never will Americans give up their liberty. But before that time comes, what sufferings, what reverses, what distress must be suffer'd. Already, in one night, have hundreds of our citizens been reduced from affluence to poverty, for it is not to be expected W—will ever again be the seat of Govt. Last night the woods round the city and G. T—were filled with women and children and old men and our flying troops....

Night, 10 oclock. The street of this quiet village, which never before witnessed confusion, is now fill'd with carriages bringing out citizens, and Baggage waggons and troops. Mrs. Bently's house is now crowded, she has been the whole evening sitting at the supper table, giving refreshment to soldiers and travellers. I suppose every house in the village is equally full. I never saw more benevolent people. "It is against our principles," said she this morning, "to have anything to do with war, but we receive and relieve all who come to us." The whole settlement are quakers. The table is just spread for the 4th or 5th time, more wanderers having just enter'd....

Farewell, dearest sister, God grant this letter may contain more news, than I may ever have occasion to write again. Farewell.

61

Tennessee Expansionists on the Adams-Onís Treaty (1819)

As new settlers began to displace Native Americans in the Old Southwest, it became increasingly important for American policy makers to safeguard U.S. interests in the region. As a result, negotiations with the Spanish over Florida and the Texas–Louisiana border were of great importance. Among those eager to secure an American presence in the West was Secretary of State John Quincy Adams, an experienced diplomat and ardent national- ist who was eager to assert American interests. Andrew Jackson's controversial invasion of Florida in 1818 provided Adams with an opportunity in his negotiations with the Span- ish. By exposing Spain's weakness in Florida, Adams successfully forced Spain to relin- quish Florida and to abandon its claim to territory north and east of the Sabine River in the Adams-Onís (or Transcontinental) Treaty. The following selection from the (Nashville) Clarion & Tennessee State Gazette *reveals the attitude of expansion-minded Tennes- seans toward the secretary of state's negotiations on the Texas border.*

Questions to Consider

1. Compare this document with John O'Sullivan's "Texas and California Annexation" (Document 86). What similarities do you note? Differences?

2. Why does the Tennessee newspaper oppose the boundary line between Spain and the United States?

3. What is the newspaper's view on the land west of the boundary?

4. From this selection, what can you deduce about American attitudes?

When we first heard the outlines of this treaty we were astonished; what we hear every day confirms our displeasure—at first we had no anticipation that the line of boundary crossed Red river—this it does, and gives Spain a territory four times as large as the state of Tennessee, besides what we believed ceded—a ter- ritory as necessary to us as any part of Upper Louisiana. In a late New York paper, there is published a communication from Wm. Darby, who surveyed the western part of Louisiana, and is probably better acquainted with the country than any man living. He says,

SOURCE: "Spanish Treaty," (Nashville) *The Clarion & Tennessee State Gazette*, 6 April 1819, p. 3.

Let any person view a good map of that part of this continent over which the new line of demarcation, between Spain and the United ... States, is to pass; and compare it with the Louisiana in the real extent of the term, will perceive that if the treaty is ratified, we have relinquished a territory of upwards 240,000 square miles of surface....

I remember when the regions now included in the states of Indiana, Missouri, the Arkansas territory, the states of Mississippi, Louisiana and Alabama, were considered relatively and remote, as at present Texas, from the Atlantic border of the United States; but the irresistible impulse of our augmenting population has brought these former expansive territories to view.

Let no man deceive himself with the main expectation that artificial lines will operate to stem the torrent of western emigration. The laws of nature will be neither arrested nor thwarted by a roll of parchment though the names of the king of Spain and his minister are both attached to its margin. The increasing and restless men of the west, will follow the courses of the rivers that flow into the Mississippi and Gulf of Mexico, regardless of future consequences ... to prevent the flow of emigration is beyond human power....

Texas is filled with Indian tribes, some are settled in fixed residence, but most are wandering hordes, who subsist by hunting and who are in almost perpetual war. As the settlements upon the Arkansaw and Red Rivers advance, the whites will come to contact with the native inhabitants; and as our former system of treating savage bands is perpetuated, savage war will continue and those savages be finally destroyed.

The positive authority of Spain exists no more in America. It is worse than folly to legislate upon a state of things which has ceased to exist—and can never again be restored. Why the United States should relinquish a part of its domain, a part, itself the extent of an EMPIRE, I cannot see; and still less can I see the sense or policy of adopting an order of things which must inevitably produce a repetition of events so much to be deprecated.

It is possible that some future event may put it in the power of some more enlightened statesman to correct blunders of the late treaty.

62

The Monroe Doctrine (1823)

The preeminent expression of America's postwar diplomatic nationalism was the 1823 Monroe Doctrine. The genesis of the document came as a response to the developing alliance system of Europe. Of particular worry was the so-called Holy Alliance, which implied that European powers might forcibly restore Spain's recently independent American states to their former owner. The British, eager to exploit trade with the new countries, requested that a joint Anglo-American statement be issued opposing European intervention in American affairs. Secretary of State John Quincy Adams rebuffed the British, reportedly stating that the United States should not "come in a cock boat in the wake of the British man-of-war." President James Monroe delivered America's unilateral position on European-American relations in his December 2 address to Congress.

Questions to Consider

1. What is the thesis of this document?
2. How powerful is the United States in comparison with major European powers at this time?
3. How does the United States view the newly independent nations of Latin America?
4. Why are European interests in the Western Hemisphere a danger to the United States?

... The citizens of the United States cherish sentiments the most friendly in favor of the favor of the liberty and happiness of their fellow-men on that side of the Atlantic. In the wars of the European powers in matters relating to themselves we have never taken any part, nor does it comport with our policy so to do. It is only when our rights are invaded or seriously menaced that we resent injuries or make preparation for our defense. With the movements in this hemisphere we are of necessity more immediately connected, and by causes which must be obvious to all enlightened and impartial observers. The political system of the allied powers is essentially different in this respect from that of America. This difference proceeds from that which exists in their respective Governments; and to the defense of our own, which has been achieved by the loss of so much blood and treasure, and matured by the wisdom of their most enlightened

SOURCE: *A Compilation of the Messages and Papers of the Presidents*, ed. James D. Richardson (Washington, DC, 1903), 2: 218–19.

citizens, and under which we have enjoyed unexampled felicity, this whole nation is devoted. We owe it, therefore, to candor and to the amicable relations existing between the United States and those powers to declare that we should consider any attempt on their part to extend their system to any portion of this hemisphere as dangerous to our peace and safety. With the existing colonies or dependencies of any European power we have not interfered and shall not interfere. But with the Governments who have declared their independence and maintained it, and whose independence we have, on great consideration and on just principles, acknowledged, we could not view any interposition for the purpose of oppressing them, or controlling in any other manner their destiny, by any European power in any other light than as the manifestation of an unfriendly disposition toward the United States. In the war between those new Governments and Spain we declared our neutrality at the time of their recognition, and to this we have adhered, and shall continue to adhere, provided no change shall occur which, in the judgment of the competent authorities of this Government, shall make a corresponding change on the part of the United States indispensable to their security.

The late events in Spain and Portugal show that Europe is still unsettled.... Our policy in regard to Europe, which was adopted at an early stage of the wars which have so long agitated that quarter of the globe, nevertheless remains the same, which is, not to interfere in the internal concerns of any of its powers; to consider the government de facto as the legitimate government for us; to cultivate friendly relations with it, and to preserve those relations by a frank, firm, and manly policy, meeting in all instances the just claims of every power, submitting to injuries from none. But in regard to those continents circumstances are eminently and conspicuously different. It is impossible that the allied powers should extend their political system to any portion of either continent without endangering our peace and happiness; nor can anyone believe that our southern brethren, if left to themselves, would adopt it of their own accord. It is equally impossible, therefore, that we should behold such interposition in any form with indifference. If we look to the comparative strength and resources of Spain and those new Governments, and their distance from each other, it must be obvious that she can never subdue them. It is still the true policy of the United States to leave the parties to themselves, in the hope that other powers will pursue the same course.

8

The Rise of Democracy

By the early 1820s, nearly every state had opened the franchise to all adult white males. The increasing democratization of American politics would soon reflect the profound changes taking place in American society. In addition to debates over the limits of national and executive power, this period witnessed divisions over responses to market change and the hardening of boundaries between races and genders in the United States. These would give rise to increasingly bitter partisan politics, eventually pitting Democrats against Whigs. The following documents offer glimpses into this increasingly democratic, and divisive, nation.

63

Fanny Wright on Equality (1830)

For reform-minded Europeans in the 1820s and 1830s, America's democratic political system, cheap available land, and lack of tradition seemed to offer an opportunity to shape a better tomorrow. One of the most renowned of these visitors was Scottish-born Frances "Fanny" Wright, who arrived in the United States in 1818 and fell in love with the country. Her behavior over the next decade would make her name a synonym for radicalism. Rumors abounded that her friendship with the Marquis de Lafayette was more than platonic and that her utopian community at Nashoba was an experiment in free love and miscegenation. Her radical critique of American life drew large crowds and incited riots in some cities. By 1830, she had settled in New York's Bowery, where this lecture took place. There, the Market Revolution had transformed the manufacturing workplace from small shops of upwardly mobile, skilled craftsmen into low-paid, semiskilled workers. The following excerpt reveals Wright's view of the meaning of democracy.

Questions to Consider

1. What is the basis of Fanny Wright's argument for equality?
2. Based on your reading of this document, why do you think Wright was so controversial?
3. How do you think a contemporary businessman would have reacted to her views?
4. Compare and contrast Fanny Wright's views with those expressed in "Sarah Grimké Argues for Gender Equality" (Document 82). What similarities and differences do you see?

… Our object, however reviled by false ambition, odious to knavery, offensive to vanity, or misconceived of by error, will ever be recognised by the great mass of this people as consistent with their national institutions, and as requisite for the practical development of the truths set forth in their declaration of independence. No! we shall not be driven to deny, nor seduced to qualify, the object, to which, as to the ultimate goal of reform, we, as Americans, are constitutionally pledged to aspire. That object—that ultimate goal is, as I have said, PRACTICAL EQUALITY OF THE UNIVERSAL AND EQUAL IMPROVEMENT OF THE CONDITION OF ALL, UNTIL, BY THE GRADUAL CHANGE IN THE VIEWS AND HABITS OF MEN, AND THE CHANGE CONSEQUENT UPON THE SAME, IN THE WHOLE SOCIAL ARRANGEMENTS OF THE BODY POLITIC, THE AMERICAN PEOPLE SHALL PRESENT, IN ANOTHER GENERATION, BUT ONE CLASS, AND, AS IT WERE, BUT ONE FAMILY—EACH INDEPENDENT IN HIS AND HER OWN THOUGHTS, ACTIONS, RIGHTS, PERSON, AND POSSESSIONS, AND ALL CO-OPERATING, ACCORDING TO THEIR INDIVIDUAL TASTE AND ABILITY, TO THE PROMOTION OF THE COMMON WEAL.

Taking this comprehensive view of all that is embraced in our *ultimate* object, every intelligent mind will distinguish that it is not attainable in this generation, and that all we can do, (though this *all* is immense,) is to exercise our own minds, and school our own feelings, in and by its contemplation, to correct such abuses as more immediately tend to exalt, at the present time, individuals or bodies of men at the expense of the mass of the community, and, first and last, and above all, to prepare the way for the entire fulfillment of what I conceive to constitute the one great constitutional duty of Americans—namely, the equal promotion of the happiness of all, by laying the foundation of a plan of

SOURCE: Frances Wright, "Parting Address as Delivered in the Bowery Theatre to the People of New York, June 1830," *Course of Popular Lectures as Delivered by Frances Wright*, 6th ed. (New York, 1836), 16–18.

education in unison with nature, with reason, with justice, and with THIS INSTRUMENT.

Such then is our ultimate object, and let us boldly declare it; such are the means—gradual and constitutional, but sure and radical, by which we propose that object to be attained. Such is our ultimate object, and let those who challenge it forego the name, even as they have forsworn the feelings of Americans. Such are the means we stand ready to adopt, and let those who blaspheme them forego the title even as they have forsworn the principles of honest man. Here—in our design or in the mode laid down for effecting that design, there is nothing to conceal, and nothing to *concede* or *extenuate*. I will take on me to speak, in this matter, in the name of my fellow citizens—constitutional is our object, righteous our means, and *determined our resolve*. We have no fear, no doubt, no hesitation, and no concealment. Why should we have? Thought here is free, speech is free, and all action free, which has in view our own benefit, combined with the benefit of our fellow man.

Behold, we have every advantage with us, which, as honest citizens, or as reasonable beings, we could ambition—a righteous object, a constitutional object, and an object feasible without violence to any, and with certain benefit to all. In Europe, the reformer, how expanded soever his mind, or generous his heart, may indeed hesitate to express the fulness of his desire. *Liberty and equality* there, is a cry whose very thought is treason, and its utterance death; but here, treason lies only in its challenge. How then should there be a point at issue with American reformers? All true and honest citizens *must*, upon reflection, have the same object—for, behold! It is engraven on their national escutcheon—it is engraven in never dying letters, in this Holy Bible of their country's faith, their country's hope, their country's love. To commence the practical illustration of the truths proclaimed to the world by the fathers of this nation's liberties, is what we ask at this day—no more could human philanthropy desire, no less could American patriotism demand.

For myself, I feel proud to declare, that no less perfect and entire is the democracy of my views and principles, than what by this charter is demanded of an American citizen; and, had I felt it otherwise, I had not claimed the noble title. I would see the righteous declaration here penned by Jefferson, signed by sages, sealed with the blood of the fathers of this nation, and solemnly sworn to by their sons on each anniversary of its birth.—I would—what shall I say? *See* its realization? That cannot be. But see such measures adopted as shall secure its realization for posterity, to the fullest extent ever conceived or conceivable by the human mind. Yes! My democracy has no reservations; my yearnings for the liberty of man acknowledge no exceptions, no prejudices, no predilections. Equal rights, equal privileges, equal enjoyments—I would see them shared by every man, by every woman, by every nation, by every race on the face of the globe. But, as I distinguish that equal condition must originate in equal knowledge, and that sound knowledge; in similar habits, and those good habits; in brotherly sympathies, and those fostered from youth up under a system of RATIONAL AND NATIONAL REPUBLICAN EDUCATION.

64

Daniel Webster's Second Reply to Robert Y. Hayne (1830)

The publication of John C. Calhoun's "Exposition and Protest," advancing the doctrine of nullification, highlighted different views over the division of powers between the state and federal governments. The issue emerged in the halls of Congress late in 1829, when Senator Samuel A. Foot of Connecticut pressed for the temporary restriction of western land sales. The debate soon became an argument over national and states' rights when South Carolina Senator Robert Y. Hayne linked the issues the following January. Massachusetts Senator Daniel Webster responded with a blistering attack on the "Exposition and Protest." Perhaps the nation's best trial lawyer, having won several cases before the Supreme Court (including McCulloch v. Maryland, *the* Dartmouth College *case, and* Gibbons v. Ogden), *Webster contended that South Carolina's problems resulted from its slave economy, not the tariff of 1828. Following Hayne's response came Webster's final oration, excerpted here, which contained the essence of nationalism as it had begun to develop in the antebellum North.*

Questions to Consider

1. How does Daniel Webster attack states' rights?
2. Why is the federal union "most dear" to Webster?
3. According to Webster, what is the basis of the federal union?
4. Compare the views contained in this document with those found in "South Carolina Nullifies the Tariff" (Document 69). In what ways do they differ?

... I profess, Sir, in my career hitherto, to have kept steadily in view the prosperity and honor of the whole country, and the preservation of our Federal Union. It is to that Union we owe our safety at home, and our consideration and dignity abroad. It is to that Union that we are chiefly indebted for whatever makes us most proud of our country. That Union we reached only by the discipline of our virtues in the severe school of adversity. It had its origin in the necessities of disordered finance, prostrate commerce, and ruined credit. Under its benign influences, these great interests immediately awoke, as from the dead, and sprang forth with newness of life. Every year of its duration has teemed with fresh

SOURCE: "Second Speech on Foot's Resolution," *The Writings and Speeches of Daniel Webster* (Boston, 1903), 6: 3–75.

proofs of its utility and its blessings; and although our territory has stretched out wider and wider, and our population spread farther and farther, they have not outrun its protection or its benefits. It has been to us all a copious fountain of national, social, and personal happiness.

I have not allowed myself, Sir, to look beyond the Union, to see what might lie hidden in the dark recess behind. I have not coolly weighed the chances of preserving liberty when the bonds that unite us together shall be broken asunder. I have not accustomed myself to hang over the precipice of disunion, to see whether, with my short sight, I can fathom the depth of the abyss below; nor could I regard him as a safe counsellor in the affairs of this government, whose thoughts should be mainly bent on considering, not how the Union may be best preserved, but how tolerable might be the condition of the people when it should be broken up and destroyed. While the Union lasts we have high, exciting, gratifying prospects spread out before us, for us and our children. Beyond that I seek not to penetrate the veil. God grant that in my day, at least, that curtain may not rise! God grant that on my vision never may be opened what lies behind! When my eyes shall be turned to behold for the last time the sun in heaven, may I not see him shining on the broken and dishonored fragments of a once glorious Union; on States dissevered, discordant, belligerent; on a land rent with civil feuds, or drenched, it may be, in fraternal blood! Let their last feeble and lingering glance rather behold the gorgeous ensign of the republic, now known and honored throughout the earth, still full high advanced, its arms and trophies streaming in their original lustre, not a stripe erased or polluted, nor a single star obscured, bearing for its motto, no such miserable interrogatory as "What is all this worth?" nor those words of delusion and folly, "Liberty first and Union afterwards"; but everywhere, spread all over in characters of living light, blazing on all its ample folds, as they float over the sea and over the land, and in every wind under the whole heavens, that other sentiment, dear to every true American heart,—Liberty and Union, now and for ever, one and inseparable!

65

Commentary on Elections in Jacksonian America (1832)

Of the several foreign visitors who described American life in the antebellum period, few were more critical than Frances Trollope. The novelist visited America between 1827 and 1831, spending most of her time in Cincinnati but also touring much of the rest of the country with her husband and three children. Upon her return to Great Britain, she wrote Domestic Manners of the Americans, *which appeared in 1832. Her American experience undoubtedly colored her views: on the Trollopes' trip to the United States, the English radical Frances Wright had convinced them to invest in a Cincinnati business venture; the scheme failed. Frances Trollope's humorous observations of American society depict a rough, egalitarian country that offended her bourgeois sensibilities. American reviewers vilified Trollope for her criticisms of their democratic experiment. In the following selection she wittily observes the popular nature of American politics and, in the process, questions the sincerity of American political convictions.*

Questions to Consider

1. What is the thesis of this document?
2. What does Frances Trollope consider so contradictory about American politics?
3. Why does she question the sincerity of American politicians?
4. How do you think an American contemporary would respond to this account?

... When a candidate for any office starts, his party endow him with every virtue, and with all the talents. They are all ready to peck out the eyes of those who oppose him, and in the warm and mettlesome south-western states, do literally often perform this operation; but as soon as he succeeds, his virtues and his talents vanish, and, excepting those holding office under his appointment, every man Jonathan of them sets off again full gallop to elect his successor. When I first arrived in America Mr. John Quincy Adams was president, and it was impossible to doubt, even from the statement of his enemies, that he was every way calculated to do honor to the office. All I ever heard against him was, that "he was

SOURCE: Frances Trollope, *Domestic Manners of the Americans* (New York, 1832), 206–8.

too much of a gentleman"; but a new candidate must be set up, and Mr. Adams was out-voted for no other reason, that I could learn, but because it was "best to change." "Jackson for ever!" was, therefore, screamed from the mouths, both drunk and sober, till he was elected; but no sooner in his place, than the same ceaseless operation went on again, with "Clay for ever" for its war-whoop.

I was one morning paying a visit, when a party of gentlemen arrived at the same house, on horseback. The one whose air proclaimed him the chief of his party, left us not long in doubt as to his business, for he said, almost in entering,

"Mr P—, I come to ask for your vote."

"Who are you for, sir?" was the reply.

"Clay for ever!" the rejoinder; and the vote was promised.

This gentleman was candidate for a place in the state representation, whose members have a vote in the presidential election.

I was introduced to him as an Englishwoman: he addressed me with: "Well, madam, you see we do these things openly and above-board here; you mince such matters more, I expect."

After his departure his history and standing were discussed. "Mr M. is highly respectable, and of very good standing; there can be no doubt of his election if he is a thorough-going Clay-man," said my host.

I asked what his station was.

The lady of the house told me that his father had been a merchant, and when this future legislator was a young man, he had been sent to some port in the Mediterranean as his supercargo. The youth, being a free-born high-spirited youth, appropriated the proceeds to his own uses, traded with great success upon the fund thus obtained, and returned, after an absence of twelve years, a gentleman of fortune and excellent standing. I expressed some little disapprobation of this proceeding, but was assured that Mr M. was considered by every one as a very "honorable man."

Were I to relate one-tenth part of the dishonest transactions recounted to me by Americans, of their fellow-citizens and friends, I am confident that no English reader would give me credit for veracity; it would, therefore, be very unwise to repeat them, but I cannot refrain from expressing the opinion that nearly four years of attentive observation impressed on me, namely, that the moral sense is on every point blunter than with us. Make an American believe that his next door neighbor is a very worthless fellow, and I dare say (if he were quite sure he could make nothing by him) he would drop the acquaintance; but as to what constitutes a worthless fellow, people differ on the opposite sides of the Atlantic, almost by the whole decalogue. There is, as it appeared to me, an obtusity on all points of honorable feeling....

66

The American System (1832)

The profound economic changes that became evident after the War of 1812 demanded a political response. Some insisted on trying to protect citizens from the uncertainties of the new economy. Others believed that the issue should be left to state governments and private enterprise, while still others argued that the federal government should play a role in shaping these changes. More nationally minded Republicans had begun to advance an agenda that came to be known as the American System. It called for a national bank to provide fiscal stability, a tariff to protect key industries and raise revenues, and federally funded internal improvements to develop a national transportation infrastructure. Henry Clay's name would become synonymous with the American System. A native of Virginia, he built a spectacular political career in Kentucky. Elected speaker of the House in his first term, he was a prominent member of the Republican pro-war faction who demanded American entry into the War of 1812. After helping to negotiate the treaty ending the war, he served as President John Quincy Adams's secretary of state before returning to the U.S. Senate in 1831. The following excerpt contains Clay's defense of the American System.

Questions to Consider

1. According to Henry Clay, what impact has the American System had upon the United States?

2. What appear to be the major criticisms of the American System?

3. How do you think Andrew Jackson ("Andrew Jackson's Bank Veto Message," Document 67) responded to Clay's American System? Why?

… On a general survey, we behold cultivation extended, the arts flourishing, the face of the country improved, our people fully and profitably employed, and the public countenance exhibiting tranquillity, contentment, and happiness. And if we descend into particulars, we have the agreeable contemplation of a people out of debt; land rising slowly in value, but in a secure and salutary degree; a ready though not extravagant market for all the surplus productions of our industry; innumerable flocks and herds browsing and gamboling on ten thousand hills and plains, covered with rich and verdant grasses; our cities expanded, and whole villages springing up, as it were, by enchantment; our exports and imports increased and increasing; our tonnage, foreign and coastwise, swelling and fully

SOURCE: "On the American System," 2, 3, & 6 February 1832, *Works of Henry Clay*, ed. Calvin Colton (New York, 1904), 7: 437–44.

occupied; the rivers of our interior animated by the perpetual thunder and light-ning of countless steamboats; the currency sound and abundant; the public debt of two wars nearly redeemed; and, to crown all, the public treasury overflowing, embarrassing Congress, not to find subjects of taxation, but to select the objects which shall be liberated from the impost. *If the term of seven years were to be selected, of the greatest prosperity which this people have enjoyed since the establishment of their present Constitution, it would be exactly that period of seven years which immediately followed the passage of the tariff of 1824.*

This transformation of the condition of the country from gloom and distress to brightness and prosperity, has been mainly the work of American legislation, fostering American industry, instead of allowing it to be controlled by foreign legislation, cherishing foreign industry. The foes of the American system, in 1824, with great boldness and confidence, predicted, first, the ruin of the public revenue, and the creation of a necessity to resort to direct taxation; the gentle-man from South Carolina (General Hayne), I believe, thought that the tariff of 1824 would operate a reduction of revenue to the large amount of eight millions of dollars; secondly the destruction of our navigation; thirdly, the desolation of commercial cities; and, fourthly, the augmentation of the price of objects of con-sumption, and further decline in that of the articles of our exports. Every predic-tion which they made has failed, utterly failed. Instead of the ruin of the public revenue, with which they then sought to deter us from the adoption of the American system, we are now threatened with its subversion, by the vast amount of the public revenue produced by that system....

While we thus behold the entire failure of all that was foretold against the system, it is a subject of just felicitation to its friends, that all their anticipations of its benefits have been fulfilled, or are in progress of fulfillment. The Honorable gentleman from South Carolina has made an allusion to a speech made by me, in 1824, in the other House, in support of the tariff, and to which, otherwise, I should not have particularly referred. But I would ask any one, who can now command the courage to peruse that long production, what principle there laid down is not true? What prediction then made has been falsified by practical experience?

It is now proposed to abolish the system, to which we owe so much of the public prosperity, and it is urged that the arrival of the period of the redemption of the public debt has been confidently looked to as presenting a suitable occa-sion to rid the country of the evils with which the system is alleged to be fraught.... But the people of the United States have not coupled the payment of their public debt with the destruction of the protection of their industry against foreign laws and foreign industry. They have been accustomed to regard the extinction of the public debt as relief from a burden, and not as the infliction of a curse. If it is to be attended or followed by the subversion of the American system, and an exposure of our establishments and our productions to the unguarded consequences of the selfish policy of foreign powers, the payment of the public debt will be the bitterest of curses....

If the system of protection be founded on principles erroneous in theory, pernicious in practice, above all, if it be unconstitutional, as is alleged, it ought to be forthwith abolished, and not a vestige of it suffered to remain. But before we sanction this sweeping denunciation, let us look a little at this system, its magnitude, its ramifications, its duration, and the high authorities which have sustained it. We shall see that its foes will have accomplished comparatively nothing, after having achieved their present aim of breaking down our iron-founderies, our woolen, cotton, and hemp manufactories, and our sugar planta-tions. The destruction of these would, undoubtedly, lead to the sacrifice of immense capital, the ruin of many thousands of our fellow-citizens, and incalcu-lable loss to the whole community.... Why, sir, there is scarcely an interest, scarcely a vocation in society, which is not embraced by the beneficence of this system.... We might well pause and contemplate, if human imagination could conceive the extent of mischief and ruin from its total overthrow, before we proceed to the work of destruction....

67

Andrew Jackson's
Bank Veto Message (1832)

By 1832 the Second Bank of the United States had become one of the most controversial issues in American politics. To many, the institution was important for fiscal management in a rapidly changing economy. But to Andrew Jackson and his supporters, the Bank represented the emergence of a "moneyed aristocracy" that would use it to deprive the com-mon man of liberty and the ability to improve his economic lot. Jackson also had political reasons for opposing the Bank. Bank President Nicholas Biddle had championed cautious fiscal policies that alienated many of Jackson's supporters in the South and Southwest, who wanted greater access to credit. Biddle also had close associations with many of Jackson's leading opponents. Henry Clay, Jackson's opponent for the presidency in 1832, was a Bank supporter. He had pushed a recharter bill through Congress to force Jackson's hand on a controversial issue during an election year. Jackson's veto dominated the fall election campaign, which Jackson won. The veto galvanized his opponents, who created the Whig party two years later.

Questions to Consider

1. What is Andrew Jackson's perspective in this document?
2. Why does Jackson veto the Bank recharter bill?

3. Whom does Jackson identify as a threat to American liberty?

4. How do you suppose the failure to recharter the Bank affected the American economy?

Washington, July 10, 1832

To the Senate:

The bill "to modify and continue" the act entitled "An act to incorporate the subscribers to the Bank of the United States" was presented to me on the 4th July instant. Having considered it with that solemn regard to the principles of the Constitution which the day was calculated to inspire, and come to the conclusion that it ought not to become a law, I herewith return it to the Senate, in which it originated, with my objections.

A bank of the United States is in many respects convenient for the Government and useful to the people. Entertaining this opinion, and deeply impressed with the belief that some of the powers and privileges possessed by the existing bank are unauthorized by the Constitution, subversive of the rights of the States, and dangerous to the liberties of the people, I felt it my duty at an early period of my Administration to call the attention of Congress to the practicability of organizing an institution combining all its advantages and obviating these objections. I sincerely regret that in the act before me I can perceive none of those modifications of the bank charter which are necessary, in my opinion, to make it compatible with justice, with sound policy, or with the Constitution of our country.

The present corporate body, denominated the president, directors, and company of the Bank of the United States, will have existed at the time this act is intended to take effect twenty years. It enjoys an exclusive privilege of banking under the authority of the General Government, a monopoly of its favor and support, and, as a necessary consequence, almost a monopoly of the foreign and domestic exchange. The powers, privileges, and favors bestowed upon it in the original charter, by increasing the value of the stock far above its par value, operated as a gratuity of many millions to the stockholders.

An apology may be found for the failure to guard against this result in the consideration that the effect of the original act of incorporation could not be certainly foreseen at its time of its passage. The act before me proposes another gratuity to the holders of the same stock, and in many cases to the same men, of at least seven millions more. This donation finds no apology in any uncertainty as to the effect of the act. On all hands it is conceded that its passage will increase at least 20 or 30 per cent more the market price of the stock, subject to the payment of annuity of $200,000 per year secured by the act, thus adding in a moment one-fourth to its par value. It is not our own citizens only who are to receive the bounty of our Government. More than eight millions of the stock of this bank are held by foreigners. By this act the American Republic

SOURCE: Andrew Jackson, "Veto Message," *A Compilation of the Messages and Papers of the Presidents*, ed. James D. Richardson (Washington, DC, 1903), 2: 576–81.

proposes virtually to make them a present of some millions of dollars. For these gratuities to foreigners and to some of our own opulent citizens the act secures no equivalent whatever. They are the certain gains of the present stockholders under the operation of this act, after making full allowance for the payment of the bonus.

Every monopoly and all exclusive privileges are granted at the expense of the public, which ought to receive a fair equivalent. The many millions which this act proposes to bestow on the stockholders of this existing bank must come directly or indirectly out of the earnings of the American people. It is due to them, therefore, if their Government sell monopolies and exclusive privileges, that they should at least exact for them as much as they are worth in open market. The value of monopoly in this case may be correctly ascertained. The twenty-eight millions of stock would probably be at an advance of 50 per cent, and command in market at least $42,000,000, subject to the payment of the present bonus. The present value of the monopoly, therefore, is $17,000,000, and this act proposes to sell for three millions, payable in fifteen annual installments of $200,000 each.

It is not conceivable how the present stockholders can have any claim to the special favor of the Government. The present corporation has enjoyed its monopoly during the period stipulated in the original contract. If we must have such a corporation, why should not the Government sell out the whole stock and thus secure to the people the full market value of the privileges granted? Why should not Congress create and sell twenty-eight millions of stock, incorporating the purchasers with all the powers and privileges secured in this act and putting the premium upon the sales into the Treasury?

But this act does not permit competition in the purchase of this monopoly. It seems to be predicated on the erroneous idea that the present stockholders have a prescriptive right not only to the favor but to the bounty of the Government. It appears that more than a fourth part of the stock is held by foreigners and the residue is held by a few hundred of our own citizens, chiefly of the richest class....

68

The *Cherokee Phoenix* on Georgia Policy Toward the Cherokee (1832)

Territorial expansion was a key element in Jacksonian ideology. To provide land in the West, it was necessary to extinguish Indian title. Many argued that Native Americans should be removed and resettled west of the Mississippi. Such a policy would provide farmsteads for thousands of white settlers; it would also save America's original inhabitants from the pressures of white American society while providing the tribes the time to accommodate to white culture. The Cherokee, who lived in the southern Appalachians, had already adopted many aspects of Euro-American culture, including similar farming techniques, slavery, a newspaper, a constitution, and evangelical Protestantism. Despite these reforms, land hunger, coupled with gold discoveries led Georgia's political leaders to put increasing pressure on the Cherokee. The issue of Indian removal divided the nation. Jackson's supporters, especially in the South, were eager to remove the Native Americans, while many northern evangelicals and reformers believed the Cherokee provided evidence that nonwhites could adjust to American culture. Excerpted here is an editorial from the Cherokee Phoenix *that analyzes the policies of states' rights governor Wilson Lumpkin.*

Questions to Consider

1. What does Georgia propose for the Cherokee?
2. What does the *Cherokee Phoenix* advocate for the Cherokee?
3. Compare the sentiments expressed in this document with those found in "Cato Petitions for his Freedom" (Document 47). What comparisons can you draw between white views of African Americans and Native Americans?
4. What can you deduce from this document about who could be considered "American" in the 1830s?

… From the message [Governor Lumpkin of Georgia], it can be no longer doubted, that the occupancy of the vacant lands of the Cherokees, by the state of Georgia, will now soon be attempted; we deem it therefore necessary to say a word to the effects of this forcible occupation of our lands, in the event of the non-interference of the federal government. His Excellency ᾿s called the attention of the legislature to the serious deliberation of the condition of the

SOURCE: (New Echota, Cherokee Territory) *Cherokee Phoenix*, 24 November 1832 (n.p.).

Cherokees: Special and appropriate legislation he deems necessary to secure in them their rights of property. If each Indian had five hundred bushels of corn, and the Governor was to take by force four hundred of it, would it not be a mockery of justice to deliberate seriously … to secure what was left? Such an act we have no doubt would be pronounced outrageous and atrocious. But the hardships arising out of the land case are much greater…. Shall we go to Arkansas? But it is said, there no wood is to be found.—Shall we go to Milledgeville [capital of Georgia]? It is said there justice & precepts have parted. The grave deliberations of the legislature recommended by his Excellency will be productive of enormous injustice to the Cherokees, and their endless sufferings. To this confiscation of our property, we will not submit, we would choose to be placed in the silent regions of death, and be gathered to our fathers, than to remain depressed by Georgia oppression.

The Guard of Governor Lumpkin at the Sixes Gold Mine has again spilt Cherokee blood. A Cherokee by the name of Nicojack was discovered digging for gold, when one of the guard fired, and severely wounded the Indian in the arm and leg.—He has nearly recovered.

69

South Carolina Nullifies the Tariff (1832)

During the 1820s, a new system of party alignments changed American politics, while a revolution in market patterns, transportation, and industry transformed the economy. These issues converged in the 1828 "Tariff of Abominations," which raised levies on a variety of foreign goods. A number of southern politicians despised the new tariff's high duties, believing that it favored northern manufacturers at the South's expense. Such sentiments were especially strong in South Carolina, where agricultural depression had eroded the local economy. In response, Vice President John C. Calhoun articulated the theory of nullification in 1828. When Congress failed to lower the tariff in 1832, South Carolina invoked the doctrine. An excerpt from the nullification ordinance follows.

Questions to Consider

1.   What actions is South Carolina taking? Why?

2.   What appears to be South Carolina's view of the relationship of federal and state power?

3. Why does South Carolina seem so fearful of the federal government?

4. Compare the views contained in this document with those found in "Daniel Webster's Second Reply to Robert Y. Hayne" (Document 64). In what ways do they differ?

… We, therefore; the People of the State of South Carolina in Convention assembled, do declare and ordain, and it is hereby declared and ordained, that the several Acts and parts of Acts of the Congress of the United States, purporting to be laws for the imposing of duties and imposts on the importation of foreign commodities, and now having actual operation and effect within the U. States, and more especially an act entitled "an act in alteration of the several acts imposing duties on imports," approved on the nineteenth day of May, one thousand eight hundred and twenty-eight, and also an act entitled "an act to alter and amend the several acts imposing duties on imports," approved on the fourteenth day of July, one thousand eight hundred and thirty-two, are unauthorized by the Constitution of the U. States, and violate the true meaning and intent thereof, and are Null, Void, and no Law, nor binding upon this State, its officers or Citizens; and all promises, contracts, obligations made or entered into or to be made or entered into the purpose to secure the duties imposed by the said acts, and all judicial proceedings which shall be hereafter had in affirmance thereof, are and shall be held utterly Null and Void:

And it is further ordained, That it shall not be lawful for any of the constituted authorities, whether of this State or of the United States, to enforce the payment of duties imposed by the said Acts within the limits of this State; but that it shall be the duty of the legislature to adopt such measures and pass such acts as may be necessary to give full effect to this Ordinance, and to prevent the enforcement and arrest the operation of the said acts and parts of acts of the Congress of the United States, within the limits of this State, from and after the 1st day of February next, and the duty of the other constituted authorities, and of all persons residing or being within the limits of this State and they are hereby required and joined to obey and give effect to this Ordinance and such acts and measures of the Legislature as may be passed or adopted in obedience thereto.…

And we, the People of South Carolina, to the end, that it may be fully understood by the Government of the United States, and the People of the co-States, that we are determined to maintain this, our Ordinance and Declaration, at every hazard, do further declare, that we will not submit to the application of force, on the part of the Federal Government, to reduce this State to obedience; but that we will consider the passage by Congress, of any act, authorizing the employment of a military or naval force against the State of South Carolina, her constituted authorities or citizens; or any act, abolishing or closing the ports of this State, or any of them, or otherwise obstructing the free ingress and egress of vessels, to and from the said ports; or any other act on the part of the Federal Government, to coerce

SOURCE: "An Ordinance to Nullify Certain Acts of Congress of the United States," *Charleston Mercury*, 29 November 1832, p. 2.

the State, shut up her ports, destroy or harrass her commerce, or to enforce the acts hereby declared to be null and void, otherwise than through the civil tribunals of the country, as inconsistent with the longer continuance of South Carolina in the Union: and that the people of this State will thenceforth hold themselves absolved from all further obligation to maintain or preserve their political connexion with the people of the other States, and will forthwith proceed to organize a separate Government, and do all other acts and things, which sovereign and independent States may of right do.

70

Images of Jacksonian Politics

Like Thomas Jefferson, Andrew Jackson's presidency stirred strong political passions. Emerging from humble beginnings, Jackson epitomized the period's growing democratic impulses and adult white males voters' intensifying interest in politics. While many lauded his championing of the common man, others saw a heavy-handed leader who threatened the fabric of government. The following images include cartoonists' depictions of Jackson's stance on the Second Bank of the United States and his style of leadership, as well as George Caleb Bingham's painting The County Election. *A native Virginian, much of Bingham's work focuses on the everyday lives of people in his adopted home of Missouri.*

Questions to Consider

1. How do you think Henry Clay ("The American System," Document 66) would respond to the images *The Downfall of Mother Bank* and *King Andrew I*?

2. Explain which image (*The Downfall of Mother Bank* and *King Andrew I*) best depicts Jackson's presidency?

3. Compare and contrast the two cartoons of Jackson. What does each image reveal about the hopes and fears of Americans during Jackson's presidency?

4. What can you deduce from Bingham's *The County Election* about mid-nineteenth-century racial and gender roles?

5. What can you deduce from *The County Election* about mid-nineteenth-century politics?

The Downfall of Mother Bank

SOURCE: The Library of Congress

King Andrew I

SOURCE: [LC-USZ62-1562]/Library of Congress Prints and Photographs Divison

The County Election

SOURCE: Saint Louis Art Museum, Gift of Bank of America

9

Society and Economy
in the North

The first half of the nineteenth century was characterized by a market revolution that transformed American life. Improvements in transportation, communication, manufacturing, and finance served to integrate disparate segments of the United States economy into an emerging world system. By 1860, the new economy had displaced much of the old. This profound alteration contributed to enormous social change. The North, in particular, was most deeply affected by these changes. Market change brought new arrangements that displaced centuries of social tradition, affecting ideology, class structure, gender roles, and race relations. The documents presented here reveal some of the forces that contributed to this metamorphosis as well as their impact on northern society.

71

Promoting the Erie Canal (1818)

As the United States expanded westward, demands for internal improvements became an increasingly important issue. Congress passed a bill to fund road construction after the War of 1812, but President James Madison vetoed it, arguing that a constitutional amendment would be necessary for such legislation. As a result, internal improvements became the prerogative of the individual states. The most important of these transportation projects was New York's Erie Canal. Championed by Governor De Witt Clinton, the waterway was to connect the Great Lakes with the Atlantic by way of the Mohawk River system. By 1825, the canal had opened and was an immediate success. Charles G. Haines was one of the canal's leading proponents. A native of New Hampshire, the young law student had just begun to serve as private secretary to Governor Clinton when he wrote the following excerpt.

Questions to Consider

1. What does Charles Haines believe that the Erie Canal can do for the nation?
2. What advantages will the canal bring to the Great Lakes region and upstate New York?
3. According to Haines, in what ways will New York City will be affected?
4. How accurate is Haines in assessing the positive impact of the canal on New York?

... The people of this state early perceived the benefits of Internal Trade, and previous to the late war with England, the GRAND CANAL from the Hudson to Lake Erie was contemplated. Such an undertaking was alone suitable to a state of peace. It was accordingly postponed to that period when more favorable auspices should await its prosecution. That period arrived, when DE WITT CLINTON was unanimously called to the chief magistracy of the state. The eyes of the people were fixed upon him, with an expectation that the Great Western Canal would be vigorously prosecuted to its final completion. The work will be prosecuted and triumphantly finished....

The length of the canal, from the Hudson to the Lakes, is calculated at three hundred and fifty-three miles, according to the report of the commissioners appointed by the New-York Legislature, on the 17th April, 1816. They observed, that in their opinion, "the dimensions of the Western or Erie Canal

SOURCE: Charles G. Haines, *Considerations on the Great Western Canal, from the Hudson to Lake Erie* (Brooklyn, NY, 1818), 4–5, 7–12, 28.

and Locks, should be as follows, viz.:—width on the water surface, forty feet; at the bottom, twenty-eight feet, and depth of water, four feet; the length of a lock ninety feet, and its width, twelve feet in the clear. Vessels carrying one hundred tons may navigate a canal of this size—and all the lumber produced in the country, and required for the market, may be transported upon it." The aggregate rise and fall is in feet 661 35, and the elevation of Lake Erie above the Hudson, is calculated to be in feet 564 85.—The number of locks will be seventy-seven. The canal has been divided into three great sections. The western section reaches from Lake Erie to Seneca River; the middle section leads from Seneca River to Rome, and the eastern, from Rome to Hudson....

We have before taken a view of the principal advantages that must result to our union, and to our republican institutions, by attaching the various sections of the country more immediately together, by means of internal communication. Our Great canal, in this respect, will produce a train of exclusive and permanent benefits, which could not, from local causes, pertain to any similar undertakings within the scope of ourselves or of the nation. When you connect the Hudson with the Lakes, by such a communication, you virtually place the Atlantic seaboard and the great western interior by the side of each other. From the ocean, you can pass through this whole chain of inland seas, navigable to vessels of the largest burthen. Nor should we stop here—New-York and New-Orleans could be brought, in point of intercourse, near each other. At trifling expense, and with no great effort of labor, you could open a communication by water, through which a vast commerce could be carried on from Lake Michigan to the Illinois River, which empties into the Mississippi above St. Louis, and traverses nearly the whole extent of that rising and fertile territory, which will soon be admitted as a state among the other sisters of the union. Even in high waters, there is now a navigation for small craft, between the waters of the Illinois and the southern extremity of Lake Michigan through Chenango Creek....

Pause for a moment, and consider the mighty population which will yet cluster on the shores of this chain of Lakes, and the unnumbered streams which roll their tributary bounties into their bosoms! The great western world which reposes upon their wide-stretched shores, needs no description of ours, to enhance its value in the estimation of the American people. It will yet contain a population, unequalled by any in the world for industry, enterprize and independence; a population bound together by those ties of union and interest, created and fortified by a grand system of internal improvements, of which the Great western canal will be the bulwark. In the animating spectacle here presented in perspective, we see a great republican community, cemented by the strongest considerations that ever influenced a political body—assimilated in manners, laws, sentiments and maxims, with their eyes fixed on their connection with the seaboard, as the life and support of their prosperity and happiness.—Yes, in this noble race of citizens, we see the cradle of liberty, laws, and the arts; we see the hallowed light of our liberal institutions beaming in its native purity, blended with the mild lustre of virtue, magnanimity and intelligence....

While referring to the advantages resulting to the nation, and to the state, from the Western Canal, we ought not to forget its effects on the prosperity of our own city. New-York is now, and ever must be, the great depot of that vast trade circulating between the country bordering on the Lakes, and the Atlantic seaboard. Would the increase of this trade to ten times its present extent be of no consequence to her interests? Does New-York forget that she is yet to contend with New-Orleans, for the character of the first commercial city of the new world? We shall not here draw a comparison between the natural advantages of the two places; but we do say, that without the Western Canal, the competition will be fearful, before the lapse of half a century. It is by drawing to her control the trade of the west and the north; it is by aiding the State Government, in every liberal undertaking, for the promotion of internal commerce, that New-York is to stand, without a rival on this side [of] the ocean. The Canal will render her a commercial emporium, second to none on the globe. It will pour into her bosom a tide of commerce, which must leave its bounties by the way, to enrich and adorn, like the floods of the Nile. In trade, in wealth, and in arts, it will render her the London of America....

72

Differing Views of a Changing Society (1827, 1836)

The Market Revolution that swept over many parts of the nation in the first half of the nineteenth century brought dramatic changes to American society. In the eighteenth century, most Americans lived in tiny rural communities where they produced most goods for home or local consumption. However, changes in transportation, communication, finance, and manufacturing pulled many immigrants and rural Americans into a system of exchange that enabled them to produce goods for distant markets. The effects of such change varied greatly. The first image is of the notorious Five Points slum on the lower east side of Manhattan. The area became the home to New York's poorest laborers, many of whom were recent immigrants from Ireland. The second image offers a very different interpretation of the market revolution. The town shown here, Lockport, New York, resulted from the best-known transportation improvement of the era, the Erie Canal.

Questions to Consider

1. Based on your examination of these images, was the Market Revolution a positive or negative development?

2. Does Catlin's depiction of Five Points seem realistic? Why?

3. What conclusions can be drawn about the Erie Canal's impact from "View of the Upper Village of Lockport, Niagara Co., NY"?

4. Does the image of Lockport seem realistic?

10. The Five Points, Junction of Baxter, Worth and Park Sts., New York, N. Y., c. 1829. [11]

George Catlin, *Five Points*

SOURCE: The Five Points, Junction of Baxter, Worth and Park Streets, New York, c.1829 (litho) by American School, (19th century) Private Collection/ Peter Newark Western Americana/ The Bridgeman Art Library Nationality / copyright status: American / out of copyright

VIEW OF THE UPPER VILLAGE OF LOCKPORT NIAGARA CO. N.Y.

From above the Race showing the ten combined locks on the Erie Canal.

View of the Upper Village of Lockport, Niagara Co., NY

SOURCE: [LC-USZ62-49239]/Library of Congress Prints and Photographs Division

73

Charles G. Finney Describes the Rochester Revival (1830–1831)

The Second Great Awakening was one of the most important cultural movements of the early nineteenth century. The waves of emotionally charged religious reform were so intense that upstate New York became known as the "Burned-Over District." One of the most "Burned-Over" areas was Rochester, New York. Located on Lake Ontario, Rochester had been a frontier village before the completion of the Erie Canal. The waterway brought access to distant markets and immediately transformed the community into one of America's most dynamic cities. But rapid change brought community stress, as hordes of newcomers sought a niche in a community with no firmly established structures. Charles Grandison Finney's visit in 1830 would change all of that. A religious experience caused him to leave the legal profession in 1821; and by the mid-1820s, his vivid sermons demanded that sinners in the audience repent or face eternal damnation. In his memoirs, excerpted here, Finney describes the techniques he used to win converts.

Questions to Consider

1. What is the author's perspective toward Rochester and its need for conversion?

2. Why does Charles G. Finney seem so eager to convert Rochester's leading citizens?

3. How did the author make use of social pressure to gain converts?

4. Compare and contrast the portrayal of religion found in this document with that contained in "Description of a Conversion Experience at Cane Ridge, Kentucky" (Document 52). How do you account for the differences?

... I had never, I believe, except in rare instances, until I went to Rochester, used as a means of promoting revivals, what has since been called "the anxious seat." I had sometimes asked persons in the congregation to stand up; but this I had not frequently done. However, in studying upon the subject, I had often felt the necessity of some measure that would bring sinners to a stand. From my own experience and observation I had found, that with the higher classes especially,

SOURCE: *Memoirs of Rev. Charles G. Finney* (New York, 1876), 288–90.

the greatest obstacle to be overcome was their fear of being known as anxious inquirers. They were too proud to take any position that would reveal them to others as anxious for their souls.

I had found also that something was needed, to make the impression on them that they were expected at once to give up their hearts; something that would call them to act, and act as publicly before the world, as they had in their sins; something that would commit them publicly to the service of Christ. When I had called them simply to stand up in the public congregation, I found that this had a very good effect; and so far as it went, it answered the purpose for which it was intended. But after all, I had felt for some time, that something more was necessary to bring them out from among the mass of the ungodly, to a public renunciation of their sinful ways, and a public committal of themselves to God.

At Rochester, if I recollect right, I first introduced this measure…. I made a call, I think for the first time, upon all that class of persons whose convictions were so ripe that they were willing to renounce their sins and give themselves to God, to come forward to certain seats which I requested to be vacated, and offer themselves up to God, while we made them subjects of prayer. A much larger number came forward than I expected, and among them was another prominent lady; and several others of her acquaintance, and belonging to the same circle of society, came forward. This increased the interest among that class of people; and it was soon seen that the Lord was aiming at the conversion of the highest classes of society. My meetings soon became thronged with that class. The Lawyers, physicians, merchants, and indeed all the most intelligent people, became more and more interested, and more and more easily influenced.

Very soon the work took effect, extensively, among the lawyers in that city. There has always been a large number of the leading lawyers of the state, resident at Rochester. The work soon got hold of numbers of these. They became very anxious, and came freely to our meetings of inquiry; and numbers of them came forward to the anxious seat, as it has since been called, and publicly gave their hearts to God.…

This revival made a great change in the moral state and subsequent history of Rochester. The great majority of the leading men and women in the city, were converted.

74

American Mania for Railroads (1834)

The invention of the railroad was one of the most significant transportation developments in human history. A primary symbol of the Industrial Revolution, the locomotive freed people from their reliance on water transportation while expediting long-distance movement. In this selection from Society, Manners and Politics in the United States, *Michel Chevalier, a French visitor who toured the United States from 1833 to 1835, observed some of the United States' earliest rail projects. Chevalier's interest in America and its railroads grew out of his belief that America held the key to understanding the future. He argued that the nation's "most visible emblem" was the locomotive. The developing rail network that attracted Chevalier's attention did indeed herald the American future as it shifted patterns of trade, and accelerated regional economic specialization, particularly in the pre–Civil War North.*

Questions to Consider

1. Why is Michel Chevalier so enthusiastic about railroad development in the United States?

2. What are some problems with the Boston to New Orleans route Chevalier described?

3. Compare and contrast the views expressed in this document with those contained in Haines's "Promoting the Erie Canal" (Document 71). Why are internal improvements so important to America?

4. What does the support for internal improvements say about antebellum America?

... The distance from Boston to New Orleans is 1600 miles, or twice the distance from Havre to Marseilles. It is highly probable, that within a few years this immense line will be covered by a series of railroads stretching from bay to bay, from river to river, and offering to the ever-impatient Americans the service of their rapid cars at the points where the steamboats leave their passengers. This is not a castle in the air, like so many of those grand schemes which are projected amidst the fogs of the Seine, the Loire, and the Garonne; it is already half completed. The railroad from Boston to Providence is in active progress; the work goes on a l'Americaine, that is to say, rapidly. From New York to Philadelphia,

SOURCE: Michel Chevalier, *Society, Manners and Politics in the United States*, trans. from 3rd ed. by Thomas G. Bradford (Boston, 1839), 83–87.

there will soon be not only one open to travel, but two in competition with each other, the one on the right, the other on the left bank of the Delaware; the passage between the two cities will be made in seven hours, five hours on the railroad, and two in the steamboat, in the beautiful Hudson and the magnificent Bay of New York, which the Americans, who are not afflicted by modesty, compare with the Bay of Naples. From Philadelphia, travellers go to Baltimore by the Delaware and Chesapeake, and by the Newcastle and Frenchtown railroad, in eight hours; from Baltimore to Washington, a railroad has been resolved upon, a company chartered, the shares taken, and the work begun, all within the space of a few months. Between Washington and Blakely, in North Carolina, 60 miles of railroad are completed, from Blakely northwards. A company has just been chartered to complete the remaining space, that is, from Richmond to the Potomac, a distance of 70 miles, and the Potomac bears you to the Federal city by Mt. Vernon, a delightful spot, the patrimony of George Washington, where he passed his honored old age, and where his body now reposes in a modest tomb. Between Washington and Blakely, those who prefer the steamboats, may take another route; by descending the Chesapeake to Norfolk, they will find another railroad, 70 miles in length, of which two thirds are now finished, and which carries them to Blakely, and even beyond. Blakely is a new town, which you will not find on any map, born of yesterday; it is the eldest, and as yet the only daughter of the Petersburg and Blakely railroad. From Blakely to Charleston the distance is great, but the Americans are enterprising, and there is no region in the world in which railroads can be constructed so easily and so cheaply; the surface has been graded by nature, and the vast forests which cover it, will furnish the wood of which the railroad will be made; for here most of these works have a wooden superstructure. From Charleston, a railroad 137 miles in length, as yet the longest in the world, extends to Augusta, whence to Montgomery, Alabama, there is a long interval to be supplied. From this last town steamboats descend the River Alabama to Mobile, and those who do not wish to pay their respects to the Gulf of Mexico, on their way to New Orleans, will soon find a railroad which will spare them the necessity of offering this act of homage to the memory of the great Cortez.

Within ten years this whole line will be completed, and traversed by locomotive engines, provided the present crisis terminates promptly and happily, as I hope it will. Ten years is a long time in these days, and a plan, whose execution requires ten years, seems like a romance or a dream. But in respect to railroads, the Americans have already something to show. Pennsylvania, which by the last census, in 1830, contained only 1,348,000 inhabitants, has 325 miles of railroads actually completed, or which will be so within the year, without reckoning 76 miles which the capitalists of Philadelphia have constructed in the little States of New Jersey and Delaware. The total length of all the railroads in France is 95 miles, that is, a little more than what the citizens of Philadelphia, in their liberality, have given to their poor neighbors. In the State of New York, whose population is the most adventurous and the most successful in their speculations, there are at present only four or five short railroads, but if the sixth part of those which are projected and authorized by the legislature, are executed,

New York will not be behind Pennsylvania in this respect. The merchants of Baltimore, which at the time of the Declaration of Independence contained 6,000 inhabitants, and which now numbers 100,000, have taken it into their heads to make a railroad between their city and the Ohio, a distance of above 300 miles. They have begun it with great spirit, and have now finished about one third of the whole road. In almost every section east of the Ohio and the Mississippi, there are railroads projected, in progress, or completed, and on most of them locomotive steam-engines are employed. There are some in the Alleghenies, whose inclined planes are really terrific, from their great inclination; these were originally designed only for the transportation of goods, but passenger-cars have been set up on them, at the risk of breaking the necks of travellers....

75

"Americans on the Move" (1835)

Numerous foreign travelers, eager to report on the progress of the American experiment, came to the United States during the antebellum period. None of these visitors has become better known for his sage observations of 1830s America than has French nobleman Alexis de Tocqueville. Tocqueville came to America with his associate, M. Gustave de Beaumont, in 1831 to study American prisons; the men remained until the following year. During his short stay, Tocqueville had the opportunity to travel extensively and meet with luminaries such as Albert Gallatin and Edward Livingston. His observations of the young nation gained great notoriety in both Europe and the United States. In Democracy in America, *Tocqueville described a people who, despite their differences, shared strong religious values; believed in their nation's special mission; and, most noticeably, were fervently egalitarian. In this selection, Tocqueville describes Americans as "venturous conservatives" engaged in a restless quest to make money.*

Questions to Consider

1. Why are Americans in "constant motion"?
2. How would Tocqueville describe the typical American?
3. Why does he believe Americans are eager to make money?
4. Does Tocqueville's description of Americans seem consistent with the description found in Crèvecouer's "What Is an American?" (Document 25)?

Does it seem consistent with traits described by Frances Trollope in "Commentary on Elections in Jacksonian America" (Document 65)?

Nothing tends to materialize man, and to deprive his work of the faintest trace of mind, more than extreme division of labor. In a country like America, where men devoted to special occupations are rare, a long apprenticeship cannot be required from anyone who embraces a profession. The Americans, therefore, change their means of gauging a livelihood very readily; and they suit their occupations to the exigencies of the moment, in the manner most profitable to themselves. Men are to be met with who have successively been barristers, farmers, merchants, ministers of the gospel, and physicians. If the American be less perfect in each craft than the European, at least there is scarcely any trade with which he is utterly unacquainted. His capacity is more general, and the circle of his intelligence is enlarged.

The inhabitants of the United States are never fettered by the axioms of their profession; they escape from all the prejudices of their present station; they are not more attached to one line of operation than to another; they are not more prone to employ an old method than a new one; they have no rooted habits, and they easily shake off the influence which the habits of other nations might exercise upon their minds from conviction that their country is unlike any other, and that its situation is without a precedent in the world. America is a land of wonders, in which everything is in constant motion, and every movement seems an improvement. The idea of novelty is there indissolubly connected with the idea of amelioration. No natural boundary seems to be set to the efforts of man: and what is not yet done is only what he has not yet attempted to do.

This perpetual change which goes on in the United States, these frequent vicissitudes of fortune, accompanied by such unforeseen fluctuations in private and in public wealth, serve to keep the minds of citizens in a perpetual state of feverish agitation, which admirably invigorates their exertions, and keeps them in a state of excitement above the ordinary level of mankind. The whole life of an American is passed like a game of chance, a revolutionary crisis, or a battle. As the same causes are continually in operation throughout the country, they ultimately impart an irresistible impulse to the national character. The American, taken as a chance specimen of his countrymen, must then be a man of singular warmth in his desires; enterprising, fond of adventure, and above all, of innovation. The same bent is manifest in all that he does; he introduces it into his political laws, his religious doctrines, his theories of social economy, and his domestic occupations; he bears it with him in the depths of the backwoods, as well as in the business of the city. It is this same passion, applied to maritime commerce, which makes him the cheapest and the quickest trader in the world.

As long as the sailors of the United States retain these inspiriting advantages, and the practical superiority which they derive from them, they will not only continue to supply the wants of the producers and consumers of their own country, but they will tend more and more to become, like the English, the

SOURCE: Alexis de Tocqueville, *Democracy in America*, trans. Henry Reeve (New York, 1900), 1: 432–34.

factors of all other peoples. This prediction has already begun to be realized; we perceive that the American traders are introducing themselves as intermediate agents in the commerce of several European nations; and America will offer a still wider field to their enterprise....

It is unquestionable that the Americans of the North will one day supply the wants of the Americans of the South. Nature has placed them in contiguity, and has furnished the former with every means of establishing a permanent connection with those States, and of gradually filling their markets. The merchants of the United States could only forfeit these natural advantages if he were very inferior to the merchant of Europe; to whom he is, on the contrary, superior in several respects. The Americans of the United States already exercise a very considerable moral influence upon all the peoples of the New World. They are the source of intelligence, and all the nations which inhabit the same continent are already accustomed to consider them as the most enlightened, the most powerful, and the most wealthy members of the great American family. All eyes are therefore turned towards the Union; and the States of which the body is composed are the models which the other communities try to imitate to the best of their power; it is from the United States that they borrow their political principles and their laws....

76

A Petition to Integrate the Schools (1842)

The absence of slavery in the North did not mean that African Americans living there experienced anything close to full citizenship. Only about one-third of American states allowed free black men to vote; although most northern states allowed for rights of expression and assembly, the threat of mob violence often circumscribed the assertion of African American rights. Nantucket Island offered something of a haven to free blacks. A part of Massachusetts, one of the more progressive states on race relations, the African American community included a number of small businesses as well as close ties to the local Quaker community. Here, the island's African Americans protest the separate-but-equal educational practices. Economic boycotts and moral suasion would ultimately lead to the integration of Nantucket schools in 1847.

Questions to Consider

1. What principles do the "Colored Inhabitants" cite as reasons for an integrated school system?

2. Why would the creator of the image "Types of Mankind" found in Document 85 ("Mid-Nineteenth Century Images of Race and Nation") disagree with this address?

3. What can you deduce from this document about Nantucket's views of American identity?

4. Compare the sentiments of this document with those expressed in *Brown* v. *Board of Education*. What similarities do you note? Differences?

Transcript of an Address by the Colored Inhabitants of Nantucket in the Inquirer of March 05, 1842

Having availed ourselves of the opportunity of witnessing your proceedings at the Town Hall, a short time ago, we were forcibly struck by the matter which was then the subject of your deliberations, and on which you were called to act. It will not be necessary for us to say anything in relation to the power of the School Committee, nor of the duty which necessarily devolves upon them, by virtue of their being a School Committee—the agents of the whole community—to attend to the department of what is called "Common School Education," and to see that the law in reference to their charge is carried out. ... In bringing the subject of our claim before our fellow citizens, we wish, by no means, to convey the idea that they have inflicted a recent wound on us, as an oppressed portion of the citizens of this town, but a wound of some years standing, the sensation of which, if it be chafed, is apt to become keen. We look upon ourselves, and we feel as an INJURED PORTION of this community, and injured indeed in such a way that no member of this Commonwealth can possibly be benefitted by it.... We have a code of laws, which are supposed to be agreeable with the spirit of the Constitution in general. Having made the above remarks, we now take for granted that the Constitution and laws of this Commonwealth make no distinction among its citizens on account of complexion or symmetry. If this be acknowledged, then we infer that the Constitution and law of this State recognize the equality of its citizens in respect to rights. — Again, whatever system may be formed or arrangements made for the benefit of the members of this Commonwealth, let it be the Common School system, or any other system by which its inhabitants may be benefitted or improved, the inference is, that all are to enjoy the advantages to be derived from them on equal terms, in the same manner, and in the same amount. This inference, we presume our citizens will acknowledge to be reasonable and just, unless any one will attempt to show that God created man with as great a variety of rights as there are distinctions of color and form, and that society has a right to proportion the privileges of its members upon such considerations. This assumption is so big with absurdity that it needs no argument to make its inconsistency apparent.

SOURCE: "Transcript of an address by the Colored Inhabitants of Nantucket," *Nantucket Inquirer*, 5 March 1842.

Again, the town school privileges of us who are called the colored portion of the citizens, as members of this society, and as far as Constitution and Law are concerned, are identical with those of citizens in general, because there is no proscriptive act that we know of to prevent the colored citizens enjoying the Common School system of education, in the same manner, and in the same amount, that it is enjoyed by our more favored fellow citizens. —But do we enjoy it because it is lawful that we should? While our more favored fellow citizens have all the facilities of obtaining a good education in a graduation of Schools, viz. Infant, Primary, Grammar, High School. &c., with every advantage that is calculated to inspire the youthful mind with aspirations to excel; in a word, while they enjoy every benefit that the Common School system holds out, while we are all rejected, and that contrary to our laws, because it has pleased the good Creator to make our complexions differ from those of others of our fellow citizens. If this be the ground of our exclusion, as we have stated, and we think that our statement is undeniable, then we will most respectfully, ask this intelligent and Christian community who know this is to be the ground of our exclusion, is it right, is it just? But it will be asked, Have you not got a School to which you can send your children? To which we answer, we are weary of this kind of honor of distinction; we want no exclusive school privileges; we are citizens of this great republic; our veins are full of republican blood; we contend not for, neither do we desire, any rights or privileges that are not common to the rest of the members of this community.... we are all, irrespective of complexional difference, entitled to the same privileges, and to the same amount of education which our common school system holds out to the rest of our fellow citizens, and that it is in the highest degree improbable, that the colored children can obtain that amount of education which our common school system is designed to furnish; and for the accomplishment of which system of education, you have needed several gradations to which the colored children are denied access, on the ground, as we understand it, that God has made their skins rather browner that the morbid state of public opinion can very well bear! We might here multiply words, but in whatever light the subject be viewed, when we reflect that we are by the Constitution and laws acknowledged to be citizens, and consequently entitled to all the rights and privileges in common with other citizens, and then that for a mere accident, the difference of complexion, we are denied the right or privilege of education in common with our fellow citizens; we must pronounce it to be unkind, unjust. Again, it is said that some of the colored citizens do not wish to enjoy equal privileges of education with their lighter complexioned brethren. Granted; let it be so, and then what will this prove? Will it prove that rights and privileges go by the hundred? We mean such rights and privileges as we have been speaking of. —Is the common school privilege, a privilege which, before it can be enjoyed by any citizen, he must necessarily go around and pray every family or parent to agree with him, before he can offer his claim; or is it a right that belongs to every citizen in particular, separate and apart from whatever course his neighbor may see fit to pursue? ... We here submit these remarks to the inhabitants of the town of Nantucket, hoping that the day is not far distant, when the good sense and christianity of this republic will proceed to make its distinctions in Society on just and reasonable grounds, and not according to the color of the skin....

77

Women Workers Protest "Lowell Wage Slavery" (1847)

In 1822, the Boston Associates created a cotton mill complex at the falls of the Merrimack River in northeastern Massachusetts; they named the village Lowell. The mills soon attracted labor from nearby rural New England, and most of these workers were young women. Although some of the women came to Lowell to escape rural boredom, more worked in the mills because of declining economic opportunities in the countryside. Lowell's founders sought to avoid the excesses of British industrial towns by providing educational and cultural opportunities for their workers. As such, Lowell was part finishing school and part industrial employer. Countless visitors came to marvel at the idyllic industrial village. The following account, however, reveals another side of the Lowell experience.

Questions to Consider

1. What is the difference between the "romance" and the "reality" for the "Lowell girls"?
2. Why are the factory girls unable to appreciate lectures and the books that are available?
3. In what ways does this article characterize the effects of working in Lowell?
4. How do you suppose Charles Haines ("Promoting the Erie Canal," Document 71) would respond to this document?

Aristocratic strangers, in broad cloths and silks, with their imaginations excited by the wonderful stories—romances of Factory Life—which they have heard, have paid hasty visits to Lowell, or Manchester, and have gone away to praise, in prose and verse, the beauty of our "Factory Queens," and the comfort, elegance and almost perfection, of the arrangements by which the very fatherly care of Agents, Superintendents, Overseers, &c., has surrounded them. To these nice

SOURCE: "Factory Life—Romance and Reality," (Boston) *Voice of Industry*, 3 December 1847, p. 2.

visitors everything in and around a Lowell Cotton Mill is bathed in an atmosphere of rose-colored light....

These lovers of the Romance of Labor—they don't like the reality very well—see not the pale and emaciated ones. They see not those who wear Consumption's hectic flush. They think little of the weariness and pain of those fair forms, as they stand there, at the loom and spindle, thirteen long hours, each day! They know not how long these hours of toil seem to them, as they look out upon the fields, and hills, and woods, which lie beyond the Merrimack, steeped in golden sunlight and radiant with beauty.... Six days shalt thou labor and do all thy work, and on the seventh thou shalt go to church, is the Commandment as improved by the mammon worshiping Christianity of modern Civilization. The factory girl is required to go to meeting on Sunday, where long, and too often unmeaning, word-prayers are repeated, and dull prosey sermons "delivered," and where God is worshiped, according to law, by pious Agents and Overseers, while the poor Irishman is blasting rocks for them in the Corporation's canal, that the mills may not be stopped on Monday.

There are lectures of various kinds, some of them free, and others requiring only a trifling fee to secure admission, to all who wish it. Then there are also libraries of well selected books, to which all can have access.

Those who recollect the fable of Tantalus in the old Mythology, will be able to appreciate the position of a large portion of the population with respect to these exalted privileges.... The unremitted toil of thirteen long hours, drains off the vital energy and unfits for study or reflection. They need amusement, relaxation, rest, and not mental exertion of any kind. A really sound and instructive lecture cannot, under such circumstances, be appreciated, and the lecturer fails, to a great extent, in making an impression.—"Jim Crow" performances are much better patronized than scientific lectures, and the trashy, milk-and-water sentimentalities of the *Lady's Book* and *Olive Branch,* are more read than the works of Gibbon, or Goldsmith, or Bancroft.

If each factory girl could suspend her labors in the Mill for a few months each year, for the purpose of availing herself of the advantages for intellectual culture by which she is surrounded, much good might be derived.... But day by day they feel their over-tasked systems give way.—A dizziness in the head or a pain in the side, or the shoulders or the back, admonishes them to return to their country homes before it is too late. But too often these friendly monitions are unheeded. They resolve to toil a little longer.—But nature cannot be cheated, and the poor victim of a false system of Industrial Oppression is carried home—to die.... There are now in our very midst hundreds of these loving, self-sacrificing martyr-spirits. They will die unhonored and unsung, but not unwept; for the poor factory girl has a home and loved ones, and dark will be that home, and sad those loved ones when the light of her smile shines on them no more.

78

"On Irish Emigration" (1852)

The economic transformation of antebellum America brought sweeping demographic changes as well. The demands of early industrialism created a huge need for unskilled labor, and it was often filled by immigrants. The majority who arrived before 1850 came from Ireland, their numbers further swelled by the potato famine of 1845–1848. The enormous quantity of immigrants who poured into America elicited a variety of responses, ranging from nativism to the creation of an immigration bureaucracy to process the newly arrived. In the following account, Edward Everett Hale discusses this bureaucracy. Hale, a Unitarian minister, was a frequent contributor to local newspapers who espoused a "New Civilization" that envisioned an improvement of all human relationships. Hale's original letters first appeared in the Boston Daily Advertiser, *a newspaper edited by his father, and later were reprinted as* Letters on Irish Emigration.

Questions to Consider

1. Why are shippers so interested in transporting Irish immigrants to America?

2. Why were immigrants examined?

3. What can you deduce from this selection about the U.S. economy?

4. Compare and contrast the views of Irishmen contained in this document with those found in George Catlin's *Five Points* (Document 72). How do you account for the similarities? Differences?

… The competition between different lines of packets and different shipping houses, had been enough to scatter through the most barbarous parts of Ireland full information as to the means of passage to America. The most remote villages receive the advertisements of different lines, just as we find in our most remote villages the inducements which the same lines scatter to Irishmen to send out remittances and passage tickets for their friends.

The correspondence from this country carries a great deal of detailed information, and at present it is the principal means of supply for the expenses of the voyage. An emigrant who has succeeded here, sends out for his friends, and sends money enough to bring them. Or, which amounts to the same thing, he buys here passage tickets which he sends to them.…

SOURCE: Edward E. Hale, *Letters on Irish Emigration* (Boston, 1852), 6–10, 24–26. Published letters in the *Boston Daily Advertiser*.

The importance of this business to ship owners will readily be seen. Ships of large accommodations for freighting, which carry out our bulky raw produce, and bring back the more condensed manufactures of England, have just the room to spare, which is made into accommodations for these passengers. In Mr. Robert B. Minturn's testimony before the "Lords' Committee" June 20, 1848, he says that the amounts paid for the passage of emigrants go very far towards paying the expense of voyages of ships from America to Europe and back.

By far the larger number of these emigrants collect at Liverpool therefore,— the large commerce of the port offering all the facilities for the cheapest passage. Of 223,078 who sailed from the United Kingdom to the United States in 1850, 165,828 were from Liverpool, 31,297 were from Irish ports, and 11,448 from Scotch ports. The ease of passage from Ireland to Liverpool carries most of the Irish emigration that way. The English Commissioners suppose that almost all the Liverpool emigration is Irish; certainly much more than nine-tenths of it. Our own returns at New York confirm this supposition.

Vessels engaged in this trade, are now subject to a double inspection. In Great Britain they are examined by English Officers, that it may be known that they comply with the British statute,—and here, that they may comply with ours. The experience of the awful suffering of emigrants in 1847, when of 90,000 who embarked for Canada in British vessels, 15,000 died on the way, or after arrival, called the attention of the English Government to the necessity of a more stringent law for passenger vessels....

THREE-FOURTHS at least of the emigrants arriving in this country land at the port of New York.... the subsequent inspection, though rapid, is complete enough to prevent much danger of deception. The Captain is bound to report, within twenty-four hours of his arrival, to the Mayor of the city, the number of his passengers who are citizens, and the number who, being foreigners, have never been bonded, their place of birth, last residence, age, name and occupation. He shows this report to the Health officer. The officer then questions him and the ship's physician as to the health of the passengers, whether any of them are lunatic, idiot, deaf, dumb, blind or infirm, if so whether they are accompanied by relatives who can take care of them; and again with regard to the deaths on the passage. All these particulars the Captain is bound to specify in his report to the Mayor, and if he fail to specify them correctly, the Commissioners of emigration on the report of their Health Officer would prosecute him for the penalty provided. Such penalties, when recovered, are a part of their available funds.

While the Health Officer obtains the details of the Captain's report, the emigrants are mustered on deck for his personal examination. He then goes below with his men,—examines the emigrant decks, that he may see those who are not well enough to go on deck,—and satisfy himself that no persons are concealed on board, so far as such an examination will satisfy him. This visit enables him to observe, in a measure, whether the United States statute regarding the treatment of emigrants on board any vessel has been violated. This statute applies to all vessels arriving here; the examination made in England having been made, of course, with reference to the provisions of the English laws. Any violation of the American statute would be reported by the Emigrant Commissioners to the United States Attorney.

This examination finished, he goes on deck, with his men, to inspect those reported as in health who are assembled there. You know that in some instances there have been more than a thousand on a single vessel. The inspection is rapid indeed. A rope is drawn across the vessel, leaving a passage between the Health Officer and one of his boatmen, wide enough for one emigrant at a time to pass through. They pass quickly through, from the throng where they are assembled, and are counted as they go. If the quick eye of the Health Officer detects a blind, deaf, dumb or idiotic person,—or one who has any aspect of sickness, he stops him, questions him,—and if he do not pass such questioning satisfactorily, he is reported. The main object of this personal examination, however, with that made below, is to obtain evidence that the ship has not brought more than the number of passengers allowed by law.

At this same visit the Health Officer and his men distribute among the emigrants papers of simple advice, which are prepared by the Commissioners in different languages.

If, now, among those ascertained to be sick, there are any suffering under diseases classed as contagious, they are landed at the Quarantine Hospital. The whole vessel and passengers, of course, are subjected to the Quarantine arrangements of the Port. If there be other sick passengers, unable to provide for themselves, the Commissioners of emigration are at once notified of the fact, and on the arrival of the vessel at New York, these persons are removed to the emigrant hospital at Ward's Island, of which I shall speak hereafter....

10

Social Reform

The economic and social changes that swept antebellum America were accompanied by a reform crusade that sought to morally revitalize the republic. Influenced by such diverse elements as the Second Great Awakening, republican ideas of liberty, and the perceived decline of revolutionary values, reformers strove to perfect American society and institutions. Though reformers could be found throughout America, the movement was centered in the northern states. There, a small but vocal minority agitated for an end to slavery, expanded political rights for women, reform of the penal system, and free public education to the masses, often in the face of a hostile audience. The following documents illustrate some of the reformers', and their opponents', methods and goals.

79

"Appeal to the Coloured Citizens of the World" (1829)

West Indian and southern slave insurrections of the late eighteenth and early nineteenth centuries made clear that large numbers of African Americans resisted their position. The following document contains a selection from Walker's Appeal ... to the Coloured Citizens of the World. *Author David Walker, a free black born in North Carolina, had traveled widely in the South and was well read, especially in the classics. In 1827 he left the South to settle in Boston, where he opened a clothing business and became active in the Massachusetts General Colored Association. In 1829 he produced this antislavery pamphlet. The* Appeal *not only refuted widely held myths of the happy slave and the ignorant African American, but it demanded that African Americans respond to their oppression. Walker's appeal alarmed many in both North and South; the state legislatures of Georgia, Virginia, and North Carolina held secret sessions to consider the pamphlet, while Boston mayor Harrison Gray Otis condemned Walker's views. Walker's work, which he reissued shortly before his mysterious death in 1830, prompted northern abolitionists to adopt a more aggressive stance against slavery.*

Questions to Consider

1. How does David Walker describe slavery?
2. What is Walker's appeal to slaves?
3. How do Walker's views differ from those of his white contemporaries?
4. Compare and contrast the views contained in this document with those expressed in "Mexican View of U.S. Occupation" (Document 89). What conclusions can you draw concerning mid-nineteenth-century white Americans' views toward people of other races and cultures?

... [A]ll the inhabitants of the earth, (except, however, the sons of Africa) are called men, and of course are, and ought to be free. But we, (colored people) and our children are brutes!! and of course are, and ought to be SLAVES to the American people and their children forever!! to dig their mines and work their farms; and thus go on enriching them, from one generation to another with our blood and our tears!!!!

SOURCE: David Walker, *Walker's Appeal, in Four Articles: Together with a Preamble to Coloured Citizens of the World* (Boston, 1830), 11–87.

... we, (colored people of these United States of America) are the most wretched, degraded and abject set of beings that ever lived since the world began, and that the white Americans having reduced us to the wretched state of slavery, treat us in that condition more cruel (they being an enlightened and Christian people,) than any heathen nation did any people whom it had reduced to our condition. These affirmations are so well confirmed in the minds of all unprejudiced men, who have taken the trouble to read histories, that they need no elucidation from me....

Do they not institute laws to prohibit us from marrying among the whites? I would wish, candidly, however, before the Lord, to be understood, that I would not give a pinch of snuff to be married to any white person I ever saw in all the days of my life. And I do say it, that the black man, or man of color, who will leave his own color (provided he can get one, who is good for any thing) and marry a white woman, to be a double slave to her, just because she is white, ought to be treated by her as he surely will be....

... show me a page of history, either sacred or profane, on which a verse can be found, which maintains, that the Egyptians heaped the insupportable insult upon the children of Israel, by telling them that they were not of the human family. Can the whites deny the charge? Have they not, after having reduced us to the deplorable condition of slaves under their feet, held us as descending originally from the tribes of Monkeys or Orangutans? ... So far, my brethren, were the Egyptians from heaping those insults upon their slaves, that the Pharaoh's daughter took Moses, a son of Israel for her own....

They think because they hold us in their infernal chains of slavery, that we wish to be white, or of their color—but they are dreadfully deceived—we wish to be just as it pleased our Creator to have made us, and no avaricious and unmerciful wretches, have any business to make slaves of, or hold us in slavery. How would they like for us to make slaves of, and hold them in cruel slavery, and murder them as they do to us? ...

Fear not the number and education of our enemies, against whom we shall have to contend for our lawful light; guaranteed to us by our Maker; for why should we be afraid, when God is, and will continue, (if we continue humble) to be on our side?

The man who would not fight under our Lord and Master Jesus Christ, in the Glorious and heavenly cause of freedom and of God—to be delivered from the most wretched, abject and servile slavery, that ever a people was afflicted with since the foundation of the world, to the present day—ought to be kept with all of his children or family, in slavery, or in chains, to be butchered by his *cruel enemies*....

I have been for years troubling the pages of historians, to find out what our fathers have done to the white Christians of America, to merit such condign punishment as they have inflicted upon them, and do continue to inflict upon us their children. But I must aver, that my researches have hitherto been to no effect. I have therefore, come to the immoveable conclusion, that they (Americans) have, and do continue to punish us for nothing else, but for enriching them and their country. For I cannot conceive of anything else. Nor will I ever believe otherwise, until the Lord shall convince me....

We, and the world wish to see the charges of Mr. Jefferson refuted by the blacks themselves, ... I know well, that there are some talents and learning among the colored people of this country, which we have not a chance to develop, in consequence of oppression; but our oppression ought not to hinder us from acquiring all we can. For we will have a chance to develop them by and by. God will not suffer us, always to be oppressed. Our sufferings will come to an end, in spite of all the Americans this side of eternity. Then we will want all the learning and talents among ourselves, and perhaps more, to govern ourselves.—"Every dog must have its day," the American's is coming to an end.

But let us review Mr. Jefferson's remarks respecting us some further. Comparing our miserable fathers, with the learned philosophers of Greece, he says: ... "Epictetus, Terence and Phaedrus, were slaves,—but they were of the race of whites. It is not their condition, then, but nature, which has produced the distinction." ... I am after those who know and feel, that we are MEN, as well as other people; to them, I say, that unless we try to refute Mr. Jefferson's arguments respecting us, we will only establish them.

... Are we MEN!!—I ask you, O my brethren! are we MEN? Did our creator make us to be slaves to dust and ashes like ourselves? Are they not dying worms as well as we? Have they not to make their appearance before the tribunal of Heaven, to answer for the deeds done in the body, as well as we? Have we any other Master but Jesus Christ alone? Is he not their Master as well as ours?—What right then, have we to obey and call any other Master, but Himself? How we could be so submissive to a gang of men, whom we cannot tell whether they are as good as ourselves or not, I never could conceive. However, this is shut up with the Lord, and we cannot precisely tell—but I declare, we judge men by their works.

The whites have always been an unjust, jealous, unmerciful, avaricious and blood-thirsty set of beings, always seeking after power and authority....

80

William Lloyd Garrison on Slavery (1831)

William Lloyd Garrison's name remains synonymous with the abolitionist movement. A native of Newburyport, Massachusetts, Garrison bounced from printing job to printing job before working for Quaker abolitionist Benjamin Lundy on the Genius of Universal Emancipation *in Baltimore. By 1830, Garrison had left Lundy due to philosophical differences over emancipation and set out to publish his own newspaper. The following selection comes from Garrison's first issue of* The Liberator, *published in January 1831. In it, Garrison makes clear his uncompromising views toward slavery. Two years later, Garrison was instrumental in creating the New England Anti-Slavery Society. Garrison's views brought him approbation in both the North and the South; in 1835, Boston officials requested that he soften his public statements. When he refused, a mob threatened his life and local officials jailed him for his own safety. Despite these setbacks, he remained resolute in his convictions. His support for female membership in the society led to a split among American abolitionists in the early 1840s.*

Questions to Consider

1. Why does William Lloyd Garrison advocate emancipation and enfranchisement for the slaves?

2. Why will he be uncompromising on the issue?

3. Why would Garrison's views be seen as controversial in the 1830s?

4. Would Garrison agree with David Walker ("Appeal to the Coloured Citizens of the World," Document 79) about the status of African Americans?

During my recent tour for the purpose of exciting the minds of the people by a series of discourses on the subject of slavery, every place that I visited gave fresh evidence of the fact that a greater revolution in public sentiment was to be effected in the free states—and particularly in New England—than at the south. I found contempt more bitter, opposition more active, detraction more relentless, prejudice more stubborn, and apathy more frozen, than among slave owners themselves. Of course, there were individual exceptions to the contrary. This state of things afflicted, but did not dishearten me. I determined, at every hazard, to lift up

SOURCE: "To the Public," (Boston) *The Liberator*, 1 January 1831, p. 1.

the standard of emancipation in the eyes of the nation, within sight of Bunker Hill and in the birth place of liberty. That standard is now unfurled; and long may it float, unhurt by the spoliations of time or the missiles of a desperate foe—yea, till every chain be broken, and every bondman set free! Let southern oppressors tremble—let their secret abettors tremble—let their northern apologists tremble—let all the enemies of the persecuted blacks tremble.

... Assenting to the "self-evident truth" maintained in the American Declaration of Independence, "that all men are created equal, and endowed by their Creator with certain inalienable rights—among which are life, liberty and the pursuit of happiness," I shall strenuously contend for the immediate enfranchisement of our slave population....

I am aware, that many object to the severity of my language; but is there not cause for severity? I will be as harsh as truth, and as uncompromising as justice. On this subject, I do not wish to think, or speak, or write, with moderation. No! no! Tell a man whose house is on fire, to give a moderate alarm; tell him to moderately rescue his wife from the hands of the ravisher; tell the mother to gradually extricate her babe from the fire into which it has fallen;—but urge me not to use moderation in a cause like the present. I am in earnest—I will not equivocate—I will not excuse—I will not retreat a single inch—AND I WILL BE HEARD. The apathy of the people is enough to make every statue leap from its pedestal, and to hasten the resurrection of the dead.

It is pretended, that I am retarding the cause of emancipation by the coarseness of my invective, and the precipitancy of my measure. The charge is not true. On this question my influence,—humble as it is,—is felt at this moment to a considerable extent, and shall be felt in coming years—not perniciously, but beneficially—not as a curse, but as a blessing; and posterity will bear testimony that I was right. I desire to thank God, that he enables me to disregard "the fear of man which bringeth a snare," and to speak this truth in its simplicity and power.

And here I close with this fresh dedication:

"Oppression! I have seen thee, face to face,
And met thy cruel eye and cloudy brow;
But thy soul-withering glance I fear not now—
For dread to prouder feelings doth give place
Of deep abhorrence! Scorning the disgrace
Of slavish knees that at thy footstool bow,
I also kneel—but with far other bow
Do hail thee and thy herd of hirelings base:—
I swear, while life-blood warms my throbbing veins,
Still to oppose and thwart, with heart and hand,
Thy brutalizing sway—till Afric's chains
Are burst, and Freedom rules the rescued land,—
Trampling Oppression and his iron rod:
Such is the vow I take—So HELP ME GOD!"
William Lloyd Garrison.
Boston, January 1, 1831.

81

Evidence Against the Views of the Abolitionists (1833)

Sentiments of antislavery and racism had long coexisted in American history. However, the emergence of immediate abolitionism by 1830 posed a challenge not merely to the continued existence of slavery, but to concepts of white supremacy itself. The new abolitionism assailed the immorality of holding slaves, while at times going so far as to assert the equality of the different races. Their views clashed with those who held that whites and blacks were the result of separate creations. By 1830, early social scientists had entered the debate, generally arguing that blacks were inferior to whites. The ensuing excerpt is typical of accounts of the time that sought to use comparative anatomy to debunk arguments of African American equality.

Questions to Consider

1. What evidence does the author present to prove African American inferiority?

2. How do you suspect Cato ("Cato Petitions for his Freedom," Document 47), Fanny Wright ("On Equality," Document 63), or William Lloyd Garrison ("On Slavery," Document 80) would have responded to the views expressed in this document?

3. To what extent does Jefferson Davis ("Jefferson Davis Responds to the Emancipation Proclamation," Document 117) reflect the sentiments found in this document?

4. How does this document use concepts of African American racial inferiority to reinforce the institution of slavery?

It will be recollected that the chief arguments of the "total abolitionists" are grounded upon the supposition, 1st, That negroes and white men belong to one and the same species, and 2d, that their known want of intellect and mental capacity arises from their deficiency of education and from the peculiar habits that slavery has entailed upon them. The inferences from which are 1st that they should be placed upon a public, as well as *private footing* of equality with white men; and 2nd, that an exemption from the above deteriorating causes will show the pristine equality of negro intellect with that of white men.

SOURCE: Richard H. Colfax, *Evidence Against the Views of the Abolitionists, Consisting of Physical and Moral Proofs, of the Natural Inferiority of the Negroes* (New York, 1833), 6–8, 30–33.

Perhaps no cause however desperate in this debating age has found a dearth of advocates and consequently a number of writers have taken upon themselves the fearful task of proving the negro to be "God's own image, like ourselves, though carved "In ebony!" to our *entire satisfaction*. Now inasmuch as we feel ourselves competent to overturn the premises of such writers and their credulous satellites, we expect those who have not enlisted under their banners, to examine into the absurdity of their conclusions. As to the "total abolitionists,"—they have pampered themselves with a surfeit of new ideas which having been already swallowed, must remain, *it status quo* it rests with us to prevent them from digesting their meal. This can be done quite effectually, as we believe, by demonstrating to the public, that the physical and mental differences between negroes and white men, are sufficient to warrant us in affirming that they have descended from distinct origins, and that therefore no alteration of the social condition of the negro can be expected to create any change in his *nature*.

From which three positions, if well substantiated the aggregate inference will be that the negroes are totally incapable of self government, and utterly unworthy of those privileges which the "immediate abolitionists" would confer upon them. If this can be made to appear independently of those arguments and considerations which grow out of the constitutional privileges and political situation of the slave holding states, then do we have "assurance doubly sure" that the views of the abolitionists and *amalgamationists* are as inexpedient as they are execrable.

... the negroes, whether physically or morally considered, are so inferior as to resemble the brute creation as nearly as they do the white species, and if after leaving the abstract views of this question which we have taken, we resort either to past history or to present facts, and find that modern negroes are fair specimens of what their race has always been, is it not strictly just and perfectly consonant with sound reason to infer that *no alteration of their present social condition would be productive of the least benefit to them*, insomuch as no change of their nature can be expected to result there from.

If their physical organization will continually prevent them from attaining a level with the whites, how unreasonable is it in those enemies to our country, called "abolitionists," to unloose within the bosom of his this now happy community, a body of *such* people, a race incapable of receiving education and of comprehending the *terrors* of religion much less of perceiving the value of our majestic system of Law. But more than this, when it is objected to this proposal that if it should go into effect we would eternally have our prisons filled and our public charities consumed because of the inability of the negroes to obtain respectable employments, (the result of a well founded prejudice,) it is further proposed that the two races should by intermarriage &c. amalgamate with each other. Would it not be as reasonable to expect the negroes to *amalgamate* with that equally valuable race of inferiors—the orang-outangs?

The negroes themselves could not feel more righteous indignation at this latter proposal, than we do at the other. "Among the Romans," observes Mr. Jefferson, emancipation required but *one effort*. The slave, when made free, might mix with, without *standing* the blood of his master. But with us a second is necessary, unknown to history, *When freed he is to be removed beyond the reach of mixture.*" But how agreeably and no less ingeniously have the devout members of the Anti-slavery Society removed all difficulties, "Liberate the Negro *first*," they exclaim, "consider upon the ways, means, and expediency afterwards, and lastly make him by marriage, or otherwise, one of your family." Truly, by complying with this advice, we should after the lapse of a few generations, could we live as long, behold a promising race, bearing about as much affinity to the present Americans, as the offspring of an African and an orang outang would to a negro. We were never before aware of the existence of so much intellect among even the whites, that it should become a desideratum to lessen their superiority. But let us view the detestable and disgusting scheme of amalgamation in all its bearings, let us analize the *principle* which dictated it, the *persons* who proposed it and above all let us consider who are to be benefited by this revolting attempt to destroy our nationality. How ridiculous will seem the project! how contemptible the advocates! how unworthy the object! *provided* always that the negroes *are*, as we know them to be; which indeed appears to be a matter of much uncertainty, among the Abolitionists.

… There is consequently but one alternative; let the blacks be removed "nonens volens" from among us, and when all danger is past—Let the traitors be branded, held up to the execration of all true hearted patriots; they will then be quite ready to seek refuge beneath that Constitution whose principles they have outraged and abused, whose founders they have villified, whose very existence they have threatened. And (like the "impure birds of the night," shrinking from public gaze and the light of day,) they will meet their just reward.…

82

Sarah Grimké Argues for Gender Equality (1837)

The passion to perfect society that was so much a part of the Second Great Awakening spurred the rise of abolitionism in the North; and when female representatives were denied positions of influence, it helped to ignite demands for women's rights. One of the earliest proponents of women's rights was Sarah Grimké. A native of South Carolina, she and her younger sister Angelina had by the 1820s moved to Philadelphia, where they emerged as outspoken critics of slavery. Both sisters soon became deeply involved in the movement, writing antislavery tracts and—in defiance of accepted convention—serving as public speakers. By 1838, Sarah had begun to shift her attention to demanding greater rights for women. The following selection is from her Letters on the Equality of the Sexes, *which were addressed to fellow abolitionist Mary Parker.*

Questions to Consider

1. In what ways might Grimké seek greater equality for women?
2. How might men of the time react to this document?
3. How might Sarah Grimké respond to the views contained in "Eliza Lucas, A Modern Woman" (Document 18)? What changes seem to have occurred in women's status from the early eighteenth century to the mid-nineteenth century?
4. How might Sarah Grimké respond to the views of Judith Sargent Murray in "On the Equality of the Sexes" (Document 48)? What changes seem to have occurred in women's status from the late eighteenth century to the mid-nineteenth century?

… During the early part of my life, my lot was cast among the butterflies of the *fashionable* world; and of this class of women, I am constrained to say, both from experience and observation, that their education is miserably deficient; that they are taught to regard marriage as the one thing needful, the only avenue to distinction; hence to attract the notice and win the attentions of men, by their external charms, is the chief business of fashionable girls. They seldom think that men will be allured by intellectual acquirements, because they find, that where any mental superiority exists, a woman is generally shunned and regarded as stepping out of her "appropriate sphere," which, in their view, is to dress, to dance, to set out to the best possible advantage her person, to read the novels which inundate the press, and which do more to destroy her character as a rational creature, than any thing else. Fashionable women regard themselves, and are regarded by men, as pretty toys or as mere instruments of pleasure; and the vacuity of mind, the heartlessness, the frivolity which is the necessary result of this false and debasing estimate of women, can only be fully understood by those who have mingled in the folly and wickedness of fashionable life; and who have been called from such pursuits by the voice of the Lord Jesus, inviting their weary and heavy laden souls to come unto Him and learn of Him, that they may find something worthy of their immortal spirit, and their intellectual powers; that they may learn the high and holy purposes of their creation, and consecrate themselves unto the service of God; and not as is now the case, to the pleasure of man.

There is another and much more numerous class in this country, who are withdrawn by education or circumstances from the circle of fashionable amusements, but who are brought up with the dangerous and absurd idea, that *marriage* is a kind of preferment; and that to be able to keep their husband's house, and

SOURCE: Sarah M. Grimké, "Letter VIII: On the Condition of Women in the United States, 1837," *Letters on the Equality of the Sexes and the Condition of Woman* (Boston, 1838), 46–55.

render his situation comfortable, is the end of her being. Much that she does and says and thinks is done in reference to this situation; and to be married is too often held up to the view of girls as the sine qua non of human happiness and human existence. For this purpose more than for any other, I verily believe the majority of girls are trained. This is demonstrated by the imperfect education which is bestowed upon them, and the little pains taken to cultivate their minds, after they leave school, by the little time allowed them for reading and by the idea being constantly inculcated, that although all household concerns should be attended to with scrupulous punctuality at particular seasons, the improvement of their intellectual capacities is only a secondary consideration, and may serve as an occupation to fill up the odds and ends of time....

Let no one think, from these remarks, that I regard a knowledge of house-wifery as beneath the acquisition of women. Far from it: I believe that a complete knowledge of household affairs is an indispensable requisite in a woman's education,—that by the mistress of a family, whether married or single, doing her duty thoroughly and *understandingly*, the happiness of the family is increased to an incalculable degree, as well as a vast amount of time and money saved. All I complain of is, that our education consists so almost exclusively in culinary and other manual operations....

The influence of women over the minds and character of *children* of both sexes, is allowed to be far greater than that of men. This being the case by the very ordering of nature, women should be prepared by education for the performance of their sacred duties as mothers and as sisters....

There is another way in which the general opinion, that women are inferior to men, is manifested, that bears with tremendous effect on the laboring class, and indeed on almost all who are obliged to earn a subsistence, whether it be by mental or physical exertion—I allude to the disproportionate value set on the time and labor of men and of women. A man who is engaged in teaching, can always, I believe, command a higher price for tuition than a woman—even when he teaches the same branches, and is not in any respect superior to the woman. This I know is the case in boarding and other schools with which I have been acquainted, and it is so in every occupation in which the sexes engage indiscriminately. As for example, in tailoring, a man has twice, or three times as much for making a waistcoast or pantaloons as a woman, although the work done by each may be equally good. In those employments which are peculiar to women, their time is estimated at only half the value of that of men. A woman who goes out to wash, works as hard in proportion as a wood sawyer, or a coal heaver, but she is not generally able to make more than half as much by a day's work. The low remuneration which women receive for their work, has claimed the attention of a few philanthropists, and I hope it will continue to do so until some remedy is applied for this enormous evil. I have known a widow, left with four or five children, to provide for, unable to leave home because her helpless babes demand her attention, compelled to earn a scanty subsistence, by making coarse shirts at 12 1–2 cents a piece, or by taking in washing, for which she was paid by some wealthy persons 12 1–2 cents per dozen. All these things evince the low estimation in which woman is held. There is yet another and more disastrous consequence arising from this unscriptual notion—women being educated, from earliest childhood, to regard themselves as inferior creatures, have not that self-respect which conscious equality would engender, and hence when their virtue is assailed, they yield to temptation with facility, under the idea that it rather exalts than debases them to be connected with a superior being....

I cannot close this letter, without saying a few words on the benefits to be derived by men, as well as women, from the opinions I advocate relative to the equality of the sexes. Many women are now supported, in idleness and extravagance, by the industry of their husbands, fathers, or brothers, who are compelled to toil out their existence, at the counting house, or in the printing office, or some other laborious occupation, while the wife and daughters and sisters take no part in the support of the family, and appear to think that their sole business is to spend the hard bought earnings of their male friends. I deeply regret such a state of things, because I believe that if women felt their responsibility, for the support of themselves, or their families it would add strength and dignity to their characters, and teach them more true sympathy for their husbands, than is now generally manifested,—a sympathy which would be exhibited by actions as well as words. Our brethren may reject my doctrine, because it runs counter to common opinions, and because it wounds their pride; but I believe they would be 'partakers of the benefit' resulting from the Equality of the Sexes, and would find that woman, as their equal, was unspeakably more valuable than woman as their inferior, both as a moral and an intellectual being.

Thine in the bonds of womanhood,

Sarah M. Grimke.

83

The Temperance Crusade (1818, 1846)

One of the most important reforms championed by members of America's Benevolent Empire was the temperance movement. In the late eighteenth and early nineteenth centuries, the Americans consumed considerable quantities of alcohol, in part because of the lack of a viable alternative beverage. By the 1820s and 1830s, improved hygiene made potable water increasingly available. At the same time, religious criticism of the use of alcohol fused with the growing numbers of reformers who were concerned that alcohol consumption was ruinous to health, destructive of family life, contributed to vice, and undermined the drinker's ability to compete in the rapidly changing market economy. Temperance advocates made very effective use of images to depict the perils posed by alcohol. The following image was one of the best known of the era, detailing the steps from an innocent first drink to perdition.

Questions to Consider

1. Do you notice any religious themes in the images below?
2. What are some of the vices associated with the consumption of alcohol?
3. Who are the victims of alcohol abuse?
4. How can the views portrayed here be reconciled with concepts of individual liberty as understood by nineteenth-century Americans?
5. What impact does alcohol appear to have on one's health?

Drunkard's Looking-Glass
SOURCE: Library Company of Philadelphia

Drunkard's Looking-Glass
SOURCE: Library Company of Philadelphia

The Drunkard's Progress. From the First Glass to the Grave
SOURCE: [LC-USZC4-1629]/Library of Congress Prints and Photographs Division

84

"Declaration of Sentiments," Seneca Falls Convention (1848)

The women's rights movement had its roots in abolitionism, which attracted a large number of female supporters from the outset. By the late 1830s, female abolitionists horrified gender-integrated audiences with their accounts of the treatment of slaves. Congregational clergy and conservative abolitionist criticisms of such practices had led Sarah Grimké to proclaim the equality of the sexes. The World Anti-Slavery Convention in London brought the issue to a head when convention organizers refused to allow delegates Lucretia Mott and Elizabeth Cady Stanton to participate. Seven years later, in 1848, Stanton and Mott organized the Seneca Falls Convention. The following selection is taken from the convention "Declaration of Sentiments." Many of those present at Seneca Falls remained active in the movement through the rest of the century.

Questions to Consider

1. Why does the Seneca Falls Convention use the Declaration of Independence as the framework for its "Sentiments"?

2. What is the evidence that man has denied woman her rights?

3. What does the declaration advocate for women?

4. For what reasons would some women who advocated the "Declaration of Sentiments" also have supported William Lloyd Garrison in the abolitionist movement ("William Lloyd Garrison on Slavery," Document 80)?

When, in the course of human events, it becomes necessary for one portion of the family of man to assume among the people of the earth a position different from that which they have hitherto occupied, but one to which the laws of nature and of nature's God entitle them, a decent respect to the opinions of mankind requires that they should declare the causes that impel them to such a course.

We hold these truths to be self-evident: that all men and women are created equal; that they are endowed by their Creator with certain inalienable rights; that among these are life, liberty, and the pursuit of happiness; that to secure these rights governments are instituted, deriving their just powers from the consent of the governed. Whenever any form of government becomes destructive of these ends, it is the right of those who suffer from it to refuse allegiance to it, and to insist upon the institution of a new government, laying its foundation on such principles, and organizing its powers in such form, as to them shall seem most likely to effect their safety and happiness. Prudence, indeed, will dictate that governments long established should not be changed for light and transient causes; and accordingly all experience hath shown that mankind are more disposed to suffer, while evils are sufferable, than to right themselves by abolishing forms to which they were accustomed. But a long train of abuses and usurpations, pursuing invariably the same object evinces a design to reduce them under absolute despotism, it is their duty to throw off such government, and to provide new guards for their future security. Such has been the patient sufferance of the women under this government, and such is now the necessity which constrains them to demand the equal station to which they are entitled.

The history of mankind is a history of repeated injuries and usurpations on the part of man toward woman, having in direct object the establishment of an absolute tyranny over her. To prove this, let facts be submitted to a candid world.

He has never permitted her to exercise her inalienable right to the elective franchise.

He has compelled her to submit to laws, in the formation of which she had no voice.

SOURCE: "Declaration of Sentiments," *History of Woman Suffrage*, eds. Susan B. Anthony, Elizabeth Cady Stanton, and Matilda Joslyn Gage (New York, 1881), 1: 70–73.

He has withheld from her rights which are given to the most ignorant and degraded men—both natives and foreigners.

Having deprived her of this first right of a citizen, the elective franchise, thereby leaving her without representation in the halls of legislation, he has oppressed her on all sides.

He has made her, if married, in the eye of the law, civilly dead.

He has taken from her all right in property, even to the wages she earns.

He has made her, morally, an irresponsible being, as she can commit many crimes with impunity, provided they be done in the presence of her husband. In the covenant of marriage, she is compelled to promise obedience to her husband, he becoming, to all intents and purposes, her master—the law giving him power to deprive her of all liberty, and to administer chastisement.

He has so framed the laws of divorce, as to what shall be the proper causes, and in case of separation, to whom the guardianship of the children shall be given, as to be wholly regardless of the happiness of women—the law, in all cases, going upon a false supposition of the supremacy of man, and giving all power into his hands.

After depriving her of all her rights as a married woman, if single, and the owner of property, he has taxed her to support a government which recognizes her only when her property can be made profitable to it.

He has monopolized nearly all the profitable employments, and from those she is permitted to follow, she receives but a scanty remuneration. He closes against her all the avenues to wealth and distinction which he considers most honorable to himself. As a teacher of theology, medicine, or law, she is not known.

He has denied her the facilities for obtaining a thorough education, all colleges being closed against her.

He allows her in Church, as well as State, but a subordinate position, claiming Apostolic authority for her exclusion from the ministry, and, with some exceptions, from any public participation in the affairs of the Church.

He has created a false public sentiment by giving to the world a different code of morals for men and women, by which moral delinquencies which exclude women from society, are not only tolerated, but deemed of little account in man.

He has usurped the prerogative of Jehovah himself, claiming it as his right to assign for her a sphere of action, when that belongs to her conscience and to her God.

He has endeavored, in every way that he could, to destroy her confidence in her own powers, to lessen her self-respect, and to make her willing to lead a dependent and abject life.

Now, in view of this entire disfranchisement of one-half the people of this country, their social and religious degradation—in view of the unjust laws above mentioned, and because women do feel themselves aggrieved, oppressed, and fraudulently deprived of their most sacred rights, we insist that they have immediate admission to all the rights and privileges which belong to them as citizens of the United States.

In entering upon the great work before us, we anticipate no small amount of misconception, misrepresentation, and ridicule; but we shall use every instrumentality within our power to effect our object. We shall employ agents, circulate tracts, petition the State and National legislatures, and endeavor to enlist the pulpit and the press in our behalf. We hope this Convention will be followed by a series of Conventions embracing every part of the country.

11

Manifest Destiny

In the first half of the nineteenth century, the United States had expanded from a collection of states with a tenuous hold over territories west of the Appalachians to an increasingly self-confident colossus stretching from the Atlantic to the Pacific. By the 1840s, the mentality that supported such expansion had been labeled "Manifest Destiny." According to this belief, America possessed a special purpose that legitimized its westward expansion. Supporters of the doctrine argued that the acquisition of new lands did more than provide opportunity for white Americans; it replaced "backward" and "savage" customs with "superior" American institutions. Opponents argued that America needed to first perfect its institutions within its existing borders. The following selections reveal the sentiments of the expansionists and their opponents.

85

Mid-Nineteenth Century Images of Race and Nation

One of the defining characteristics of the American experience has been the contact between white and non-white culture. Throughout history, American intellectuals grappled with how to come to terms with these cultural differences. By the mid-nineteenth century, early social scientific beliefs on cultural evolution occurring in progressive stages combined with emerging American nationalism's emphasis on the superiority of American institutions. The results justified white Americans' sense of ethnic and racial superiority and legitimized the conquest and subjugation of non-white land and peoples. The first set of images depicts an early view of racial hierarchy. The following image is a mid-nineteenth-century romantic painting of America's triumphant march across the continent. Both sets of images clearly demonstrate the sense of "progress" inherent in mid-century American thought and depict white American sense of superiority.

Questions to Consider

1. What can you deduce about white attitudes toward Africans and African Americans from the first set of images?
2. How do you think the first set of images might be used to justify slavery?
3. What are the symbols of progress depicted in the romantic painting?
4. What can you deduce about American nationalism from this set of images?

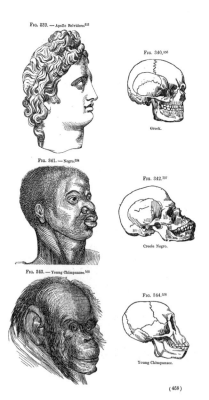

Types of Mankind

SOURCE: Courtesy of Department of Special Collections and University Archives, Stanford University Lib

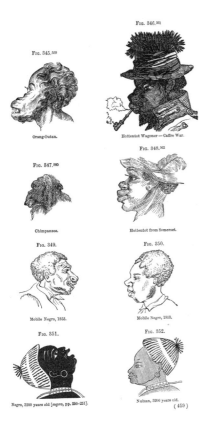

Types of Mankind

SOURCE: Courtesy of Department of Special Collections and University Archives, Stanford University Lib

American Progress

SOURCE: [LC-USZ62-737]/Library of Congress Prints and Photographs Division

86

Texas and California Annexation (1845)

Territorial expansion had been a virtual act of faith for many white Americans since the arrival of the first settlers. By the 1840s, the sense of a special mission shared by many Americans, coupled with economic depression, led to renewed calls for expansion. The issue divided the parties: Democrats argued in favor of expansion, while the Whigs opposed the acquisition of added territories. The following selection first appeared in the New York–based United States Magazine and Democratic Review *in the summer of 1845. Its author, John L. O'Sullivan, trumpets his view of America's "Manifest Destiny" and captures the boisterous spirit of the expansionists. O'Sullivan established the* Review *in 1837 to foster America's "democratic genius." By the mid-1840s, he also served as editor of the* New York Morning News, *which he had founded with future Democratic presidential candidate Samuel J. Tilden. Territorial expansion became the leading issue in the 1844 election campaign, and differences over the annexation of Texas fueled sectional tensions.*

Questions to Consider

1. How does John O'Sullivan define *Manifest Destiny*?
2. According to O'Sullivan, why was Texas acquired?
3. What does America offer the unsettled regions, especially California?
4. How do you suppose O'Sullivan would respond to the views expressed in "Tecumseh on White Encroachment" (Document 59) or "Appeal to the Coloured Citizens of the World" (Document 79)?

IT IS TIME NOW for opposition to the annexation of Texas to cease....

Texas is now ours. Already, before these words are written, her convention has undoubtedly ratified the acceptance, by her congress, of our proffered invitation into the Union; and made the requisite changes in her already republican form of constitution to adapt it to its future federal relations. Her star and her stripe may already be said to have taken their place in the glorious blazon of our common nationality; and the sweep of our eagle's wing already includes within its circuit the wide extent of her fair and fertile land....

Why, were other reasoning wanting, in favor of now elevating this question of the reception of Texas into the Union, out of the lower region of our past party dissensions, up to its proper level of a high and broad nationality, it surely is to be found, found abundantly, in the manner in which other nations have undertaken

SOURCE: John L. O'Sullivan, "Annexation," *United States Magazine and Democratic Review* (July 1845): 5–10.

to intrude themselves into it, between us and the proper parties to the case, in a spirit of hostile interference against us, for the avowed object of thwarting our policy and hampering our power, limiting our greatness and checking the fulfillment of our manifest destiny to overspread the continent allotted by Providence for the free development of our yearly multiplying millions....

The independence of Texas was complete and absolute. It was an independence, not only in fact, but of right. No obligation of duty toward Mexico tended in the least degree to restrain our right to effect the desired recovery of the fair province.... If Texas became peopled with an American population, it was by no contrivance of our government, but on the express invitation of that of Mexico herself; accompanied with such guaranties of state independence, and the maintenance of a federal system analogous to our own, as constituted a compact fully justifying the strongest measures of redress on the part of those afterward deceived in this guaranty, and sought to be enslaved under the yoke imposed by its violation.

She was released, rightfully and absolutely released, from all Mexican allegiance, or duty of cohesion to the Mexican political body, by the acts and fault of Mexico herself, and Mexico alone. There never was a clearer case. It was not revolution; it was resistance to revolution....

Nor is there any just foundation for the charge that annexation is a great pro-slavery measure—calculated to increase and perpetuate that institution. Slavery had nothing to do with it. Opinions were and are greatly divided, both at the North and South, as to the influence to be exerted by it on slavery and the slave states. That it will tend to facilitate the disappearance of slavery from all the northern tier of the present slave states, cannot surely admit of serious question. The greater value in Texas of the slave labor now employed in those states, must soon produce the effect of draining off that labor southwardly, by the same unvarying law that bids water descend the slope that invites it....

The Spanish-Indian-American population of Mexico, Central America, and South America, afford the only receptacle capable of absorbing that race whenever we shall be prepared to slough it off—to emancipate it from slavery, and (simultaneously necessary) to remove it from the midst of our own. Themselves already of mixed and confused blood, and free from the "prejudices" which among us so insuperably forbid the social amalgamation which can alone elevate the Negro race out of a virtually servile degradation....

California will, probably, next fall away from the loose adhesion which, in such a country as Mexico, holds a remote province in a slight equivocal kind of dependence on the metropolis. Imbecile and distracted, Mexico never can exert any real government authority over such a country....

The Anglo-Saxon foot is already on its borders. Already the advance guard of the irresistible army of Anglo-Saxon emigration has begun to pour down upon it, armed with the plough and the rifle, and marking its trail with schools and colleges, courts and representative halls, mills and meetinghouses. A population will soon be in actual occupation of California, over which it will be idle for Mexico to dream of dominion. They will necessarily become independent....

Their right to independence will be the natural right of self-government belonging to any community strong enough to maintain—distinct in position, origin and character, and free from any mutual obligations of membership of a common political body, binding it to others by the duty of loyalty and compact of public faith. This will be their title to independence; and by this title, there can be no doubt that the population now fast streaming down upon California will both assert and maintain that independence.

Whether they will then attach themselves to our Union or not, is not to be predicted with any certainty. Unless the projected railroad across the continent to the Pacific be carried into effect, perhaps they may not; though even in that case, the day is not distant when the empires of the Atlantic and Pacific would again flow together into one, as soon as their inland border should approach each other. But that great work, colossal as appears the plan on its first suggestion, cannot remain long unbuilt.

Its necessity for this very purpose of binding and holding together in its iron clasp our fast-settling Pacific region with that of the Mississippi Valley .... these considerations give assurance that the day cannot be distant which shall witness the conveyance of the representatives from Oregon and California to Washington within less time than a few years ago was devoted to a similar journey by those from Ohio; while the magnetic telegraph will enable the editors of the *San Francisco Union*, the *Astoria Evening Post*, or the *Nootka Morning News*, to set up in type the first half of the President's inaugural before the echoes of the latter half shall have died away beneath the lofty porch of the Capitol, as spoken from his lips....

87

American Description of Mexican Women in Santa Fe (1845)

The expansion-minded spirit of Manifest Destiny that characterized the United States in the 1830s and 1840s contributed to growing interest in the Southwest and the Pacific Coast. American interest in New Mexico was primarily economic. Traders followed the roughly nine-hundred-mile Santa Fe Trail from Independence, Missouri, to the remote Mexican town of Santa Fe, where the exchange of goods brought enormous profits. The arrival of American merchants contributed to the increasingly multiethnic community there. George W. Kendall was one of those who made the trip to Santa Fe. A newspaper editor and journalist who had worked on many of the nation's leading newspapers, Kendall had moved in 1837 to New Orleans, where he established the Times-Picayune. *In 1841, he joined a Republic of Texas–sanctioned expedition to Santa Fe. The following selection offers Kendall's observations on Mexican women. He would later send reports on the Mexican-American War back to the* Picayune, *thus becoming one of America's first war correspondents.*

Questions to Consider

1. What can you deduce from the Republic of Texas' authorizing an expedition to Santa Fe in 1841?

2. What does this document tell you about nineteenth-century attitudes concerning ethnicity and gender?

3. What can you deduce from this document about nineteenth-century sexual mores?

4. How do you think Sarah Grimké ("Sarah Grimké Argues for Gender Equality," Document 82) would respond to the attitudes expressed here?

... The dress worn by the females of Northern Mexico, in fact all over the country, is a cotton or linen chemise and a blue or red short woollen petticoat—frequently, among the more wealthy, the latter is made of a gaudy, figured merino, imported expressly for the purpose. These simple articles of raiment are usually made with no little degree of neatness, the chemise, in particular, being in many cases elaborately worked with flowers and different conceits, while the edges are tastefully decorated with ruffles or laces, if it lies within the power of the wearer to procure them. On first entering the country, the Anglo-Saxon traveller, who has been used to see the gentler sex of his native land in more full, and perhaps I should say more becoming costume, feels not a little astonished at the Eve-like and scanty garments of the females he meets; he thinks that they are but half-dressed, and wonders how they can have the indelicacy, or, as he would deem it at home, brazen impudence, to appear before him in dishabille so immodest. But he soon learns that it is the custom and fashion of the country—that, to use a common Yankee expression, the women "don't know any better." He soon looks, with an eye of some leniency, at such little deficiencies of dress as the absence of a gown, and is not long in coming to the honest conclusion, as the eye becomes more weaned from the fastidiousness of early habit and association, that a pretty girl is quite as pretty without as with that garment. By-and-by, he is even led to think that the dress of the women, among whom fate, business, or a desire to see the world may have thrown him, is really graceful, easy—aye, becoming: he next wonders how the females of his native land can press and confine, can twist and contort themselves out of all proportion, causing the most gracefully-curving lines of beauty to become straight and rigid, the exquisite undulations of the natural form to become flat or angular, or conical, or jutting, and all in homage to a fickle and capricious goddess—a heathen goddess, whose worshippers are Christians! He looks around him, he compares, he deliberates—the result is altogether in favour of his new-found friends.

Among the Mexican women, young and old, corsets are unknown, and by a majority of them, probably unheard of. I travelled nearly seven hundred miles through the country, without seeing a single gown—all the females were dressed in the same style, with the same *abandon*. The consequence any one may readily imagine: the forms of the gentler sex obtain a roundness, a fulness, which the divinity of tight lacing never allows her votaries. The Mexican belles certainly

SOURCE: G. W. Kendall, *Narrative of the Texan Santa Fe Expedition* (Bristol, England, 1845), 233–36.

have studied, too, their personal comfort in the costume they have adopted, and it is impossible to see the prettier of the dark-eyed *senoras* of the northern departments without acknowledging that their personal appearance and attractions are materially enhanced by the *negligé* style. Moore's beautiful lines to Nora Creina appear to apply especially to the Mexican girls, for their dress certainly leaves

—every beauty free
To sink or swell as Heaven pleases.

But by all this the reader must not understand that the traveller sees no full-dressed ladies in Mexico. In the great city of the Montezumas, in fact in all the larger towns where foreigners and French milliners have settled, he sees them habited after the fashion of his own land, although he cannot but notice that a large portion of those so attired feel constrained and ill at ease under the infliction. I have seen, in one of the larger cities, a lady with the body and sleeves of a fashionable frock hanging dangling at her back, without even attempting to conceal what many would call a gross departure from all rules and reasons.

Bonnets are never worn, either by rich or poor, high or low; but in their stead the *mantilla* and *reboso*, more especially the latter, are in general use among all classes. The latter is a species of long, narrow scarf, made of cotton, and in a majority of cases figured with two colours only, blue and white. These indispensable articles in the toilet of the Mexican female serve not only the uses of parasol and bonnet, but also of shawl, veil, and workbag. The manner of wearing them is extremely graceful—sometimes upon the head, at others over the shoulders, and again round the waist, with the ends hanging across the arms; in the streets they are worn almost invariably over the head, and so archly and coquettishly does the fair Mexican draw the reboso around her face, that the inquisitive beholder is frequently repaid with no other than the sight of a dark and lustrous eye peering out from amid its folds.

The ends of the reboso are frequently used as an apron, to carry any little articles that cannot be held in the hands, and seldom is a female seen without one of them, from the extreme north of Mexico to its southern-most boundaries. From childhood it is worn, and long habit has so accustomed them to its use that it is not laid aside when engaged in common household labour....

88

Life on the Overland Trail (1846)

By the mid-1840s, Manifest Destiny and the promise of a new life had led thousands of Americans to leave their homes and head overland to the West. So great was the lure of the West that by 1860, approximately 350,000 people had traversed the Oregon Trail alone.

Life on the trail offered challenges for which many migrants were unprepared; approximately 10 percent of those who traveled the Oregon Trail died en route. The letter excerpted here was written by Tamsen Donner, who was traveling with her husband and three children to California in 1846. This excerpt provides a glimpse of life on the trail. The Donners' fortunes would take a turn for the worse later that year, when an early snow trapped their party in the high Sierras. Tamsen—as well as 40 other members of the 87-person Donner party—died that winter, their bodies cannibalized by the starving survivors.

Questions to Consider

1. How would you describe gender roles on the Overland Trail?

2. What raw materials are available for use by those crossing the Great Plains? How are they used?

3. Does Donner seem optimistic or pessimistic?

4. How do you think the authors of the "'Declaration of Sentiments,' Seneca Falls Convention" (Document 84) would respond to Tamsen Donner's letter?

"Near the Junction of the North and South Platte," June 16, 1846
My Old Friend: —

We are now on the Platte, 200 miles from Fort Larimee. Our journey, so far, has been pleasant. The roads have been good, and food plentiful. The water for a part of the way has been indifferent—but at no time have our cattle suffered for it. Wood is now very scarce, but *"Buffalo chips"* are excellent—they kindle quick and retain heat surprisingly. We had this evening Buffalo steaks broiled upon them that had the same flavor they would have had upon hickory coals.

We feel no fear of Indians. Our cattle graze quietly around our encampment unmolested. Two or three men will go hunting twenty miles from camp;—and last night two of our men lay out in the wilderness rather than ride their horses after a hard chase. Indeed if I do not experience something far worse than I have yet done, I shall say the trouble is all in getting started.

Our waggons have not needed much repair, but I cannot yet tell in what respects they may be improved. Certain it is they cannot be too strong. Our preparations for the journey, in some respects, might have been bettered. Bread has been the principal article of food in our camp. We laid in 150 lbs. of flour and 75 lbs. of meat for each individual, and I fear bread will be scarce. Meat is abundant. Rice and beans are good articles on the road—cornmeal, too, is very acceptable. Linsey dresses are the most suitable for children. Indeed if I had one it would be comfortable. There is so cool a breeze at all times in the prairie that the sun does not feel so hot as one would suppose.

We are now 450 miles from Independence. Our route at first was rough and through a timbered country which appeared to be fertile. After striking the prairie we found a first rate road, and the only difficulty we had has been crossing creeks. In that, however, there has been no danger. I never could have believed

SOURCE: Tamsen E. Donner, "Letter from Tamsen E. Donner, June 16, 1846," *Overland in 1846: Diaries and Letters of the California-Oregon Trail*, ed. Dale Morgan (Lincoln, NE, 1993), 2: 561–64. Reprinted by permission of the University of Nebraska Press. ©1963 by Dale Morgan.

we could have travelled so far with so little difficulty. The prairie between the Blue and Platte rivers is beautiful beyond description. Never have I seen so varied a country—so suitable for cultivation. Every thing was new and pleasing. The Indians frequently come to see us, and the chiefs of a tribe breakfasted at our tent this morning. All are so friendly that I cannot help feeling sympathy and friendship for them. But on one sheet, what can I say?

Since we have been on the Platte we have had the river on one side, and the ever varying mounds on the other—and have traveled through the Bottom lands from one to ten miles wide with little or no timber. The soil is sandy, and last year, on account of the dry season, the emigrants found grass here scarce. Our cattle are in good order, and where proper care has been taken none has been lost. Our milch [milk] cows have been of great service—indeed, they have been of more advantage than our meat. We have plenty of butter and milk.

We are commanded by Capt. Russel—an amiable man. George Donner is himself yet. He crows in the morning, and shouts out "Chain up, boys!—chain up!" with as much authority as though he was "something in particular." John Denton is still with us—we find him a useful man in camp. Hiram Miller and Noah James are in good health and doing well. We have of the best of people in our company, and some, too, that are not so good.

Buffalo show themselves frequently. We have found the wild tulip, the primrose, the lupine, the ear-drop, the larkspur, and creeping hollyhock, and a beautiful flower resembling the bloom of the beech tree, but in bunches large as a small sugar-loaf, and of every variety of shade, to red and green. I botanize and read some, but cook a "heap" more.

There are 420 waggons, as far as we have heard, on the road between here and Oregon and California.

Give our love to all enquiring friends—God bless them.

Yours truly
Mrs. George Donner

89

Mexican View of U.S. Occupation (1847)

American expansion created conflict with Mexico during the 1830s and 1840s. A newly independent Mexico encouraged American immigrants to settle in Texas during the 1820s, but sought to curtail further settlement in the ensuing decade as the number of North American immigrants threatened to overwhelm the province. This policy, along with the Mexican government's attempt to exert greater control over its northern province, caused Texans of both

Anglo and Mexican origin to successfully revolt in 1836. The Republic of Texas remained independent until annexed by the United States in 1845, just days before James K. Polk, a fervent expansionist from Tennessee, became president. The ensuing war, instigated by the new American administration's eagerness to add California and the Southwest to the nation, ended with American armies occupying Mexico City in 1847. In the ensuing letter, José Fernando Ramirez, a leading political and intellectual figure of mid-nineteenth-century Mexico, describes the Mexican response to the Yankee conquerors' behavior.

Questions to Consider

1. How does José Fernando Ramirez characterize the American occupation of Mexico City?
2. How did the Mexicans resist?
3. Whom does Ramirez blame for the city's occupation?
4. How do you think Ramirez would respond to the sentiments found in John O'Sullivan's views on "Texas and California Annexation" (Document 86)?

Mexico City, September 30, 1847

My dear friend:

I have not received any word from you to which I can reply, because, since the unfortunate inhabitants of this city are being treated as enemies, there has been no opportunity to get mail in from the outside. Where it is being held heaven only knows. We have hopes that the mail will eventually be permitted to come in, and then I shall know what I have to reply to.

What shall I tell you? Well, to be frank, nothing because this city is no longer the center of political life. According to reports, the center has been transferred to many other centers that will exhaust whatever political life is left to us by our enemy who is oppressing and humiliating us. How I would like to bring home this lesson to certain politicians who have talked incessantly about despotism, etc! Here they would see and get a taste of what it means to live without guarantees! It is all so frightful. I must say that those who have conquered us, brutally savage as they are, have conducted themselves in a manner different from that of European armies belonging to nations that bear the standard of civilization. This does not mean that they do not commit countless excesses every day. But we have here a phenomenon consisting of mingled barbarism and restraint. This has been the situation for several days, and there is no way to account for it.

Open fighting ceased the third day after the city was occupied; but the undercover struggle goes on, and it is assuming a fearful aspect. The enemy's forces are growing weaker day by day because of assassinations, and it is impossible to discover who the assassins are. Anyone who takes a walk through the streets or goes a short distance away from the center of the city is a dead man. I have been told that a small cemetery has been found in a pulque tavern where deadly liquor was dispensed for the purpose of assuring an increasing number of

SOURCE: José Fernando Ramirez, *Mexico During the War with the United States*, ed. Walter V. Scholes, trans. by Elliot B. Scherr (Columbia, MO, 1970), 160–62. Reprinted by permission of Marie V. Scholes.

victims. Seven corpses were discovered inside the establishment, but the tavern keeper could not be found. I am also told that the number of those who have been taken off this way amounts to 300, without counting those dying of sickness and wounds. Five days ago a funeral cortege with the bodies of four officers passed by my residence. The plague has begun to show its signs, and the monuments that those filthy soldiers have scattered along the streets of their quarters unmistakably testify to the fact that dysentery is destroying them. I have never before seen such sodden drunkenness, nor any more scandalous or impudent than the drunkenness that holds these men in its grip. Nor have I ever seen more unrestrained appetites. Every hour of the day, except during the evenings, when they are all drunk, one can find them eating everything they see.

The Palace and almost all public buildings have been savagely ransacked and destroyed. I think it only right to say, however, that our disgraceful rabble were the ones who began it all. When the enemy's troops entered the Palace, the doors had already been broken down and the building had been plundered. Three days later the embroidered velvet canopy was sold for four pesos at the Palace entrance. The Government records and other items were sold for two reales. The infamous and eternally accursed Santa Anna abandoned us all, both individuals and property, to the mercy of the enemy and did not leave even one sentinel to defend us.

In Durango you probably know more of what is going on than I do, and you no doubt can see how horrible our future is. I am forwarding to you some documents, two of which I want you to keep as testimony of the iniquitous and shameful rule that the Americans have imposed upon us. The sad thing about all this is that the punishment has been deserved.

Forward the enclosed letters and tell the members of my family that we are all in good health. Do not forget your friend, who holds you in great esteem.

90

Mormons Describe Entering the Salt Lake Valley (1848)

While many Americans joined reform movements during the turbulent 1830s, others sought refuge in new religions. One of the most prominent of these new faiths was the Church of Jesus Christ of Latter Day Saints. Founded by Joseph Smith in the Burned-Over District of New York, the faith followed the teaching found in the Book of Mormon. *The Mormons, as they came to be known, established a tight-knit community structure that emphasized hard work and loyalty to the faith. While the Mormons prospered, their sense of exclusiveness alienated many of their contemporaries. Their communal living arrangements coupled with the emerging practice of polygamy in 1843 contributed to increased persecution. These attacks ultimately led the Mormons to seek refuge in the remote Salt Lake valley in the present-day state of Utah. In this excerpt Oliver B. Huntington describes the last days of the trek before entering Utah. A native of Watertown, New York, and early convert, Huntington would become one of Utah's most successful beekeepers and an important chronicler of early Latter Day Saints history.*

Questions to Consider

1. What appears to be the leading motivation for the Mormons' move west?
2. What appear to be the major obstacles in the approach to Salt Lake?
3. Why do forts guard the approaches to Salt Lake?
4. Based on your reading of this document and Document 88 ("Life on the Overland Trail"), what can you conclude about the trek west?

September 20, 1848

We entered on the 20th day of September A.D. 1848 A fine clear fair day— and the Fort, as we emerged from the Kanion, had a rather singular appearance; or rather the whole Valley was the great scene of curiosity wonder and astonishment, and Fort contributed much to the grandure of the view before us. After arriving at the summit of the last Mountain (which is the worst of the three, and up which all doubled teams) our road was, for several miles—in fact even to the Fort (By this time I may call it, city, as it faintly appeared at first view, not being able to distinguish wheat and hay and other stacks from houses) quite descending—and for about 1/4 a mile from the summit of the Mt. we locked both hindwheels and then 2 yoke could but let the wagon and load down with safty—so great was the descent. The way was harder rougher and narrower as we approached the Valley until within 6 miles of the Fort or City of the Great Salt Lake After passing through a natural gate of but 2 or three rods wide with inaccessible mountains on either side, and the road in the bed of the creek (just there) we soon emerged into an open Paradise, as it will comparatively seem to one who may travel the dreary road that leads to it.

In a moment, release comes to the weary traveller; he sees at once the thin only icilated spot of civilized rest for or within 1000 miles in any direction: a sudden feeling of joy, grandure and gratitude suddenly filled each heart, which brought a few moments of death like stillness, well fited for a large range of the mind: then suddenly every heart and tongue was buisy in rendering praises to the beatiful land of rest immediately in view; embracing the most healthful climate and most productive soil, yet known by any of us.

It was a gradual desent from the first entrance into the valley to within a mile of the forts or city, and about one fourth of this distance on either side of

SOURCE: Oliver Boardman Huntington, Diaries, 1843–1932, *American Memory* 10: 31–36.

the road was fast traveling people constantly meeting eagerly gazing in the face of every individual to descri[be] some friend or fond acquaintance, so eager were they that they could not wait our arrival in camp. There were hundreds of as joyful hearts as earth ever witnessed before. Every heart was full to overflowing, as each strained countainance bespoke plainer than words. We will follow the camps and companies of this emigration to their last camping ground as a traveling party.

Aside from the Forts, there was but one house in the whole Valley. The forts were built on a square covering about 10 acres each and adjoining each other. Three completed and the fourth was in process of building and nearly finished The east side of the old fort which the Pioneers built was of logs; the remainder was of Adobe or as they are commonly called Do-by, the last syllable spoken like "bee" short, which are a large species of brick baked or dried in the sun; they are quite hard and have been known to last near 200 years. On the North south, east and west side [of] each was a large gate to each fort. The outside wall of the fort was the outside wall of the houses. Thus properly, the forts were formed by the joining of houses, and windows were regular built portholes. We'll return to the great train of wagons which was headed by Brigham Young in a coach or an ould Stage, such as are used to carry passenges traveling in the United States Entering the east gate of the old fort and passing directly out at the west gate, we formed in a large carell about 100 yards west of the north fort. About noon our carell was formed. Then the teams were driven over the river jourdin about a mile for feed. Haeppy happy hour thought more than one thousand reflecting minds;—long sought for through years of direful calameties and imparalelled suffering. A home beyond Mobs and strife;—rest from persecution.

91

Local Reaction to the Gold Rush (1848)

The Spanish first colonized California in the eighteenth century, extending missions and settlements up the coast to protect the northern approaches to Mexico. By the early nineteenth century, a small but profitable ranching community had emerged, supplying Yankee traders with tallow and skins for the China trade. Such opportunities attracted a small American community to the area. The war with Mexico escalated American interest in the region, but it was the January 1848 discovery of gold in the American River Valley near Sacramento that rapidly transformed California. The following article from the San Francisco California Star *captures the mood in early gold rush California. The* California

Star ceased publication just four days after this article, when its staff abandoned their jobs in San Francisco to strike out for the gold fields.

Questions to Consider

1. What can you deduce from this selection about economic conditions in mid-nineteenth-century America?
2. How multicultural is the gold rush?
3. What are the principal occupations of those panning for gold?
4. In what ways do you think the gold rush shaped the future of California?

Many of our countrymen are not disposed to do us justice as regards the opinion we have at different times expressed of the employment in which over two thirds of the white population of the country are engaged. There appears to have gone abroad a belief that we should raise our voices against what some one has denominated an "infatuation." We are very far from it, and would invite a calm recapitulation of our articles touching the matter, as in themselves amply satisfactory. We shall continue to report the progress of the work, to speak within bounds, and to approve, admonish, or openly censure whatever, in our opinion, may require it at our hands.

It is quite unnecessary to remind our readers of the "prospects of California" at this time, as the effects of this gold washing enthusiasm, upon the country, through every branch of business are unmistakably apparent to every one. Suffice it that there is no abatement, and that active measures will probably be taken to prevent really serious and alarming consequences.

Every seaport as far south as San Diego, and every interior town, and nearly every rancho from the base of the mountains in which the gold has been found, to the Mission of San Luis, south, has become suddenly drained of human beings. Americans, Californians, Indians and Sandwich Islanders [Hawaiians], men, women and children, indiscriminately. Should there be that success which has repaid the efforts of those employed for the last month, during the present and next, as many are sanguine in their expectations, and we confess to unhesitatingly believe probably, not only will witness the depopulation of every town, the desertion of every rancho, and the desolation of the once promising crops of the country, but it will also draw largely upon adjacent territories—awake Sonora, and call down upon us, despite her Indian battles, a great many of the good people of Oregon. There are at this time over one thousand souls busied in washing gold, and the yield per diem may be safely estimated at from fifteen to twenty dollars, each individual.—

We have by every launch from the embarcadera of New Helvetia, returns of enthusiastic gold seekers—heads of families, to effect transportation of their households to the scene of their successful labors, or others, merely returned to more fully equip themselves for a protracted, or perhaps permanent stay.—

SOURCE: (San Francisco) *California Star*, June 10, 1848.

Spades, shovels, picks, wooden bowls, Indian baskets (for washing), etc., find ready purchase, and are very frequently disposed of at extortionate prices.

The gold region, so called, thus far explored, is about one hundred miles in length and twenty in width. These imperfect explorations contribute to establish the certainty of the placera extending much further south, probably three or four hundred miles, as we have before stated, while it is believed to terminate about a league north of the point at which first discovered. The probable amount taken from these mountains since the first of May last, we are informed is $100,000, and which is at this time principally in the hands of the mechanical, agricultural and laboring classes.

There is an area explored, within which a body of 50,000 men can advantageously labor. Without maliciously interfering with each other, then, there need be no cause for contention and discord, where as yet, we are gratified to know, there is harmony and good feeling existing. We really hope no unpleasant occurrences will grow out of this enthusiasm, and that our apprehensions may be quieted by continued patience and good will among the washers.

92

Images of Chinese Immigrants (1852, 1860)

The gold rush that attracted thousands to California included large numbers of Chinese. Most of these immigrants were from Guangdong in southeastern China. The region was a center of the Taiping rebellion, which sought to overthrow the Chinese emperor. Approximately 20 million died as a result of the conflict. The Chinese immigrants who fled were overwhelmingly male, as the 1860 census recorded that 33,149 of California's 34,933 "Asiatics" were men. The Chinese, accounted for nearly 10 percent of the state's population, and were the subject of racial stereotypes. The images below depict the work and leisure of this overwhelmingly male group of outsiders.

Questions to Consider

1. What can you deduce from these images about mid-nineteenth-century white American racial attitudes?

2. What can you deduce from these images about mid-nineteenth-century white American attitudes toward gambling?

3. How do you think the artist who created "Types of Mankind" (Document 85) would respond to the first image, which depicts whites and Chinese working together?

4. How do you think William Lloyd Garrison ("On Slavery," Document 80) would categorize the Chinese?

Gum Shan Meets El Dorado (c. 1852)

SOURCE: Courtesty of the California History Room, California State Library, Sacramento, California

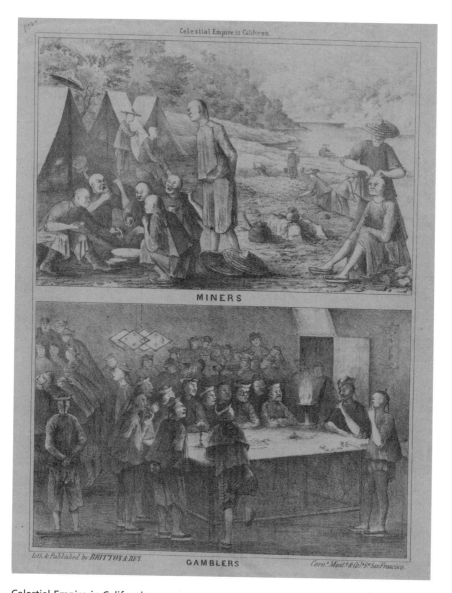

Celestial Empire in California

SOURCE: Courtesy of The Bancroft Library University of California, Berkeley

93

"Civil Disobedience" (1849)

The Mexican War was one of America's most unpopular foreign ventures. Ostensibly begun because of Mexico's invasion of Texas, the war was primarily the result of America's desire to acquire territory. Opposition to the war was particularly strong in New England, where many viewed the conflict as an unjust expansion of slavery. Henry David Thoreau was among those prominent in his opposition to the war. Like his fellow Transcendentalists, he eschewed rationalism, believing that the material world could be transcended and a higher form of reality realized through intuition. Thoreau's philosophy led him to live alone at Walden Pond outside of Concord, Massachusetts. The declaration of the Mexican War, however, demanded a response. In July 1846, Thoreau protested the war by refusing to pay his taxes—an act that briefly landed him in jail. Three years later, he commented at length on "passive resistance" in "Civil Disobedience." His suggestions, some of which are found in the following selection, became a model for later leaders such as India's Mahatma Gandhi and civil rights advocate Martin Luther King Jr.

Questions to Consider

1. What kind of peaceful revolution does Thoreau advocate?
2. Why is Thoreau wary of the rich when it comes to righteous causes?
3. According to Thoreau, why do people need government?
4. Based on this document, what are Thoreau's views toward American democracy?

… Under a government which imprisons any unjustly, the true place for a just man is also a prison. The proper place to-day, the only place which Massachusetts has provided for her freer and less desponding spirits, is in her prisons, to be put out and locked out of the State by her own act, as they have already put themselves out by their principles. It is there that the fugitive slave, and the Mexican prisoner on parole, and the Indian come to plead the wrongs of his race should find them; on that separate, but more free and honorable, ground, where the State places those who are not with her, but against her,—the only house in a slave State in which a free man can abide with honor. If any think that their influence would be lost there, and their voices no longer afflict the ear of the State, that they would not be as an enemy within its walls, they do not

SOURCE: Henry David Thoreau, "Civil Disobedience," *The Writings of Henry David Thoreau*, vol. 4, *Cape Cod and Miscellanies* (New York, 1968; reprint edition of 1906 ed.), 356–87.

know by how much truth is stronger than error, nor how much more elo-
quently and effectively he can combat injustice who has experienced a little in
his own person. Cast your whole vote, not a strip of paper merely, but your
whole influence. A minority is powerless while it conforms to the majority; it
is not even a minority then; but it is irresistible when it clogs by its whole
weight. If the alternative is to keep all just men in prison, or give up war and
slavery, the State will not hesitate which to choose. If a thousand men were not
to pay their tax-bills this year, that would not be a violent and bloody measure,
as it would be to pay them, and enable the State to commit violence and shed
innocent blood. This is, in fact, the definition of a peaceable revolution, if any
such is possible. If the tax-gatherer, or any other public officer, asks me, as one
has done, "But what shall I do?" my answer is, "If you really wish to do anything, resign your office." When the subject has refused allegiance, and the officer has resigned his office, then the revolution is accomplished. But even suppose
blood should flow. Is there not a sort of blood shed when the conscience is
wounded? Through this would a man's real manhood and immortality flow
out, and he bleeds to an everlasting death. I see this blood flowing now.

I have contemplated the imprisonment of the offender, rather than the seizure of his goods,—though both will serve the same purpose,—because they
who assert the purest right, and consequently are most dangerous to a corrupt
State, commonly have not spent much time in accumulating property. To such
the State renders comparatively small service, and a slight tax is wont to appear
exorbitant, particularly if they are obliged to earn it by special labor with their
hands. If there were one who lived wholly without the use of money, the State
itself would hesitate to demand it of him. But the rich man—not to make any
invidious comparison—is always sold to the institution which makes him rich.
Absolutely speaking, the more money, the less virtue; for money comes between
a man and his objects, and obtains them for him; and it was certainly no great
virtue to obtain it. It puts to rest many questions which he would otherwise be
taxed to answer; while the only new question which it puts is the hard but
superfluous one, how to spend it. Thus his moral ground is taken from under
his feet. The opportunities of living are diminished in proportion as what are
called the "means" are increased. The best thing a man can do for his culture
when he is rich is to endeavor to carry out those schemes which he entertained
when he was poor. Christ answered the Herodians according to their condition.
"Show me the tribute-money," said he;—and one took a penny out of his
pocket;—if you use money which has the image of Caesar on it, and which he
has made current and valuable, that is, if you are men of the State, and gladly
enjoy the advantages of Caesar's government, then pay him back some of his
own when he demands it. "Render therefore to Caesar that which is Caesar's,
and to God those things which are God's,"—leaving them no wiser than before
as to which was which; for they did not wish to know.

When I converse with the freest of my neighbors, I perceive that, whatever
they may say about the magnitude and seriousness of the question, and their
regard for the public tranquility, the long and the short of the matter is, that
they cannot spare the protection of the existing government, and they dread

the consequences to their property and families of disobedience to it. For my own part, I should not like to think that I ever rely on the protection of the State. But, if I deny the authority of the State when it presents its tax-bill, it will soon take and waste all my property, and so harass me and my children without end. This is hard. This makes it impossible for a man to live honestly, and at the same time comfortably, in outward respects. It will not be worth the while to accumulate property; that would be sure to go again. You must hire or squat somewhere, and raise but a small crop, and eat that soon. You must live within yourself, and depend upon yourself always tucked up and ready for a start, and not have many affairs....

94

The Question of Cuban Annexation (1853)

Although Manifest Destiny is generally considered a western phenomenon, many southerners were eager to expand into the Caribbean. Every president since Thomas Jefferson had expressed an interest in Cuba, and James K. Polk had authorized $100,000,000 for its purchase from Spain. By the early 1850s, American expansionism combined with southern desire to add slave territory led to another round of overtures to procure Cuba, culminating in the Ostend Manifesto in 1854. In the editorial presented here, the DeBow's Review *offers its insights on the matter. Under the editorial leadership of James Dunwoody Brownson DeBow, the* Review *advertised itself as the leading periodical chronicling the "agricultural, commercial, and industrial progress and resources" of the American South during the mid-nineteenth century.*

Questions to Consider

1. What are the arguments for annexation? What are the arguments against?

2. How do you think John L. O'Sullivan ("Texas and California Annexation," Document 86) would have responded to this editorial?

3. How do you think Henry David Thoreau ("Civil Disobedience," Document 93) would have responded to this editorial?

4. How do you think Francis Pickens ("Inaugural Address of South Carolina Governor Francis Pickens," Document 113) would have responded to this editorial?

The present and prospective condition of Cuba is one of deep interest. Appearances indicate that Spain cannot long continue to hold possession of that island unless she changes, and that greatly, her policy in reference to it. Should the Spanish Government extend to the people of Cuba the privileges they so much desire; allow them an equal participation in the offices of honor and profit, instead of bestowing them exclusively upon natives of Old Spain; remove the burdens placed upon commerce, and otherwise modify the harsh features of their present policy, Spain might for years retain possession of the island of Cuba. Nor would she sustain any loss in thus changing her policy, because the increased trade and commerce of Cuba, resulting from a more liberal policy, would more than compensate the Spanish Government for the concession it might make. But we are apprehensive that Spain will obstinately refuse to ameliorate the condition of that people until a successful resistance shall have been made to the Spanish authorities, and Spain shall have lost her dominion over the island of Cuba.... There are many satisfactory reasons why Cuba should not be annexed to the United States, unless it becomes a matter of necessity to annex her in order to prevent her coming under the control of Great Britain or France. The geographical position of Cuba is such that she must either belong to Spain, become an independent government, or be annexed to our republic. In no event could our government permit her to be acquired by any European power, and any such attempt would necessarily involve the nation making it in a war with the United States.

... Whilst we think that the United States should not interfere in a struggle between Spain and the people of Cuba, even to assist those struggling for freedom, yet we could not and would not permit any European nation to interfere in behalf of Spain. All our sympathies would be with those contending for freedom; and although we could not vie them any direct assistance, without violating our most sacred and wisest maxims of policy; and without departing from the examples set us by our ablest, most distinguished, and best statements, yet if any other government should interpose for the purpose of crushing the rising spirit of liberty on this continent, we would be in duty bound to put a stop to such interference at the hazard of war, if that were necessary. This is and long has been the American doctrine, and it is well that the governments of England and France should distinctly understand the position we occupy on this subject.

In the event of a revolution in Cuba, our citizens would have the undoubted right, if they saw fit to exercise it, of emigrating to that island and taking part in the struggle, but in so doing they would forfeit the privileges of American citizens, and would voluntarily place themselves beyond the protection of our government.... They would in no point of view be responsible to any other government than their own and the government of Spain, and neither England nor France would have any right to intercept them, or in any other way interfere them.... Our country does not desire a war with either Spain, England

SOURCE: "Cuba and the United States: The Policy of Annexation Discussed," *DeBow's Review and Industrial Resources* 14 (January 1853): 63.

or France, on account of Cuba, but our rights as an American nation we will maintain. We will not permit any interference on the part of any European government on this continent and their oppressors.... If it should become necessary to annex Cuba to the United States in order to prevent its coming under the control of England or France, then we say, let it be done, but in no other point of view do we see that it would be good policy for us to annex it. The most desirable position which, we think, Cuba could occupy, would be that of an independent republic, rich in her tropical productions, having free and unrestricted commerce with all nations, enjoying their friendship and sharing largely in their trade. In this way she would be as beneficial to the United States as if she were annexed, without any of the evils resulting from annexation.... Cuba is unlike Texas in almost every respect. Texas was in a great degree uninhabited. Cuba is densely populated. Texas furnished an outlet for overgrowing population. Cuba is already full, and would afford no homes for the enterprising emigrants from the United States. The present slave population, with its annual increase under the humane system of slavery which would follow its annexation, would be amply sufficient for all its wants. It would not, then, give us an outlet for our rapidly increasing slave population. The people of Texas had laws, institutions, manners and feelings similar to our own. In fact, Texas was colonized from this country. Such is not the case with Cuba. They are different from us in nearly every respect, and would not easily coalesce with us. Though under the same government, they would remain a distinct people....

One of the principal objections to the acquisition of Cuba is that it will renew in all its fierceness the slavery agitation, which came so near destroying this confederacy. If Cuba is annexed, it being a slaveholding state, the North will insist upon the annexation of Canada..... Are we of the South willing to take Canada for the sake of getting Cuba? This is the true question.

... It cannot be expected that either England or France would quietly see so great a maritime nation as the United States acquire Cuba, which is said to be the "key of the Gulf of Mexico." The same reasons which would cause us to oppose its acquisition of Cuba by England or France would cause them to oppose the acquisition of us.... We say then that there is every reason to believe that the acquisition of Cuba would lead to long, bloody and disastrous war, ruinous to all the nations engaged in it, and calculated to lead to no beneficial result.... Let us pause and consider well the consequences before we take the fearful leap. Let the fate of other republics be a warning to us of the dangers of unlimited extension, and of wars of conquest.

12

Slavery and the Old South

The republic's Founders envisioned a nation of liberty, assuming that slavery would gradually wither away. Economic forces, however, conspired to make slavery profitable in the South. By the 1830s, many southerners argued that the "peculiar institution" was essential to their way of life. The persistence of slavery made the region increasingly distinct from the North and brought condemnation from reformers on both sides of the Atlantic. White southerners responded to these attacks by portraying their culture as an idyllic society to be emulated, not maligned. Individuals of African descent provided a much different view of southern society. The following excerpts include these varying viewpoints about the Old South.

95

The Alabama Frontier (1821)

The War of 1812 proved disastrous for American Indians of the trans-Appalachian West. Andrew Jackson's victory against the Creeks at Horseshoe Bend in March 1814 opened Alabama to white settlement. Following the war, settlers eager to obtain rich lands in the expanding cotton kingdom swarmed to areas like north Alabama's Tennessee River Valley. By 1819, Alabama had attracted enough people to become a state. While most of the settlers came in search of farmland, many of the newcomers clustered together in towns that emerged from the wilderness virtually overnight. One of the boom towns on the South's urban frontier was Florence, Alabama. In the following letter, Anne Royall boosts the prospects of this new community and conveys the optimism shared by many early settlers. Royall, sometimes referred to as "America's first woman journalist," wrote a series of letters describing early Alabama.

Questions to Consider

1. To what audience is this document directed?
2. What natural advantages does Florence, Alabama, possess?
3. How does Anne Royall suggest that the town still retains a sense of rugged frontier individualism?
4. What can you deduce from this document about frontier attitudes?

... Florence is one of the new towns of this beautiful and rapid rising state. It is happily situated for commerce at the head of steamboat navigation, on the north side of Tennessee river, in the county of Lauderdale, five miles below the port of the Muscle Shoals, and ten miles from the line of the state of Tennessee.

Florence is to be the great emporium of the northern part of this state. I do not see why it should not; it has a great capital and is patronized by the wealthiest gentlemen in the state. It has a great state at its back; another in front, and a noble river on all sides, the steamboats pouring every necessary and every luxury into its lap. Its citizens, bold, enterprising, and industrious—much more so than any I have seen in the state.

Many large and elegant brick buildings are already built here, (although it was sold out, but two years since,) and frame houses are putting up daily. It is not uncommon to see a framed building begun in the morning and finished by night.

Several respectable mercantile houses are established here, and much business is done on commission also. The site of the town is beautifully situated on an eminence, commanding an extensive view of the surrounding country, and Tennessee River, from which it is three quarters of a mile distant. It has two springs of excellent and never failing water. Florence has communication by water with Mississippi, Missouri, Louisiana, Indiana, Illinois, Ohio, Kentucky, West Pennsylvania, West Virginia, and East Tennessee, and very shortly will communicate with the Eastern States, through the great canal!!! The great Military road that leads from Nashville to New Orleans, by way of Lake Ponchartrain, passes through this town, and the number of people who travel through it, and the numerous droves of horses for the lower country, for market, are incredible. Florence contains one printing press, and publishes a paper weekly called the *Florence Gazette;* it is ably patronized, and edited by one of our first men, and said to be the best paper in the state. Florence is inhabited by people from almost all parts of Europe and the United States; here are English, Irish, Welsh, Scotch, French, Dutch, Germans, and Grecians. The first Greek I ever saw was in this town. I conversed with him on the subject of his country, but found him grossly ignorant. He butchers for the town, and has taken to his arms a mulatto woman for a

SOURCE: Anne Royall to her sister, 10 July 1821, Letter 45, Anne Royall, *Letters from Alabama on Various Subjects* (Washington, DC, 1830), 144–46.

wife. He very often takes an airing on horseback of a Sunday afternoon, with his wife riding by his side, and both arrayed in shining costume.

The river at Florence is upwards of five-hundred yards wide; it is ferried in a large boat worked by four horses, and crosses in a few minutes.

There are two large and well kept taverns in Florence, and several Doggeries. A Doggery is a place where spirituous liquors are sold; and where men get drunk, quarrel, and fight, as often as they choose, but where there is nothing to eat for man or beast. Did you ever hear any thing better named. "I sware!" said a Yankee ped-dlar, one day, with both his eyes bunged up, "that are Doggery, be rightly named. Never seed the like on't. If I get to hum agin it 'il be a nice man 'il catch me in these here parts. Awfullest place one could be at." It appeared the inmates of the Doggery enticed him under pretence of buying his wares, and forced him to drink; and then forced him to fight; but the poor little Yankee was sadly beaten. Not content with blacking up his eyes, they over-turned his tin-cart, and scattered his tins to the four winds; frightened his horse, and tormented his very soul out about lasses, &c. He was a laughable object—but to hear his dialect in laying off the law, was a complete farce, particularly when Pat came to invite him into the same Doggery to drink friends—"I ben't a dog to go into that are dog house."

The people, you see, know a thing or two, here; they call things by their right names. But to proceed—there may be about one hundred dwelling houses and stores, a court house, and several warehouses in Florence. The latter are however on the river. One of the longest buildings I ever saw, is in Florence. It was built by a company of gentlemen, and is said to have cost $90,000, and is not yet finished. The proprietors, being of this place, are men of immense wealth, and are pushing their capital with great foresight and activity. For indus-try and activity, Florence outstrips all the northern towns in the state. More peo-ple travel this road than all our western roads put together....

96

The Trial of Denmark Vesey (1822)

The Old South's dependence on slave labor provided opportunity for wealth among its white inhabitants, but at the expense of the African American slaves who toiled on their behalf. White southerners chose to believe that their slaves were content with their status, but their anxiety over the possibility of a slave insurrection belied underlying fears. Slave insurrections had been infrequent in America, but the success of the revolt on Saint Domingue [Haiti] in the 1790s was an example of what could happen. Before the discov-ery of the Vesey plot in 1822, many white citizens in Charleston, South Carolina, chose to ignore the potential for revolt. *Denmark Vesey was probably born in Africa and arrived in Charleston in 1783. Having purchased his freedom with winnings from a local lottery, Vesey found that his freedom and wealth still left him without status in race-conscious Charleston. Vesey, other free blacks in the city, and an undetermined number of slaves responded by plotting to launch an insurrection on July 14, 1822. White authorities uncovered the plot in late May and arrested Vesey on June 22. The following account is from his trial transcript. He and thirty-four fellow conspirators were later executed.*

Questions to Consider

1. What can you deduce from this account about white attitudes toward African Americans?
2. Why do you think an account of the Denmark Vesey trial was published?
3. Why do you think the transcript is so clear in describing Vesey as a "free black man"?
4. Are the attitudes expressed in this document consistent with what David Walker ("Appeal to the Coloured Citizens of the World", Document 79)? said about white American society?

THE TRIAL OF DENMARK VESEY,
A FREE BLACK MAN—COL. G.W. CROSS
ATTENDING AS HIS COUNSEL

Evidence

William, the slave of Mr. Paul, testified as follows:—Mingo Harth told me *that Denmark Vesey was the chiefest man, and more concerned than any one else*—Denmark Vesey is an old man in whose yard my master's negro woman Sarah cooks—he was her father in law, having married her mother Beck, and though they have been parted some time, yet he visited her at her house near the Indendant's, (Major Hamilton) where I have often heard him speak of the rising—*He said he would not like to have a white man in his presence—that he had a great hatred for the whites,* and that if all were like him they would resist the whites—he studies all he can to put it into the heads of the blacks to have a rising against the whites, and tried to induce me to join—he tries to induce all his acquaintances—this has been his chief study and delight for a considerable time—my last conversation with him was in April—he studies the Bible a great deal and tries to prove from it that slavery and bondage is against the Bible. I am persuaded that Denmark Vesey was chiefly concerned in business....

SOURCE: "The Trial of Denmark Vesey, a Free Black Man," *An Official Report of the Trials of Sundry Negroes charged with an Attempt to Raise an Insurrection in the State of South Carolina*, comp. by Lionel H. Kennedy and Thomas Parker (Charleston, 1822), 85–90.

Frank, Mrs. Ferguson's slave gave the following evidence—I know Denmark Vesey and have been to his house—I have heard him say that the negroe's situation was so bad he did not know how they could endure it, and was astonished they did not rise and fend for themselves, and he advised me to join and rise—he said he was going about to see different people, and mentioned the names of Ned Bennett and Peter Poyas as concerned with him—that he had spoken to Ned and Peter on this subject; and that they were to go about and tell the blacks that they were free, and must rise and *fight for themselves*—that they would take the Magazines and Guard-Houses, and the city and be free—that he was going to send *into the country* to inform the people there too—he said he wanted me to join them—I said I could not answer—he said if I would not go into the country for him he could get others—he said himself, Ned Bennett, Peter Poyas and Monday Gell were the principals men and himself the head man. He said they were the principal men to go about and inform the people and fix them, &c. that *one party would land on South-Bay, one about Wappoo, and about the farms*—that the party which was to land on South-Bay was to take the Guard-House and get arms and then they would be able to go on—that the attack was to commence about 12 o'clock at night—*that great numbers would come from all about*, and it must succeed as so many were engaged in it—that they would kill all the whites—that they would leave their master's houses and assemble together near the lines, march down and meet the party which would land on South-Bay—...

The court *unanimously* found Denmark Vesey GUILTY, and passed upon him the sentence of DEATH. After his conviction, a good deal of testimony was given against him during the succeeding trials.—

97

A Reaction to the Nat Turner Revolt (1831)

In the antebellum South, slave revolts occurred with enough frequency to alarm whites who lived in areas with large populations of enslaved peoples. The bloody uprising on Saint Domingue (Haiti) between 1792 and 1802, followed by the Gabriel Prosser revolt in Virginia (1800) and the Vesey plot in South Carolina (1822) inflamed these fears. But the insurrection that had the greatest impact occurred in the summer of 1831 in South-hampton County, Virginia. The revolt's leader, Nat Turner, was instrumental in organiz-ing the slaves' attempt to gain their freedom. An extraordinary individual who had learned to read at a young age, Turner looked to the Bible for refuge from his bondage. Convinced that he had a divine mission, he hatched his plot in August 1831. The revolt failed after the insurgents had killed over 60 whites; at least 120 African Americans would be killed in retribution. Turner and many of his co-conspirators subsequently paid with their lives. The insurrection, which many southerners blamed on abolitionist agitation, caused southern leaders to become increasingly defensive of the institution. The following woodcut offers a white interpretation of the events.

Questions to Consider

1. How does the woodcut depict the insurrection?
2. What can you deduce from this image about white attitudes toward gender?
3. What does this selection reveal about white attitudes toward African Americans?
4. Why is Nat Turner's revolt significant?

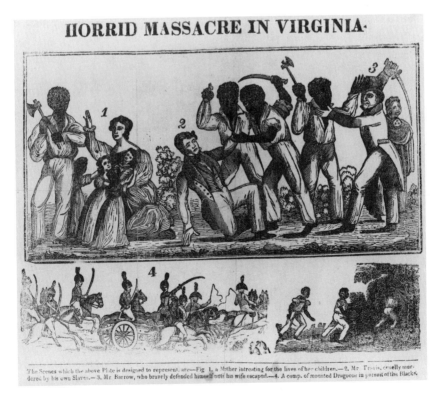

Horrid Massacre in Virginia (1831)

SOURCE: [LC-USZ62-38902]/Library of Congress Prints and Photographs Division

98

The Plantation Labor Force (1838–1839)

Plantation slaves performed a variety of tasks. While a handful of slaves worked in the "big house" and some others worked as artisans, most toiled in the fields. Male and female field hands were subject to a highly organized hierarchy that carefully governed their work patterns. Generally organized into gangs or assigned to complete specific tasks, they were carefully watched by either white overseers or slave drivers. The following selection describes the power that overseers and drivers had over the slaves. Author Fanny Kemble was among the most intriguing characters of the antebellum period. A member of one of the leading acting families in British history, she was one of the first great actresses to appear on American stages and was also an accomplished poet and playwright. Her marriage to slave owner Pierce Butler brought her to his Georgia plantation and provided her with a firsthand view of slavery. She and Butler divorced in 1849. Having given up the stage, she continued her writing, finally publishing Journal of a Residence on a Georgian Plantation in 1838–39 *in 1863. An excerpt from the work follows.*

Questions to Consider

1. What does Fanny Kemble find disturbing about slavery?
2. How is the slave workforce organized?
3. How would southern white slaveholders respond to this document?
4. In what ways might Kemble's gender have influenced her views toward slavery?

At the upper end of the row of houses, and nearest to our overseer's residence, is the hut of the head driver. Let me explain, by the way, his office. The negroes, as I before told you, are divided into troops or gangs, as they are called; at the head of each gang is a driver, who stands over them, whip in hand, while they perform their daily task, who renders an account of each individual slave and his work every evening to the overseer, and receives from him directions for their next day's tasks. Each driver is allowed to inflict a dozen lashes upon any refractory slave in the field, and at the time of the offense; they may not, however, extend the chastisement, and if it is found ineffectual, their remedy lies in reporting the unmanageable individual either to the head

SOURCE: Frances Anne Kemble, *Journal of a Residence on a Georgian Plantation in 1838–1839* (New York, 1863), 42–43, 263.

driver or the overseer, the former of whom has power to inflict three dozen lashes at his own discretion, and the latter as many as he himself sees fit, within the number of fifty; which limit, however, I must tell you, is an arbitrary one on this plantation, appointed by the founder of the estate, Major—, Mr.—'s grandfather, many of whose regulations, indeed I believe most of them, are still observed in the government of the plantation. Limits of this sort, however, to the power of either driver, head driver, or overseer, may or may not exist elsewhere; they are, to a certain degree, a check upon the power of these individuals; but in the absence of the master, the overseer may confine himself within the limit or not, as he chooses; and as for the master himself, where is his limit? He may, if he likes, flog a slave to death, for the laws which pretend that he may not are a mere pretense, inasmuch as the testimony of a black is never taken against a white; and upon this plantation of ours, and a thousand more, the overseer is the *only* white man, so whence should come the testimony to any crime of his? With regard to the oft-repeated statement that it is not the owner's interest to destroy his human property, it answers nothing; the instances in which men, to gratify the immediate impulse of passion, sacrifice not only their eternal, but their evident, palpable, positive worldly interest, are infinite. Nothing is commoner than for a man under the transient influence of anger to disregard his worldly advantage; and the black slave, whose preservation is indeed supposed to be his owner's interest, may be, will be, and is occasionally sacrificed to the blind impulse of passion....

In considering the whole condition of the people on this plantation, it appears to me that the principal hardships fall to the lot of the women—that is, the principal physical hardships. The very young members of the community are of course idle and neglected; the very, very, old, idle and neglected too; the middle-aged men do not appear to me overworked, and lead a mere animal existence, in itself not peculiarly cruel or distressing, but involving a constant element of fear and uncertainty, and the trifling evils of unrequited labor, ignorance the most profound (to which they are condemned by law), and the unutterable injustice which precludes them from all the merits and all the benefits of voluntary exertion, and the progress that results from it....

99

Labor at the Tredegar
Iron Works (1847)

Although the antebellum southern economy was primarily agrarian, it did contain some significant manufacturing establishments. Perhaps the most important of these was the Tredegar Iron Works in Richmond, Virginia. In 1833, local entrepreneurs brought engineer Rhys Davies and several experienced iron workers from Wales to establish the Works. In 1841, Tredegar came under the leadership of West Point graduate Joseph Reid Anderson. Its rolling mills would soon become important suppliers of rails for railroads and munitions for the military. During the Civil War, Tredegar was the leading producer of Confederate cannons and also clad the CSS Virginia *with the iron plates that made the ship famous. The following newspaper article describes an 1847 strike at the Works and discusses the future of industry and labor in the South's fledgling industries.*

Questions to Consider

1. According to this article, why did Tredegar's workers go on strike in 1847?
2. How did Anderson respond to the strike?
3. Why do you think the *Charleston Mercury* is interested in how labor is used in Richmond?
4. How might Richard Colfax, author of "Evidence Against the Views of the Abolitionists" (Document 81), have responded to the views expressed in this article?

By the Richmond papers we perceive that the workmen at the Tredegar Iron Works have "struck," that is, refused to perform their accustomed service. The proprietor, Mr. Anderson, supposed this movement was to extort higher wages, and solicitous of justifying his course, published the rates paid, which proved to be considerably higher than those allowed for similar services in Northern establishments. The workmen, in their response, stated that their objections were not to the wages, but to associating with the colored workmen in the same establishment, and unless these were discharged, they would no longer work for him. Our Northern Abolitionists, with all their hypocritical sympathy for the blacks, justify this "strike," and deal out their accustomed denunciations of Southern

SOURCE: "Abolition Movement in Virginia," *Charleston* [South Carolina] *Mercury*, 10 June 1847, 2.

institutions, demonstrating that it is not love for the slave, but hatred of the slave holder, which actuates them. Mr. Anderson, with a decision and firmness which merits the support and the thanks of the South has refused to compromise his right to employ that kind of labor which he deems most conductive to his interest; and as the whites refuse to divide, has resolved to patronize hereafter the black race exclusively, who have to be fed and clothed as well as the other portions of the human family. He is now rapidly filling up the vacant places at his furnaces and foundry with the sable sons of Africa, the color of whose skins will suffer no detriment by coming in contact with Coal and Iron, and both of which they can prepare and manufacture profitably without legislative *protection*. Mr. Anderson's experiment has been most successful, and has been agreeably surprised at the skill and alacrity with which the negroes have taken hold of what has been considered hitherto the mysteries of the trade, as if it was their peculiar province to deal with such dark articles. We are highly gratified at the triumphant success of Mr. Anderson, and consider it of the greatest importance to the South, as demonstrating that there are other sources of revenue, and means of subsistence, for our blacks beside cotton, rice, tobacco and sugar. Virginia, the "Old Dominion," awaking to her true interests is destined to become a great manufacturing State. Her mineral resources, and her immense water power, are strong inducements to develop her capacities in that direction. As her agricultural productions become less remunerating, she is fortunate in having such profitable materials for the employment of her capital and labor. A mistaken idea has prevailed that our black population is not adapted to manufacturing purposes, and the South was thoughtlessly falling into a false policy. As we became manufacturing, white operatives were imported, superseding our negro workmen, composing a large portion of our population, all of which had to be provided for. The inevitable effect of this course was to expel the black race, and to force their masters to emigrate, or reluctantly to sell them. We rejoice therefore, at the late strike in Richmond. It will awaken the South to the contemplation of a grave question, pregnant with the most momentous consequences, and on which the prosperity and welfare of our people may greatly depend. The Blacks are a most important part of our population. They compose the entire laboring class. They are human beings and with other members of the family, must be fed and clothed. They merit the guardian care of the Southern community. They are capable of performing all the functions to which labor can be profitably directed; and as the sounds of profit from labor change, it is the policy of the country where they reside, not to expel them, but reserve the new vocations for them. The coal and iron business seems to be peculiarly adapted to them; and as Mr. Anderson's experiment, thus far, has resulted so encouragingly, we hope that the entire South will unite in countenancing the policy in which he has taken the lead; and effectually dispel the mistaken notions that our Blacks may not be as profitably employed in all the channels of mining and manufacturing, as in those of agriculture. We shall thus open new channels of profitable employment for our *peculiar*, *contented*, and *most efficient* class of laborers.

100

Martin Delany and African American Nationalism (1852)

The sense of American nationalism that was so pervasive in the middle of the nineteenth century was exclusively white. Americans of African descent, subject to pervasive and dehumanizing discrimination yet affected by many of the same intellectual currents as whites, would develop their own form of nationalism. The leading Black Nationalist of the time was Martin Delany. A free black from Virginia, Delany settled in Pittsburgh to apprentice as a medical doctor. He eventually won acceptance to Harvard Medical School in 1850 but left following student protests against his presence. By this time he had already begun publishing material for abolitionist presses and briefly coedited Frederick Douglass's North Star. *Often considered the father of Black Nationalism, Delany published the following account in 1852. After a brief time in Canada and an exploration of the Niger Valley of West Africa, Delany returned to serve in the Civil War. Following the war, he moved to Charleston, South Carolina, where he became involved in local Republican politics and was an outspoken advocate of African American self-reliance.*

Questions to Consider

1. Compare and contrast the nationalism expressed by Martin Delany with that of John L. O'Sullivan ("Texas and California Annexation," Document 86).

2. How does Martin Delany plan to promote Black Nationalism?

3. How might white Americans of the mid-nineteenth century have responded to this proposal?

4. To what extent have African Americans adopted views of race and nation that parallel those expressed by white contemporaries?

APPENDIX

A PROJECT FOR AN EXPEDITION OF ADVENTURE, TO THE EASTERN COAST OF AFRICA

Every people should be the originators of their own designs, the projector of their own schemes, and creators of the events that lead to their destiny—the consummations of their desires.

Situated as we are, in the United States, many, and almost insurmountable obstacles present themselves. We are four-and-a-half millions in numbers, free and bond; six hundred thousand free, and three-and-a-half millions bond.

We have native hearts and virtues, just as other nations; which in their pristine purity are noble, potent, and worthy of example. We are a nation within a nation;—as the Poles in Russia, the Hungarians in Austria, the Welsh, Irish, and Scotch in the British dominions.

But we have been, by our oppressors, despoiled of our purity, and corrupted in our native characteristics, so that we have inherited their vices, and but few of their virtues, leaving us in character, really a *broken people*.

Being distinguished by complexion, we are still singled out—although having merged in the habits and customs of our oppressors—as a distinct nation of people; as the Poles, Hungarians, Irish, and others, who still retain their native peculiarities, of language, habits, and various other traits. The claims of no people, according to established policy and usage, are respected by any nation, until they are presented in a national capacity.

To accomplish so great and desirable an end, there should be held, a great representative gathering of the colored people of the United States; not what is termed a national Convention, represented en masse, such as have been, for the last few years, held at various times and places; but a true representation of the intelligence and wisdom of the colored freemen; because it will be futile and an utter failure, to attempt such a project without the highest grade of intelligence.

No great project was ever devised without the consultation of the most mature intelligence, and discreet discernment and precaution.

To effect this, and prevent intrusion and improper representation, there should be a CONFIDENTIAL COUNCIL held; and circulars issued, only to such persons as shall be *known* to the projectors to be equal to the desired object....

By this Council to be appointed, a Board of Commissioners, to consist of three, five, or such reasonable number as may be decided upon, one of whom shall be chosen as Principal or Conductor of the Board, whose duty and business shall be, to go on an expedition to the EASTERN COAST of Africa, to make researches for a suitable location on that section of the coast, for the settlement of colored adventurers from the United States, and elsewhere. Their mission should be to all such places as might meet the approbation of the people; as South America, Mexico, the West Indies, &c....

The Council shall appoint a permanent Board of Directors, to manage and supervise the doings of the Commissioners, and to whom they shall be amenable for their doings, who shall hold their office until successors shall be appointed.

SOURCE: Martin R. Delany, *The Condition, Emigration, and Destiny of the Colored People of the United States, Politically Considered* (Philadelphia, 1852), 209–14.

A National Confidential Council, to be held once in three years; and sooner, if necessity or emergency should demand it; the Board of Directors giving at least three months' notice, by circulars and newspapers....

MANNER OF RAISING FUNDS

The National Council shall appoint one or two Special Commissioners, to England and France, to solicit, in the name of the Representatives of a Broken Nation, of four-and-a-half millions, the necessary outfit and support, for any period not exceeding three years, of such an expedition. Certainly, what England and France would do, for a little nation—mere nominal nation, of five thousand civilized Liberians, they would be willing and ready to do, for five millions; if they be but authentically represented, in a national capacity. What was due to Greece, enveloped by Turkey, should be due to us, enveloped by the United States; and we believe would be respected, if properly presented. To England and France, we should look for sustenance, and the people of those two nations—as they would have everything to gain from such an adventure and eventual settlement on the Eastern Coast of Africa—the opening of an immense trade being the consequence. The whole Continent is rich in minerals, and the most precious metals, as but a superficial notice of the topographical and geological reports from that country, plainly show to any mind versed in the least, in the science of the earth....

101

A Slave Describes Sugar Cultivation (1853)

Cotton production dominated the economy of the Old South, but large numbers of slaves also labored to bring in cash crops such as sugar. In the following account, Solomon Northup describes the sugar harvest and production during his days of bondage. Born free in Minerva, New York, Northup lived a relatively uneventful life until he was kidnapped not far from his home and sold into slavery in March 1841. Following an unsuccessful attempt to commandeer the slave ship on which he traveled, he spent twelve years working for several different masters in Louisiana. In January 1853, Northup returned to New

York after a prominent member of the family that had once owned his father secured the kidnapped slave's freedom. Northup returned to Glens Falls, New York, and later that year published his account, an excerpt of which follows.

Questions to Consider

1. According to Solomon Northup, what did the slaves do to plant and harvest sugarcane?
2. What is gang labor?
3. Was it common to sell the services of a slave to others?
4. How might the creator of the image "Types of Mankind" (Document 85) have responded to this account?

… In consequence of my inability in cotton-picking, Epps was in the habit of hiring me out on sugar plantations during the season of cane-cutting and sugar-making. He received for my services a dollar a day, with the money supplying my place on his cotton plantation. Cutting cane was an employment that suited me, and for three successive years I held the lead row at Hawkins', leading a gang of from fifty to an hundred hands.…

The ground is prepared in beds, the same as it is prepared for the reception of the cotton seed, except it is ploughed deeper. Drills are made in the same manner. Planting commences in January, and continues until April. It is necessary to plant a sugar field only once in three years. Three crops are taken before the seed or plant is exhausted.

Three gangs are employed in the operation. One draws the cane from the rick, or stack, cutting the top and flags from the stalk, leaving only that part which is sound and healthy. Each joint of the cane has an eye, like the eye of a potato, which sends forth a sprout when buried in the soil. Another gang lays the cane in the drill, placing two stalks side by side in such manner that joints will occur once in four or six inches. The third gang follows with hoes, drawing earth upon the stalks, and covering them to the depth of three inches.

In four weeks, at the farthest, the sprouts appear above the ground, and from this time forward grow with great rapidity. A sugar field is hoed three times, the same as cotton, save that a greater quantity of earth is drawn to the roots. By the first of August hoeing is usually over. About the middle of September, whatever is required for seed is cut and stacked in ricks, as they are termed. In October it is ready for the mill or sugar-house, and then the general cutting begins. The blade of a cane-knife is fifteen inches long, three inches wide in the middle, and tapering towards the point and handle. The blade is thin, and in order to be at all serviceable must be kept very sharp. Every third hand takes the lead of two others, one of whom is on each side of him. The lead hand, in the first place, with a blow of his knife shears the flags from the stalk. He next cuts off the top down as far as it is green. He must be careful to sever all the green from the ripe

SOURCE: Solomon Northup, *Twelve Years a Slave* (Auburn, NY, 1853), 208–11.

part, inasmuch as the juice of the former sours the molasses, and renders it unsalable. Then he severs the stalk at the root, and lays it directly behind him. His right and left hand companions lay their stalks when cut in the same manner, upon his. To every three hands there is a cart, which follows, and the stalks are thrown into it by the younger slaves, when it is drawn to the sugar-house and ground....

In the month of January the slaves enter the field again to prepare for another crop. The ground is now strewn with the tops, and flags cut from the past year's cane. On a dry day fire is set to this combustible refuse, which sweeps over the field, leaving it bare and clean, and ready for the hoes. The earth is loosened about the roots of the old stubble, and in process of time another crop springs up from the last year's seed. It is the same the year following; but the third year the seed has exhausted its strength, and the field must be ploughed and planted again. The second year the cane is sweeter and yields more than the first, and the third year more than the second....

102

A Defense of Southern Society (1854)

As northern and European reformers increasingly criticized the institution of slavery, southerners grew more defensive of their society and its "peculiar institution." The discomfort felt by southerners like Thomas Jefferson about the institution was replaced by the ideas of people like Thomas R. Dew, who argued that slavery was a "positive good." George Fitzhugh was among the most effective defenders of southern society during the years immediately preceding the Civil War. Trained in the law, he served in the attorney general's office during the Buchanan administration; but it was his comparative essays on northern and southern economies and society that made him well known. An 1856 trip to the North brought him to the home of Gerrit Smith, a relative and staunch abolitionist, and led to a meeting with Harriet Beecher Stowe, the author of Uncle Tom's Cabin. *The visit transformed the Virginia native into a more aggressive defender of southern civilization. In the following selection from* The Sociology for the South, *Fitzhugh compared the laissez-faire economy of the North with southern paternalism.*

Questions to Consider

1. According to George Fitzhugh, why does the South have the better way of life?

2. Why is the South's economy so strong in comparison to the North's?

3. Why is the South's society better than the North's?

4. How might a northerner respond to this document?

... At the slaveholding South all is peace, quiet, plenty and contentment. We have no mobs, no trades unions, no strikes for higher wages, no armed resistance to the law, but little jealousy of the rich by the poor. We have but few in our jails, and fewer in our poor houses. We produce enough of the comforts and necessaries of life for a population three or four times as numerous as ours. We are wholly exempt from the torrent of pauperism, crime, agrarianism, and infidelity which Europe is pouring from her jails and alms houses on the already crowded North. Population increases slowly, wealth rapidly. In the tide water region of Eastern Virginia, as far as our experience extends, the crops have doubled in fifteen years, whilst the population has been almost stationary. In the same period in the lands, owing to improvements of the soil and the many fine houses erected in the country, have nearly doubled in value. This ratio of improvement has been approximated or exceeded wherever in the South slaves are numerous. We have enough for the present, and no Malthusian spectres frightening us for the future. Wealth is more equally distributed than at the North, where a few millionaires own most of the property of the country. (These millionaires are men of cold hearts and weak minds; they know how to make money, but not how to use it, either for the benefit of themselves or of others.) High intellectual and moral attainments, refinement of head and heart, give standing to a man in the South, however poor he may be. Money is, with few exceptions, the only thing that ennobles at the North. We have poor among us, but none who are over-worked and under-fed. We do not crowd cities because lands are abundant and their owners kind, merciful and hospitable. The poor are as hospitable as the rich, the negro as the white man. Nobody dreams of turning a friend, a relative, or a stranger from his door. The very negro who deems it no crime to steal, would scorn to sell his hospitality. We have no loafers, because the poor relative or friend who borrows our horse, or spends a week under our roof, is a welcome guest. The loose economy, the wasteful mode of living at the South, is a blessing when rightly considered; it keeps want, scarcity and famine at a distance, because it leaves room for retrenchment. The nice, accurate economy of France, England and New England, keeps society always on the verge of famine, because it leaves no room to retrench, that is to live on a part only of what they now consume. Our society exhibits no appearance of precocity, no symptoms of decay. A long course of continuing improvement is in prospect before us, with no limits which human foresight can descry. Actual liberty and equality with our white population has been approached much nearer than in the free States. Few of our whites ever work as day laborers, none as cooks, scullions, ostlers, body servants, or in other menial capacities. One free citizen does not lord it over another; hence that feeling of independence and equality that distinguishes us; hence that pride of character, that self-respect, that give us ascendence when we come in contact with Northerners. It is a distinction to be a Southerner, as it once was to be a Roman citizen....

SOURCE: George Fitzhugh, *The Sociology for the South; Or, The Failure of Free Society* (Richmond, VA, 1854), 253–55.

103

Images of Slave Life (1858, 1860)

Despite a wealth of writings and images on the institution of slavery, few mid-nineteenth-century depictions of the institution offer a balanced, let alone sympathetic interpretation of the daily lives of slaves. The first image is a woodcut of slaves picking cotton. The staple crop was central to the southern economy, leading contemporaries to declare that cotton was king. The reliance on cotton as an export contributed greatly to the invigoration and expansion of slavery in the nineteenth century. The second image depicts a slave funeral. The great evangelical revivals of the late eighteenth and nineteenth centuries with their messages of spiritual equality and liberation were especially attractive to many African Americans, who fashioned their own interpretation of Christianity in the process.

Questions to Consider

1. In what ways do these two images depict the enslaved African American family?

2. Compare and contrast these images with that found in Document 97 ("A Reaction to the Nat Turner Revolt"). In what ways do black and white gender roles appear to differ?

3. How do you think Fanny Kemble ("The Plantation Labor Force," Document 98) and George Fitzhugh ("A Defense of Southern Society," Document 102) would respond to these images?

4. How would you expect the artist who created the image "Types of Mankind" (Document 85) to respond to the depiction of the slave funeral?

Picking cotton on a Georgia plantation (1858)

SOURCE: [LC-USZ62-76385]/Library of Congress Prints and Photographs Division

Creator

SOURCE: The Historic New Orleans Collection

104

The Southern Yeomen (1860)

The Old South has been commonly stereotyped as a land of planters, plantation mistresses, and slaves. Most of the antebellum white southerners, however, were not slave owners. In Social Relations in Our Southern States, Daniel R. Hundley sought to dispel the traditional myths about southern society and emphasize the role that the yeomen played in the South. An Alabama native who grew up on the family plantation, Hundley attended a variety of educational institutions before receiving a law degree from Harvard in 1853. Following his graduation he moved to Chicago, where he dabbled in a wide variety of business ventures. The widespread unemployment and financial ruin created by the Panic of 1857 led Hundley to champion a "charity fund" to relieve increasing urban poverty. Despite his Chicago career, Hundley retained his southern contacts, wintering each year in his native state. Hundley never expressed serious interest in politics before 1860 and remained committed to the Union until Lincoln's election—an event that he believed doomed the nation. In the following document, Hundley describes the southern yeomanry that formed the bulk of the region's white population.

Questions to Consider

1. Why does Daniel Hundley marvel at the yeoman farmer?
2. Why does he distinguish between the yeoman and "poor White Trash"?
3. Why do the distinctions between master and slave blur when the yeoman owns slaves?
4. How do you think Solomon Northup ("A Slave Describes Sugar Cultivation," Document 101) would respond to this excerpt?

… For while princes, presidents, and governors may boast of their castles and lands, their silken gowns and robes of ceremony—all which can be made the sport of fortune, and do often vanish away in a moment, leaving their sometime owners poor indeed—the COMMON PEOPLE, as the masses are called, possess in and of themselves a far richer inheritance, which is the ability and the will to earn an honest livelihood (not by the tricks of trade and the lying spirit of barter, nor yet by trampling on any man's rights, but) by the toilsome sweat of their own brows, delving patiently and trustingly in old mother earth, who under the blessing of God, never deceives or disappoints those who put their trust in

SOURCE: Daniel R. Hundley, *Social Relations in Our Southern States* (New York, 1860), 192–98.

her generous bosom. And of all the hardy sons of toil, in all free lands the Yeomen are most deserving of our esteem....

But you have no Yeoman in the South, my dear Sir? Beg your pardon, our dear Sir, but we have hosts of them. I thought you had only poor White Trash? ...

Know, then, that the Poor Whites of the South constitute a separate class to themselves; the Southern Yeomen are as distinct from them as the Southern Gentleman is from the Cotton Snob. Certainly the Southern Yeomen are nearly always poor, at least so far as this world's goods are to be taken into the account. As a general thing they own no slaves; and even in case they do, the wealthiest of them rarely possess more than from ten to fifteen. But even when they are slaveholders, they seem to exercise but few of the rights of ownership over their human chattels, making so little distinction between master and man, that their negroes invariably become spoiled, like so many frequently see black and white, slave and freeman, camping out together, living sometimes in the same tent or temporary pine-pole cabin; drinking ... out of the same tin dipper or long-handled gourd their home-distilled apple brandy; dining on the same homely but substantial fare, and sharing one bed in common, videlicet, the cabin floor.

Again should you go among the hardy yeomanry of Tennessee, Kentucky, or Missouri, whenever or wherever they own slaves (which in these States is not often the case) you will invariably see the negroes and their masters ploughing side by side in the fields; or bared to the waist, and with old-fashioned scythe vying with one another who can cut down the broadest swath of yellow wheat, or of the waving timothy; or bearing the tall stalks of maize and packing them into the stout-built barn, with ear and fodder on, ready for the winter's husking....

And yet, notwithstanding the Southern Yeoman allows his slaves so much freedom of speech and action, is not offended when they call him familiarly by his Christian name, and hardly makes them work enough to earn their salt, still he is very proud of being a slaveholder; and when he is not such, his greatest ambition is to make money enough to buy a negro....

13

Origins of the Civil War

Despite social, cultural, and economic differences, the North and South had managed to negotiate their disputes successfully during the first half-century of the nation's existence. After the Mexican War, this spirit of compromise quickly disintegrated into an increasingly hostile exchange. Northerners, alarmed by the spread of slavery, became vocal in their criticism of the South, while southerners decried attempts to undermine their way of life. The events of the 1850s exacerbated these differences. As the political middle collapsed, politicians from both sections championed more radical solutions to the issues that divided the nation, deepening the cleavage between the sections. The following excerpts shed light on these issues and the hostility they generated.

105

An African American Minister Responds to the Fugitive Slave Law (1851)

The Compromise of 1850 sought to defuse sectional tensions by addressing all of the major issues that divided North and South and meeting at least some of each section's demands. Southern slaveholders demanded a stronger fugitive slave law. As part of the compromise, the federal government pledged to support the recovery of runaway slaves. The resulting law provided financial incentives for judges to find African Americans as fugitive slaves, barred alleged runaways from testifying on their own behalf, and imposed penalties on anyone who assisted fugitives. The law and its subsequent enforcement brought a howl of protest from many northerners while threatening the freedom of northern blacks. Samuel R. Ward was among those in jeopardy. Because he had escaped slavery at an early age, Ward had little memory of the institution. Licensed to preach in 1839, he served primarily white congregations in upstate New York. Active in antislavery circles as a writer and speaker, he placed himself at great jeopardy by publicly speaking against the law. Fearful for his safety, he fled to Canada in 1851. The following selection from his autobiography details his decision to do so.

Questions to Consider

1. What effect did the Fugitive Slave Law have upon free blacks in the North?
2. What can you discern about northern racism from this document?
3. How do you think William Lloyd Garrison ("William Lloyd Garrison on Slavery," Document 80) would respond to this document? How would those who supported the prosecution of Denmark Vesey ("The Trial of Denmark Vesey," Document 96) respond to this document?

... In the summer of 1851, business called me to travel in various parts of the country. I visited numerous districts of New York, Pennsylvania, Ohio, Illinois, Wisconsin, Michigan, and Indiana, as well as Connecticut, Rhode Island, Massachusetts, and New Hampshire. Smarting as we were under the recently passed Fugitive Law—and these irritations being inflamed and aggravated by the dragging of some poor victim of it from some Northern town to the South and to slavery, every month or so—of course this law became *the theme* of most I said and wrote. In October, Mrs. Ward accompanied me in a tour through Ohio. We were about finishing that tour, when we saw in the papers an account of the Gorsuch case, in Christiana, Pennsylvania. That was a case in which the Reverend Mr. Gorsuch went armed to the house of a Negro, in the suburbs of the town named, in search of a slave who had escaped from him. The owner of the house denied him admittance. Several Negroes, armed, stood ready inside the house to defend it against the *reverend* slave-catcher and his party—the latter declaring his slave was in that house, avowing his determination to have him, if he went to h—ll after him; and, intending to intimidate the Negroes, fired upon the house with a rifle. Fortunately none of the besieged party were killed; but, they returned Mr. Gorsuch's fire, and *he* dropped a corpse!

The authorities arraigned these poor Negroes for murder. They seemed determined to have their blood. Upon reading this, I handed the paper containing the account to my wife; and we concluded that resistance was fruitless, that the country was hopelessly given to the execution of this barbarous enactment, and that it were vain to hope for the reformation of such a country. At the same time, my secular prospects became exceedingly involved and embarrassed; and willing as I might be to be one of a forlorn hope in the assault upon slavery's citadel, I had

SOURCE: Samuel R. Ward, *Autobiography of a Fugitive Negro* (London, 1855), 115–17.

no reasonable prospect of doing so, consistently with my duty to my family. The anti-slavery cause does not, cannot, find bread and education for one's children. We then jointly determined to wind up our affairs, and go to Canada; and, with the remnant of what might be left to us, purchase a little hut and garden, and pass the remainder of our days in peace, in a free British country....

106

Southern Review
of *Uncle Tom's Cabin* (1852)

During the decade preceding the Civil War, long-standing differences between North and South became more pronounced and increasingly difficult to compromise. Slavery proved the most divisive of these issues. The publication of Harriet Beecher Stowe's Uncle Tom's Cabin *in 1852 further inflamed regional discord. Stowe grew up in New England before moving with her family to Cincinnati in 1832, where her father, Congregationalist minister Lyman Beecher, had accepted the leadership of Lane Theological Seminary. While living in Cincinnati, she had the opportunity to observe the institution of slavery more closely, while also embarking on a writing career. The Fugitive Slave Law of 1850 intensified Stowe's opposition to slavery. In 1852 she produced* Uncle Tom's Cabin, *a fictional account of the "peculiar institution" as seen through slaves' eyes. The following selection is a review of Stowe's work that appeared in the* Southern Literary Messenger. *Formerly edited by Edgar Allan Poe, the journal—based in Richmond, Virginia—was the South's leading literary periodical.*

Questions to Consider

1. Why does the *Southern Literary Messenger* point out that a "female writer" authored *Uncle Tom's Cabin*?
2. How is the book characterized in the review?
3. Why is the author of the review fearful of the book's influence?
4. What is the significance of *Uncle Tom's Cabin?*

... [W]e beg to make a distinction between lady writers and female writers. We could not find it in our hearts to visit the dullness or ignorance of a

SOURCE: *Southern Literary Messenger* 18 (October 1852): 630–38.

well-meaning lady with the rigorous discipline which it is necessary to inflict upon male dunces and blockheads. But where a writer of the softer sex manifests, in her productions, a shameless disregard of truth and of those amenities which so peculiarly belong to her sphere of life, we hold that she has forfeited the claim to be considered a lady, and with that claim all exemption from the utmost stringency of critical punishment....

... [Mrs. Stowe] wished, by the work now under consideration, to persuade us of the horrible guilt of Slavery, and with the kindest feelings for us as brethren, to teach us that our constitution and laws are repugnant to every sentiment of humanity. We know that among other novel doctrines in vogue in the land of Mrs. Stowe's nativity—the pleasant land of New England—which we are old-fashioned enough to condemn, is one which would place woman on a footing of political equality with man, and causing her to look beyond the office for which she was created—the high and holy place of maternity—would engage her in the administration of public affairs; thus handing over the State to the perilous protection of diaper diplomatists and wet-nurse politicians. Mrs. Stowe, we believe, belongs to this school of Woman's Rights, and on this ground she may assert her prerogative to teach us how wicked are we ourselves and the Constitution under which we live....

But whatever her designs may have been, it is very certain that she has shockingly traduced the slaveholding society of the United States, and we desire to be understood as acting entirely on the defensive, when we proceed to expose the miserable misrepresentations of her story....

... many of the allegations of cruelty towards the slaves, brought forward by Mrs. Stowe, are absolutely and unqualifiedly false.... We are of opinion too that heart-rending separations [of families] are much less frequent under the institution of slavery than in countries where poverty rules the working classes with despotic sway....

But let it be borne in mind that this slanderous work has found its way to every section of our country and has crossed the water to Great Britain, filling the minds of all who know nothing of slavery with hatred for that institution and those who uphold it. Justice to ourselves would seem to demand that it should not be suffered to circulate longer without the brand of falsehood upon it. Let it be recollected, too, that the importance Mrs. Stowe will derive from Southern criticism will be one of infamy. Indeed she is only entitled to criticism at all, as the mouthpiece of a large and dangerous faction which if we do not put down with the pen, we may be compelled one day (God grant that day may never come!) to repel with the bayonet. There are questions that underlie the story of "Uncle Tom's Cabin" of far deeper significance than any mere false coloring of Southern society, and our readers will probably see the work discussed, in other points of view, in the next number of the *Messenger,* by a far abler and more scholar-like hand than our own. Our editorial task is now ended, and in dismissing the disagreeable subject, we beg to make a single suggestion to Mrs. Stowe—that, as she is fond of referring to the Bible, she will turn over, before writing her next work of fiction, to the twentieth chapter of Exodus and there read these words—"THOU SHALT NOT BEAR FALSE WITNESS AGAINST THY NEIGHBOR."

107

American (Know Nothing) Party Platform (1856)

The large numbers of immigrants who flooded America in the decades before the Civil War elicited a strong nativist response. For many native born, the Irish in particular came to epitomize the threat these newcomers posed. Nativists were convinced that Roman Catholics could not be good American citizens since they were bound to follow the dictates of the Pope. In addition, many condemned the living conditions and use of alcohol associated with many immigrants. Fearful that the Democrats were becoming a tool of urban immigrants and seeing no viable alternative, the American party emerged in the 1840s. Because many of its members kept their membership secret, many of its adherents stated that they "know nothing" when asked about the party. By the mid-1850s, the American party had become a powerful political force in many northeastern states. Many of its members would eventually gravitate to the Republicans.

Questions to Consider

1. What appear to be the most important values of American party adherents?
2. What does the platform advocate relative to the relationship between national and state power?
3. How do the sentiments expressed compare with those found in Document 21 ("Pennsylvania Assembly Comments on German Immigration")? What can you conclude from this comparison?
4. How would a Know Nothing define American Identity?

AMERICAN PLATFORM OF PRINCIPLES ADOPTED AT PHILADELPHIA, THURSDAY, FEBRUARY 21, 1856

1. An humble acknowledgement to the Supreme Being, for his protecting care vouchsafed to our fathers in their successful Revolutionary struggle, and

SOURCE: "American Platform of Principles," *The True American's Almanac and Politician's Manual for 1857* (New York, 1857).

hitherto manifested to us, their descendants, in the preservation of the liberties, the independence and the union of these States.

2. The perpetuation of the Federal Union and Constitution, as the palladium of our civil and religious liberties, and the only sure bulwarks of American Independence.

3. Americans must rule America, and to this end native-born citizens should be selected for all State, Federal, and municipal offices of government employment, in preference to all others. Nevertheless,

4. Persons born of American parents residing temporarily abroad, should be entitled to all the rights of native-born citizens.

5. No person should be selected for political station (whether of native or foreign birth), who recognizes any allegiance or obligation of any description to any foreign prince, potentate or power, or who refuses to recognize the Federal and State Constitution (each within its sphere) as paramount to all other laws, as rules of political action.

6. The unequalled recognition and maintenance of the reserved rights of the several States, and the cultivation of harmony and fraternal good will between the citizens of the several States, and to this end, non-interference by Congress with questions appertaining solely to the individual States, and non-intervention by each State with the affairs of any other State.

7. The recognition of the right of native-born and naturalized citizens of the United States, permanently residing in any Territory thereof, to frame their constitution and laws, and to regulate their domestic and social affairs in their own mode, subject only to the provisions of the Federal Constitution, with the privilege of admission into the Union whenever they have the requisite population for one Representative in Congress: Provided, always, that none but those who are citizens of the United States, under the Constitution and laws thereof, and who have a fixed residence in any such territory, ought to participate in the formation of the Constitution, or in the enactment of laws for said Territory or State.

8. An enforcement of the principles that no State or Territory ought to admit others than citizens to the right of suffrage, or of holding political offices of the United States.

9. A change in the laws of naturalization, making a continued residence of twenty-one years, of all not heretofore provided for, an indispensable requisite for citizenship hereafter, and excluding all paupers, and persons convicted of crime, from landing upon our shores; but no interference with the vested rights of foreigners.

10. Opposition to any union between Church and State; no interference with religious faith or worship, and no test oaths for office.

11. Free and thorough investigation into any and all alleged abuses of public functionaries, and a strict economy in public expenditures.

12. The maintenance and enforcement of all laws constitutionally enacted until said laws shall be repealed, or shall be declared null and void by competent judicial authority.

13. Opposition to the reckless and unwise policy of the present Administration in the general management of our national affairs, and more especially as shown in removing "Americans" (by designation) and Conservatives in principle, from office, and placing foreigners and Ultraists in their places; as shown in a truckling subserviency to the stronger, and an insolent and cowardly bravado towards the weaker powers; as shown in re-opening sectional agitation; by the repeal of the Missouri Compromise; as shown in granting to unnaturalized foreigners the right of suffrage in Kansas and Nebraska question; as shown in the corruptions which pervade some of the Departments of the Government; as shown in disgracing meritorious naval officers through prejudice or caprice; and as shown in the blundering mismanagement of our foreign relations.

14. Therefore, to remedy existing evils, and prevent the disastrous consequences otherwise resulting therefrom, we would build up the "American Party" upon the principles hereinbefore stated.

15. That each State Council shall have authority to amend their several Constitutions, so as to abolish the several degrees and substitute a pledge of honor, instead of other obligations, for fellowship and admission into the party.

16. A free and open discussion of all political principles embraced in our platform.

108

Charles Sumner on "Bleeding Kansas" (1856)

The 1850s brought a new, less-compromising generation of politicians to prominence in both the North and South. Among this new group was Charles Sumner of Massachusetts. Holding undergraduate and law degrees from Harvard, Sumner spent the years immediately after his education touring Europe, where he met many of the leading statesmen and learned to speak French, German, and Italian. Sumner's involvement in politics began with his vigorous denunciations of the Mexican War. By 1848, he was condemning many of Massachusetts' leading textile magnates for their comfortable association with the "slaveocracy." A coalition of Free Soilers and Democrats sent him to the Senate in 1851.

A brilliant orator, he hurled his initial attacks at the Compromise of 1850. The passage of the Kansas-Nebraska Act led him to join the Republican Party. In the spring of 1856, he delivered his "Crime of Kansas" speech, which is excerpted here. Within weeks, 1 million copies had been printed in the North. South Carolina Congressman Preston Brooks responded to the verbal attack against his uncle, A. Pierce Butler, by assaulting Sumner, who sat helpless at his Senate desk. The assault further polarized the sections.

Questions to Consider

1. Why does Sumner link slavery and the southern way of life to South Carolina's Senator Pierce Butler?

2. Why does Sumner appeal to Kansas residents to vote?

3. Does Sumner envision a resolution to the growing sectional division within the country?

4. Why does Sumner use the imagery of sexual exploitation in his speech? What does this say about contemporary views of race? Sex?

Before entering upon the argument, I must say something of a general character, particularly in response to what has fallen from senators who have raised themselves to eminence on this floor in the championship of human wrong: I mean the senator from South Carolina [Mr. Butler] and the senator from Illinois [Mr. Douglas], who though unlike as Don Quixote and Sancho Panza, yet, like this couple, sally forth together in the same adventure, I regret much to miss the elder senator from his seat; but the cause against which he has run a tilt, with such ebullition of animosity, demands that the opportunity of exposing him should not be lost; and it is for the cause that I speak. The senator from South Carolina has read many books of chivalry and believes himself a chivalrous knight, with sentiments of honor and courage. Of course he has chosen a mistress to whom he has made his vows and who, though ugly to others, is always lovely to him; though polluted in the sight of the world of the world, is chaste in his sight. I mean the harlot Slavery. To her his tongue is always profuse in words. Let her be impeached in character, or any proposition be made from the extension of her wantonness, and no extravagance of manner or hardihood of assertion is then too great for this senator. The frenzy of Don Quixote in behalf of his wench ... is all surpassed. The asserted rights of slavery which shock equality of all kinds, are cloaked by a fantastic claim of equality. If the slave States cannot enjoy what, in mockery of the great fathers of the republic, he misnames equality under the Constitution,—in other words the full power in the national territories to compel fellow-men to unpaid toil, separate husband and wife, and to sell little children at the auction-block, then, sir, the chivalric senator will conduct the State of South Carolina out of the Union! Heroic knight! exalted senator! a second Moses come for the second exodus!

SOURCE: "Speech on Kansas," *Memoirs and Letters of Charles Sumner*, ed. Edward L. Pierce (London, 1893), 3: 446–52.

Not content with this poor menace, ... the senator, in the unrestrained chivalry of his nature, has undertaken to apply opprobrious words to those who differ from him.... He calls them "sectional and fanatical"; and resistance to the usurpation of Kansas he denounces as "an uncalculating fanaticism." To be sure, these charges lack all grace of originality and all sentiment of truth; but the adventurous senator does not hesitate. He is the uncompromising, unblushing representative on this floor of a flagrant sectionalism now domineering over the republic; and yet with a ludicrous ignorance of his own position, unable to see himself as others see him, or with an effrontery which even his white head ought not to protect from rebuke, he applies to those here who resist his sectionalism the very epithet which designates himself. The men who strive to bring back the government to its original policy, when freedom and not slavery was national, while slavery and not freedom was sectional, he arraigns as sectional. This will not do; it involves too great a perversion of terms. I tell that senator that it is to himself, and to the "organization" of which he is the "committed advocate," that this epithet belongs. I now fasten it upon them. For myself, ... I affirm that the Republican party of the Union is in no just sense sectional, but, more than any other party, national; and that it now goes forth to dislodge from the high places that tyrannical sectionalism of which the senator from South Carolina is one of the maddest zealots.

... the senator from South Carolina [Mr. Butler], who, omnipresent in this debate, overflows with rage at the simple suggestion that Kansas has applied for admission as a State, and with incoherent phrase discharges the loose expectoration of his speech, now upon her representative, and then upon her people.... the senator touches nothing which he does not disfigure with error,—sometimes of principle, sometimes of fact. He shows an incapacity of accuracy, whether in stating the Constitution or in stating the law, whether in details of statistics or diversions of scholarship. He cannot open his mouth but out here flies another blunder....

But it is against the people of Kansas that the sensibilities of the senator are particularly aroused. Coming, as he announces, "from a State,"—ay, sir, from South Carolina,—he turns his lordly disgust from this newly formed community, which he will not recognize even as "a member of the body politic." Pray, sir, by what title does he indulge in this egotism? Has he read the history of the "State" which he represents? ... He cannot forget its wretched persistence in the slave trade, as the very apple of its eye, and the condition of its participation in the Union. He cannot forget its constitution, which is republican only in name, confirming power in the hands of the few.... Were the whole history of South Carolina blotted out of existence .... civilization might lose—I do not say how little, but surely less than it has already gained by the example of Kansas in that valiant struggle against oppression....

The contest which, beginning in Kansas, reaches us, will be transferred soon from Congress to that broader stage, where every citizen is not only spectator but actor; and to their judgment I confidently turn. To the people about to exercise the electoral franchise in choosing a chief magistrate of the republic, I appeal to vindicate the electoral franchise in Kansas. Let the ballot-box of the

Union with multitudinous might protect the ballot-box in that Territory. Let the voters everywhere, while rejoicing in their own rights, help guard the equal rights of distant fellow-citizens, that the shrines of popular institutions now desecrated may be sanctified anew.... In just regard for free labor, ... in Christian sympathy with the slave, ... in rescue of fellow citizens now subjugated to tyrannical usurpation; in dutiful respect for the early fathers, ... in the name of the Constitution outraged, of the laws trampled down, of justice banished, of humanity degraded, of peace destroyed, of freedom crushed to earth, and in the name of the Heavenly Father, whose service is perfect freedom,—I make this last appeal.

109

Chicago Tribune on the Dred Scott v. Sanford Decision (1857)

The sectional tensions over slavery spread from the political to the judicial arena in 1857, when the Supreme Court ruled on the case of Dred Scott v. Sanford. *Scott, a slave born in Southampton County, Virginia, moved with owner Peter Blow to St. Louis, Missouri, in 1827. Purchased by army surgeon John Emerson in 1833, Scott went wherever his new master was stationed, spending three years in Illinois and two in the Wisconsin Territory. In 1846, a white friend sued for Scott's freedom, arguing that residence in a free territory emancipated the slave. The case ultimately came before the Supreme Court, presided over by Roger B. Taney, a Maryland native appointed by Andrew Jackson. The court divided along sectional lines, with Chief Justice Taney ruling that (1) African Americans' inherent inferiority precluded them, whether slave or free, from the rights of a citizen—including bringing a case before the Supreme Court; (2) the Missouri Compromise was an abridgment of property rights and was therefore, unconstitutional; (3) a territory could not prohibit the introduction of slaves. The following excerpt provides the reaction of the* Chicago Tribune.

Questions to Consider

1. How does the *Chicago Tribune* view the Supreme Court's decision?
2. What does the newspaper suggest that citizens do?
3. In what ways did the Supreme Court's decision help to further divide the nation?

4. How might Richard Colfax ("Evidence Against the Abolitionists," Document 81) have responded to this article?

5. How might Francis Pickens ("Inaugural Address of South Carolina Governor Francis Pickens," Document 113) have responded to this article?

... We must confess we are shocked at the violence and servility of the Judicial Revolution caused by the decision of the Supreme Court of the United States. We scarcely know how to express our detestation of its inhuman dicta, or to fathom the wicked consequences which may flow from it. The blood of the early day—of the times that tried men's souls—was all healthful and strong, and lived, or was shed, for Liberty as freely as water. That is now changed legally. This decision has sapped the constitution of its glorious and distinctive features, and seeks to pervert it into a barbarous and unchristian channel.

Jefferson feared this Supreme Court, and foretold its usurpation of the legislative power of the Federal Government. His prophecy is now reality. The terrible evil he dreaded is upon us.

To say or suppose, that a Free People can respect or will obey a decision so fraught with disastrous consequences to the People and their Liberties, is to dream of impossibilities. No power can take away their rights. They will permit no power to abridge them. No servility of Judges or of Presidents, no servility of Congresses can taint their spirit or subdue it. The contest has come, and in that contest, the Supreme Court, we are sorry to say, will be shorn of its moral power—will lose that prestige, that authority, which instinctively insures respect and commands obedience. By its own bad act it has impaired its organization. Fortunate will it be, if that act does not destroy its utility....

That there has been for long years a conspiracy against Freedom in this Republic, and that certain members of the Supreme Court were engaged in it, we do not doubt. How this has happened, or why, it is needless to discuss now. It is enough to know, that a continued residence at Washington—the breathing in of its central and polluted atmosphere makes, or tends to make, those in authority, at once obedient and servile to the ruling dynasty, and callous to the purer and higher instincts and principles of the people. The Judiciary has proven no exception. We would, therefore, apply the remedy which JEFFERSON urged, and JACKSON recommended—decentralization. Strip the President of every power which the people can exercise. Let every office which they are able to fill, be filled by them. Confide into their hands the election of the Judges of the United States, and thus infuse into these Judges a knowledge of their interests, a spirit and a purposeful kindred with theirs, an independence of the Executive worthy of them.

SOURCE: "The Past and Present," *Chicago Tribune*, 12 March 1857, p. 2.

110

Sensible Hints to the South (1858)

*By 1858, a small but growing number of southern leaders questioned the South's contin-
ued relationship with the Union. Led by William Lowndes Yancey, Edmund Ruffin, and
Robert B. Rhett, these "fire-eaters" had first advocated leaving the Union in 1850. In
May 1858, the fire-eaters would use the meeting of the Southern Commercial Convention
in Montgomery, Alabama, to advocate for secession and reopening of the African slave
trade. In the following selection,* DeBow's Review *reprints an editorial about the Convention's disunionist sentiments. Under the editorial leadership of James Dunwoody
Brownson DeBow, the* Review *advertised itself as the leading periodical chronicling the
"agricultural, commercial, and industrial progress and resources" of the American South
during the mid-nineteenth century.*

Questions to Consider

1. What advice does the editorial offer concerning the possible secession of
   southern states from the Union?

2. How seriously does the author of this selection appear to take the
   "fire-eaters"?

3. What conclusions can you draw from this document about the economic
   relationship between the North and South?

4. Based on the outcome of the Civil War, how accurate an appraisal does the
   author offer of the industrial capabilities of each region?

A Virginia paper offers the following;

If the delegates to the Southern Convention will take note of a few particulars on their way, perhaps they may find food for reflection more valuable than
has hitherto been submitted in resolutions and manifestoes.

They will start in some stage or railroad coach made in the North; an
engine of Northern manufacture will take their train or boat along; at every
meal they will sit down in Yankee chairs, to a Yankee table, spread with a
Yankee cloth. With a Yankee spoon they will take from Yankee dishes,
sugar, salt, and coffee which have paid tribute to Yankee trade, and with
Yankee knives and forks they will put into their mouths the only thing Southern they will get on the trip.

SOURCE: *DeBow's Review and Industrial Resources,* 24 (June 1858): 573.

At night they will pull off a pair of Yankee boots with a Yankee boot-jack; and throwing a lot of Yankee toggery on a Yankee chair, lie down to dream of Southern independence, in a Yankee bed, with not even a thread of cotton around them that has not gone through a Yankee loom or come out of a Yankee shop.

In the morning they will get up to fix themselves by a 12 by 14 Yankee looking glass, with a Yankee brush and comb, after perhaps shushing off a little of the soil of the South from their faces, with water drawn in a Yankee bucket, and put in a Yankee pitcher, on a Yankee wash-stand, the partner in honorable exile with a lot of Yankee wares that make up the sum of the furniture.

Think of these things, gentlemen, and ask yourselves is there no remedy for this dependence? Ask yourselves if there be not some mode of action which will bring about a change and keep your cotton, your wheat, and your tobacco crops from going out of the South, to buy for you the things you must have to be up with the age?

Great steamships, and grand expansions, and magnificent speeches will do well enough, but there are little things, and a thousand of them, too, which might have a little attention, and perhaps lead to some small advantages. Could there not be some purpose, some real resolution to encourage not only by precept but by example a little home industry? Could you not buy sometimes a little Southern cotton goods without allowing them to go forward to the North, to get baptism into the true faith of Southern trade? Could you not induce the young maidens and matrons, who call you husbands and fathers, to look upon it as requisite to their principles, that country merchants should get their stocks in Southern ports, instead of turning up their nose at anything that does not come direct from the fashionable haunts of New York, and Boston, and Philadelphia, and Baltimore, for Baltimore is as little Southern as any of them? Could you not induce your legislature to ameliorate the hard public necessities than by crippling it in its infancy and weakness, by heavy license laws and serve exaction? We beg you to think of these little things and do something.

111

Frederick Douglass on John Brown (1859)

Sectional tensions were further inflamed in 1859 by John Brown's efforts to secure the federal armory in Harper's Ferry, Virginia (now West Virginia), in order to procure arms for a slave insurrection. Following Brown's capture by troops led by Robert E. Lee, he was tried for treason against the state of Virginia in Charlestown. An early convert to the abolition movement (he had helped to finance the publication of Walker's "Appeal"—Document 79), Brown had drifted for much of his life before landing in Kansas at the height of the Bleeding Kansas controversy. There in May 1856, he and a group of followers murdered five proslavery settlers at Pottawatomie Creek in southeastern Kansas. He later headed east, where—with secret abolitionists—he hatched his plan to instigate a slave insurrection. In the following selection excerpted from Douglass' Monthly, Frederick Douglass, perhaps the North's most prominent abolitionist, discusses the case of John Brown. Born a slave in Maryland, in his youth Douglass had been taught to read by his master's daughter. He escaped slavery in 1838 and within a few years became active in the antislavery movement. He was a forceful lecturer with a captivating presence, and his involvement in the movement dispelled the myth of the ignorant African American—often to the surprise of many white abolitionists.

Questions to Consider

1. What documents and books does Douglass cite to legitimize Brown's actions?
2. Do you think John Brown is a freedom fighter or a terrorist? Explain.
3. How do you think Martin Delany ("Martin Delany and African American Nationalism," Document 100) would have responded to the sentiments expressed here?
4. How do you think Francis Pickens ("Inaugural Address of South Carolina Governor Francis Pickens," Document 113) responded to the Brown raid? How do you think he responded to the sentiments expressed in this editorial?

One of the most painful incidents connected with the name of this old hero, is the attempt to prove him insane. Many journals have contributed to this effort from a friendly desire to shield the prisoner from Virginia's cowardly vengeance.

SOURCE: Frederick Douglass, "Capt. John Brown Not Insane," *Douglass' Monthly* (Rochester, NY), 2 November 1859, p. 1.

This is a mistaken friendship, which seeks to rob him of his true character and dim the glory of his deeds, in order to save his life. Was there the faintest hope of securing his release by this means, we would choke down our indignation and be silent. But a Virginia court would hang a crazy man without a moment's hesitation, if his insanity took the form of hatred of oppression; and this plea only blasts the reputation of this glorious martyr of liberty, without the faintest hope of improving his chance of escape.

It is an appalling fact in the history of the American people, that they have so far forgotten their own heroic age, as readily to accept the charge of insanity against a man who has imitated the heroes of Lexington, Concord, and Bunker Hill.

It is an effeminate and cowardly age, which calls a man a lunatic because he rises to such self-forgetful heroism, as to count his own life as worth nothing in comparison with the freedom of millions of his fellows. Such an age would have sent Gideon to a mad-house, and put Leonidas in a strait-jacket. Such a people would have treated the defenders of Thermopylae as demented, and shut up Caius Marcus in bedlam. Such a marrowless population as ours has become under the debaucheries of Slavery, would have struck the patriot's crown from the brow of Wallace, and recommended blisters and bleeding to the heroic Tell. Wallace was often and again as desperately forgetful of his own life in defense of Scotland's freedom, as was Brown in striking for the American slave; and Tell's defiance of the Austrian tyrant, was as far above the appreciation of cowardly selfishness as was Brown's defiance of the Virginia pirates. Was Arnold Winkelried insane when he rushed to his death upon an army of spears, crying "make way for Liberty!" Are heroism and insanity synonyms in our American dictionary? Heaven help us! when our loftiest types of patriotism, our sublimest historic ideals of philanthropy, come to be treated as evidence of moon struck madness. Posterity will owe everlasting thanks to John Brown for lifting up once more to the gaze of a nation grown fat and flabby on the garbage of lust and oppression, a true standard of heroic philanthropy, and each coming generation will pay its installment of the debt. No wonder that the aiders and abettors of the huge, overshadowing and many-armed tyranny, which he grappled with in its own infernal den, should call him a mad man; but for those who profess a regard for him, and for human freedom, to join in the cruel slander, "is the unkindest cut of all."

Nor is it necessary to attribute Brown's deeds to the spirit of vengeance, invoked by the murder of his brave boys. That the barbarous cruelty from which he has suffered had its effect in intensifying his hatred of slavery, is doubtless true. But his own statement, that he had been contemplating a bold strike for the freedom of the slaves for ten years, proves that he had resolved upon his present course long before he, or his sons, ever set foot in Kansas. His entire procedure in this matter disproves the charge that he was prompted by an impulse of mad revenge, and shows that he was moved by the highest principles of philanthropy. His carefulness of the lives of unarmed persons—his humane and courteous treatment of his prisoners—his cool self-possession all through his trial—and especially his calm, dignified speech on receiving his sentence, all conspire to show that he was neither insane or actuated by vengeful passion; and we hope that the country has heard the last of John Brown's madness. The explanation of his conduct is perfectly natural and simple on its face. He believes the Declaration of Independence to be true, and the Bible to be a guide to human conduct, and acting upon the doctrines of both, he threw himself against the serried ranks of American oppression, and translated into heroic deeds the love of liberty and hatred of tyrants, with which he was inspired from both these forces acting upon his philanthropic and heroic soul. This age is too gross and sensual to appreciate his deeds, and so calls him mad; but the future will write his epitaph upon the hearts of a people freed from slavery, because he struck the first effectual blow.

Not only is it true that Brown's whole movement proves him perfectly sane and free from merely revengeful passion, but he has struck the bottom line of the philosophy which underlies the abolition movement. He has attacked slavery with the weapons precisely adapted to bring it to the death. Moral considerations have long since been exhausted upon slaveholders. It is in vain to reason with them. One might as well hunt bears with ethics and political economy for weapons, as to seek to "pluck the spoiled out of the hand of the oppressor" by the mere force of moral law. Slavery is a system of brute force. It shields itself behind *might,* rather than right. It must be met with its own weapons. Capt. Brown has initiated a new mode of carrying on the crusade of freedom, and his blow has sent dread and terror throughout the entire ranks of the piratical army of slavery. His daring deeds may cost him his life, but priceless as is the value of that life, the blow he has struck, will, in the end, prove to be worth its mighty cost. Like Samson, he has laid his hands upon the pillars of this great national temple of cruelty and blood, and when he falls, that temple will speedily crumble to its final doom, burying its denizens in its ruins.

112

Cartoonists Depict the Issues of the Day (1860)

The 1860 presidential election was one of the most momentous in American history. The divisions that dominated the political landscape of the 1850s could no longer be contained; armed conflict marred the contest over popular sovereignty in Kansas; politicians had resorted to violence in the Sumner-Brooks affair. The issues of the 1850s shattered the Second Party system of Democrats and Whigs and left a divided Democratic Party and several fledgling new parties. The emergence of the Republican Party, with its purely north-ern appeal, was perceived as a dire threat to many southerners. The division of the Demo-crats and subsequent selection of a main Democratic candidate and a deep southern candidate further complicated the ensuing election campaign. A fourth ticket also ran, prom-ising nothing more than the preservation of the Union. The ensuing images depict the major issues of the day as portrayed by cartoonists.

Questions to Consider

1. What does the cartoonist see as the central issue in "The Political Quadrille"?

2. Who are the different candidates appealing to in the first image?

3. In "Dividing the National Map," what is the cartoonist predicting will happen as a result of the presidential election?

4. How accurate is this prediction?

The Political Quadrille: Music by Dred Scott
SOURCE: [LC-USZ62-14827]/Library of Congress Prints and Photographs Division

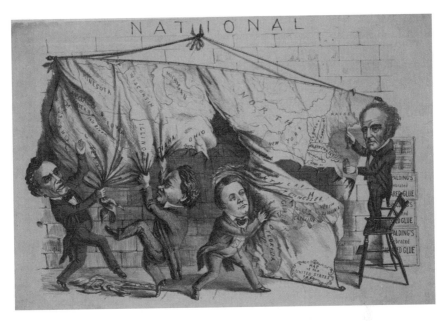

Dividing the National Map
SOURCE: [LC-USZC4-7997]/Library of Congress Prints and Photographs Division

113

Inaugural Address of South Carolina Governor Francis Pickens (1860)

Abraham Lincoln's election brought a howl of protest from the South. In South Carolina, a convention of delegates began meeting in December to consider whether the state should secede. The following selection contains excerpts of an address delivered by Governor Francis W. Pickens shortly before South Carolina left the Union. A member of a prominent state family, Pickens had been an outspoken supporter of his state during the 1832–1833 nullification crisis. Years of service in Congress made him increasingly wary of compromise with the North; and by 1850, he had emerged as one of his state's leading secessionists. By the mid-1850s, however, he was becoming more cautious on the issue. After serving two years as American minister to Russia, he returned to South Carolina in the fall of 1860. He initially warned against immediate secession and, with the support of the state's conservative secessionists, was elected governor.

Questions to Consider

1. Why is Francis Pickens wary of the Republican control of Congress and the presidency?

2. What does he advocate for South Carolina and the South?

3. What can you deduce from this document about South Carolina in 1860?

4. Compare and contrast Governor Pickens's views with those expressed in "South Carolina Nullifies the Tariff" (Document 69). What similarities do you note? Differences?

Gentlemen of the Senate and House of Representatives:

You have called me to preside as Chief Magistrate of South Carolina at a critical juncture in our public affairs. I deeply feel the responsibilities of the position I am about to assume.

For seventy-three years this State has been connected by a federal compact with co-States, under a bond of union, for great national objects, common to all. In recent years there has been a powerful party organized upon principles of ambition and fanaticism, whose undisguised purpose is to divert the Federal Government from external, and turn its power upon the internal interests and domestic institutions of these States. They have thus combined a party exclusively in the Northern States, whose avowed objects not only endanger the peace, but the very existence of near one-half the States of this Confederacy; and in the recent election for President and Vice President of these States, they have carried the election upon principles that make it no longer safe for us to rely upon the powers of the Federal Government or the guarantees of the Federal Compact. This is the great overt act of the people in the Northern States at the ballot-box, in the exercise of their sovereign power at the polls, from which there is no higher appeal recognized under our system of Government, in its ordinary and habitual operations—They thus propose to inaugurate a Chief Magistrate at the head of the army and navy, with vast powers, not to preside over the common interests and destinies of all the States alike, but upon issues of malignant hostility and uncompromising war to be waged upon the rights, the interests and the peace of half the States of this Union.

In the Southern States these are two entirely distinct and separate races, and one has been held in subjugation to the other by peaceful inheritance from worthy and patriotic ancestors, and all who know the races well know that it is the only form of Government that can preserve both, and administer the blessings of civilization with order and in harmony.

Anything tending to change or weaken this government and the subordination between the races, not only endangers the peace, but the very existence of our security. We have for years warned the Northern people of the dangers they were producing by their wanton and lawless course. We have often appealed to our sister States of the South to act with us in concert upon some firm but moderate system, by which we might be able, if possible, to save the Federal

SOURCE: "The News From Columbia," *Charleston* [South Carolina] *Mercury*, 18 December 1860, p. 1

Constitution, and yet feel safe under the general compact of Union. But we could obtain no fair hearing from the North, nor could we see any concerted plan proposed by our co-States of the South, calculated to make us feel safe and secure.

Under all these circumstances, we now have no alternative left but to interpose our sovereign power as an independent State, to Protect the rights and ancient privileges of the people of South Carolina.

This State was one of the original parties to the Federal Compact of the Union. We agreed to it as a state under peculiar circumstances, when we were surrounded with great external pressure for purposes of national protection and for the general welfare of all the States equally and alike; and when it ceases to do this it is no longer a perpetual Union. It would be an absurdity to suppose it was a perpetual Union for our ruin. The Constitution is a compact between Co-states, and not with the Federal Government. On questions vital, and involving the peace and safety of the parties to the compact from the very nature of the instrument, each State must judge of the mode and measure of protection necessary for her peace and the preservation of local and domestic institutions, South Carolina will therefore decide for herself, and will, as she has a right to do, resume her original powers of government as an independent State, and, as such will negotiate with other powers such treaties, leagues or covenants, as she may deem proper....

There is one thing certain, and I think it due to the country say in advance, that South Carolina is resolved to assert her separate independence, and, as she acceded separately to the compact of the Union, so she will most assuredly secede, separately and alone, be the consequences what they may; and I think it right to say, with no unkind feeling whatever, that on this point there can be no compromise, let it be offered from where it may. The issues are too grave, and too momentous, to admit of any counsel that looks to anything but direct and straight forward independence. In the present emergency, the most decided measures are the safest and wisest. To our sister States who are identified with us in interest and feeling, we will cordially and kindly look for co-operation and for a future Union; but it must be after we have asserted and resumed our original and inalienable rights and powers of sovereignty and independence. We can then form a government with them, having a common interest with people of homogenous feelings, united together by all the ties that can bind States in one common destiny. From the position we may occupy towards the Northern States, as well as from our own internal structure of society, the government may, from necessity, become strongly military in its organization. When we look back upon the inheritance, the common glories and triumphant power of this wonderful Confederacy, no language can express the feelings of the human heart, as we turn from the contemplation, and sternly look to the great future that opens before us. It is our sincere desire to separate from the States of the North in peace, and leave them to develop their own civilization, according to their own sense of duty and of interest. But if, under the guidance of ambition and fanaticism, they decide otherwise, then be it so. We are prepared for any event, and, in humble reliance upon that Providence who presides over the destiny of men and of nations, we will endeavor to do our duty faithfully, bravely and honestly.

I am now ready to take the oath of office, and swear undivided allegiance to South Carolina.

114

Northern Participation in the Slave Trade (1862)

Most of what historians have written about antebellum slavery focuses on the South. Far less is known about the extent to which northerners may have participated in the African slave trade, despite its being illegal since 1808. This selection clearly debunks the myth that all northerners opposed slavery as it offers a detailed description of prominent New Yorkers' role in the trade. It appeared in the first issue of the Continental Monthly, *a Boston journal that contained a decided pro-Union editorial policy. Despite its high-brow approach to the major issues of the day and the inclusion of essays by leading writers such as Horace Greeley, the monthly journal would cease publication in 1864.*

Questions to Consider

1. What appear to be the primary motives for New Yorkers involved in the slave trade?

2. Based on what this selection, what conclusions might you draw on the level of corruption in New York at this time?

3. Does the author of this selection believe the U.S. government had done all it could to stop the trade?

The principal slave captains and chief officers of vessels engaged in the slave-trade have their residences and boarding-places in the eastern wards of the city, most of them being between James and Houston Streets. They are known to every one who has an investment in the business. Indeed, they are all members of a secret fraternity, having its signs, grips, and pass-words. While I was in Eldridge-street jail, said one of them, Captain Loretti was captured and brought

SOURCE: "The Slave-Trade in New York," *Continental Monthly: Devoted to Literature and National Policy,* 1, no. 1 (January 1862): 88–90.

there. He did not know any one, but I shook hands with him, and we became acquainted at once.

The arrival of a slave captain from one voyage is the signal for preparation for another. Negotiations are carried on, generally in the first-class hotels. The contracts for the City of Norfolk and several other notorious slavers were made at the Astor House. The risk of detection is less at such a public place than it would be at a private office. A man who had failed in business on Greenwich Street was recently engaged in fitting out these vessels for their African voyage. He was first sent to procure apparatus for the refining of palm oil. This was but a blind, the practice being to take out the machinery, and employ the boiler for culinary purposes, until the vessels had got out to sea, and there was no farther necessity for duping inquisitive persons. This man was also commissioned to purchase wooden ware, champagne, and other necessary articles. Such were the business agents and their duty; all was liberally paid for and promptly supplied. As soon as a vessel is ready and officered for the voyage, measures are taken to procure a crew. Slave-traders employ for this the services of "runners", who constitute a caste of pariahs of the most degraded kind. A conscientious scruple would seem never to enter into their calculations. They would hardly recognize a precept of the decalogue except by the circumstance of its violation. Earning their livelihood thus basely, debauchery and crime constitute their every-day history. These persons keep a record of the names of men who have served on slave ships, or been guilty of mutiny, or other villany. So accurate is their information and so expert are they in their estimate of character, that they seldom commit a blunder, or furnish a seaman who is not the man for the vocation. The crew which they select are indeed picked men. They are of every nationality, and are taken from the seamen's boarding-houses in the lower wards of the city. A few years since, the information was received in New York that a yacht was lying in Long Island Sound, and that circumstances warranted the suspicion that she was intended for the slave-trade. The marshal, with a display of enthusiastic zeal for the execution of the laws, proceeded to the place with a strong force of assistants, and took charge of the yacht; but subsequent investigations failed to criminate her. The reputed owner declared that he had fitted her out for a pleasure excursion; that was all. The vessel was discharged, and a few months afterward landed a cargo of negroes on the coast of Georgia. So easy has it been to deceive the Federal officers....

The obtaining of a clearance at the custom-house was not a very difficult matter. Slavers were never detained by any extraordinary curiosity on the part of those having cognizance of their departure.

They had but to assume a transparent disguise, raise the American flag, and keep up the show till they arrived at the intermediate port. Here the national ensign was changed, the papers of the vessel were altered, and necessary arrangements were made for receiving a cargo of slaves.

Factories or agencies are maintained on the African coast, where the vessels obtain their living freight. The captains seldom go on shore except for purpose of observation. Each vessel generally takes with her from New York a Spaniard to transact the business. The complement being obtained, it only remains to get away and beyond the cruisers. The action of the Federal government, some years since, in relation to the visitation of vessels, has been effectual in impairing the energy of the British squadron, which has been maintained on the coast of Africa, pursuant to the treaty of Washington. As for the American squadron, it never co-operated heartily in the matter of suppressing the slave-trade; and the vessels were generally absent for the purpose of obtaining coal, or for repairs, whenever there was opportunity of making a capture.

But the capitalists of New York do not depend entirely upon these precautions. Their vessels are occasionally taken; and then the men on board must be protected, or they will disclose everything. Not only are appliances used to make an examination result in a discharge, but a corps of attorneys is kept under pay to defend those who fall within the clutches of the law. The impunity which has attended these men is notorious....

After remaining some twelve weeks at the jail, Captain Latham determined not to await a trial. He obtained the aid of one of the marshals assistants; a friend of his, who has a place of business in Wall Street, advancing three thousand dollars. One of his attorneys was also in the secret. A writ of habeas corpus was obtained from the recorder, and dismissed for want of jurisdiction. This was all done to elude suspicion. A ticket for a passage to Havana was procured; and on the day that the steamer was to sail, a carriage, in which were Sanchez, the marshals assistant, and a friend, drove to the jail.... The names of the prominent slavetraders, their residences and places of business, are known to the marshal. Several of them have fled from the city; among them, a woman of wealth residing in St. Marks Place. Their operations have been largely curtailed, and it has become almost impossible for a slaver to leave New York .... it is to be hoped that the slave-trade will be exterminated in every Northern port. Some legislation by Congress to increase the powers of the marshals, and efficient action on the part of the executive, are all that is now required to sweep the infamous commerce from the ocean.

14

The Civil War

B y the time Abraham Lincoln assumed the presidency in March 1861, seven
states of the Deep South had left the Union. Determined to maintain the
integrity of the Union, the new president soon challenged the secessionists, an
act that caused four states of the upper South to join the Confederacy. Many
thought it would be a short war, but it quickly developed into a bloodbath that
required enormous sacrifices on the home front to support the struggle in the field.
By 1863, northern war aims had evolved from a conflict to save the Union into a
crusade to end slavery. The following documents reveal the motives of those
involved in the war and help illustrate the transformation of the conflict.

115

Mary Boykin Chesnut, the Attack on Fort Sumter (1861)

*The Lincoln administration first tested secession in South Carolina, where Fort Sumter in
Charleston harbor remained in Union hands. South Carolina officials, determined to con-
fiscate federal property, declared their refusal to allow the Union to provision the fort.
On April 4 President Lincoln, resolved to hold federal property in the South, ordered
that Fort Sumter (as well as Fort Pickens in Florida) be resupplied. South Carolina,
with the support of the Confederate government, decided to resist these efforts. Mary
Boykin Chesnut was the daughter of Mary Boykin and Stephen Miller (one of South*

Carolina's leading political figures); she married James B. Chesnut, Jr., whose father was one of the state's largest landowners. Following James's election to the U.S. Senate in 1858, Mary quickly established herself in the social circles of other southern politicians' wives. In 1860, the Chesnuts left the nation's capital to return to South Carolina, where James played a prominent role in the state's secession. Her diary, from which this account is excerpted, provides an excellent description of Charleston society just before and during the attack on Fort Sumter.

Questions to Consider

1. Why does Mary B. Chesnut's diary move from excitement of the attack to a more subdued assessment the following day?

2. What does Chesnut anticipate about the coming war?

3. Why does Chesnut comment on the reaction of the slaves?

4. In what ways do Chesnut's views contrast with those of "The Southern Homefront" (Document 121)? How do you account for these differences?

April 12th.—Anderson will not capitulate. Yesterday's was the merriest, maddest dinner we have had yet. Men were audaciously wise and witty. We had an unspoken foreboding that it was to be our last pleasant meeting. Mr. Miles dined with us to-day. Mrs. Henry King rushed in saying, "The news, I come for the latest news. All the men of the King family are on the Island," of which fact she seemed proud....

I do not pretend to go to sleep. How can I? If Anderson does not accept terms at four, the orders are, he shall be fired upon. I count four, St. Michael's bells chime out and I begin to hope. At half-past four the heavy booming of a cannon. I sprang out of bed, and on my knees prostrate I prayed as I never prayed before.

There was a sound of stir all over the house, pattering of feet in the corridors. All seemed hurrying one way. I put on my double-gown and a shawl and went, too. It was to the housetop. The shells were bursting. In the dark I heard a man say, "Waste of ammunition." I knew my husband was rowing about in a boat somewhere in that dark bay, and that the shells were roofing it over, bursting toward the fort. If Anderson was obstinate, Colonel Chesnut was to order the fort on one side to open fire. Certainly fire had begun. The regular roar of the cannon, there it was. And who could tell what each volley accomplished of death and destruction?

The women were wild there on the housetop. Prayers came from the women and imprecations from the men. And then a shell would light up the scene. To-night they say the forces are to attempt to land. We watched up there, and everybody wondered that Fort Sumter did not fire a shot....

April 13th.—Nobody has been hurt after all. How gay we were last night. Reaction after the dread of all the slaughter we thought those dreadful cannon were making. Not even a battery the worse for wear. Fort Sumter has been on

SOURCE: Mary Boykin Chesnut, *A Diary from Dixie*, eds. Isabella D. Martin and Myrta Lockett Avary (New York, 1905), 30–41.

fire. Anderson has not yet silenced any of our guns. So the aides, still with swords and red sashes by way of uniform, tell us. But the sound of those guns makes regular meals impossible. None of us go to table. Tea-trays pervade the corridors going everywhere. Some of the anxious hearts lie on their beds and moan in solitary misery. Mrs. Wigfall and I solace ourselves with tea in my room. These women have all a satisfying faith. "God is on our side," they say. When we are shut in Mrs. Wigfall and I ask "Why?" "Of course, He hates the Yankees, we are told. You'll think that well of Him."

Not by one word or look can we detect any change in the demeanor of these negro servants. Lawrence sits at our door, sleepy and respectful, and profoundly indifferent. So are they all, but they carry it too far. You could not tell that they even heard the awful roar going on in the bay, though it has been dinning in their ears night and day. People talk before them as if they were chairs and tables. They make no sign. Are they stolidly stupid? or wiser than we are; silent and strong, biding their time?

… [April 15th—] Mrs. Frank Hampton knows already what civil war means. Her brother was in the New York Seventh Regiment, so roughly received in Baltimore. Frank will be in the opposite camp….

116

"A War to Preserve the Union" (1861)

A child of the frontier, Abraham Lincoln was born in Kentucky and lived in Indiana before finally settling in Illinois. Primarily self-taught, he began a legal career in Springfield in the mid-1830s and quickly gained notoriety as a trial lawyer. A Whig, he served in the Illinois legislature from 1834 until 1842 and was elected to the U.S. Congress in 1846. He joined the new Republican Party in 1856 and two years later ran against Stephen A. Douglas for the U.S. Senate. Although he lost this race, it propelled him to national prominence. When Abraham Lincoln became president in March 1861, seven states of the Deep South had already left the Union. With Congress in recess, Lincoln had to act unilaterally to meet the secession crisis. His decisions to supply Fort Sumter and his later call for troops led to the secession of four more southern states. In the selection excerpted here, the president informs a special session of Congress of his motives and war aims.

Questions to Consider

1. What was Lincoln's initial response to the seizure of federal property throughout the South?

2. What is Lincoln's purpose in fighting the war?

3. Is Lincoln convinced that most southerners support secession and the attack on federal property?

4. To what extent do Lincoln's views reflect those expressed by Daniel Webster in his "Second Reply to Robert Y. Hayne" (Document 64)?

MESSAGE TO CONGRESS IN SPECIAL SESSION, JULY 4, 1861

Fellow-citizens of the Senate and House of Representatives: Having been convened on an extraordinary occasion, as authorized by the Constitution, your attention is not called to any ordinary subject of legislation.

At the beginning of the present presidential term, four months ago, the functions of the Federal Government were found to be generally suspended within the several States of South Carolina, Georgia, Alabama, Mississippi, Louisiana, and Florida, excepting only those of the Post-office Department.

Within these States all the forts, arsenals, dockyards, custom-houses, and the like, including the movable and stationary property in and about them, had been seized, and were held in open hostility to this government, excepting only Forts Pickens, Taylor, and Jefferson, on and near the Florida coast, and Fort Sumter, in Charleston Harbor, South Carolina. The forts thus seized had been put in improved condition, new ones had been built, and armed forces had been organized and were organizing all avowedly with the same hostile purpose.

The forts remaining in the possession of the Federal Government in and near these States were either besieged or menaced by warlike preparations, and especially Fort Sumter was nearly surrounded by well-protected hostile batteries, with guns equal in quality to the best of its own, and outnumbering the latter as perhaps ten to one....

Finding this condition of things, and believing it to be an imperative duty upon the incoming executive to prevent, if possible, the consummation of such attempt to destroy the Federal Union, a choice of means to that end became indispensable. This choice was made and was declared in the inaugural address. The policy chosen looked to the exhaustion of all peaceful measures before a resort to any stronger ones. It sought only to hold the public places and property not already wrested from the government, and to collect the revenue, relying for the rest on time, discussion, and the ballot-box....

[T]he assault upon and reduction of Fort Sumter was in no sense a matter of self-defense on the part of the assailants.... They knew that this government desired to keep the garrison in the fort, not to assail them, but merely to maintain visible possession, and thus to preserve the Union from actual and immediate dissolution.... By the affair at Fort Sumter, with its surrounding circumstances, that point was reached. Then and thereby the assailants of the government began the conflict of arms, without a gun in sight or in expectancy to return their fire,

SOURCE: "Message to Congress in Special Session, July 4, 1861," *Complete Works of Abraham Lincoln*, eds. John G. Nicolay and John Hay (Lincoln, PA, 1894), 6: 297–325.

save only the few in the fort sent to that harbor years before for their own protection, and still ready to give that protection in whatever was lawful. In this act, discarding all else, they have forced upon the country the distinct issue, "immediate dissolution or blood."

And this issue embraces more than the fate of these United States. It presents to the whole family of man the question whether a constitutional republic or democracy—a government of the people by the same people—can or cannot maintain its territorial integrity against its own domestic foes. It presents the question whether discontented individuals, too few in numbers to control administration according to organic law in any case, can always, upon the pretenses made in this case, or on any other pretenses, or arbitrarily without any pretense, break up their government, and thus practically put an end to free government upon the earth. It forces us to ask: "Is there, in all republics, this inherent and fatal weakness?" "Must a government, of necessity, be too strong for the liberties of its own people, or too weak to maintain its own existence?"

117

Jefferson Davis Responds to the Emancipation Proclamation (1862)

Many southerners insisted that the election of a Republican president would lead to the emancipation of slaves. During the first phase of the Civil War, however, the North fought only to preserve the Union. By late 1862, the need for additional manpower, the determination to undermine the South economically, and the desire to make the war a moral crusade led Lincoln to announce his plan for emancipation. On January 1, 1863, the Emancipation Proclamation freed all slaves behind Confederate lines, in effect making the war a crusade against slavery. In the following selection, Confederate President Jefferson Davis responds to the proclamation in his annual message to the Confederate Congress. Jefferson Davis had enjoyed an impressive career before becoming the Confederacy's only president. A West Pointer, the Kentucky native briefly served in the military before becoming a Mississippi planter. He served his adopted state in the Congress, the Senate, and as secretary of war in the Franklin Pierce administration.

Questions to Consider

1. In what ways does Jefferson Davis react to the Emancipation Proclamation?
2. How does he use the occasion to justify secession and reestablish the fear of the Republican Party?

3. What can you deduce about southern attitudes toward slavery?
4. What can you deduce about southern attitudes toward race?

The public journals of the North have been received, containing a proclamation, dated on the 1st day of the present month, signed by the President of the United States, in which he orders and declares all slaves within ten of the States of the Confederacy to be free, except such as are found within certain districts now occupied in part by the armed forces of the enemy. We may well leave it to the instincts of that common humanity which a beneficent Creator has implanted in the breasts of our fellowmen of all countries to pass judgment on a measure by which several millions of human beings of an inferior race, peaceful and contented laborers in their sphere, are doomed to extermination, while at the same time they are encouraged to a general assassination of their masters by the insidious recommendation "to abstain from violence unless in necessary self-defense." Our own detestation of those who have attempted the most execrable measure recorded in the history of guilty man is tempered by profound contempt for the impotent rage which it discloses. So far as regards the action of this Government on such criminals as may attempt its execution, I confine myself to informing you that I shall, unless in your wisdom you deem some other course more expedient, deliver to the several State authorities all commissioned officers of the United States that may hereafter be captured by our forces in any of the States embraced in the proclamation, that they may be dealt with in accordance with the laws of those States providing for the punishment of criminals engaged in exciting servile insurrection. The enlisted soldiers I shall continue to treat as unwilling instruments in the commission of these crimes, and shall direct their discharge and return to their homes on the proper and usual parole.

In its political aspect this measure possesses great significance, and to it in this light I invite your attention. It affords to our whole people the complete and crowning proof of the true nature of the designs of the party which elevated to power the present occupant of the Presidential chair at Washington and which sought to conceal its purpose by every variety of artful device and by the perfidious use of the most solemn and repeated pledges on every possible occasion....

The people of this Confederacy, then, cannot fail to receive this proclamation as the fullest vindication of their own sagacity in foreseeing the uses to which the dominant party in the United States intended from the beginning to apply their power, nor can they cease to remember with devout thankfulness that it is to their own vigilance in resisting the first stealthy progress of approaching despotism that they owe their escape from consequences now apparent to the most skeptical. This proclamation will have another salutary effect in calming the fears of those who have constantly evinced the apprehension that this war might end by some reconstruction of the old Union or some renewal of close political relations with the United States. These fears have never been shared by me, nor have I ever been able to perceive on what basis they could rest. But the proclamation affords the fullest guarantee of the impossibility of such a result; it has established a state of things which can lead to but

SOURCE: "The President's Message," *Richmond Daily Dispatch*, 15 January 1863, p. 2.

one of three possible consequences—the extermination of the slaves, the exile of the whole white population from the Confederacy, or absolute and total separation of these States from the United States.

This proclamation is also an authentic statement by the Government of the United States of its inability to subjugate the South by force of arms, and as such must be accepted by neutral nations, which can no longer find any justification in with holding our just claims to formal recognition. It is also in effect an intimation to the people of the North that they must prepare to submit to a separation, now become inevitable, for that people are too acute not to understand a restoration of the Union has been rendered forever impossible by the adoption of a measure which from its very nature neither admits of retraction nor can coexist with union....

118

Images of African Americans in the Civil War (1863, 1865)

Legislation passed in July 1862 and the ensuing Emancipation Proclamation opened the Union army to African Americans. Despite wretched treatment in the army and the threat of execution if captured by Confederate forces, black soldiers quickly demonstrated their willingness to fight. Approximately 180,000 African Americans served in the Union army, roughly 10 percent of the total number of soldiers. African Americans who served suffered extraordinarily high casualty rates, as nearly one-third of those who served lost their lives. The first image depicts a Union recruiting poster; despite intense white racism, the Union recognized that African Americans offered an important source of recruits needed for the war effort. The second image, a photograph taken after the battle of Cold Harbor in 1864, shows the types to work reserved for many African Americans as well as the carnage of the war.

Questions to Consider

1. Why were African Americans eager to fight in the Civil War?

2. Why does the all African American unit depicted in the recruiting poster include a white officer?

3. What can you deduce from these images about northern attitudes toward African Americans?

4. How are the attitudes toward African Americans displayed in these images different from those displayed by Jefferson Davis ("Jefferson Davis Responds to the Emancipation Proclamation," Document 117)?

Come and Join US Brothers, (1863)

SOURCE: Come and Join Us Brothers', Union recruitment poster aimed at black volunteers (colour litho), American School, (19th century) / Private Collection / Peter Newark American Pictures/The Bridgeman Art Library

African Americans Collecting Bones of Soldiers, Cold Harbor, Virginia, 1865

SOURCE: [LC-DIG-ppmsca-12615]/Library of Congress Prints and Photographs Division

119

George Pickett on the "Charge" (1863)

The Battle of Gettysburg in July 1863 represented the high-water mark of Confederate military success in the Eastern Theater. Confederate General Robert E. Lee believed that if his Army of Northern Virginia could successfully take the war into the North, Union support for the war might collapse. On July 1, Lee's forces met the Union army at Gettysburg, a small Pennsylvania crossroads town with easy proximity to Washington D.C., Baltimore, and Philadelphia. After initially failing to turn the Union flanks, Lee ordered a frontal assault against Union positions in the hills south of town. The following letter to his new bride, LaSalle, provides General George Pickett's description of the battle. Pickett had finished last in his class at West Point and served in the Mexican War before joining the Confederate army.

Questions to Consider

1. Does "Old Peter" (General James Longstreet) think that the planned assault on Union positions is a good idea?
2. What appears to be the author's reaction to the charge?
3. What is the significance of this document?
4. Compare this document with the depictions offered in "Images of African Americans in the Civil War" (Document 118) and "General William T. Sherman on War" (Document 122). What conclusions can you draw about Civil War combat from these documents?

MY letter of yesterday, my darling, written before the battle, was full of hope and cheer; even though it told you of the long hours of waiting from four in the morning, when Gary's pistol rang out from the Federal lines signaling the attack upon Culp's Hill, to the solemn eight-o'clock review of my men, who rose and stood silently lifting their hats in loving reverence as Marse Robert, Old Peter and your own Soldier reviewed them—on then to the deadly stillness of the five hours following, when the men lay in the tall grass in the rear of the artillery line, the July sun pouring its scorching rays almost vertically down upon them, till one o'clock when the awful silence of the vast battlefield was broken by a cannon-shot which opened the greatest artillery duel of the world. The firing lasted two hours. When it ceased we took advantage of the blackened

SOURCE: George Edward Pickett, "George Edward Pickett to LaSalle Corbell Pickett, July 4, 1863," *The Heart of a Soldier; as Revealed in the Intimate Letters of General George Pickett*, ed. LaSalle Corbell Pickett (New York, 1913), 97–100.

field and in the glowering darkness formed our attacking column just before the brow of Seminary Ridge.

I closed my letter to you a little before three o'clock and rode up to Old Peter for orders. I found him like a great lion at bay. I have never seen him so grave and troubled. For several minutes after I had saluted him he looked at me without speaking. Then in an: agonized voice, the reserve all gone, he said:

"Pickett, I am being crucified at the thought of the sacrifice of life which this attack will make. I have instructed Alexander to watch the effect of our fire upon the enemy, and when it begins to tell he must take the responsibility and give you your orders, for I can't."

While he was yet speaking a note was brought to me from Alexander. After reading it I handed it to him, asking if I should obey and go forward. He looked at me for a moment, then held out his hand. Presently, clasping his other hand over mine without speaking he bowed his head upon his breast. I shall never forget the look in his face nor the clasp of his hand when I said:—"Then, General, I shall lead my Division on." I had ridden only a few paces when I remembered your letter and (forgive me) thoughtlessly scribbled in a corner of the envelope, "If Old Peter's nod means death then good-by and God bless you, little one," turned back and asked the dear old chief if he would be good enough to mail it for me. As he took your letter from me, my darling, I saw tears glistening on his cheeks and beard. The stern old war-horse, God bless him, was weeping for his men and, I know, praying too that this cup might pass from them. I obeyed the silent assent of his bowed head, an assent given against his own convictions,—given in anguish and with reluctance.

My brave boys were full of hope and confident of victory as I led them forth, forming them in column of attack, and though officers and men alike knew what was before them,—knew the odds against them,—they eagerly offered up their lives on the altar of duty, having absolute faith in their ultimate success.

Over on Cemetery Ridge the Federals beheld a scene never before witnessed on this continent,—a scene which has never previously been enacted and can never take place again—an army forming in line of battle in full view, under their very eyes—charging across a space nearly a mile in length over fields of waving grain and anon of stubble and then a smooth expanse—moving with the steadiness of a dress parade, the pride and glory soon to be crushed by an overwhelming heartbreak.

Well, it is all over now. The battle is lost, and many of us are prisoners, many are dead, many wounded, bleeding and dying. Your Soldier lives and mourns and but for you, my darling, he would rather, a million times rather, be back there with his dead, to sleep for all time in an unknown grave.

Your sorrowing
Soldier.

In Camp, July 4, 1863.

120

New York City Draft Riots (1863)

The loss of life occasioned by the Civil War demanded that the federal government take extraordinary measures. Perhaps none represented a greater intrusion of federal power into the lives of ordinary people than the decision to draft young men into the army. While such a measure was considered a wartime necessity in many parts of the North, the decision was unpopular among some groups. For recently arrived immigrants, especially the Irish, the Republican Party with its vestiges of anti-immigrant "Know Nothingism" was their enemy. Since most immigrants were poor urban dwellers whose status was artificially elevated by the intense racism aimed at free blacks, the transition to a war against slavery potentially meant additional competition for jobs and status. Finally, the working poor realized that a draft was likely to fall much more heavily on them than on other groups in society. Nowhere was the situation more acute than in New York City, and in no immigrant group were these feelings more prevalent than among the Irish. Fear of the draft, coupled with lingering urban problems, led to the worst riots in American history. The following account from the New York Herald *describes the cause of the disturbances.*

Questions to Consider

1. According to this account, what are the underlying causes of the riots?
2. After reading this document, what can you deduce about Civil War era attitudes concerning class, race, and ethnicity?
3. Compare and contrast this account with that found in the image "Five Points" (Document 72). What similarities do you note? Differences? What conclusions might be drawn concerning middle-class Americans' view of property rights?

Now that the smoke and the dust and the noise and confusion of the late riots in this city have cleared away we may without much difficulty get at their true character, their causes and the elements involved in them. We are all satisfied that while under the general panic which they created throughout Manhattan Island they were greatly magnified—that, in brief, what was supposed to be a prodigious mountain has dwindled down to a contemptible molehill.

These riots were commenced by a body of laboring men in an active, lawless demonstration against the draft, including a number of enraged individuals turned over to the army by the first day's working of the wheel in the disaffected

SOURCE: "The Late Riots—A Mountain Reduced to a Molehill," *New York Herald*, 24 July 1863, p. 4.

district. Carrying everything before them in the outset, and finding neither policemen nor soldiers on hand in sufficient numbers to check them, the rioters were rapidly joined by all the thieves, burglars, pickpockets, incendiaries and jailbirds of all descriptions in the neighborhood, until a large proportion of the villains and vagabonds of every part of the island and every hole and corner of the city had joined the original mob, and completely changed its character into various hordes of rogues and ruffians, seizing the occasion for a carnival of terrorism, fire, blood and plunder.

A single regiment of our State militia on Monday morning would have been sufficient to quell the original disturbance. Certainly the troops and policemen collected by Monday afternoon, if managed with anything like skill and system, would have been sufficient in a few hours to put down every vestige of a lawless assemblage. But between our supreme federal military officer, General Wool, and Governor Seymour and Mayor Opdyke, all of whom made a great parade of doing wonderful things, while, in fact, they were doing little or nothing, there was so much of confusion in the management of our soldiers and policemen that it was not until Wednesday that the war was turned decisively against the rioters.

It is due, however, to Commissioner Acton, of the Metropolitan board, to say that from the moment he assumed the general direction of the police to the end of the disturbances, his conduct was that of a skilful, fearless, energetic and able officer. He has nobly earned the gratitude of the whole community. Captain Wilson, too, of the Fort Washington Precinct, operated among the rioters after the fashion of General Grant, breaking up one gang here, another there, and so on from point to point with his faithful squad, giving the enemies of law and order no rest, but smiting them hip and thigh, right and left, till his work was done. There were several other detachments of the police which did good service against great odds in various encounters with the rioters; but still there is a considerable number of these grenadier Metropolitans who seem to be fit for little else in their vocation than to escort the ladies safely across Broadway "among those horrid omnibuses."

Mayor Opdyke would doubtless have done something had not this functionary been deprived of the power to do anything by our tinkering Albany politicians. They have by their tinkering, in fact, given us such divided counsels and departments in our city government as to render it almost completely helpless in any emergency like that of a carnival of rogues and ruffians. It is to be hoped that this fact will not be forgotten by our city members at the next meeting of the State Legislature.

But these late riots which have so disgraced our city have been exaggerated by our radical abolition organs into a grand rebel conspiracy in behalf of Jeff. Davis. Nothing could be more absurd, except the absurd speculations of some of the newspapers of rebeldom. The *Richmond Dispatch*, for instance, supposes that these New York disturbances are but the beginnings of a general Northern rebellion against the Lincoln despotism, and that by these outbreaks the Davis confederacy is to be lighted to its national independence. Such are the straws that drowning men will snatch at. It will not be long before these Southern newspaper philosophers discover their folly and stupidity in believing for a moment the partisan claptrap of our abolition organs in regard to these late riots. They are ended; for we are sure that President Lincoln, in returning to the business of the draft, will, in a liberal application of the law, render it acceptable even to the working man, who has nothing but his daily labor to depend upon for the subsistence of his family.

The New York riots are ended. They will not be renewed; and the sooner the newspaper organs of Jeff. Davis at Richmond dismiss the idea that he has a great political conspiracy in the North moving for his support the sooner will the misery and the suspense of Davis and his fellows be ended.

121

The Southern Home Front (1863)

By 1863, the initial enthusiasm of two years earlier had given way to the harsh reality of struggle and privation for many southerners. The ever-tightening Union naval blockade, the need for huge quantities of food to feed a modern army, the lack of a reliable transportation infrastructure to easily move supplies, and the lack of manpower to work southern farms all contributed to the growing shortages. These deprivations would contribute to bread riots in Richmond, Virginia, during the spring of 1863. In the ensuing document, "A Richmond Lady", Sallie Putnam recounts the difficulties faced during the war and how women on the home front sought to contribute to the Confederate war effort.

Questions to Consider

1. Does the author of this selection remain enthusiastic about the war effort?
2. What can you deduce about public support for the war from this document?
3. In what ways has life changed in Richmond?
4. What can you deduce about the importance of social class from this document? In what ways have attitudes changed?

At this time our Richmond workshops were turning out large supplies of valuable arms and weapons of warfare, and our Nitre Bureau was made effective in

SOURCE: A Richmond Lady [Sallie A. Putnam], *Richmond During the War: Four Years of Personal Observation* (New York, 1867).

contributions of valuable ammunition. While our financial interests were going to ruin, and our navy doing comparatively nothing for our assistance, our people were striving, by their own energies, and by the development of their personal resources, to neutralize, as far as possible, the maladministration of certain departments of the government, which, properly conducted, might have remedied many of the evils and inconveniences entailed upon us. While the men were in the field, branches of female industry were faithfully attended to. We were carried back to the times of our grandmothers.

Our women were actively interested in discovering the coloring properties of roots, barks, and berries, and experimenting with alum, copperas, soda, and other alkalies and mineral mordants in dying cotton and wool for domestic manufacture. On approaching a country house rather late, the ear would be greeted, not with the sound of the piano or the Spanish guitar, but with the hum of the spinning-wheel brought out from the hiding-place to which it had been driven before the triumph of the mechanical skill, and the "bang-bang" of the old-fashioned and long-disused loom. The whereabouts of the mistress of the mansion might be inferred from the place whence the sound proceeded; for she was probably herself engaged in, or superintending, the work of a servant, in the weaving or spinning-room.... With commendable pride we beheld the Southern gentlemen clad in the comfortable homespun suit, and our ladies wearing domestic dresses that challenged comparison with the plaids and merinos of commercial manufacture. To the rustic and virtuous simplicity of the times the honored wife of our President nobly conformed.

The winter evenings' exercises of knitting for the soldiers were varied by the braiding of straw for bonnets and hats, many of which would compare favorably with those of English manufacture. For gloves, knitting was resorted to, and they were also made of soft, thin cloth, and those rather rude in appearance, were cheerfully exhibited as ingenious evidences that necessity develops resources.

Kid gloves were rarely seen. On a gentleman they were considered as only little more than disgusting relics of dandyism. Confederate simplicity was rigidly austere. The Paris gloves remaining in possession of our ladies were carefully preserved to be the accompaniment to well-cared-for silks and laces of the abundance of days gone by and a costume so magnificent was only donned for some momentous occasion.

Our style of living was quite as simple as our dress. Hotels and boarding-houses, in consequence of the high prices and scarcity of provisions, had ceased to furnish a "*table d'hote*," and "keeping apartments" was the fashionable mode of living in Richmond. "We are living in the Paris style," did not mean, however, the luxury of a suit of magnificent apartments where could be served to all the delicacies and luxuries of the season, but generally the renting of a single room, which served at the same time the purposes of kitchen, dormitory, and parlor for the lucky family that could secure even such comfortable accommodations. The simple dinner was cooked in a sauce-pan on the grate, and often consisted only of potatoes and a very small quantity of meat and bread, varied with occasionally a fowl, and tea.

At weddings we were served with unfrosted cake, and drank the health of the fair bride in domestic wine, if wine at all could be procured. We knew nothing of dyspepsia, and the thousand ailments of an overcharged stomach were unheard of. We practiced a compulsory system of "Banting," and amused ourselves at the many laughable, yet instructive inconveniences to which we were subjected. When invited to breakfast with an intimate friend, the inducement to accept the kind invitation was frequently, "I'll give you a cup of nice pure coffee," and for dinners we would sometimes ask, "Will you give me something sweet?" (meaning a dessert.) "Yes." "Then I'll come." There was something romantic, something novel in this mode of life, and the remembrance, though associated with much that is painful, is on the whole rather pleasant.

We were taught many lessons of forbearance and economy, the value of which to us must be tested by their influence on our future lives. We were, in our poverty, prepared fully to realize the truth—

"Man wants but little here below—"

but our trials only served to make us regret every piece of economy practiced when goods were plentiful, and at such prices that we could with ease obtain them.

The situation of the refugees was often painful in the extreme. It was no unusual thing to have presented at our doors a basket in the hands of a negro servant who sold on commission articles disposed of by the necessitons to obtain food. Handsome dresses, patterns of unmade goods, purchased perhaps before the commencement or in the beginning of the war, a piece of silver, or sets of jewelry, accompanied by a note anonymously sent, attested to the poverty and noble pride of some woman who doubtless wore a cheerful face, and when asked if she desired peace, would reply, "Only with liberty." In the stores of our jewelers were frequently seen diamonds and pearls, watches and valuable plate for sale, placed there by some unfortunate, who disposed of these articles of former wealth, luxury and taste, to procure necessary articles of food and raiment.

122

General William T. Sherman on War (1864)

In the Western Theater, Union commanders not only achieved important victories, but developed new military strategies in the process. One of the most effective of these generals was William T. Sherman. An Ohio native, Sherman was a graduate of West Point and later served in the Mexican-American War. During the Civil War, Sherman quickly rose through the ranks; in March 1864, he succeeded Ulysses Grant as commander of Union armies in the West. Sherman sought to defeat an enemy by destroying its economic infrastructure; his interest in Atlanta, Georgia, resulted from its strategic significance as a transportation hub and supply center. In the following account, Sherman responds to Atlanta's leaders with a description of his view of warfare and his role in it.

Questions to Consider

1. Why was William T. Sherman fighting the war?
2. What is his definition of war, and how does he hope to prosecute it?
3. Why does Sherman have little sympathy for the mayor of Atlanta?
4. How might Sallie Putnam ("The Southern Home Front," Document 121) have responded to General Sherman?

Headquarters Military Division of the Mississippi,
In the Field, Atlanta, Georgia, September 12, 1864

James M. Calhoun, Mayor, E. E. Rawson and S. C. Wells,
representing City Council of Atlanta.

GENTLEMEN: I have your letter of the 11th, in the nature of petition to revoke my orders removing all the inhabitants from Atlanta. I have read it carefully, and give full credit to your statements of the distress that will be occasioned, and yet shall not revoke my orders, because they were not designed to meet the humanities of the case, but to prepare for the future struggles in which millions of good people outside of Atlanta have a deep interest. We must have peace, not only at Atlanta, but in all America. To secure this, we must stop the war that now desolates our once happy and favored country. To stop war, we must defeat the rebel armies which are arrayed against the laws and Constitution that all must respect and obey. To defeat those armies, we must prepare the way to reach them in their recesses, provided with the arms and instruments which enable us to accomplish our purpose. Now, I know the vindictive nature of our enemy, that we may have many years of military operations from this quarter; and, therefore, deem it wise and prudent to prepare in time. The use of Atlanta for warlike purposes is inconsistent with its character as a home for families. There will be no manufactures, commerce, or agriculture here, for the maintenance of families, and sooner or later want will compel the inhabitants to go. Why not go now, when all the arrangements are completed for the transfer, instead of waiting till the plunging shot of contending armies will renew the scenes of the past month? Of course, I do not apprehend any such thing at this moment, but you do not suppose this army will be here until the war is over. I cannot discuss this subject with you fairly, because I cannot impart to you what

SOURCE: William T. Sherman, "William T. Sherman to James M. Calhoun (Mayor), E. E. Rawson and S. C. Wells, 12 September 1864," *Memoirs* (New York, 1892), 2: 125–27.

we propose to do, but I assert that our military plans make it necessary for the inhabitants to go away, and I can only renew my offer of services to make their exodus in any direction as easy and comfortable as possible.

You cannot qualify war in harsher terms than I will. War is cruelty, and you cannot refine it; and those who brought war into our country deserve all the curses and maledictions a people can pour out. I know I had no hand in making this war, and I know I will make more sacrifices to-day than any of you to secure peace. But you cannot have peace and a division of our country. If the United States submits to a division now, it will not stop, but will go on until we reap the fate of Mexico, which is eternal war. The United States does and must assert its authority, wherever it once had power; for, if it relaxes one bit to pressure, it is gone, and I believe that such is the national feeling. This feeling assumes various shapes, but always comes back to that of Union. Once admit the Union, once more acknowledge the authority of the national Government, and, instead of devoting your houses and streets and roads to the dread uses of war, I and this army become at once your protectors and supporters, shielding you from danger, let it come from what quarter it may. I know that a few individuals cannot resist a torrent of error and passion, such as swept the South into rebellion, but you can point out, so that we may know those who desire a government, and those who insist on war and its desolation.

You might as well appeal against the thunder-storm as against these terrible hardships of war. They are inevitable, and the only way the people of Atlanta can hope once more to live in peace and quiet at home, is to stop the war, which can only be done by admitting that it began in error and is perpetuated in pride.

We don't want your negroes, or your horses, or your houses, or your lands, or any thing you have, but we do want and will have a just obedience to the laws of the United States. That we will have, and, if it involves the destruction of your improvements, we cannot help it.

You have heretofore read public sentiment in your newspapers, that live by falsehood and excitement; and the quicker you seek for truth in other quarters, the better. I repeat then that, by the original compact of Government, the United States had certain rights in Georgia, which have never been relinquished and never will be; that the South began war by seizing forts, arsenals, mints, custom-houses, etc., etc., long before Mr. Lincoln was installed, and before the South had one jot or tittle of provocation. I myself have seen in Missouri, Kentucky, Tennessee, and Mississippi, hundreds and thousands of women and children fleeing from your armies and desperadoes, hungry and with bleeding feet. In Memphis, Vicksburg, and Mississippi, we fed thousands upon thousands of the families of rebel soldiers left on our hands, and whom we could not see starve. Now that war comes home to you, you feel very different. You deprecate its horrors, but did not feel them when you sent car-loads of soldiers and ammunition, and moulded shells and shot, to carry war into Kentucky and Tennessee, to desolate the homes of hundreds and thousands of good people who only asked to live in peace at their old homes, and under the Government of their inheritance. But these comparisons are idle. I want peace, and believe it can only be reached through union and war, and I will ever conduct war with a view to perfect and early success.

But, my dear sirs, when peace does come, you may call on me for any thing. Then will I share with you the last cracker, and watch with you to shield your homes and families against danger from every quarter.

Now you must go, and take with you the old and feeble, feed and nurse them, and build for them, in more quiet places, proper habitations to shield them against the weather until the mad passions of men cool down, and allow the Union and peace once more to settle over your homes at Atlanta. Yours in haste,

—**W. T. Sherman, Major-General commanding.**

123

Lincoln's Second Inaugural Address (1865)

By March 1865, Union military successes in Virginia and Georgia had brought the North to the brink of victory. With victory in sight, postwar issues now became increasingly central to the national agenda. In the midst of the debates over the nation's future, President Abraham Lincoln delivered his second inaugural address, which follows.

Questions to Consider

1. How have President Lincoln's views changed since he proclaimed "A War to Preserve the Union" (Document 116)? What has remained unchanged?
2. How would you describe President Lincoln's views toward the South?
3. What does the president see as the major issues confronting the nation after the war?
4. What can you deduce about the religious sensibilities of President Lincoln?

FELLOW-COUNTRYMEN: At this second appearing to take the oath of the presidential office, there is less occasion for an extended address than there was at the first. Then a statement, somewhat in detail, of a course to be pursued,

SOURCE: "Second Inaugural Address, March 4, 1865," *Complete Works of Abraham Lincoln*, eds. John G. Nicolay and John Hay, New and Enlarged Edition (New York, 1894), 11: 44–47.

seemed fitting and proper. Now, at the expiration of four years, during which public declarations have been constantly called forth on every point and phase of the great contest which still absorbs the attention and engrosses the energies of the nation, little that is new could be presented. The progress of our arms, upon which all else chiefly depends, is as well known to the public as to myself; and it is, I trust, reasonably satisfactory and encouraging to all. With high hope for the future, no prediction in regard to it is ventured.

On the occasion corresponding to this four years ago, all thoughts were anxiously directed to an impending civil war. All dreaded it—all sought to avert it. While the inaugural address was being delivered from this place, devoted altogether to saving the Union without war, insurgent agents were in the city seeking to destroy it without war—seeking to dissolve the Union, and divide effects, by negotiation. Both parties deprecated war; but one of them would make war rather than let the nation survive; and the other would accept war rather than let it perish. And the war came.

One-eighth of the whole population were colored slaves, not distributed generally over the Union, but localized in the southern part of it. These slaves constituted a peculiar and powerful interest. All knew that this interest was, somehow, the cause of the war. To strengthen, perpetuate, and extend this interest was the object for which the insurgents would rend the Union, even by war; while the government claimed no right to do more than to restrict the territorial enlargement of it.

Neither party expected for the war the magnitude or the duration which it has already attained. Neither anticipated that the cause of the conflict might cease with, or even before, the conflict itself should cease. Each looked for an easier triumph, and a result less fundamental and astounding. Both read the same Bible, and pray to the same God; and each invokes his aid against the other. It may seem strange that any men should dare to ask a just God's assistance in wringing their bread from the sweat of other men's faces; but let us judge not, that we be not judged. The prayers of both could not be answered—that of neither has been answered fully.

The Almighty has his own purposes. "Woe unto the world because of offenses! For it must needs be that offenses come; but woe to that man by whom the offense cometh." If we shall suppose that American slavery is one of those offenses which, in the providence of God, must needs come, but which, having continued through his appointed time, he now wills to remove, and that he gives to both North and South this terrible war, as the woe due to those by whom the offense came, shall we discern therein any departure from those divine attributes which the believers in a living God always ascribe to him? Fondly do we hope—fervently do we pray—that this mighty scourge of war may speedily pass away. Yet, if God wills that it continue until all the wealth piled by the bondsman's two-hundred and fifty years of unrequited toil shall be sunk, and until every drop of blood drawn with the lash shall be paid by another drawn with the sword, as was said three thousand years ago, so still it must be said, "The judgements of the Lord are true and righteous altogether."

With malice toward none; with charity for all; with firmness in the right, as God gives us to see the right, let us strive on to finish the work we are in; to bind up the nation's wounds; to care for him who shall have borne the battle, and for his widow, and his orphan—to do all which may achieve and cherish a just and lasting peace among ourselves, and with all nations.

15

Reconstruction

After the Civil War, the nation faced the enormous task of reconstructing the republic. In particular, policymakers had to determine the status of the former Confederate states and what to do with the recently freed slaves. Devastated by the war, the South also had to cope with the influx of northern troops, reformers, and profiteers, many of whom had their own ideas concerning the region's future. The diversity of opinions over Reconstruction deeply divided the North and occasionally brought a violent response from some southern whites. The ensuing selections reveal how Americans of different races and regions responded to Reconstruction.

124

A Northern Teacher's View of the Freedmen (1863–1865)

Early in the Civil War, Union troops occupied the sea islands along South Carolina's coast near Beaufort. All property—plantations, cotton, and slaves—was confiscated and placed under the jurisdiction of Secretary of the Treasury Salmon P. Chase. Of particular concern was the welfare of the slaves, who at this early stage of the war were considered contraband if they were behind Union lines and were not returned to their owners. Sensing the opportunity to use these islands as an experiment for the future reconstruction of the

South, Chase permitted benevolent organizations to send teachers, many of them women, to help educate the former slaves. In October 1863, the New England Freedmen's Aid Society sponsored Elizabeth Hyde Botume as a teacher in this experiment. Hyde became more than a teacher in the several years she spent among the ex-slaves, as her book, First Days Amongst the Contrabands, *revealed. Excerpted here is Hyde's description of the freedmen.*

Questions to Consider

1.   In what ways did the slaves react to freedom?

2.   What are the initial problems facing the freedmen?

3.   What social, political, and economic issues confronting Reconstruction does Elizabeth Hyde Botume observe?

4.   What can you deduce about race relations?

… Contrabands were coming into the Union lines, and thence to the town, not only daily, but hourly. They came alone and in families and in gangs, —slaves who had been hiding away, and were only now able to reach safety. Different members of scattered families following after freedom, as surely and safely guided as were the Wise Men by the Star of the East.

On New Year's Day I walked around amongst these people with Major Saxton. We went to their tents and other quarters. One hundred and fifty poor refugees from Georgia had been quartered all day on the wharf. A wretched and most pitiable gang, miserable beyond description. But when we spoke to them, they invariably gave a cheerful answer. Usually to our question, "How do you do?" the response would be, "Thank God, I live!"

Sometimes they would say, "Us ain't no wusser than we been."

These people had been a long time without food, excepting a little hominy and uncooked rice and a few ground-nuts. Many were entirely naked when they started, and all were most scantily clothed and we had already had some extremely cold days, which we, who were fresh from the North, found hard to bear.

It was the same old story. These poor creatures were covered only with blankets, or bits of old carpeting, or pieces of bagging, "crocus," fastened with thorns or sharp sticks….

I went first to the negro quarters at the "Battery Plantation," a mile and a half away. A large number of Georgia refugees who had followed Sherman's army were quartered here. Around the old plantation house was a small army of black children, who swarmed like bees around a hive. There were six rooms in the house, occupied by thirty-one persons, big and little. In one room was a man whom I had seen before. He was very light, with straight red hair and a sandy complexion, and I mistook him for an Irishman. He had been to me at

SOURCE: Elizabeth Hyde Botume, *First Days Amongst the Contrabands* (Boston, 1893), 78–79, 82–83, 117–18, 168–69, 176–77.

one time grieving deeply for the loss of his wife, but he had now consoled himself with a buxom girl as black as ink. His sister, a splendidly developed creature, was with them. He had also four sons. Two were as light as himself, and two were very black. These seven persons occupied this one room. A rough box bedstead, with a layer of moss and a few old rags in it, a hominy pot, two or three earthen plates, and a broken-backed chair, comprised all the furniture of the room. I had previously given one of the women a needle and some thread, and she now sat on the edge of the rough bedstead trying to sew the dress she ought, in decency, to have had on....

The winter of 1864–1865 was a sad time, for so many poor creatures in our district were wretchedly ill, begging for help, and we had so little to give them. Many of the contrabands had pneumonia. Great exposure, with scanty clothing and lack of proper food, rendered them easy victims to the encroachments of any disease. I sent to Beaufort for help. The first doctor who came was exasperatingly indifferent. He might have been a brother of a "bureau officer," who was sent down especially to take care of the contrabands, and who wished all the negroes could be put upon a ship, and floated out to sea and sunk. It would be better for them and for the world. When we expressed our surprise that he could speak so of human beings, he exclaimed, "Human beings! They are only animals, and not half as valuable as cattle."

When the doctor came, I went from room to room and talked with the poor sick people, whose entire dependence was upon us. Finally I could endure his apathy and indifference no longer.

"Leave me medicines, and I will take care of these people as well as I can," I said....

I could not, however, excuse the doctor, a man in government employ, drawing a good salary with no heart in his work. Beaufort was reported to be a depot for officials whom government did not know what to do with....

Early in February we went to Savannah with General and Mrs. Saxton, and members of the general's staff, and other officers. How it had become known that we were to make this trip I cannot tell, but we found a crowd of our own colored people on the boat when we went aboard. To our exclamations of surprise they said with glee,—

"Oh, we're goin' too, fur us has frien's there."

We found the city crowded with contrabands who were in a most pitiable condition. Nearly all the negroes who had lived there before the war had gone away. A large number went on with the army; those left were the stragglers who had come in from the "sand hills" and low lands. The people from the plantations too had rushed into the city as soon as they knew the Union troops were in possession.

A crowd of poor whites had also congregated there. All were idle and destitute. The whites regarded the negroes as still a servile race, who must always be inferior by virtue of their black skins. The negroes felt that emancipation had lifted them out of old conditions into new relations with their fellow beings. They were no longer chattels, but independent creatures with rights and privileges like their neighbors....

Nothing in the history of the world has ever equalled the magnitude and thrilling importance of the events then transpiring. Here were more than four millions of human beings just born into freedom; one day held in the most abject slavery, the next, "de Lord's free men." Free to come and to go according to the best lights given them. Every movement of their white friends was to them full of significance, and often regarded with distrust. Well might they sometimes exclaim, when groping from darkness into light, "Save me from my friend, and I will look out for my enemy."

Whilst the Union people were asking, "Those negroes! what is to be done with them?" they, in their ignorance and helplessness, were crying out in agony, "What will become of us?" They were literally saying, "I believe, O Lord! help thou mine unbelief."

They were constantly coming to us to ask what peace meant for them? Would it be peace indeed? or oppression, hostility, and servile subjugation? This was what they feared, for they knew the temper of the baffled rebels as did no others.

125

Charleston, South Carolina, at the Conclusion of the Civil War (1865)

The Civil War brought destruction to the South. With much of the fighting taking place in southern states, armies of both sides laid waste to the countryside and burned or destroyed communities as they struggled to win the war. While often not directly involved in the fighting, the civilian population felt the brunt of the conflict. The war also brought a dislocation of trade and business activities in the South, often resulting in shortages of food and clothing. Furthermore, the Civil War shattered the plantation economy of primarily cotton production based on the labor of African American slaves. When the Confederacy surrendered in April 1865, the southern states faced significant social, political, and economic adjustments. At the war's conclusion, some northern journalists traveled throughout the South to report on conditions and people's reactions to the beginnings of Reconstruction. Sidney Andrews was one of these journalists; his observations appeared in the Chicago Tribune *and the* Boston Advertiser. *The reports from his three-month southern tour attracted such attention that they were compiled in book form,* The South Since the War, *which is excerpted here. His direct and well-written accounts were among the best commentaries on the immediate postwar South.*

Questions to Consider

1. What conditions did Andrews find in Charleston?

2. In what ways did residents of Charleston react to northerners? To Reconstruction policies? Would this be expected?

3. What issues and attitudes does Andrews reveal that become critical in Reconstruction?

4. In what ways does the photograph of African Americans collecting skeletons after the Battle of Cold Harbor ("Images of African Americans in the Civil War," Document 118) compare with Andrews's description of Charleston?

A city of ruins, of desolation, of vacant houses, of widowed women, of rotting wharves, of deserted warehouses, of weed-wild gardens, of miles of grass-grown streets, of acres of pitiful and voiceful barrenness,—that is Charleston, wherein Rebellion loftily reared its head five years ago, on whose beautiful promenade the fairest of cultured women gathered with passionate hearts to applaud the assault of ten thousand upon the little garrison of Fort Sumter!...

We will never again have the Charleston of the decade previous to the war. The beauty and pride of the city are as dead as the glories of Athens. Five millions of dollars could not restore the ruin of these four past years; and that sum is so far beyond the command of the city as to seem the boundless measure of immeasurable wealth. Yet, after all, Charleston was Charleston because of the hearts of its people. St. Michael's Church, they held, was the center of the universe; and the aristocracy of the city were the very elect of God's children of earth. One marks now how few young men there are, how generally the young women are dressed in black. The flower of their proud aristocracy is buried on scores of battlefields. If it were possible to restore the broad acres of crumbling ruins to their foretime style and uses, there would even then be but the dead body of Charleston....

Of Massachusetts men, some are already in business here, and others came on to "see the lay of the land," as one of them said. "That's all right," observed an ex-rebel captain in one of our after-dinner chats,—"that's all right; let's have Massachusetts and South Carolina brought together, for they are the only two States that amount to anything."

"I hate all you Yankees most heartily in a general sort of way," remarked another of these Southerners; "but I find you clever enough personally, and I expect it'll be a good thing for us to have you come down here with your money, though it'll go against the grain of us pretty badly."

There are many Northern men here already, though one cannot say that there is much Northern society, for the men are either without families or have left them at home. Walking out yesterday with a former Charlestonian, ... he pointed out to me the various "Northern houses"; and I shall not exaggerate if I say that this classification appeared to include at least half the stores on each of the principal streets. "The presence of these men," said he, "was at first

SOURCE: Sidney Andrews, *The South Since the War* (Boston, 1866), 1–9.

very distasteful to our people, and they are not liked any too well now; but we know they are doing a good work for the city."

I fell into some talk with him concerning the political situation, and found him of bitter spirit toward what he was pleased to denominate "the infernal radicals." When I asked him what should be done, he answered: "You Northern people are making a great mistake in your treatment of the South. We are thoroughly whipped; we give up slavery forever; and now we want you to quit reproaching us. Let us back into the Union, and then come down here and help us build up the country." ...

It would seem that it is not clearly understood how thoroughly Sherman's army destroyed everything in its line of march,—destroyed it without questioning who suffered by the action. That this wholesale destruction was often without orders, and often against most positive orders, does not change the fact of destruction. The Rebel leaders were, too, in their way, even more wanton, and just as thorough as our army in destroying property. They did not burn houses and barns and fences as we did; but, during the last three months of the war, they burned immense quantities of cotton and rosin....

The city is under thorough military rule; but the iron hand rests very lightly. Soldiers do police duty, and there is some nine-o'clock regulation; but, so far as I can learn, anybody goes anywhere at all hours of the night without molestation. "There never was such good order here before," said an old colored man to me. The main street is swept twice a week, and all garbage is removed at sunrise. "If the Yankees was to stay here always and keep the city so clean, I don't reckon we'd have 'yellow jack' here any more," was a remark I overheard on the street. "Now is de fust time sense I can 'mem'er when black men was safe in de street af'er nightfall," states the negro tailor in whose shop I sat an hour yesterday.

On the surface, Charleston is quiet and well-behaved; and I do not doubt that the more intelligent citizens are wholly sincere in their expressions of a desire for peace and reunion. The city has been humbled as no other city has been; and I can't see how any man, after spending a few days here, can desire that it shall be further humiliated enough for health is another thing. Said one of the Charlestonians on the boat, "You won't see the real sentiment of our people, for we are under military rule; we are whipped, and we are going to make the best of things; but we hate Massachusetts as much as we ever did." This idea of making the best of things is one I have heard from scores of persons. I find very few who hesitate to frankly own that the South has been beaten. "We made the best fight we could, but you were too strong for us, and now we are only anxious to get back into the old Union and live as happily as we can," said a large cotton factor. I find very few who make any special profession of Unionism; but they are almost unanimous in declaring that they have no desire but to live as good and quiet citizens under the laws.

126

African Americans Seek Protection (1865)

The emancipation of 4 million slaves in the South brought significant social, political, and economic adjustment for both African Americans and whites. Despite obtaining freedom from their masters and the rigors of plantation life, the former slaves lost their source of shelter, food, clothing, and occupation. In short, they had little but their freedom. Realizing that they remained at the mercy of their previous owners, many African Americans gathered in conventions in cities throughout the South to discuss the best methods of protecting their fragile freedom. Some of these conventions petitioned Congress for assistance; others turned to local officials for help. Excerpted here is a petition from a convention of African Americans meeting in Alexandria, Virginia, in August 1865. This petition, the typical result of the conventions, demonstrates the precarious position of the freedmen and how they proposed to protect themselves.

Questions to Consider

1. What types of protection does this convention seek?
2. For what reasons was the convention critical of "loyalty oaths" and the Freedmen's Bureau?
3. What does this document reveal about the situation for the freedmen at this time?
4. In what ways did Elizabeth Hyde Botume's description of the freedmen ("A Northern Teacher's View of the Freedmen," Document 124) anticipate this convention's call for protection?

We, the undersigned members of a convention of colored citizens of the State of Virginia, would respectfully represent that, although we have been held as slaves, and denied all recognition as a constituent of your nationality for almost the entire period of the duration of your government, and that by your permission we have been denied either home or country, and deprived of the dearest rights of human nature; yet when you and our immediate oppressors met in deadly conflict upon the field of battle—the one to destroy and the other to save your government and nationality, we, with scarce an exception, in our inmost souls

SOURCE: "The Late Convention of Colored Men," *New York Times*, 13 August 1865, p. 3.

espoused your cause, and watched, and prayed, and waited, and labored for your success....

When the contest waxed long, and the result hung doubtfully, you appealed to us for help, and how well we answered is written in the rosters of the two hundred thousand colored troops now enrolled in your service; and as to our undying devotion to your cause, let the uniform acclamation of escaped prisoners, "Whenever we saw a black face we felt sure of a friend," answer.

Well, the war is over, the rebellion is "put down," and we are declared free! Four-fifths of our enemies are paroled or amnestied, and the other fifth are being pardoned, and the President has, in his efforts at the reconstruction of the civil government of the States, late in rebellion, left us entirely at the mercy of these subjugated but unconverted rebels, in everything save the privilege of bringing us, our wives and little ones, to the auction block. He has, so far as we can understand the tendency and bearing of his action in the case, remitted us for all our civil rights, to men, a majority of whom regard our devotions to your cause and flag as that which decided the contest against them! This we regard as destructive of all we hold dear, and in the name of God, of justice, of humanity, of good faith, of truth and righteousness, we do most solemnly and earnestly protest. Men and brethren, in the hour of your peril you called upon us, and despite all time-honored interpretation of constitutional obligations, we came at your call and you are saved; and now we beg, we pray, we entreat you not to desert us in this the hour of our peril!

We know these men—know them well—and we assure you that, with the majority of them, loyalty is only "lip deep," and that their professions of loyalty are used as a cover to the cherished design of getting restored to their former relation with the Federal Government, and then, by all sorts of "unfriendly legislation," to render the freedom you have given us more intolerable than the slavery they intended for us.

We warn you in time that our only safety is in keeping them under Governors of the military persuasion until you have so amended the Federal Constitution that it will prohibit the States from making any distinction between citizens on account of race or color. In one word, the only salvation for us besides the power of the Government, is in the possession of the ballot. Give us this, and we will protect ourselves. No class of men relatively as numerous as we were ever oppressed when armed with the ballot. But, 'tis said we are ignorant. Admit it. Yet who denies we know a traitor from a loyal man, a gentleman from a rowdy, a friend from an enemy?...

... All we ask is an equal chance with the white traitors varnished and japanned* with the oath of amnesty. Can you deny us this and still keep faith with us? "But," say some, "the blacks will be overreached by the superior knowledge and cunning of the whites." Trust us for that. We will never be deceived a second time. "But," they continue, "the planters and landowners will have them in their power, and dictate the way their votes shall be cast."

---

* A varnish that yields a hard brilliant finish.

We did not know before that we were to be left to the tender mercies of these landed rebels for employment. Verily, we thought the Freedmen's Bureau was organized and clothed with power to protect us from this very thing, by compelling those for whom we labored to pay us, whether they liked our political opinions or not!...

We are "sheep in the midst of wolves," and nothing but the military arm of the Government prevents us and all the truly loyal white men from being driven from the land of our birth. Do not then, we beseech you, give to one of these "wayward sisters" the rights they abandoned and forfeited when they rebelled until you have secured our rights by the aforementioned amendment to the Constitution.

Let your action in our behalf be thus clear and emphatic, and our respected President, who, we feel confident, desires only to know your will, to act in harmony therewith, will give you his most earnest and cordial cooperation; and the Southern States, through your enlightened and just legislation, will speedily award us our rights. Thus not only will the arms of the rebellion be surrendered, but the ideas also.

127

Thaddeus Stevens on Reconstruction and the South (1865)

The debate over Reconstruction began during the Civil War and became increasingly acute as the North moved toward victory. The lines were quickly drawn between the president and Congress, though various factions within the Republican Party argued vociferously for certain positions. Some of the more important issues centered on how the secessionist states should be reunited with the Union; what political and social status should be conveyed to the 4 million freedmen; how the whites who supported the Confederacy should be treated; and lastly, who should control Reconstruction. Presidential Reconstruction, begun by Abraham Lincoln in December 1863 and slightly modified when Andrew Johnson assumed the presidency, was declared too lenient by Republicans. Within Congress, a powerful group called the Radical Republicans challenged Presidential Reconstruction and began advocating their own agenda. Among the leaders of the Radical Republicans was Thaddeus Stevens, a representative from Lancaster, Pennsylvania, whose quick wit, honesty, political savvy, and belief that Reconstruction offered an opportunity to establish a better country made him a powerful supporter of Congressional Reconstruction. Excerpted here is Stevens's speech on the status of the South and what Congressional Reconstruction should encompass.

Questions to Consider

1. What political actions does Thaddeus Stevens propose for the South?

2. What does Stevens believe Congress should do for the freedmen?

3. In what ways do Stevens's proposals help shape Reconstruction policies?

4. In what ways might Stevens have reacted to Elizabeth Hyde Botume's description of the freedmen ("A Northern Teacher's View of the Freedmen," Document 124) and the freedmen's appeal for protection ("African Americans Seek Protection," Document 126)?

... No one doubts that the late rebel states have lost their constitutional relations to the Union, and are incapable of representation in Congress, except by permission of the Government. It matters but little, with this admission whether you call them States out of the Union, and now conquered territories, or assert that because the Constitution forbids them to do what they did do, that they are therefore only dead as to all national and political action, and will remain so until the government shall breathe into them the breath of life anew and permit them to occupy their former position. In other words, that they are not out of the Union, but are only dead carcasses lying within the Union. In either case, it is very plain that it requires the action of Congress to enable them to form a State government and send representatives to Congress. Nobody, I believe, pretends that with their old constitutions and frames of government they can be permitted to claim their old rights under the Constitution. They have torn their constitutional States into atoms, and built on their foundations fabrics of a totally different character. Dead men cannot raise themselves. Dead States cannot restore their own existence "as it was." Whose especial duty is it to do it? In whom does the Constitution place the power? Not in the judicial branch of government, for it only adjudicates and does not prescribe laws. Not in the Executive, for he only executes and cannot make laws. Not in the Commander-in-Chief of the armies, for he can only hold them under military rule until the sovereign legislative power of the conqueror shall give them law....

Congress alone can do it. But Congress does not mean the Senate, or the House of Representatives, and President, all acting severally. Their joint action constitutes Congress.... Congress must create States and declare when they are entitled to be represented. Then each House must judge whether the members presenting themselves from a recognized State possess the requisite qualifications of age, residence, and citizenship; and whether the election and returns are according to law. The Houses, separately, can judge of nothing else. It seems amazing that any man of legal education could give it any larger meaning.

It is obvious from all this that the first duty of Congress is to pass a law declaring the condition of these outside or defunct States, and providing proper civil governments to them. Since the conquest they have been governed by martial law. Military rule is necessarily despotic, and ought not to exist longer than is absolutely necessary. As there are no symptoms that the people of these provinces will be prepared to participate in constitutional government for some years, I know

SOURCE: "Reconstruction," *Congressional Globe*, 39th Congress, 1st Session, part 1 (18 December 1865), 72–74.

of no arrangement so proper for them as territorial governments. There they can learn the principles of freedom and eat the fruit of foul rebellion. Under such governments, while electing members to the Territorial Legislatures, they will necessarily mingle with those to whom Congress shall extend the right of suffrage. In Territories Congress fixes the qualifications of electors; and I know of no better place nor better occasion for the conquered rebels and the conqueror to practice justice to all men, and accustom themselves to make and obey equal laws....

According to my judgment they ought never to be recognized as capable of acting in the Union, of being counted as valid States, until the Constitution shall have been so amended as to make it what its framers intended; and so as to secure perpetual ascendancy to the party of the Union; and so as to render our republican Government firm and stable forever. The first of those amendments is to change the basis of representation among the States from Federal numbers to actual voters....

But this is not all that we ought to do before these inveterate rebels are invited to participate in our legislation. We have turned, or are about to turn, loose four million slaves without a hut to shelter them or a cent in their pockets. The infernal laws of slavery have prevented them from acquiring an education, understanding the commonest laws of contract, or of managing the ordinary business of life. This Congress is bound to provide for them until they can take care of themselves. If we do not furnish them with homesteads, and hedge them around with protective laws; if we leave them to the legislation of their late masters, we had better have left them in bondage. Their condition would be worse than that of our prisoners at Andersonville. If we fail in this great duty now, when we have the power, we shall deserve and receive the execration of history and of all future ages.

128

A White Southern Perspective on Reconstruction (1868)

Congressional or Radical Reconstruction imposed a new set of requirements on the South. It divided the region into five military districts and outlined how new governments were to be created—especially granting suffrage to African Americans. Complying with these guidelines, every southern state was readmitted into the Union by 1870. A Republican Party coalition of African Americans, recently arrived northerners (carpetbaggers), and southern whites (scalawags) controlled nearly all these state governments. Many former supporters of the Confederacy found these Republican governments to be offensive, corrupt, and expensive (they raised taxes to pay for new services like public education). One of the most

*outspoken and uncompromising opponents of Radical Reconstruction was Howell Cobb.
Born into a wealthy Georgia cotton plantation family, Cobb devoted his life to public
service. He served in the House of Representatives, was elected speaker in 1849, was governor of Georgia, served as secretary of the treasury under President James Buchanan, was a
prominent secessionist, helped form the Confederate government, and was an officer in the
war. Following the war Cobb maintained a self-imposed silence on political matters, which
he broke with the letter excerpted here. Many white southerners would have agreed with
Cobb's attack on Radical Reconstruction.*

Questions to Consider

1. What are Howell Cobb's reasons to oppose Reconstruction policies?

2. Which policies does he particularly dispute? Why?

3. In what ways did white southerners react to Reconstruction?

4. How might Cobb have reacted to Thaddeus Stevens's speech ("Thaddeus Stevens on Reconstruction and the South," Document 127)?

Macon [GA], 4 Jany., 1868

We of the ill-fated South realize only the mournful present whose lesson teaches us to prepare for a still gloomier future. To participate in a national festival would be a cruel mockery, for which I frankly say to you I have no heart, however much I may honor the occasion and esteem the association with which I would be thrown.

The people of the South, conquered, ruined, impoverished, and oppressed, bear up with patient fortitude under the heavy weight of their burdens. Disarmed and reduced to poverty, they are powerless to protect themselves against wrong and injustice; and can only await with broken spirits that destiny which the future has in store for them. At the bidding of their more powerful conquerors they laid down their arms, abandoned a hopeless struggle, and returned to their quiet homes under the plighted faith of a soldier's honor that they should be protected so long as they observed the obligations imposed upon them of peaceful law-abiding citizens. Despite the bitter charges and accusations brought against our people, I hesitate not to say that since that hour their bearing and conduct have been marked by a dignified and honorable submission which should command the respect of their bitterest enemy and challenge the admiration of the civilized world. Deprived of our property and ruined in our estates by the results of the war, we have accepted the situation and given the pledge of a faith never yet broken to abide it. Our conquerors seem to think we should accompany our acquiescence with some exhibition of gratitude for the ruin which they have brought upon us. We cannot see it in that light. Since the close of the war they have taken our property of various kinds, sometimes by

SOURCE: Howell Cobb to J. D. Hoover, 4 January 1868, *Annual Report of the American Historical Association for the Year
1911, vol. 2, The Correspondence of Robert Toombs, Alexander H. Stephens, and Howell Cobb,* ed. U. B. Phillips (Washington, DC, 1913), 690–94.

seizure, and sometime by purchase,—and when we have asked for remuneration have been informed that the claims of rebels are never recognized by the Government. To this decision necessity compels us to submit; but our conquerors express surprise that we do not see in such ruling the evidence of their kindness and forgiving spirit. They have imposed upon us in our hour of distress and ruin a heavy and burthensome tax, peculiar and limited to our impoverished section. Against such legislation we have ventured to utter an earnest appeal, which to many of their leading spirits indicates a spirit of insubordination which calls for additional burthens. They have deprived us of the protection afforded by our state constitutions and laws, and put life, liberty and property at the disposal of absolute military power. Against this violation of plighted faith and constitutional right we have earnestly and solemnly protested, and our protest has been denounced as insolent;—and our restlessness under the wrong and oppression which have followed these acts has been construed into a rebellious spirit, demanding further and more stringent restrictions of civil and constitutional rights. They have arrested the wheels of State government, paralized the arm of industry, engendered a spirit of bitter antagonism on the part of our negro population towards the white people with whom it is the interest of both races they should maintain kind and friendly relations, and are now struggling by all the means in their power both legal and illegal, constitutional and unconstitutional, to make our former slaves *our masters,* bringing these Southern states under the power of *negro supremacy.* To these efforts we have opposed appeals, protests, and every other means of resistance in our power, and shall continue to do so until the bitter end. If the South is to be made a pandemonium and a howling wilderness the responsibility shall not rest upon our heads. Our conquerors regard these efforts on our part to save ourselves and posterity from the terrible results of their policy and conduct as a new rebellion against the constitution of our country, and profess to be amazed that in all this we have failed to see the evidence of their great magnanimity and exceeding generosity. Standing today in the midst of the gloom and suffering which meets the eye in every direction, we can but feel that we are the victims of cruel legislation and the harsh enforcement of unjust laws.... We regarded the close of the war as ending the relationship of enemies and the beginning of a new national brotherhood, and in the light of that conviction felt and spoke of constitutional equality.... We claimed that the result of the war left us a state in the Union, and therefore under the protection of the constitution, rendering in return cheerful obedience to its requirements and bearing in common with the other states of the Union the burthens of government, submitting even as we were compelled to do to *taxation without representation;* but they tell us that a successful war to keep us in the Union left us out of the Union and that the pretension we put up for constitutional protection evidences bad temper on our part and a want of appreciation of the generous spirit which declares that the constitution is not over us for the purposes of protection.... In such reasoning is found a justification of the policy which seeks to put the South under negro supremacy. Better, they say, to hazard the consequences of negro supremacy in the

South with its sure and inevitable results upon Northern prosperity than to put faith in the people of the South who though overwhelmed and conquered have ever showed themselves a brave and generous people, true to their plighted faith in peace and in war, in adversity as in prosperity....

With an Executive who manifests a resolute purpose to defend with all his power the constitution of his country from further aggression, and a Judiciary whose unspotted record has never yet been tarnished with a base subserviency to the unholy demands of passion and hatred, let us indulge the hope that the hour of the country's redemption is at hand, and that even in the wronged and ruined South there is a fair prospect for better days and happier hours when our people can unite again in celebrating the national festivals as in the olden time.

129

African American Suffrage in the South (1867, 1876)

One of the critical and hotly debated issues of Reconstruction was the extension of civil rights to the freedmen. The initial Reconstruction plans called for the protection of African Americans' rights, mainly to protect the former slaves from possible retaliation at the hands of their former masters. Led by some Radical Republicans, Congress implemented its plan of Reconstruction, which required the new state governments in the South to guarantee the right to vote for male African Americans. In 1867 African Americans voted for the first time, often casting their ballots for Republican candidates and helping to establish the Republican party's control of state government. For white southerners, who traditionally voted Democratic, this represented a revolutionary change and caused bitter resentment toward black voters and the Republican party. Some southern whites joined the Ku Klux Klan to intimidate Republicans, while other whites used their economic influence as landowners to intimidate African Americans. The two images below in Harper's Weekly, *a well-respected newspaper of the era, reflect the optimism of African Americans participating in the political process for the first time as well as the reality of voter manipulation. The first image was the cover of the November 16, 1867 issue, while the second image was a double-page illustration in the October 21, 1876 issue.*

Questions to Consider

1. How do the images below differ in their depiction of African Americans' right to vote?

2. What appears to be the status of African Americans voting in the first image? How is the African American portrayed in the second image different? What might you deduce from these differences?

The First Vote Harper's Weekly

SOURCE: Art Resource, NY

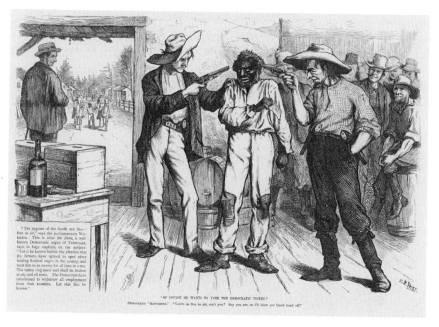

"Of Course He Wants to Vote the Democratic Ticket!"
SOURCE: Stock Montage/Getty Images

3. How does the second image portray southern whites? How do you account for this portrayal?

4. How do you think Howell Cobb ("A White Southern Perspective on Reconstruction," Document 128) would respond to these images?

130

An African American Congressman Calls for Civil Rights (1874)

A critical and hotly debated issue of Reconstruction concerned the extension of civil rights to African Americans, who faced widespread racial discrimination in the South. In the early 1870s a civil rights bill that would outlaw racial discrimination in public places was presented to Congress. Among those speaking out against this legislation was Alexander H.

Stephens, who had served earlier as vice president of the Confederacy but during Reconstruction represented Georgia in Congress. Supporting the civil rights bill was Robert B. Elliott of South Carolina. Born probably in Great Britain, Elliott came to America shortly after the Civil War. Because of his education and oratorical skills, he quickly became a prominent African American Republican politician in South Carolina. When he was elected to Congress in 1870, only a handful of African Americans held national office. In early 1874, when it became known that Elliott would rebut the former vice president of the Confederacy on the proposed civil rights bill, the galleries in the House of Representatives were packed, and many Congressmen remained at their seats. Elliott's speech, excerpted here, was an eloquent call for civil rights. Congress passed the Civil Rights Act of 1875—the last major piece of Reconstruction legislation.

Questions to Consider

1. In what ways did Robert Elliott challenge many of the congressmen who represented the South?
2. On what grounds did Elliott argue for passing the civil rights legislation?
3. According to Elliott, what is the purpose of the national government?
4. What is the significance of this speech?

Sir, it is scarcely twelve years since that gentleman [Alexander H. Stephens of Georgia] shocked the civilized world by announcing the birth of a government which rested on human slavery as its corner-stone. The progress of events has swept away that *pseudo*-government which rested on greed, pride, and tyranny; and the race whom he then ruthlessly spurned and trampled on are here to meet him in debate, and to demand that the rights which are enjoyed by their former oppressors—who vainly sought to overthrow a Government which they could not prostitute to the base uses of slavery—shall be accorded to those who even in the darkness of slavery kept their allegiance true to freedom and the Union. Sir, the gentleman from Georgia has learned much since 1861; but he is still a laggard. Let him put away entirely the false and fatal theories which have so greatly marred an otherwise enviable record. Let him accept, in its fullness and beneficence, the great doctrine that American citizenship carries with it every civil and political right which manhood can confer. Let him lend his influence, with all his masterly ability, to complete the proud structure of legislation which makes this nation worthy of the great declaration which heralded its birth, and he will have done that which will most nearly redeem his reputation in the eyes of the world, and best vindicate the wisdom of that policy which has permitted him to regain his seat upon this floor.

To the diatribe of the gentleman from Virginia, [Mr. John T. Harris] who spoke on yesterday, and who so far transcended the limits of decency and propriety as to announce upon this floor that his remarks were addressed to white men alone, I shall have no word of reply. Let him feel that a negro was

SOURCE: *Congressional Record*, 43rd Congress, 1st Session, volume 2 (6 January 1874), 410.

not only too magnanimous to smite him in his weakness, but was even charitable enough to grant him the mercy of his silence. [Laughter and applause on the floor and in the galleries.] I shall, sir, leave to others less charitable the unenviable and fatiguing task of sifting out of that mass of chaff the few grains of sense that may, perchance, deserve notice. Assuring the gentleman that the negro in this country aims at a higher degree of intellect than that exhibited by him in this debate, I cheerfully commend him to the commiseration of all intelligent men the world over—black men as well as white men.

Sir, equality before the law is now the broad, universal, glorious rule and mandate of the Republic. No State can violate that. Kentucky and Georgia may crowd their statute-books with retrograde and barbarous legislation; they may rejoice in the odious eminence of their consistent hostility to all the great steps of human progress which have marked our national history since slavery tore down the stars and stripes on Fort Sumter; but, if Congress shall do its duty, if Congress shall enforce the great guarantees which the Supreme Court has declared to be the one pervading purpose of all the recent amendments, then their unwise and unenlightened conduct will fall with the same weight upon the gentlemen from those States who now lend their influence to defeat this bill, as upon the poorest slave who once had no rights which the honorable gentlemen were bound to respect....

No language could convey a more complete assertion of the power of Congress over the subject embraced in the present bill than is here expressed. If the States do not conform to the requirements of this clause, if they continue to deny to any person within their jurisdiction the equal protection of the laws, or as the Supreme Court had said, "deny equal justice in its courts," then Congress is here said to have power to enforce the constitutional guarantee by appropriate legislation. That is the power which this bill now seeks to put in exercise. It proposes to enforce the constitutional guarantee against inequality and discrimination by appropriate legislation. It does not seek to confer new rights, nor to place rights conferred by State citizenship under the protection of the United States, but simply to prevent and forbid inequality and discrimination on account of race, color, or previous condition of servitude. Never was there a bill more completely within the constitutional power of Congress. Never was there a bill which appealed for support more strongly to that sense of justice and fair-play which has been said, and in the main with justice, to be a characteristic of the Anglo-Saxon race, The Constitution warrants it; the Supreme Court sanctions it; justice demands it.

Sir, I have replied to the extent of my ability to the arguments which have been presented by the opponents of this measure. I have replied also to some of the legal propositions advanced by gentlemen on the other side; and now that I am about to conclude, I am deeply sensible of the imperfect manner in which I have performed the task. Technically, this bill is to decide upon the civil status of the colored American citizen; a point disputed at the very formation of our present Government, when by a short-sighted policy, a policy repugnant to true republican government, one negro counted as three-fifths of a man. The logical result of this mistake of the framers of the Constitution strengthened the cancer of slavery, which finally spread its poisonous tentacles over the southern portion of the body-politic. To arrest its growth and save the nation we have passed through the harrowing operation of intestine war, dreaded at all times, resorted to at the last extremity, like the surgeon's knife, but absolutely necessary to extirpate the disease which threatened with the life of the nation the overthrow of civil and political liberty on this continent. In that dire extremity the members of the race which I have the honor in part to represent—the race which pleads for justice at your hands to-day, forgetful of their inhuman and brutalizing servitude at the South, their degradation and ostracism at the North—flew willingly and gallantly to the support of the national Government. Their sufferings, assistance, privations, and trials in the swamps and in the rice-fields, their valor on the land and on the sea, is a part of the ever-glorious record which makes up the history of a nation preserved, and might, should I urge the claim, incline you to respect and guarantee their rights and privileges as citizens of our common Republic. But I remember that valor, devotion, and loyalty are not always rewarded according to their just deserts, and that after the battle some who have borne the brunt of the fray may, through neglect or contempt, be assigned to a subordinate place, while the enemies in war may be preferred to the sufferers.

The results of the war, as seen in reconstruction, have settled forever the political status of my race. The passage of this bill will determine the civil status, not only of the negro, but of any other class of citizens who may feel themselves discriminated against. It will form the cap-stone of that temple of liberty, begun on this continent under discouraging circumstances, carried on in spite of the sneers of monarchists and the cavils of pretended friends of freedom, until at last it stands in all its beautiful symmetry and proportions, a building the grandest which the world has ever seen, realizing the most sanguine expectations and the highest hopes of those who, in the name of equal, impartial, and universal liberty, laid the foundation stones....

131

The Situation for African Americans in the South (1879)

Much of the Reconstruction legislation and policies were designed to protect the freedmen from possible retaliation at the hands of their former masters and allow African Americans to make their way in the South. In 1867, African Americans voted for the first time in the South, often casting their ballots for Republican candidates and helping to establish the Republican Party's control of state governments. For many white southerners, most of whom were Democrats, this represented revolutionary change and caused bitter resentment toward black voters and the Republican Party. A resurgence of Democratic Party power in the South toppled many Republican-controlled state governments until 1877, when—as part of a "bargain" that allowed Rutherford B. Hayes to become president—federal troops were removed from the South and the last Republican state governments collapsed. This event signaled the end of Reconstruction. Within a short time, thousands of African Americans began migrating from the South into the West. The newsmagazine The Nation *explained the motives for this "flight" in an editorial, which is excerpted here. In 1879, about 6,000 African Americans moved to Kansas, and probably as many as 20,000 came the following year. These individuals were called the "Exodusters" for making the exodus from the South.*

Questions to Consider

1. According to *The Nation*, what were the problems that African Americans faced during Reconstruction?

2. For what reasons did some African Americans leave the South?

3. What does this article reveal about race relations and economic conditions in the South after Reconstruction?

It would be difficult to conceive of a situation less favorable to healthy social progress than that in which the negroes at the South found themselves since the war. They were very poor, and very ignorant, and very timid, and surrounded by fierce, war-like, and contemptuous neighbors of a different race. Their ignorance, too, did not consist in the want of book-learning, but in the want of the common discipline of civilized life. All this was bad enough, or would have been bad enough, even if they had nothing to trouble them but the difficulty of getting a livelihood. They were, however, armed with the franchise, and were at once plunged into a sea of troubles which even the best equipped races would have found it difficult to navigate. The party which gave them the ballot had really no means of protecting them in the enjoyment of it, and yet had the strongest interest in preventing the Democrats from getting the benefit of it. Accordingly, it had to resort for this purpose to keeping alive among the negroes as long as possible a spirit of hatred and distrust towards the whites, and at the same time to nourishing the passions of the war at the North by stories, some true and some false, of negro wrongs. The whites, on their side, rather helped this plan by the savage means to which they resorted, in those States in which the negroes were in majority, to overturn or prevent negro rule. The effect of the struggle on the unfortunate colored people has, of course, been bad; the wonder it has not been worse. It has kept them in a state of permanent hostility with their white neighbors, and has filled their minds with vague expectations of advancement or elevation of some kind from the Northern Republicans.

SOURCE: "The Flight of the Negroes," *The Nation* 28 (10 April 1879): 242.

That they should have, under these circumstances, cultivated the soil as faithfully as the Southern crop returns show them to have done, and at the same time purchased so much land, and taken so much advantage of the schools, is very remarkable, and suggests some melancholy reflections as to what they might have accomplished during the past fifteen years if they had enjoyed thorough security, and had not been compelled to take part in the electioneering contests of their white countrymen the minute they crossed the threshold of civilization. The flight of several thousand of them in a sort of panic from Louisiana and Mississippi, with accounts of which the papers are now filled, is dismal reading enough, because it is largely the result of delusions of one sort or another, and the danger is that it will be fostered and used during the next year as a fine campaign incident. The immense misery that it is about to produce will, of course, cause the managers and stump-speakers little concern.

When one reads in the correspondence of the Stalwart paper which is making the most of it for party purposes, that the negroes in South Carolina are ceasing to purchase homesteads and are hoarding their money, we perceive clearly enough that the more thrifty and well-to-do are alarmed by something that is impending, rather than suffering from anything which has happened in the past. A state of things in which a poor man has been able to save money to buy a homestead as tens of thousands of negroes have done, is not one in which he is likely to think himself unhappy or ill-used. What is probably alarming this class is the accounts which have been circulated amongst them of the evils which are likely to befall them now that the Democrats have secured control of Congress. If the Stalwart reports of their condition during the past ten years, however, were true, nothing the Democrats could now do would have any terrors for them. Senator Dawes told the people of Massachusetts in 1870 that there was not a negro at the South who did not fear when he went to bed at night that he would have his throat cut or his cabin burnt before morning. The New York *Times* says that for a long time past Christmas Day and election days—that is, two days in the year—"have been appropriated [by the Southern whites] for the sole purpose of killing 'peart niggers'"; the other days of the year being reserved for "robbery and personal violence." Moreover, we learn from the same paper that during recent years, while the negroes have been raising these tremendous crops of cotton and sugar, the whites "gambled, drank whiskey, and improved their skill as marksmen by shooting offhand at a servant who did not please them." One would think that a laboring man who was murdered regularly on Christmas day and election day, and was robbed and assaulted on other days, besides occasionally serving as mark for a drunken man's rifle, would have little to fear in this world from any change in the Government. Nevertheless, there can be no doubt that the thrifty colored men at the South were pretty well off; that a very large number were, in spite of many difficulties, making their way in the world, and that the accounts from Republican sources of that are to result from Democratic rule have determined them to get by hook or by crook into a State in which the Government would be friendly to them.

The impelling motives of the poorer and more shiftless class of emigrants in abandoning their homes are not difficult to divine either. Both the planters and the laborers at the South resumed their farming at the close of the war absolutely without capital and without business habits. Little or no money passes between them and the negro subsists during the year on supplies furnished him on a credit account either by the planter or that still greater man in Southern society nowadays, the cross-roads storekeeper. This, of course, means monstrous prices, and probably a good deal of fraud in the tally. No laboring man who lived in this way anywhere, be he black or white, ever rises above the direst poverty or escapes debt. Laborers suffer terribly from the process at the North, and it would be difficult to say what legal remedy could be devised for it. It is probable, too, that all negroes suffer in nerves about election-time. Either the Democrats "intimidate" them to keep them from polls, or the Republicans assure them that they will be intimidated, and between the two they have a month every year of great anxiety and no matter which side wins, it brings no change in their condition. But if the emigration could be properly conducted, and emigrants were able to take care of themselves until they found employment or raised crops, there would be little to regret about it. In fact it would be an excellent remedy for the trouble some of the Southern States. There are too many negroes now in South Carolina, Louisiana, and Mississippi both for their own good and that of the whites. Profusion of labor generally means misery for the laborer, and the negroes' best chance of social and political advancement lies in scattering themselves in more advanced communities....